Electric Don Quixote
the definitive story of
Frank Zappa

For my parents, Agnes and John, who never stand
in the way and always pick up the pieces.
And for Robynne, the wild little lion cub.

Electric Don Quixote
the definitive story of
Frank Zappa

Neil Slaven

OMNIBUS PRESS
LONDON · NEW YORK · SYDNEY

Edited and Designed by Colin Larkin for Square One Books Ltd,
assisted by Susan Pipe & Miles Hutchinson.

Cover designed by Frost Design
Picture research by Nikki Rusell
Cover photos: LFI/Redferns

ISBN: 0.7119.6553.6
Order No: OP48002

Exclusive Distributors
Book Sales Limited,
8/9 Frith Street,
London W1D 3JB, UK.

Music Sales Corporation,
257 Park Avenue South,
New York, NY 10010, USA.

Music Sales Pty Limited,
120 Rothschild Avenue, Rosebery,
NSW 2018, Australia.

To the Music Trade only:
Music Sales Limited,
8/9 Frith Street,
London W1D 3JB, UK.

Printed in the United Kingdom by MPG Books Ltd, Bodmin, Cornwall

A catalogue record for this book is available from the British Library.[END]

CONTENTS

'. . . we of these times enjoy the
agreeable entertainment, not only
of his true and delightful adventures;
but, also the intervening episodes,
which are no less real, artful and
delicious, than the main history
itself, the twisted, reeled and
ravelled thread of which is
continued thus.'

Don Quixote, Book Four, Chapter One
Miguel de Cervantes
(translated by Tobias Smollett, 1755)

There's only one reason to write:
because you consider yourself to be
a writer, and you want people to pay
attention to what you wrote. It's
the bane of your existence that you
must write about somebody else doing
something that you can't do.

Frank Zappa, Zappa!

No bane, no gain.

Neil Slaven

FOREWORD

It seems like years since I commissioned this book. That was back in the days when I was a juggler and naïvely thought I could write, edit and produce the *Guinness Encyclopedia Of Popular Music* and simultaneously be a publisher, commissioning editor and radio broadcaster.

Neil Slaven first came to my eye as a name on the back of the famous 'Beano' album by John Mayall's Bluesbreakers featuring Eric Clapton. His name would appear on dozens more Decca and Deram albums as a (credible) record producer. The UK blues boom of the late 60s was an incredibly fertile time, and Slaven carved a niche for himself producing many albums by the Savoy Brown Blues Band, Chicken Shack and (very dear to my heart) the excellent Keef Hartley Band. In those days blues, folk rock, heavy rock and prog rock were fêted by the same audience - much the same that would have worn out imported copies of the Mothers Of Invention's *Freak Out* or *Absolutely Free*. This was back in the days of US imports and Bruce's record shop in Edinburgh and One Stop in London. They were the days when John Peel spoke in monotone, when *everything*, including Savoy Brown, Hartley and Zappa were reeeerly amyyyyzzzing. Zappa *was* really amazing, although most of us didn't understand why. Slaven was one of the very few who did - he understood and appreciated Zappa then as he does now. The closest I got to Zappa was outside the Rainbow Theatre in London. Together with thousands of confused fans I waited for the chalk board to appear: SHOW CANCELLED. I have never forgiven FZ for getting thrown into the orchestra pit on the first show instead of the second.

In the intervening years Neil Slaven has become one of the leading authorities on the blues. He regularly compiles and writes album sleeve notes and reviews records for a number of magazines and journals. With the late Mike Leadbitter he wrote *Nothing But The Blues* and the indispensable *Blues Records: A Selected Discography 1943-1966*. He has also been an important contributor to the *Guinness Encyclopedia Of Popular Music* and the *Guinness Who's Who Of Blues*. And there lies the problem; typecasting. Just as Fred Astaire was made to dance, Neil Slaven was made to tell the blues. Until now.

He was one of the earliest people to know that Zappa's cancer had returned and that it would be only a matter of time. He acted as a consultant for BBC television's documentary and got to meet a sick FZ in his home fortress. A number of books appeared shortly after his death and Slaven was hopelessly late with his. Mostly it was a case of overwriting – the more he wrote the more he realised just how much he knew and felt about FZ and how similar they were in oh so many ways. The book that takes it's time is the one worth waiting for. I refused to pressure the author because he could have lost confidence or stamped his feet and thrown in the towel. I have dealt with a few Rumplestilkskins in my time.

Frank Zappa's often brilliant combination of irreverent humour and 'serious' music has and will continue to baffle many. This musical bisexuality has made him misunderstood and hard to market. Why does somebody who has the gift of satire and comedy waste his time composing orchestral pieces? Why does a highly literate composer and brilliant musician choose to trivialise his work with pornographic humour? Because he is Frank Zappa.

At some stage, maybe not in Slaven's or my lifetime, FZ will be widely seen as a musical genius and one of the greatest contributors to music of the 20th century.

Electric Don Quixote is the best book that has ever been or is likely to be written on the phenomenon that was Frank Zappa. I would say that wouldn't I, even though I have a strong belief that in years to come, when FZ is finally recognised, the adage, 'pass me a copy of Slaven's Zappa', will be a reality.

My thanks to Andy Childs, Bob Wise and Chris Charlesworth for helping this masterpiece on its way.

COLIN LARKIN, March 1996

INTRODUCTION

When it happened, I was having a drink with friends at The Mondrian, a hotel on Sunset down the street from the Comedy Store, which 30 years before had been Ciro's. I'd been in town for ten days, researching in the basement of the new Los Angeles Library, a monolithic building that inside looks like Fort Knox in a Slide Area, and junking in second-hand bookshops and memorabilia stores for obscure interviews and press reports.

From a number of sources, I knew that Zappa's health was failing but people were still going up to the house. All week, I'd agonised about ringing to ask if I could pay my respects. But in the war between two principal character traits, timidity and arrogance, timorousness prevailed. After all, I wasn't exactly a close friend of the family.

Sunday morning was spent at the Pasadena Swap Meet, where I found a few magazines and resisted buying all the bootlegs on offer. The evening was quiet until around eight, when the radio announced that what we all knew had to happen but - please God, not yet - had taken place.

Frank Zappa was dead. And buried. Gone on his final tour.

He'd left just before 6pm on Saturday, December 4, 1993, with Gail and Moon and Dweezil and Ahmet and Diva there to see him off. The other ceremony, unheralded, took place Sunday morning, with family and close friends present. The rest of us would have to wait for the opportunity to indulge in sentiments that he always professed to be an inappropriate use of valuable time.

Well, Frank, I was upset anyway, OK? I'd only met you once and that had taken 24 years to achieve. The occasion had been less than momentous for you. Despite my advancing years, I'd been overawed and the lines of communication between my brain and my mouth had hung by a thread. Even so, you granted me several hours of your precious time as, for the umpteenth time, you ran through a long and productive career that needed days rather than hours to adequately detail. Then you introduced me to your family and showed me round the Utility Muffin Research Kitchen. You even set up the Synclavier and played some of *N-Lite*, explaining its operation to my uncomprehending ears.

Despite my being English and a journalist, you were tolerant and polite even though you were obviously in some pain, and let me gauge when my visit was over. Like many others before and since, I was leaving with the impression that I'd made a friend, even if that friend didn't have the time to indulge the need for further contact that was already coursing through my veins. We stood in the dark on the steps outside your house and shook hands. I looked into your eyes and said, 'Good luck'. It was a lame thing to say; we both knew that luck was not a factor in the inevitability to come. I drove away wondering, Why did I end up being so trite when I wanted to be profound?

But what do you say to a man whose music you've lived with half your life? Who'd probably helped to shape your view of the world and your aspirations, even though the dedication and perseverance that he showed weren't yours to command? (We'd talked about my still-unrealised ambition to compile a film history of man's inhumanity to man, using Varèse's *Arcana* as a soundtrack.) Who relentlessly pursued every one of his objectives while others wandered from indecision to self-indulgence? Whose thirst for knowledge and grasp of detail over a wide range of subjects continued unabated, in parallel with his musical explorations.

Right from the release of *Freak Out!*, Frank gathered people like myself, figuratively speaking, around him. In 1966, he chose to term himself and them freaks. Needless to say, they treated as a destination what he saw only as a point of departure. I never thought of myself as a freak, except insofar as liking the Mothers of Invention seemed to qualify me as one to friends who could only manage the stylistic leap from the Shadows to the Rolling Stones.

As far as I was concerned, they took the easy option. I liked challenging music, so I'd heard Varèse, Stravinsky and Penderecki. I didn't read music, I didn't understand what was happening. But I responded to the result, as I did to the drums of Burundi, the gongs of a Balinese gamelan orchestra or Moondog's eerie and unique percussion instruments recorded on Manhattan's Sixth Avenue. (We talked of him, too.) Even so, it was still hard to like Frank's music at first hearing. It was demanding, densely layered, sardonic and satirical. But once in a while there was a bluesy turn of phrase from the guitar which connected the Mothers with another of my musical interests.

Through all the subsequent changes of (apparent) direction and personnel, I remained doggedly loyal, buying every album, even if some got played less often than others. It wasn't possible to like every one equally but then it was inconceivable that the faith would be broken. I didn't get to see every tour but bootlegs and tape exchanges took care of that omission.

As the years passed, I became aware of a deeper purpose in the music. It was no great achievement on my part, for Frank made it plain in his sleevenotes and his interviews that there were situations in the world and especially the USA that needed to be brought to people's attention. It was equally evident that he was appalled by the blind patriotism that kept most of his countrymen wilfully ignorant of the inequities around them and the injustices committed in their name. During the 80s, he enlarged upon his mordant view of the alliances between State and Church, the military and business cartels.

Frank was no people's champion, his Mr Smith was disinclined to go to Washington; but in the end, he went anyway. Like some modern Don Quixote he entered the lists, his lances tipped with verbal venom, to defend the notion of individual freedom supposedly enshrined in the American Constitution. Cervantes' original was a deluded old man, his senses addled by tales of knight-errantry, who tilted at windmills which he elected to view as giants 'with vast extended arms'. But as the story progressed, his character, initially both the object and instrument of satire and ridicule, became broader and more complex. Instead of ignoring reality, Cervantes forced his creation to justify his existence in the real world.

Fyodor Dostoevsky thought the knight suffered from 'the nostalgia of realism'. Frank Zappa abjured nostalgia and tilted at more substantial windmills, convinced of a pernicious disparity between the aims of government and organisations who invoked 'the American Way' and the reality behind them. Many of the targets he engaged 'in fierce and unequal combat' were all too real, all too fallible and all too devious to be caught in the spotlight. Some were more fanciful than others but his arguments were always supported by rigorous logic. He admitted, 'I tend to view the whole thing as a conspiracy.'[1]

So, was the prevalence of LSD among Californian hippie communes in the 60s an experiment conducted in public with the connivance of the CIA and the government of the day? Was AIDS a military germ warfare research project that escaped from the laboratory? Was there an unnamed secret police network whose task it was to investigate and infiltrate whatever might be perceived as a threat to America's stability? Were the leaders of the religious right intent upon suppressing the right of free speech and dissent by any means necessary? Whatever the truth of these things, Frank was ready with a list of analogous events and circumstances that lent a statistical probability to what he proposed. Further examples will crop up in the pages that follow.

It's all too easy to label these accusations 'paranoia', the fantasies of a man who expunged from his life anything he deemed a waste of time or outside the scope of his enquiring mind. In order to pursue those things, almost all related to music, that interested him, Frank Zappa exercised inflexible control over his daily routine. Some commentators portrayed him as arrogant and cold, but the warmth, honesty and normality of his family life proved this to be a misconception. His was a personality that had to be judged by its own criteria. The prodigious work rate was the product of a mind rarely at rest. That he made time to publicly protest about the erosion of personal and artistic freedom was a reflection of how seriously he perceived the threat.

Much to the surprise of his detractors, who still thought of him as an exhibitionist and a freak, Frank proved a very eloquent and humorously acute adversary of organisations like the Parents Music Resource Center. For someone who claimed never to read books, he was extremely well-informed, able to cut through the emotional cant in which self-appointed protectors of the nation's morals cloaked their restrictive intentions. 'I'm really quite wild and outrageous but in ways that people wouldn't understand,' he maintained. 'Today, if you actually work 18 hours a day and you *like* it, that's pretty outrageous. And if you don't compromise and don't put up with a bunch of bullshit and you punch your way through life, which I kind of manage to do on the budget available to me, that's *out-fucking-rageous*.'[2]

It was his insistence on using such terminology and his lack of reverence for established institutions that incensed authorities in America and Britain. While others ran like prisoners in an exercise yard to stand in line at the sound of the warden's whistle, Frank defended his freedom of expression as a musician and businessman, and also that of groups for whose music he had little respect. For, long before it became enshrined in *Joe's Garage* , he'd always maintained that 'Music is the BEST'.

Above all else, there is the music. Tens of albums, hundreds of songs and fiendishly convoluted instrumental themes. His orchestral compositions adhered to Varèsian principles, with unrelated themes following in a free succession of contrast and surprise. Audiences relished songtexts that told of enema bandits and sexual deviants, as well as scathing critiques of public figures, their peccadilloes laid bare. His guitar solos he regarded as compositions in themselves, expositions of a unique playing style that matched form and content with a bravura control of effects and amplification. No one since Jimi Hendrix used feedback as creatively as Frank Zappa did. But beneath all the harsh, angular phrasing was a gift for creating starkly beautiful melodies that remain in the mind long after their conclusion.

'Watermelon In Easter Hay' says more about Frank Zappa than these words can. Play it now and when you finish the book.

This biography is an assemblage of facts and quotations that hopefully illustrate some of the character traits which shaped his music. It's just one interpretation of a mass of material sufficient to write the same story again using wholly different examples. Where possible, I've used Frank's own words to illustrate the point at issue. Like his music, which doesn't sound the same when he isn't there to direct its intricacies, his beliefs and motivations are best expressed in his own terms. Rather than attempt the impossible by preparing a laboriously detailed explanation of a complex mind, I've tried to provide the reader with the means to arrive at their own interpretation of a unique and irreplaceable personality.

What merit this manuscript contains would not have been possible without constant application to two magazines dedicated to the documentation and appraisal of Frank Zappa's words and deeds. *Society Pages*, edited by Rob Samler and Den Simms, and *T'Mershi Duween*, overseen by Fred Tomsett, are both essential to anyone with an obsessional tendency where Frank is concerned. Just as important to the comprehensiveness of the text was the permission granted by the British Broadcasting Corporation to use material from the complete transcript of the BBC2 *Late Show* interview conducted by Nigel Leigh, obtained through the kind efforts of the programme's director, Elaine Shepherd, who also located the programme schedule for *Juke Box Jury*. My gratitude is here insufficiently acknowledged.

I received significant help from a number of people who still remain friends and deserve thanks: Mary Katherine Aldin, for acting as temporary landlady and patient guide around the obscure backwaters of Los Angeles and the San Fernando Valley in search of tempting morsels of information, and for maintaining her exclusive cuttings agency; Ted Berkowitz, who witnessed at first hand Frank's diligence as a chaperone; Tony Burke, for filling a multitude of gaps with donations of magazines and tapes that facilitated accurate dating of important gigs and the musical developments that took place at them; Roy Carr for pulling the strings that set up the interview, and IPC for access to their file of reviews, news reports and articles covering Frank's war dance with the British press; Norman Darwen, for his German being better than mine; Roger Dopson, for climbing into his attic and manhandling boxes of yellowing music papers down to ground level, and Jacky, for overlooking the damage to the living room carpet; Andy Fletcher, for sterling chauffeur work on trips to Pacific Grove and Lancaster and for 'percussive maintenance'; Phil Holmes for the olive oil, the grappa and the hoe; John O'Toole, for rummaging for nuggets in his own store of magazines; Howard Thompson, for his encouragement, being a provider and eyewitness to a climactic moment in Frank's life; Alan and Pat Warner for sharing memories and keeping me abreast of the tributes; Phil Wight for delving in his *Downbeat*'s; Victoria Winston, for casting her mind back to Frank's freak days.

Finally, an act of contrition: This project would not have been completed without the tolerance and patience of Colin Larkin. I never felt the lash, but it brought out the masochist in me. Now, if I could just get this orange out of my mouth...

NEIL SLAVEN, January 1996

CHAPTER ONE
WHAT'S NEW IN BALTIMORE (1)

On December 21, 1940, the birth of Frank Vincent Zappa Jr ll (by his own terminology) was. Baltimore, in the state of Maryland, is one of America's oldest cities; guidebooks assure the visitor that an air of previous centuries pervades its elegant brownstone houses and Victorian terraces. A major port in days gone by, the harbour is now a tourist trap of fast food and colonial nostalgia. Situated some 50 miles north-east of Washington, DC, it's about as close to government as Frank was ever likely to get.

Baltimore was the birthplace of Dashiell Hammett, Billie Holiday, harmonica maestro and ego Larry Adler, Mike Leiber, one half of the Leiber & Stoller songwriting team, and Wallis Simpson, erstwhile Duchess of Windsor, the home of journalist and critic H.L. Mencken, proto-rap deejay Douglas 'Socko' Henderson and of Richard Spellman, the FBI's own nomination for archetypal agent. Among others, the town also claims Edgar Allan Poe, who died there but was born in Boston, and baseball legend Babe Ruth, champion of the Baltimore Orioles, the team named for the bird that represents the state. The Orioles was also the name of the vocal group led by Baltimore-born Sonny Til which had a 1953 hit with 'Crying In The Chapel'.

It was where, on September 14, 1814, in a fit of patriotic fervour, Francis Scott Key wrote 'The Star Spangled Banner'. The garrison of Fort McHenry, at the mouth of the Patapsco River, withstood bombardment from General Ross's British Army, hot from its destruction of Washington, thus preventing the sacking of the town and thwarting the planned invasion. Ironic then that the tune Key used, 'To Anacreon In Heaven', was English.

In 1977, preparing material for his album, *Little Criminals*, Randy Newman wrote 'Baltimore' as a doom-laden elegy to a dying city. Trouble was, he'd only ever passed through it on a train. The Baltimore of his imagination didn't exist: the townspeople told him so when next he played the city's Lyric Theatre. Film director Barry Levinson was on safer ground when he mythologised his Baltimore upbringing in *Diner*, *Tin Men* and *Avalon* (the latter with music, by way of belated atonement, by Newman). It's also the home town of *Hairspray* heroine Tracey Turnblad and her creator John Waters, Annie Reed, hankerer-after-love in *Sleepless In Seattle*, the setting for the television series, *Homicide: Life On The Streets*, and the stamping ground of Eugene Victor Tooms, the hibernating liver-eating serial-killer in *The X-Files*.

Maryland squats either side of Chesapeake Bay, a vast expanse of water frequently eulogised in the fiction of another native polymath, John Barth, comprehensively in *Tidewater Tales* and *Sabbatical* but an integral part of several other of his books. With few exceptions, Barth's texts are as dense, erudite, self-referential and playful as Frank Zappa's music. It must be something in the water.

By contrast, Frank had little good to say about his home state after he left it as an asthmatic ten-year-old in 1950. Thirty six years later, and on Valentine's Day, he came back to appear before the Maryland State Judiciary Committee. His purpose was to aid in the defeat of a bill proposed by Delegate Judith Toth to bring records, tapes and CDs under the existing pornography statutes. The rhetorically-titled 'What's New In Baltimore?' had appeared the year before on *Frank Zappa Meets The Mothers Of Prevention*. On that occasion, Frank saved his eloquence for his guitar. Like parents, places of birth can't be chosen.

His father, Francis Vincent Zappa Jr, had come from Partinico in northern Sicily, his antecedents Sicilian, Greek, Arab and French. The family name, Frank informed Nicholas Slonimsky, translated from Italian as 'the plough', but dictionaries define it as 'a hoe'. His father had been a small child when his family arrived in America on an immigrant ship. Growing up in Little Italy on Baltimore's waterfront, he did his bit for the family business, lathering chins in their barbershop. Frank's mother, Rose Marie, was first-generation American, her heritage French, Sicilian and Italian. Her family owned a restaurant along the same waterfront, where she and Frank's father may have met as children. More likely, that event took place after he graduated from college in Chapel Hill, North Carolina, and returned to Baltimore to take up a teaching post at Loyola College.

Francis Zappa never shrank from hard work. He paid his way through college cutting hair and playing guitar for frat parties. When he started a family, his 'old country' ethics dictated he should strive his hardest to support it, which he proceeded to do for the rest of his working life. Later he would declare: 'All my life I've made good money. It all went for food, clothing and environment. I've paid for everything I've wanted.[1]

Fourteen days before his son's first birthday, Japanese planes laid waste to Pearl Harbor, America's Pacific naval base in Hawaii. President Franklin D. Roosevelt declared war on Japan the following day, which prompted Japan's allies, Germany and Italy, to declare war back at him. Now it was a world conflict, with America committed both east and west. Francis resolved to do his part towards his country's victory. As his son remarked 50 years later, 'it was not a good idea to be of a Sicilian or Italian extraction at that point in American history; he had to try extra hard to be patriotic, I think.[2]

Grouped around what John Barth calls the cervix of Chesapeake Bay was a microcosm of military life. There was the Naval Academy, the Aberdeen Ordnance Proving Ground, Norfolk Navy Yard, Langley Air Force Base, Andrews Air Force Base, Fort Belvoir, Fort Eustis, Fort Story, Fort Meade, where in the late 70s the CIA's 'remote viewing' unit working on programme 'Grill Flame' was stationed – and the Edgewood Arsenal for Chemical and Biological Weapons Development, 15 miles up Highway 40 from Baltimore (and a minor plot element in Barth's *Sabbatical*).

Francis became a meteorologist at Edgewood, 'helping to figure out the best kinds of weather patterns that would be used to disperse poison gas in time of national crisis'.[3] The family moved into 15 Dexter Street, part of the project in which the Army housed its ancillary workforce. The houses were cheaply built, thin-walled and freezing in winter, swamplike (flies all green and buzzin') in summer. Little wonder Frank was a sickly child, prone to asthma, earache and sinus trouble; his teeth were none too cute, either. There was his mother's hot olive oil for his ears, the doctor's radium-tipped swab to probe his sinuses and a mad Italian dentist called Dr. Rocca. It would take a change of climate to remedy his asthma.

If the physical equipment went on the blink from time to time, Frank's mental faculties were sharp and enquiring. When he was five, he offered his father an original design for a warhead, which was declined. 'I wanted to help, and always have,' he said in 1988. 'I happen to think if you have to have defence you want your shit to work. I'm no peacenik.'[4] A year later, he and his friend Leonard Allen had discovered the constituents to make gunpowder, the first of several skills with which he would disrupt his school years.

'I certainly mixed a few potions in my time and got to be quite an expert on making explosives. It was one of my main interests in life, partly because I like fireworks.'[5] Unable to afford an A.C. Gilbert chemistry set, Francis piqued his son's interest by bringing laboratory paraphernalia home for him to play with. 'If they would have gotten me a chemistry set when I asked them to, I would have been a fucking scientist right now,' he told David Whalley.[6]

Francis would have liked his son to become a scientist or an engineer but his parents couldn't afford the necessary education. Nor could their son fail to observe what his father had to do to maintain their upkeep. He would accompany his father when, after a day's work, he fished the local creeks for crabs and catfish to supplement the family diet. More often that not, Francis' arms would be bandaged. 'You could be a human guinea pig for these things called pap tests,' his son told Bob Guccione. 'So he'd have these big bandages on his arm, and sometimes come home with two or three on his arms, and they'd itch and burn, and he'd suffer with these things, but they'd be thirty dollars more a week.'[7] The rent had to be paid.

Then there were the gas masks. Because of their proximity to the Arsenal's tanks of mustard gas, every family on the housing project was issued with them in case the tanks broke. There was a rack of four in the Zappa home now that Frank had a brother, Bobby. 'Knowing what I know now about poison gas, everybody would have died anyway. You would have kept on breathing but the rest of your body would have exploded.'[8]

Frank liked to imagine that his mask was a space helmet but he was curious to investigate the contents of the can hanging at the end of the hose connected to the face mask. Having examined the mixture of crystals and charcoal inside, he found that without the can attached, his new lightweight space helmet made it easier for him to wander the universe, the coal bin his spaceship.

Right from the start, Francis knew his son was intellectually gifted, with brains to spare. Because of his mental capacity, Frank was easily bored, at home and at school, by subjects that didn't interest him. He preferred books that told him what he wanted to know and refused Francis's suggestion that he read Shakespeare. He also liked to draw, to sketch and to paint. Once in a while, his father would take his guitar out of the closet and strum a song but Frank's attention was usually otherwise occupied.

He did, however, like some music. 'I was a massive Spike Jones fan,' he told Charles Amirkhanian, 'and when I was six or seven years old, he had a hit record called 'All I Want For Christmas Is My Two Front Teeth' and I sent him a fan letter because of that.'[9] Instead of receiving a photograph of Spike Jones, he was sent one of George Rock, the tune's vocalist, whom he thought resembled a master criminal. 'I used to really love to listen to all those records. It always seemed to me that if you could get a laugh out of something, that was good, and if you could make life more colourful than it actually was, that was good.'[10] The principle of humour in music had been learned: it would be useful in the future.

He also learned what he regarded as a physical principle of music: 'I went to my grandmother's funeral when I was little and I sat there looking at the candles. The choir was singing, and when they would sing a note, the candles would respond to it. I didn't know why . . . But it was a physical manifestation of a sound. I remembered it; I put it in the memory bank to see what I could do with it later.'[11]

With his son's health so poor, Francis got another government job, this time in ballistics, in Opa-Locka, Florida, close by the Miami Canal. It was a brief tenure but Frank's health improved in the sunshine and he grew a foot in height. That, combined with his mother's homesickness, meant that a return to Maryland could be contemplated. Not to Edgewood but to a terrace house in Park Heights Avenue in Pikesville, a north-western suburb of Baltimore and part of the city's Jewish enclave.

Frank hated city life, he missed the woods where he could ride his bike, climb trees and dream of experimenting with gunpowder. Mr & Mrs Zappa didn't like Baltimore much either and Francis looked further afield for job opportunities. He was offered a post at Dugway Proving Ground, west of Salt Lake City, Utah, where nerve gas was produced. Maps noted that there was 'no public access' to the area, which was adjoined by Skull Valley Indian Reservation. They, presumably, took their own chances.

Francis didn't take the job. Instead, he took a position in Monterey, teaching metallurgy at the Naval Post-Graduate School. So, in November 1950, the family set off in their Kaiser car for the two-week journey to California, during which Francis distributed their winter clothing to a needy black family. He didn't realise that northern California, like Maryland, had its fair share of rain and freezing fog in winter.

'Where we were living, it was damp and it was cold and it was unpleasant. We were living in Monterey, which at that time was pretty much a city in major decay.'[12] Shortly, the family moved a couple of miles further onto the Monterey peninsula to Pacific Grove, a small seaside community that had begun as a Methodist camping ground in 1875 and was the winter retreat for thousands of Golden Monarch butterflies. To eat better than the winter visitors, the Zappas had to be inventive to make ends meet. Twelve miles inland at Salinas was a lettuce-growing area to which Francis and his son would drive once in a while. The family car would follow the heavily-laden lorries, picking up any lettuce that fell in the road.

Frank's awareness of his family's circumstances added another bitter dimension to his isolation. Moving to new schools as his father went from job to job disrupted his education, most of which he found boring anyway. 'It was a little rough,' he told Kurt Loder, 'because I had a moustache when I was 11 and I weighed around 180 pounds.'[13] There was little time to form friendships in the anonymous housing projects in which the family lived. 'I never had the ethnic neighbourhood upbringing experience. I was moving around all the time and living in mixed company, so I never had that real strong meatball sandwich identity.'[14] Driven to rely on his own resources, he built model planes, conducted puppet shows using figures he had made and clothed himself, and pursued an on-going fascination with explosives that led to several potentially harmful accidents.

While he lived in Pacific Grove, Frank became interested in drumming. He attended a summer-school course intended for children hoping to join the school's drum and bugle brigade. Supervised by a teacher named Keith McKillop, the trainee *batteurs* struck planks of wood laid across chair backs. When he got home, Frank set about beating the paint off the bureau in his bedroom. To save the furniture, his parents rented a snare drum on which he was allowed to practise in the garage.

By 1953, there were six mouths to feed in the Zappa family, with the addition of another brother, Carl, and sister, Candy. Photographs from the period catch Frank on the threshold of his teenage, staring humourlessly at the camera, an incipient moustache the pelmet for a compressed, tight-lipped smile designed to satisfy the photographer and hide the dental work. His parents and brother Bob have no such reticence and grin with undisguised pleasure.

That year, Francis got a job as a metallurgist with Convair and the family moved to Pomona, midway between Los Angeles and San Bernadino. A year later, he transferred to San Diego to work on the Atlas missile project for two years, setting up home in El Cajon, east of the city. Frank's education, both state-controlled at Grossmont High School and self-promoted at home, continued apace. He was in the ninth grade at Grossmont when he designed a prize-winning poster for a Fire Prevention Week contest, entered by 30 schools. A photograph of Frank posing beside his effort appeared in the local press. A cartoon of three disgruntled children's faces was surmounted by the words, 'No Picnic'. Beneath, it said, 'Why? No Woods. Prevent Forest Fire.'[15]

It was his interest in art that led Frank to become intrigued by musical notation. 'I liked the way music looked on paper,' he told David Sheff. 'It was fascinating to me that you could see the notes and somebody who knew what they were doing would look at them and music would come out. I thought it was a miracle.'[16] The aesthetic pleasure gained from making patterns on manuscript paper didn't mean the results were necessarily playable but a percussion piece entitled 'Mice' did survive, written for a junior high school competition.

Turning on the car radio one day, he discovered vocal group music, specifically 'Gee' by the Crows. Other records that fed his fascination included 'I' by the Velvets, 'Riot In Cell Block Number Nine' by the Robins (with Richard Berry taking lead vocal), 'Johnny Darling' by the Feathers and 'Annie Had A Baby' by Hank Ballard and the Midnighters. Needless to say, his mother and father tried to discourage their son from finding the black stations on the radio dial, thus enhancing the pleasure of getting to hear the music.

After years of defacing furniture and the monotonous rataplan of a solitary snare, Frank convinced his parents to buy him a second-hand drumkit consisting of snare, hi-hat, bass drum, floor tom and ride cymbal. By now, he was attending Mission Bay High School in San Diego and had found a group of aspiring musicians who also liked R&B and came together as the Ramblers. At first, there was no drumkit for him to play, so at rehearsals at the home of the pianist, Stuart Congdon, he had to be content - make a bongo noise here - with beating on pots and pans placed between his knees.

The drumkit arrived a week before the band's first gig at San Diego's Uptown Hall, for which the sponsors, a local girl gang called the Blue Velvets, would pay them the princely sum of seven dollars. Things did not go well. On the way to the gig, Frank discovered that he'd left his only pair of sticks at home.

The band was led by Elwood 'Junior' Modeo (known as 'Bomba The Jungle Boy' on account of his Italian/Indian background). 'He was the lead guitar player,' Frank said later. 'He was really excellent and I used to love to listen to him play. I couldn't play very well, so eventually I got fired. As I should have, you know. The band deserved a better drummer than me.'[17] He told David Mead, 'My main drawback was that I didn't have good hand-to-foot co-ordination. I could play a lot of stuff on the snare and the tom-toms and the cymbal and everything, but I couldn't keep an even beat on the kick drum.'[18]

THE PRESENT-DAY COMPOSER

Alongside his interest in R&B, Frank had spent more than a year searching for a record he'd read about in *Look* magazine. The article extolled Sam Goody's New York record store and cited an album of music by the French composer Edgard (more often Edgar) Varèse as an example of the store's ability to sell anything. The album was *Complete Works Of Edgard Varèse, Volume 1*, the piece noted was *Ionisation* a six-minute composition for 13 percussionists playing 37 instruments. The article maintained it was so dissonant and ugly that no one would want to own it. Except Frank Zappa, who wanted it for that very reason.

Varèse had written *Ionisation* in 1931 as the culmination of his attempts to rid his music of everything but rhythm and intensity. Born in Paris in 1883, he studied music under D'Indy and Widor and became a protégé of Debussy and Richard Strauss. In 1915, he moved to New York where he set about expunging the diatonic music system from his writing, along with melody and harmony. In July 1921, he founded the International Composers Guild. Part of its manifesto stated, 'Dying is the privilege of the weary. The present day composers refuse to die. They have realised the necessity of banding together and fighting for the right of the individual to secure a fair and free presentation of his work.'

In a burst of creative exploration, Varèse wrote *Offrandes* (1921), *Hyperprism* (1922), *Octandre* (1923) and *Integrales* (1924). All of these works were scored for wind instruments and percussion, in line with his search for 'pure' notes played without the vibrato that could be applied to strings. *Integrales*, also on the album that Frank wanted to hear, used 14 musicians, of whom four were percussionists. From some of the 'events' within the score, it was to some extent a run-through for his next composition. *Arcana* was written between 1925 and 1927 and required a massive orchestra of 120 musicians, including 70 strings and eight percussionists playing 40 instruments.

By contrast, *Density 21.5* (1936), was written for solo flute; not just any flute but one made from platinum, a metal whose atomic density gave the work its title. This and *Integrales* were his last published compositions before Varèse suffered a creative impasse that lasted 15 years. Because of his obsession with pure sound, Varèse had taken an interest in such early electronic devices as the Theremin (featured on many 50s science fiction film soundtracks and on the Beach Boys' 'Good Vibrations'), the Dynaphone and the Ondes Martenot (an integral part of Oliver Messiaen's *Turangalila Symphony*). But it wasn't until the development of taped electronic music in the early 50s that Varèse discerned the way out of his dilemma. He was emerging from this long period of stalled creativity when the young Frank Zappa took an interest in his music.

As Frank tells it, he was staying at his friend Dave Franken's house in La Mesa, a San Diego suburb, when the pair decided to check out a sale of R&B singles at the local hi-fi store. On his way to pay for a couple of Joe Houston records, he glanced in an LP bin and saw what looked like a mad scientist with a shock of frizzy grey hair on an album cover. Closer inspection identified it as the very record for which he'd been searching, *The Complete Works Of Edgard Varèse, Volume 1*. His pocket money came up well short of the $5.95 price tag but some impassioned bargaining and the fact that it had already been used as a demonstration record for the store's hi-fi equipment closed the deal.

This was a pivotal moment, for the album was an important catalyst in his musical development. In Varèse's music, percussion played an integral part in each composition and dissonance held sway. 'The way I perceived the dissonance was, these chords are really mean. I like these chords. And the drums are playing loud in this music and you can hear the drums often in this music, which is something that you could not experience in other types of classical music.'[19]

His parents had recently bought a Decca record player in a sale at Smokey Rogers Music Store in El Cajon, along with two or three free 78s, one of which, 'The Little Shoemaker', became Mrs Zappa's favourite accompaniment to her ironing. 'It had little triangular legs on the bottom, so that it would be raised off the table and the speaker was in the bottom and it had one of those five-pound arms. It was really an ugly piece of audio gear.'[20]

It had never run at 33 1/3rpm before the Varèse album arrived in the household and it didn't take many plays for his parents to forbid him to play it in the living room. Thereafter, the machine vanished into his bedroom, where *Ionisation* was played several times a day. He gleaned what musical knowledge he could from the sleevenotes and tested friendship's fortitude by playing it to his high school classmates. 'What I used to do,' he told Paul Zollo, 'was play them parts of the Varèse album and then play them Lightnin' Slim things like 'My Starter Won't Work' or 'Have Your Way' or I'd play them some Howlin'

Wolf . . . usually that would get rid of the girls and the ignorant boys and what was left over was somebody you could have a conversation with.'[21]

Rigorous as ever in pursuit of a subject that interested him, Frank set about understanding the mechanics of music. There were books to be read, such as H.A. Clarke's *Counterpoint: Strict And Free*. But with no formal training, he exercised his habitual scepticism over the rules of counterpoint and harmony. 'I never studied counterpoint,' he told Don Menn. 'I could never understand it. I hated anything with rules, except for 12-tone, because it was so simple-minded. It was as simple-minded as the idea of getting a pen and some paper and some Higgins ink and just drawing some music.'[22]

One practical test was to find out what it was that made certain R&B records appeal more than others. Playing the Jewels' 'Angel In My Life' to Mr Kavelman, the Mission Bay band instructor, he was told that its particular charm rested in the use of parallel fourths. Mr Kavelman also told him about 12-tone music, which led to Frank's subsequent interest in the composer Webern.

For his fifteenth birthday, his mother proposed to give him $5 but Frank decided he'd rather call Varèse long-distance in New York. He got through to the apartment at 118 Sullivan Street, only to be told by Varèse's wife, Louise, that the great man was in Brussels working on what became *Poème Electronique*. In *The Real Frank Zappa Book*, he noted that when he eventually spoke to Varèse, the composer told him that he was working on a piece to be called *Deserts*. He wrote, 'When you're 15 and living in the Mojave Desert, and you find out that the World's Greatest Composer (who also looks like a mad scientist) is working in a secret Greenwich Village laboratory on a song about your hometown (so to speak), you can get pretty excited.'[23]

In the interim, his interest in things that go *bang!* if you make them had not been entirely superseded, and it had gone out in a literal blaze of glory. He and a like-minded friend had filled a large glass jar with a combination of zinc, sulphur and stink-bomb powder. With the aid of a supply of paper cups and more willing hands, he proceeded to disrupt an Open House Night with a series of foul-smelling fires. The following day, he was summoned to the principal's office for a terse lecture from the fire officer and an ultimatum: two weeks suspension or a 2,000-word essay. So he took two weeks off and returned with a list of his R&B records by song title, artist and label and those that he expected to buy in the foreseeable future. 'I laughed at them.'[24]

Further retribution was prevented when Mrs Zappa informed the probation officer (who just happened to be an Italian) that Mr Zappa was about to be transferred to Lancaster. This was a sprawling community at the northernmost limit of Los Angeles County, beyond the San Gabriel Mountains and alongside Edwards Air Force Base in the Mojave Desert.

VILLAGE OF THE SUN

Lancaster was in Antelope Valley, dubbed in typical early 50s hyperbole the 'New Empire of Urban and Industrial Progress in the Southland'. Before the arrival of the aerospace industry, Lancaster had been a small town principally devoted to the cultivation of alfalfa. As the town grew, its streets were laid out on a geometric grid, with the odd bend to keep drunk drivers alert. To this day, many outlying roads only exist as 'Avenue F-10' or 'G-14'. Downtown hides amongst the endless rows of anonymous streets. Dust from the Mojave makes Lancaster an arid, shabby town of pastel colours.

It may have been a boomtown, as men like Francis came to work on data reduction for the missile projects at Edwards, but enervation was the local pastime. The Zappa family moved in at 45438 Third Street East, alongside the Antelope Valley Fair Grounds. A hundred yards further, the street petered out into scrubland. 'I lived on a tract of little stucco houses,' as Frank put it. 'Okies dying in their yards. You know how you always have to pull up a Chevrolet and let it croak on your lawn.'[25] 'In a way I hated it while I was there, and in other ways I thought it was a really great place to be. It's not a glamourous desert, like Arizona. It's just desert, but that's nice. It's kind of ascetic, which is not something you would imagine a 15 or 16-year-old kid would be interested in.'[26]

He was enrolled at Antelope Valley Union High School, which occupied the north-east quadrant of the junction of Division Street and Lancaster Boulevard. 'It was a pretty strange place. It was not a homogenised high school environment like you would see in movies of high school life of the time.'[27] There were 2,500 students, made up of the children of the alfalfa farmers and those from the Air Force base. 'Anyone who came there to work on defence was an outcast. We felt like squatters.'[28]

As before, Frank only did well in subjects that interested him. Consequently identified as a 'problem' student, he was put into an art class where he created a ten-minute film with classical music soundtrack for which he hand-painted every frame. But opportunities for such self-expression were rare in a system that valued conformity at any price. For Frank, non-conformity was the price of lunch.

'I used to look forward to lunch time because there was a place down the street from the school that had really exceptional chilli,' he told Nigel Leigh, 'which was my favourite thing in the world to eat. I would have a bowl of chilli with crackers, a large bottle of RC cola and listen to the jukebox. That was my main interest in school. The couple that owned the chilli place, Opal and Chester, agreed to ask the man who serviced the jukebox to put in some of the song titles that I liked. Because I promised that I would dutifully keep pumping quarters into this thing so I could listen to them. So I had the ability to eat good chilli and listen to 'Three Hours Past Midnight' by Johnny

'Guitar' Watson for most of my junior and senior years.'[29]

'That's probably one of the most important musical statements I ever heard in my life,' he said in 1988. 'What Watson was doing was not just pentatonic scales,' he told David Mead. 'One of the things I admired about him was his tone, this wiry, kind of nasty, aggressive and penetrating tone, and another was the fact that the things that he would play would often come out as rhythmic outbursts over the constant beat of the accompaniment.'[30] This latter facet also recommended itself in the work of Eddie 'Guitar Slim' Jones, composer of 'The Things I Used To Do'.

The day that I was due to talk to Frank, I'd bought a CD of that track and 25 other of Jones' Specialty recordings. It prompted me to ask, what it was about Slim that interested him. 'Mostly the attitude but a little bit of the notes, too. Because the few solos that I heard on those Specialty recordings, it just seemed like he grabbed it, he got mad at it and he said, "So there!". 'The Story Of My Life', it'd be nice to hear it without the scratches because, let me tell you, I played that song so many times, it was just dust by the time I stopped listening.'

When I showed him the CD, Frank's eyes lit up for the first time in our conversation. I left the house several hours later but the Guitar Slim CD stayed in its new home.

Despite his 'difficult' status, Frank continued to grace the pages of the local press. 'Versatile AVHS Student Is Winner Of State Competition' headlined the story of his success in a painting competition, sponsored by the California Federation of Women's Clubs, on the theme 'Symphony Of Living' with an abstract painting, Family Room. The article went on, 'He is presently engaged in writing a book but his reply to a query as to whether painting or literature would be his chosen career was, "Music".'[31]

Ernest Tossi, vice-principal in charge of discipline, felt the need to build an uneasy alliance with the single-minded newcomer. 'Frank was the forerunner of student militancy and the beatniks because he was wearing sideburns and a moustache,' he said later, his words more simplistic than the hindsight that prompted them. 'Frank was an independent thinker who couldn't accept the Establishment's set of rules.' But, he added, 'To make progress you've got to be creative. In my mind, if Frank chose to go academic to a university and get a PhD, he could. I saw his test scores and I know Frank has the talent of a genius.'[32]

Frank referred to Ernest Tossi as 'my favourite confrontation with authority'. They treated one another with wary respect, the school teacher urging the teenager to obey the rules, the teenager seeking to interpret them to his own advantage. He also listened to Mr Ballard, Antelope's music instructor and band director. William Ballard indulged Frank's experimental mind by letting him write music which the school band would attempt to play. 'A high school orchestra in those days tuned up to a box which put out a tone,' he told Andy Gill. 'The B flat was used for tuning up the marching band and the orchestra tuned to the A. So I took the first violins and tuned them to the A, and took the second violins and tuned them to B flat, guaranteeing that whatever they played would be dissonant, no matter what was on the page.'[33]

Frank remained grateful to Ballard: 'He saved me a lot of effort in later life just by letting me hear things like that. Of course, the other people in the orchestra thought I was out of my fucking mind.'[34] Back at home, the Zappa family couldn't afford a piano so Frank wrote with the aid of a xylarimba.

'I had no outlet in music then to express my discontent. So my aggravation with the way things were festered throughout my high-school years,' he told Dan Ouellette. 'The only reason I got training as a musician was because the school needed a marching band at its football games.' But cigarettes had already become part of his lifelong diet. 'We had to sit in the freezing cold and wear these dorky maroon-and-grey uniforms and play every time our team scored a touchdown. So, during a break, I went under the bleachers for a smoke. I got caught and I was out of there. Not just for smoking but for smoking in uniform.'[35] Even so, Ballard and Tossi's names appear in the acknowledgements to *Freak Out!*, along with Frank's English teacher, Don Cerveris, of whom more later.

Because of his 'unruly' status, Frank was given permission to take harmony classes in the neighbouring junior college. His teacher was Mr Russell, a jazz trumpeter in his spare time, who gave him Piston's *Harmony* to study. 'I don't think he enjoyed harmony very much either, but that's what he was teaching.'[36] Walter Piston, who died in 1976, wrote a number of symphonies and books on musical theory and taught musicians such as Leonard Bernstein and Elliott Carter. All of which counted for little with Frank.

'I went through some of the exercises in there. And I was wondering why a person would really want to devote a lifetime to doing this, because after you complete it you'll sound like everybody else who used the same rules. So I learned enough of the basic stuff so I got the concept of what harmony was supposed to do, what voice leading was supposed to do, how melody was supposed to function in a harmonic climate, what rhythm was supposed to do. I learned all of that and then chucked the rest of it.'[37]

He was more intrigued by the work of Moravian composer Aloys Haba, one of the first to experiment with quarter tone intervals. Haba studied at the Universities of Prague, Vienna and Berlin, where his interest in birdsong and his country's folk music led him to write microtonal music for string quartets and small orchestras. Instruments, including harmonium, piano and trumpet, were made for him and he wrote a book propounding the use of third, fifth and twelfth tones. His most famous work was a microtonal opera,

The Mother, last performed in Florence, Italy in 1964.

Frank's constant flouting of the school authorities created friction at home. 'I was also hearing it from my father who had a security clearance and he was saying, "You must behave, otherwise I'll lose my clearance and therefore my job".'38 Despite that, when Frank was put on suspension (which happened frequently), Francis would fight the school himself. 'I got so goddamn sick and tired of going to see these guys,' he said later, 'that I in turn gave them hell and I talked the language which was very vernacular, so they could really understand what I was saying, so that they didn't care too much for Frank.'39

It's hard to think of Frank Zappa as a representative of any faction but to school authorities he was just another troublesome adolescent who regarded rebellion as a way of life. America was still reeling from 'reds under the bed' and the House Un-American Activities Committee; it was the era of *The Blackboard Jungle* and *Rebel Without A Cause*, of rock 'n' roll and 'juvenile delinquency'. As individuals and in gangs, teenagers fought authority and each other to find a different conformity from that which Senator McCarthy had pressed on their parents. 'The impact of this poor, mentally ill, alcoholic son of a bitch and what he did to the United States, that naughty old Joe McCarthy . . . I could never forgive that guy.'40

At high schools like Antelope Valley, there was social cachet to delinquency which accorded with Frank's own highly developed sense of non-conformity. While not exactly a loner, his varied interests and the single-minded way in which he pursued them, had already marked him out as something of an outsider with little inclination for the gang mentality. The only group activity he wished to indulge in was playing music and that was just a part of his on-going self-education. The second album he bought was a budget version of Igor Stravinsky's *The Rite Of Spring* by The World-Wide Symphony Orchestra. To his way of thinking, there was no difference between Varèse and Stravinsky and Howlin' Wolf, Lightnin' Slim, the Crows or the Robins. 'To me it was all good music,' he wrote later.41

To feed his need for R&B, Frank worked lunchtimes and after school in the local record store, becoming the buyer and thereby upping the valley's awareness of groups like the Dells and the Rocking Brothers, as well as Guitar Slim, Little Richard and Clarence 'Gatemouth' Brown. He also discovered that Gilbert's Dime Store sold used jukebox records for a few cents apiece and 'it was just crawling with Excello releases'.

His interest in Varèse still undiminished, Frank wrote to the composer while spending the summer of 1957 with his Aunt Mary in Baltimore, hoping for the opportunity of travelling to New York to visit him. A handwritten reply, dated July 12, 1957, read:

Dear Mr Zappa,
I am sorry not to be able to grant you your request. I am leaving for Europe next
week and will be gone until next spring. I am hoping however to see you on my return.
With best wishes,
Sincerely,
Edgard Varèse

The meeting never took place. Varèse died on November 6, 1965. Frank later framed the letter and hung it in the workroom of his Laurel Canyon home.

CHEAP THRILLS

With a disregard for convention that was already a finely-honed skill, Frank formed a racially-integrated R&B band. He called them the Blackouts, since members of the rocking teenage combo often assumed the horizontal after drinking peppermint schnapps, their tipple of choice. He and Terry Wimberly were of white immigrant stock, Wayne Lyles, Johnny and Carter Franklin were black, the Salazar brothers Mexican. The combination was guaranteed to offend the Ivy Leaguers and cheerleaders who formed the high school's social elite.

'At Lancaster the cheerleaders had such an importance, boola boola wasn't enough for them,' Frank scoffed in 1968, 'they were running what you call the student government too. They were just pigs. It was too American for me.'[42] Of course, the pariahs in this pastiche of real life American style were the black students whose parents bred turkeys down the road in Sun Village, east of Palmdale.

The Blackouts rehearsed a ten-song set that included 'Kansas City', 'Behind The Sun', 'Okie Dokie Stomp' and Little Richard's 'Directly From My Heart To You'. Their finest moment came at an NAACP benefit at Los Angeles' Shrine Auditorium, when they were the warm-up band for Earl Bostic. Another gig, sponsored by the Eagles Lodge and entitled The Summer Blowout, combined Frank's past and present with the promise that The Blackouts and Ramblers would 'wail' at Lancaster Fairgrounds Exposition Hall.[43] More memorable, and parochial, was a gig arranged at the Lancaster Women's Club. The evening before, Frank was arrested for vagrancy at 6.00 pm and spent the night in jail.

Plainly the authorities didn't want the dance to take place. But Frank was sprung by his parents and the dance went on to be a success. At the end of the evening, the Ivy Leaguers made one last attempt to express their disapproval. The 'varsity white-bread boys' shaped up for a fight as the band were loading their equipment into Johnny Franklin's Studebaker. They were dissuaded by the timely appearance of a bunch of Sun Village residents with their hands full of baseball bats and their minds on percussive maintenance.

CHAPTER TWO
CRUISING FOR BURGERS

In his final year of high school, Frank met another character who, like him, had a reputation for singular conduct and poor school attendance. Don Vliet had just left Antelope High to take over his father Glen's job, after the latter's heart attack. Don had been born in Glendale, California on January 15, 1941. He'd had an equally unique, precocious and self-directed childhood. 'I had my parents trained from the time I was a baby,' he told Kristine McKenna. 'I used to tell them they were my gas station. I remember one time I branded my mother. She used to wear those mule type shoes . . . you know, she'd clip clop across the room. One time, I was about three, I put a piece of toast under the rug. She shuffled into it, went flying and landed on the heater. It branded her with an 'H' that's never gone away.'[1]

He told interviewer John Yau that he'd picked up the harmonica at about the same age. He also claimed a harmonica-playing grandfather, Amos Vertenor Warfield, who was second cousin to Wallis Simpson, 'the gold-digger who got that English guy to give up the throne'.[2] By the time he was five, he'd created a private world in his bedroom, refused to attend school regularly and spent his time creating clay animal sculptures. When he was 12, he met the Portuguese sculptor Augustinio Rodriguez in Griffith Park one day. His evident skill with clay led to him being featured on Rodriguez' weekly television show. The following year, a local patroness offered him a six-year scholarship to study art in Italy. Glen and his mother Sue demurred on his behalf, delivering the dictum that all artists were queers.

The family, including Uncle Alan and Aunt Ione, moved to Mojave and then Lancaster, where Glen drove a Helms Bread van and Sue became an Avon lady. When Frank met him, Don had a live-in girlfriend, Laurie, who was regularly flashed by Uncle Alan. He'd leave the bathroom door open when he took a leak; as she passed by, he would extol the virtues of his appendage, referring to it as a 'beef heart'.

Frank discovered Don was the only other teenager in Lancaster with an interest in blues and R&B. Music was their strongest point of contact. Both had grown up as loners, creating their own worlds to keep at bay a reality that each scorned. The difference was that Frank used his as a shield in order to pursue his own ends, while Don's was a living environment. He had what Langdon Winner called 'an unstructured consciousness'[3], which allowed him to perceive language and art with unique insight, as his later records and paintings would prove.

Don and Frank spent their evenings playing records, memorising lyrics, singing guitar solos and testing each other's knowledge of artists, labels and catalogue numbers, while eating stale cakes from the Helms Bread van. They would end the night by cruising the desert roads in a vain search for girls. 'His main interest in life at that time was dressing sharp, having his hair done exactly right and riding around town in a baby blue Oldsmobile with a homemade werewolf head mounted underneath the plastic dome thing in the centre of the steering wheel.'[4]

The Blackouts lasted about a year and a half, after which Frank sold part of his drumkit and rented the rest to a local band called the Bluenotes. Through listening to Johnny 'Guitar' Watson and Clarence 'Gatemouth' Brown, he became interested in the guitar. 'My father had always had a guitar in the house,' Frank told Nigel Leigh, 'and it stayed in the closet. Ever since I was a little kid, I would go in and see this thing and strum on it. But I couldn't imagine how you would get anything other than the open string sound. I couldn't conceive of what the frets were for.

'The first one in the family to figure it out was my younger brother, Bobby.'[5] He'd bought 'an arch-top, f-hole, ugly mother-fucker'[6] for $1.50 at an auction; it was old and the maker's name had long since been scuffed off. 'He learned to play the guitar before I did. He knew chords, so I used to make him play chords in the background while I played lead lines. Once I'd figured out that the pitch changed when you put your finger down on the fret, I was hell on wheels.'[7] The guitar's action was so high that he couldn't play chords on it, so lead lines were all he could achieve. 'I didn't learn to play chords until after about a year but in four weeks I was playing shitty teenage leads.'[8] 'I liked it because it was so tinny-sounding,' he told David Mead. 'It was just an acoustic guitar, but it was moving closer to that wiry tone I liked with Johnny 'Guitar' Watson, especially if you picked it right next to the bridge.'[9]

An example has survived: 'Lost In A Whirlpool' is an R&B parody recorded in an Antelope High classroom on a school tape recorder. Don Vliet sings in falsetto, backed by a strummed rhythm guitar played by Bobby Zappa and Frank's fairly accomplished lead lines, perhaps played on his father's guitar to which he'd attached a DeArmond soundhole pickup. The song grew out of a story dreamt up by Frank and two of his friends, Larry Littlefield and Jeff Harris, while they all attended Mission Bay High School in San Diego. A boy addresses his girlfriend, who has flushed him down the toilet. 'There's a big brown fish lookin' at me. He ain't got no eyes, how could that motherfucker possibly see?' The boy pleads for help; 'Pour some Drano down and get the plunger right after me. I'll let you know a little secret, baby. I'm getting tired of all this pee.' Ah! schooldays.

The guitar became a permanent accessory which Frank took to school every day. It fitted right in with his 'student militant' ensemble, blue-hooded parka jacket, sunglasses, moustache and goatee. 'I know I was weird.'[10] Hardly surprising that in middle age, Frank would reminisce, 'They didn't like me, and I knew they didn't like me, and I didn't like them'.[11]

Euclid James Sherwood recalls Franks sitting out study periods on the school's front lawn, hammering out his shitty teenage leads. Sherwood, in his freshman year, shared classes with Bobby Zappa. He was another blues and R&B fan, prompting Bobby to introduce him to his older brother. He remembers attending a gig at 'the Moose Lodge or something' shortly before the Blackouts disbanded.[12] With Don Vliet and Sherwood as occasional members, they would become the Omens after the Zappa family had moved away from Lancaster.

Frank graduated from high school on Friday, June 13, 1958, with some 20 units less than the required standard. It was a measure of the school's wish to see the back of him and mirrored Frank's own feelings about state education. His father was urging him to study music at the Peabody Conservatory in Maryland but he was adamant that his school days were over.

RUN HOME SLOW

In the spring of 1959, the Zappa family moved again, this time to Claremont, east of Pasadena. Frank used the opportunity to get his own apartment in the Echo Park district of Hollywood, between the Hollywood Freeway and the Dodgers Stadium. At the time it was largely a Mexican neighbourhood and housing was cheap. For that reason, a decade later it would become popular with students and retained its youthful image to become the setting and title of a 1985 offbeat comedy film starring Tom Hulce and Susan Dey.

Some time earlier, Don Cerveris, Frank's English teacher at Antelope Valley had left to try his luck as a scriptwriter in Hollywood. They had kept in touch and now Cerveris convinced Tim Sullivan, producer of his low-budget Western, *Run Home Slow*, to hire Frank to write the music score. Unfortunately, the leading lady had a miscarriage on the third day of shooting and the production was shelved until Sullivan could raise more money. One of the themes Frank had written turned up later as 'Duke Of Prunes' on *Absolutely Free*.

In the meantime, Frank was nurturing the stomach ulcers he'd had since he was sixteen. Heeding the advice of the failed film project, he moved back to Claremont. Still in search of sexual recreation, he enrolled for a harmony course, with required keyboard practice, taught by Miss Holly at Chaffey Junior College in Alta Loma. He also sat in, unsanctioned, on a composition course taught by Mr Kohn at the Pomona College nearby. Joyce Shannon was head of the Music Department at Chaffey and remembered Frank clearly: 'He was a very exceptional music student, extremely bright. He had read the text I used on his own, which was amazing to me because it wasn't an easy book to read, and he was contemptuous of a lot of academia. He went out of his way to study both books and musical scores.'[13]

This last stab at formal education only lasted for one semester either side of the summer vacation. Its one significant outcome was that Frank met Kay Sherman, his first wife. The pair dropped out of college and lived together for a while before getting married and moving into a house at 314 West G Street. There's a fuzzy photograph of them in *The Real Frank Zappa*. Light has damaged the film but a conventionally clothed couple are seen standing on the porch; she a blonde in dark cardigan and skirt, her hand coyly placed flat beside her thigh, he with flat-top haircut, pencil tie, his light-coloured cardigan unbuttoned.

Unbuttoned could not describe their life together. Kay worked as a secretary for the First National Bank of Ontario and Frank got a job at the Nile Running Greeting Card company. 'I was in the silk-screen department with the big rubber gloves,' he told Matt Groening, 'pulling the Mylar off of these smelly things.'[14] He convinced the owner to let him prepare a few experimental designs. The front cover of one read 'Captured Russian Photo Shows Evidence of American Presence on Moon First'. Inside was a picture of a lunar crater bearing the legend, 'Jesus Saves'. Another had 'Goodbye' on the front and a black hand inside. More mentally challenging was the one with the word 'Farky' on its cover, which opened to reveal a picture of a pirate.

There were other jobs, as a copy writer and designer of ads for local businesses, including his wife's employers, as a window dresser, a jewelry salesman and a door-to-door salesman for Collier's Encyclopaedias, at which he lasted only slightly longer than the three-day training period.

Music was confined to his ongoing and then-unheard experiments with twelve-tone music and weekend bar and high school gigs with his band, the Boogie Men, consisting of Frank's vocals and lead guitar, Kenny Burgan on saxophone, Doug Rost on rhythm guitar and Al Surratt on drums. They never earned enough to afford a bass player. A local newspaper printed a photograph of them rehearsing in Frank's garage.

Frank had hired his first electric guitar, a Fender Telecaster, and found that he had to learn to play all over again. With that achieved, he bought himself a Fender Jazzmaster and had cards printed: 'F.V. Zappa Composer-Master Blues Guitarist', with his G Street address and message service. When the Boogie Men folded, he joined a 'really wretched' four-piece lounge band called Joe

Perrino and the Mellotones. Their picture appeared in the press too, with Frank looking defiant and Joe flourishing a pair of drumsticks above his timbales. The caption noted that they were 'rockin' the town from the bandstand of Tommy Sandi's Club Sahara on E Street in San Bernardino . . . They're a real action group.'15

Picture the scene: Frank Zappa in white tuxedo, bow tie, black pants and patent leather shoes, perched on a stool, strumming the 'Anniversary Waltz' and 'Happy Birthday To You', allowed to play just one 'twist number' a night. 'You had to read songs out of a (thick) brown book, flip the pages in the dark and see what the chord changes were.'16 As well as the Club Sahara, the band oozed their way through gigs at the clubs around West Covina. 'I could tolerate that for a short period of time (about ten months) but eventually I hated it so much, I just put the guitar in the case, stuck it behind the sofa and didn't play at all for about eight months.'17 And he remembered the experience, which he commemorated as 'America Drinks & Goes Home' on *Absolutely Free*.

Luckily, other work offered itself. In June 1961, he began writing music for another film, *The World's Greatest Sinner*. Written, produced and directed by Timothy Carey, described (probably by himself) as Hollywood's 'ugliest, meanest' character actor, for Frenzy Productions, the $90,000 budget meant that 80% of the film was made in Carey's El Monte garage. Was it vaulting ambition or un-American irony that invested the story of a frustrated insurance salesman who turns to music, religion and politics before finally repenting of his attempt to identify himself as God? David Koresh should have taken note.

In the March 9, 1962 *Pomona Progress-Bulletin*, under the headline, 'Ontario Man Writes Score for New Film', Frank noted that, 'The score is unique in that it uses every type of music.'18 No further explanation was given but it was revealed that 'a small rock 'n' roll group - eight musicians - recorded last November'. In early December a 20-piece chamber ensemble recorded. Then on December 17, the 55-piece Pomona Valley Symphony, augmented by other musicians from Pomona High School and Chaffey Junior College and directed by Fred E. Graff, was recorded in a 12-hour session at the Chaffey Junior College Little Theater.

Since the proceedings were recorded on two microphones, mixed to mono and recorded on portable equipment in a truck parked outside, it was little wonder that Frank later pronounced the results 'rancid'. The final indignity was that, once again, he never got paid. However, the main theme did appear as the b-side of a single by Baby Ray & The Ferns in March 1963 and even later, it was transmuted into the first, slow version of 'Holiday In Berlin' on *Burnt Weeny Sandwich*.

It's tempting to speculate whether the same resources were used when

Frank payed $300 for a concert of his own music which took place sometime in 1962 at Mount St. Mary's College. 'It was all oddball, textured weirdo stuff,' he told Don Menn. 'I was doing tape editing of electronic music and part of all the pieces had this little cheesoid Wollensack tape recorder in the background pumping out through mono speakers.'[19] Frank had also been experimenting with home movies and so there were screens on which these 16mm films were projected. This multi-media event was broadcast by radio station KPFK, which perhaps helped to defer Frank's costs. It was almost certainly the source for later bootlegs of the concert, which included such titles as *Piece No. 2* or *Visual Music for Jazz Ensemble and 16mm Projector* (written in 1957), *Piano Piece from 'Opus 5'*, *Collage One For String Instruments* and *Opus 5 For Piano, Tape Recorder And Multiple Orchestra*.

CUCAMONGA

Going west out of San Bernardino, Route 66 becomes Foothill Boulevard and 16 miles later reaches Cucamonga, where it crosses Archibald Avenue. Just north of the intersection at 8040 North Archibald in 1963 was the Pal Recording Studio, owned by Paul Buff. Buff had learned electronics in the US Marines and on his discharge had rented the three-room premises and set about constructing a recording studio. The control room contained an eight-channel Presto mixing desk, a Hammond spring echo unit and a Rec-O-Cut cutting lathe for acetates. More importantly, he built his own tape machine.

'I think he's a genius guy,' Frank told William Ruhlmann. 'He built his own five-track recorder at a time when four-track was an absolutely exotic piece of equipment in the industry. Three-track was something that they used for filmwork. Four-track was rare.'[20] Buff also had pretensions as a recording artist and set about teaching himself the rudiments of every instrument he needed to imitate the hits of the day. 'He would listen to whatever was on the tracks and he would grasp what the hook element was and then build his version of something that contained the same hook-type material.'[21]

Frank was introduced to Buff by Ronnie Williams, 'a guitar-player that I was working with in some local bands at that time. Ronnie had joined him up there and was putting guitar parts on some of his things and then Ronnie brought me over and I worked with him on some stuff.'[22] 'Some stuff' turned out to be 14 singles over the course of two years by sundry real and invented artists. The first record from the alliance was 'Breaktime' and '16 Tons', the a-side written by Buff, Williams and Zappa and released as by the Masters on Emmy 10082, a label owned by Buff. 'Gotta Find My Roogalator', written by Frank and sung by Paul Jameson, followed on Penthouse 503, of which only promotional copies survive.

Ten singles on various labels were issued during 1963, including 'Love Of My Life' and 'Tell Me' (Daani 101) by Ron Roman, 'Dear Jeepers' and

'Letter From Jeepers' (Donna 1380) by Bob Guy, 'Cradle Rock' and 'Everytime I See You' (Donna 1381) by the Heartbreakers, 'The Big Surfer 'and 'Not Another One' (Vigah! 001) by Brian Lord and the Midnighters, 'Hey Nelda' and 'Surf Along' (Vigah! 002) by Ned and Nelda and 'Tijuana Surf' and 'Grunion Run' (Original Sound 39) by the Hollywood Persuaders.

Bob Guy introduced horror movies on a local television station; Frank wrote the Jeepers songs in imitation of John Zacherle's single, 'Dinner With Drac'. Brian Lord was a San Bernardino DJ who imitated President John F. Kennedy. Vigah! was another of Paul Buff's labels and he subsequently leased the record to Capitol for $800. It received a catalogue number, Capitol 4981, and would have been released in June 1963. It never reached the stores, though. One of the record's jokes involving the Peace Corps backfired when Medgar Evers, a field secretary in the NAACP, was murdered in Jackson, Mississippi on June 12. Thirty-one years after the event and exactly two calendar months after Frank went on his last tour, Byron De La Beckwith, 73, was finally convicted of Evers' murder, having been twice acquitted back in 1964.

The other Vigah! release parodied Paul and Paula's 'Hey Paula', a saccharine teen hit produced by Major Bill Smith, a Texas entrepreneur. The Heartbreakers were two local 14-year-old Mexican kids, while the Hollywood Persuaders consisted of Frank and Paul Buff, who played all the instruments on Tijuana Surf. 'Grunion Run', a Zappa composition, was also covered by the Jim Musil Combo.

Since Frank and Paul were both multi-instrumentalists of a sort, the pair wrote and constructed their backing tracks with occasional assistance from musicians that Frank would meet on the local club circuit. One of these was Ray Collins, a veteran of several R&B groups including Chicano doo-woppers Little Julian Herrera & The Tigers, who encountered Frank playing in The Sportsman, a Pomona bar that didn't even have a stage. 'I figured that any band that played 'Work With Me Annie' was all right,' he said. He sang with the band that night and told Frank of an idea for a song based on a catch-phrase used by Steve Allen on his networked TV show.

Frank wrote the song and recruited Collins to sing it. 'How's Your Bird' and 'The World's Greatest Sinner' were released on Donna 1378 as by Baby Ray & The Ferns, a group that consisted of Frank, Ray Collins, Paul Buff and Dick Barber, the last of whom went on to become the Mothers' road manager and 'snorker'. Collins also co-wrote with Frank the Ned and Nelda single and 'Memories Of El Monte', an affectionate parody of 50s doo-wop released by the Penguins on Original Sound 27.

It may have been through the Baby Ray record that Frank appeared on the *Steve Allen Show*. It was reported in the local press under the headline, 'Ontario Composer, Steve Allen To Play Wacky Duet'. This was a concerto for two performers and a bicycle. 'It's very funny,' Frank was quoted. 'You play a bicycle by plucking the spokes and blowing through the handlebars.'[23] He was photographed with the show's host, dressed in acceptable dark suit and tie, clutching a violin bow.

Other techniques of 'cyclophony', it appeared, included stroking the spokes with the violin bow, twirling the pedals and letting the air out of the tyres. This was abetted by a man in the control room 'fooling around' with a tape recorder and a jazz group supplying 'toneless background noise'. The news item also noted that 'The World's Greatest Sinner' had recently had its premiere at the Vista-Continental Theater in Hollywood.

Another project in the summer of 1963 was the formation of the Soots, which brought Frank and Don Vliet together, along with guitarist Alex St. Clair and Vic Mortenson on drums. The group made several recordings, including 'Metal Man Has Won His Wings', 'Cheryl's Canon' and 'Slippin' And Slidin'', Don's take on Little Richard. 'Metal Man' featured Don, recorded in the hallway that served for a vocal booth, emitting a series of falsetto whoops and barely audible barked asides that are almost swamped by Frank's extended guitar solo. However, the repeated chanting of the song's title is clear enough to question how bootleggers could have called this 'Metal Man Has Hornet Wings' for so long. The lyrics were derived from a comic book that was pinned to a notice-board beside the studio door. The tapes were sent to Dot Records and on September 19, 1963, a standard rejection letter (addressed to 'Mr V. Zappa') arrived from Dot A&R man, Milt Rogers.[24]

Providentially, at the end of the year Frank's other film score was resurrected when *Run Home Slow* finally went into production with actress Mercedes McCambridge in a leading role. Better still, Frank received $2,000, part of which paid for the Gibson ES-5 Switchmaster guitar which he used on the Mothers' first three albums. Most of what was left went into the purchase of Pal Studios. Paul Buff had been in financial difficulties for some months, unable to keep up the lease payments. Frank agreed to take over these payments and to rent and/or buy the studio equipment. The contract, dated August 1, 1964, detailed the minutiae of the deal, whereby Frank payed Buff $1,000, a reduction of $212 on the supposed value of the equipment, and payed a rental of $50 per month until individual items were sold.

'He showed me how to work the stuff and I went from being kind of an incompetent commercial artist to a full-time obsessive overdub maniac, working in this studio.'[25] Little or none of what was recorded over the next four or five months has been released, apart from 'Charva', featuring Frank on vocal, piano, bass and drums, which appears on the *Mystery Disc* included in *The Old Masters Box One*. The original five-track masters are unplayable on current equipment but two-track mixes of such things as 'Lonely Lips' by

Sonny Wilson could only be released if the original participants could be located.

Frank renamed the establishment Studio Z and threw an opening night party attended by Ray Collins, Motorhead Sherwood and Don Vliet, among others. A short sound collage from the event also turns up on the above-mentioned *Mystery Disc*. The colour scheme was changed to olive green and turquoise blue and Frank painted 'Record Your Band' and '$13.50 Per Hour' on the walls each side of the front door.

At about this time, his marriage to Kay finally cracked under the strain that his lifestyle and pursuits had put upon it. Frank filed for divorce and moved into Studio Z. It was to be a rigorous life, for there were no domestic facilities and only an industrial sink to wash in. He was quickly joined by Motorhead Sherwood, who combined the attributes of saxophonist, car mechanic and food scrounger. Through his efforts, their staple diet consisted of peanut butter, instant mashed potatoes, coffee and honey, with the occasional trip to the grocery store to exchange empty pop bottles for cigarettes.

A few weeks after Studio Z opened for business, Frank bought a job-lot of film scenery from an auction at the F.K. Rockett Studios. For $50 he acquired a two-sided cyclorama, a kitchen, a library interior and a building exterior. He repainted all the sets himself, including the two-dimensional rocket ship illustrated in *The Real Frank Zappa*. This was to be part of the scenery for *Captain Beefheart vs. The Grunt People*, a science-fiction film script written with Don Vliet in mind. 'The Birth Of Captain Beefheart', included on the *Mystery Disc* in *The Old Masters Box One*, was a sample of the dialogue.

Another project was 'a stupid piece of trash' called 'I Was A Teenage Maltshop', an attempt at the world's first 'rock opera'. The opening theme was played on the piano by Frank, accompanied by Motorhead Sherwood's acoustic guitar and Vic Mortenson on drums. After Captain Beefheart had introduced himself and predicted that 'we've got a heck of a little teenage opera for you – really', two unidentified female voices deliver a cheer-leaders' version of 'Status Back Baby' before 'Ned The Mumbler' makes his appearance. Described by Beefheart as 'a teenage Lone Ranger', Frank sings over a slow blues and then a fast rock vamp. 'Ned Has A Brainstorm' consists of a short burst of overdubbed guitar nonsense followed by an early version of what would become 'Toads Of The Short Forest'.

THE STREETS OF FONTANA

At the time, one of his few sources of income was a weekend gig back in Sun Village. The Village Inn was a barbecue hut where Frank would play with some of his old high school friends, including Johnny Franklin on bass, for the princely sum of $7 a night. A taped excerpt of one such gig, with 'Toby' on drums, Motorhead Sherwood on tenor sax and 'Frankie Zappo' on guitar, was also included on the *Mystery Disc* already mentioned. These occasions enabled him to keep in touch with the ex-Blackouts, who now called themselves the Omens. Motorhead was in the band and remembers that during that time, Frank 'would come up for battles of the bands all the time'.[26] Years later, memories of the period formed the basis for 'Village Of The Sun', a song that appeared on the live album, *Roxy & Elsewhere*.

Less remunerative but more fun were the gigs he and Ray Collins performed as a sardonic parody of a folk duo, calling themselves 'The Sin City Boys'. 'We sang 'Puff The Magic Dragon' as 'Joe The Puny Greaser' and we played a perverted version of 'The Streets Of Laredo' called 'The Streets Of Fontana'. We weren't setting out to make any kind of impact on people. We were just doing it for a laugh, to have fun.'[27] Ranging further afield, they also appeared on 'Talent Night' at The Troubadour in Los Angeles. 'We went down there, and we're singing songs about pimples and all kinds of other far-out things. It seems like a lot of that was the basis of some of the things that the Mothers eventually wound up doing.'[28]

On that occasion, they appeared as 'Loeb & Leopold', named after the young Illinois homosexuals, Richard Loeb and Nathan Leopold Jr., who were sentenced to life imprisonment in 1924 for the murder two years previously of Robert Franks. The story of how they did the deed as an expression of their 'superiority' was fictionalised by novelist Meyer Levin and filmed in 1959 as *Compulsion* by Richard Fleischer, with Bradford Dillman and Dean Stockwell in the leading roles.

As he'd proved on 'Ned The Mumbler', Frank was still a reluctant vocalist, largely because of his professed inability to sing and play guitar simultaneously. But for a short while he assumed the double role, forming a power trio he called The Muthers with bassist Paul Woods and Les Papp on drums. The band worked clubs and bars in the Pomona area, particularly at The Saints & Sinners on Holt Boulevard in nearby Ontario. 'We were playing 'In The Midnight Hour' to an audience of Mexican labourers, entertained by four go-go girls in black fishnet stockings.'[29] When they weren't ogling the dancers' latticed thighs, the audience looked askance at the group's appearance. They affected 'longish' hair; 'that is to say, it was aiming downward and about three inches long. In that day and age for that part of the country, I was a mutant . . . I was wearing striped shirts unheard-of to a population that thrives on the white short-sleeved T-shirt, because that's what you wore to work.'[30]

There was a constant police presence in the club, one officer on weekdays and two at weekends. One night, a policeman sidled up and asked Frank if he would be interested in making some training films for the San Bernadino vice squad. When Frank indicated that he was, the officer gave him his card and left; Frank thought no more about it. Around the same time, the Sunday supplement of the *Ontario Daily Report* wrote a feature on Frank's studio and his attempts to set up *Captain Beefheart vs. The Grunt People*. A casting call went out for locals to fill the lesser roles, one of whom, Frank subsequently found out, was another member of the vice squad.

Some weeks later, this same man returned to the studio, posing as a used car salesman. He and his friends were having a party on the following Wednesday and could Frank supply him with a sex film for the evening? Frank opined that a film would be too expensive but that an audio tape might have the same effect. The 'salesman' gave him a list of the sex acts they'd like to listen to and Frank told him to return the following day with $100 in his hand for the tape of his desires.

Frank enlisted the help of one of the girls, Lorraine Belcher, to simulate the requisite manoeuvres. 'So I stayed up most of the night manufacturing this bogus sex tape, fake bedsprings, squeeks and grunts. I overdubbed a musical background and spent hours cutting the laughs out of this thing.' The following day, the 'salesman' came back and offered him $50. 'I said to him, "No, that's not what the deal was, so goodbye". The tape never changed hands. I never sold him anything. But the next thing I knew, the door flies open, photographers are rushing in and the place is raided.'[31] The play-acting 'salesman' turned out to be Sergeant Jim Willis, vice investigator of the San Bernadino County Sheriff's Office and nemesis of local cottaging gays, with his playmates, Jim Mayfield, Phillip Ponders and Detective Stan McCloskey. Between them, they confiscated every tape and film reel on the premises, of which Frank got back less than half.

'Vice Squad Raids Local Film Studio' screamed the headline in the *Ontario Daily Report*. Ted Harp, fearless reporter, burst a brain cell coming up with the sub-heading, '2 A-Go-Go To Jail' for his coverage of what amounted to entrapment, a favourite pastime of US enforcement agencies. Frank, 'a self-styled movie producer', and Lorraine Belcher, 'his buxom, red-haired companion', were booked on suspicion of conspiracy to manufacture pornographic materials and suspicion of sex perversion. To make pornography was a misdemeanour but 'conspiracy' made it a felony with a '10 to 20' sentence. 'I mean, I had no intention of ever becoming a pornographer. I'd never seen pornography, didn't have any idea what it was. I knew that such a thing did exist but I had never seen any.'[32]

Frank's father had to take out a bank loan to pay for his son's bail. Once out, Frank contacted Art Laboe, owner of the Original Sound label, and obtained a $1500 advance against the royalties for 'Memories Of El Monte' and 'Grunion Run'. This he used to bail out Lorraine Belcher and to engage the services of an attorney. At the subsequent trial, the judge asked to hear the offending tape. 'We went into the judge's chambers and played this tape for him. He started laughing, he thought it was the most ridiculous thing. He was going to blow the whole thing off. But there was this 26-year-old district attorney who, if he'd had his way, I would've gotten the death penalty.

'I pled *Nolo contendere*, which means, just like many people in America, "I'm too broke to fight the law." And so, the net result was a sentence of six months in jail with all but ten days suspended. Plus three years probation, during which I was not to be in the company of any unmarried woman under the age of 21, and not violate any of the traffic laws of the state of California and so on.'[33]

The convicted felon was committed to Tank 'C' of the San Bernadino County Jail. Frank would later say that he found the experience 'educational'. 'I had no plans of ever becoming a criminal of any sort in my life, (so) it just was quite a shock for me to find myself in jail. You can't appreciate what a jail is and what goes on there unless somebody sticks you in one. In a way, I guess I have to thank Detective Willis and the evil machinery of the San Bernardino County legal system for giving me a chance to see, from that perspective, what the penal system is like in this country, and . . . how ineffectual and how stupid it is.'[34]

It was summertime and very hot and there was no ventilation in the cells. The lights were kept on all night, sleep was almost impossible and the warders harassed their charges by day. The food was virtually inedible, especially something that was called 'chop suey'. 'There's no telling what it was, but there was a certain amount of vegetable content and a certain amount of protein content, and a certain amount of gravy. It would have taken a research grant to ascertain exactly what 'chop suey' really was . . . I remember one day they handed me this aluminium bowl with some cream of wheat (which) arrived tipped over. The cream of wheat fell out in one moulded helmet-like kind of thing, flipped over, and there was a cockroach stuck in the bottom. So I pulled this out, didn't eat the cream of wheat but saved the cockroach and put it in an envelope with a letter to Motorhead's mother. The jail censor caught it and threatened me with solitary confinement if I ever tried anything like that again.'[35]

The jail's scum-infested shower, just one stall for 44 men, was immortalised in 'San Ber'doo'. 'There was scum, composed perhaps of some soap material but other unknown substances, very thick scum on the pan of this shower which had never been cleaned. And even though it was hot and even though you were forced to wear this horrible boiler suit while you were in there, no way was I taking a shower in that thing.'[36]

After paying his debt to society, Frank returned to Studio Z, but his stay was short-lived. A real estate development which involved the widening of Archibald Avenue was waiting to proceed and not surprisingly, Frank had fallen behind with his rent. He wasn't particularly welcome at his parents' home, either. 'My father didn't buy the concept of long hair as brain-ends.'[37] It was then that Ray Collins came to the rescue. He rang Frank to ask if he'd like to join a band he'd been singing with for the last three months called the Soul Agents.

Playing 'straight commercial rhythm and blues', the Soul Agents had been formed by bass player Roy Estrada and drummer Jimmy Carl Black. Black came from Anthony, a town on the Texas/New Mexico border. He'd joined the Air Force in 1958 and after leaving the service stayed on in Wichita, Kansas for a couple of years as a professional drummer. In 1964, he moved west to Los Angeles and became a starving musician, a role he would diligently pursue over the next few years. He met Roy Estrada in a pawnshop one day as he was hocking some cymbals to get money for food. The Soul Agents grew out of their meeting.

The rest of the band was made up of saxophonist Dave Coronado and guitarist Ray Hunt. Hunt and Collins quickly developed a mutual antipathy which the guitarist compounded by playing wrong chords while Collins was singing. The singer got the best of the ensuing fight and the Soul Agents needed a new guitarist. Frank made the trip to the Broadside, a bar in Pomona where the band had a weekend residency. It was back to 'Gloria' and 'Mustang Sally' and 'Louie Louie'. But not for long.

Frank enjoyed working with the band and thought they were too good just to play in bars, good enough to learn the songs which he'd been stockpiling. 'So I said, "OK you guys, I've got this plan: we are going to get rich. You probably won't believe this now, but if you bear with me, we'll go out and do it."[38] The only dissenting voice came from Dave Coronado, who was nominal leader of the band. 'He was a wise gentleman,' Frank told me. 'He said, 'If you play original material, you'll get fired from bar-band gigs and you won't be able to eat'. We started playing original material and we started getting fired. So he was right and we were wrong.' Coronado went off to his job at a bowling alley and the band learned how to starve.

They practised at Studio Z for about a week before being turfed out by the developers. Armed with their original repertoire and a new name, Captain Glasspack and His Magic Mufflers, they prepared to take on the British Invasion that was then at its height. If you didn't sound like the Beatles or the Rolling Stones, you didn't get hired. 'We weren't going about it that way. We'd play something weird and we'd get fired. I'd say, "Hang on", and we'd move to another go-go bar - the Red Flame in Pomona, the Shack in Fontana, the Tom Cat in Torrence . . . It was a strange time. We even got thrown out of after-hours jam sessions.'[39]

The problem was a simple one: if a band didn't play recognisable songs, the punters weren't happy; if the punters weren't happy, they didn't drink; if they didn't drink, the bar owners didn't make any money. Even when the band got a gig, Frank wasn't happy. 'If you're the kind of musician who thinks it's a good idea to play for beer, it would've been heaven. A lot of these places would calculate your wages based on a certain number of dollars plus all the beer you can drink. Which meant that you were getting a lot of water in your diet, too. It was kind of a humiliating environment.'[40]

Eventually, they ended up back at the Broadside in Pomona. Frank decided it was time for the band to change its name again. 'At the time, if you were a good musician, you were a motherfucker. And 'Mothers' was short for a collection of motherfuckers. And actually, it was kind of presumptuous to name the band that because we weren't that good musicians. But by bar band standards in the area, we were light years ahead of our competition. But in terms of real musicianship, I suppose we were right down there in the swamp.'[41]

It was May, the time when nuts are gathered and American children remember their mothers. And which day did Frank choose, quite by chance, to rename his musicians?

CHAPTER THREE
PROJECT/OBJECT

The symbolism of the date and the name change may not have been arbitrary as Frank has since indicated. 'It just happened by sheer accident to be Mothers Day,' he said in 1968, 'although we weren't aware of it at the time. When you are nearly starving to death, you don't keep track of holidays.'[1] Indeed. But, irrespective of his calorific intake, Frank had already begun to lay plans for the future and what decisions the prevailing circumstances allowed him to make were taken knowingly. The resonance of the date and the sleight-of-hand in denying it are typical of how he would later manipulate public perceptions of his career.

In another 1968 interview, he admitted, 'The Mothers project was carefully planned some 18 months before it actually got off the ground. I had been looking for the right people for a long time.' While he'd been in advertising, he went on, he'd done some motivational research. He felt he'd identified a niche in the marketplace for a form of music of his own devising. 'I composed a composite, gap-filling product to plug most of the gaps between so-called serious music and so-called popular music.'[2] Is this the man who renamed his band by 'sheer accident' on the one day of the year that gave the new name significance?

Six years later, his master plan was enumerated once again in a press kit. 'Perhaps the most unique aspect of the Mothers' work is the *conceptual continuity* of the group's *output macro-structure*. The basic blueprints were executed in 1962-63. Preliminary experimentation in early and mid-1964. Construction of the *project/object* began in late 1964. The *project/object* contains *plans* and *non-plans*, also precisely calculated *event-structures* designed to accommodate the mechanics of fate and all bonus statistical improbabilities thereto.'[3]

The *project/object* was the means by which Zappa incorporated every aspect of his work into an undefined grand design. It meant that every record and performance, every musician and member of the audience, every critical reaction to each gig, record, video and interview was integrated into a unifiable whole. Beneath all this was the continuity of his compositions, which followed consistent themes and experiments that, in turn, were adapted and augmented by the influence of random events and circumstances chosen by him for being either apposite or contradictory.

The press-kit was itself an *event-structure* that had as much to reveal about manipulation as it did about a co-ordinated programme of events. If at the start there was calculation, it was Zappa's ability to provoke reaction and turn it to his advantage. 'Audiences just couldn't identify with or relate to the music, so we got into the habit of insulting them . . . and we accumulated a big reputation in that way. Nobody came to hear us play, they came in to see how much abuse they could take. We managed to get jobs on that basis but it didn't last very long because we'd eventually end up by abusing the owner of the club.'[4]

Hindsight jacked up the mythology but the reality of the time was that the Mothers starved for ten months before journeying west to try their luck in Hollywood. Frank took an apartment at 1819 Bellevue Avenue, back in Echo Park, which he described as 'a grubby little place on the side of a hill'. He got a job as a salesman in the singles department of Wallich's Music City on the corner of Sunset and Vine in Hollywood.

Through Don Cerveris he'd met Mark Cheka, a middle-aged artist from New York who lived in West Hollywood at the time with a waitress from the Ash Grove, L.A.'s premier folk club on Melrose Avenue. In the hope that Cheka's 'artistic' temperament might qualify him to become the Mothers' manager, Frank enticed him to the Broadside one night, a journey of some 50 miles, to assess their potential. Cheka was probably nonplussed by the band's appearance: Frank had encouraged the band to modify their attire to reflect their performance. 'I felt you couldn't play the sort of music we were playing and look the way some of the guys did - with processed pompadours.'[5]

The pompadours were in fact a disguise that Jimmy Carl Black and Roy Estrada adopted when they returned to their homes in Santa Ana in Orange County, 'which is a bad place to be unless you belong to the John Birch Society'.[6] As well as intolerance in the suburbs, the British Invasion held sway in Hollywood clubs and bars and if you didn't have long hair, you weren't hired. Frank himself had a problem there too because, as he told Sally Kempton, 'due to an unfortunate circumstance, all my hair had been cut off'.[7] Without long hair and a manager, the Mothers didn't stand much chance.

TINSEL TOWN REBELLION

Mark Cheka accepted the challenge but soon discovered that he too would need help. He turned to a friend, Herb Cohen, whose tenacity and taste for confrontation were ideal qualities for the task of representing Frank and the Mothers. Cohen had considerable experience in the entertainment business and much else besides. Originally from New York, where he was born in 1933, he joined the Merchant Marine at 17 as a deckhand, fireman and sometime union organiser. During a brief stint of Army service, he was posted to San Francisco, where he met and lived with folk singer Odetta. He got involved in the local folk scene, promoting gigs during the years that Senator McCarthy painted folk singers with a decidedly pink brush.

At about the time that the Zappa family was moving to Lancaster, Herb Cohen was in Los Angeles, managing a club called the Purple Onion. Over the next two years he turned it into a folk club, thus antagonising the owner who wanted his investment to be a 'classy' collar-and-tie establishment. Borrowing money from Theodore Bikel, one of the singers he'd been booking into the Onion, in 1958 Cohen opened his own coffee-house/folk club, the Unicorn.

There were a lot of earnest coffee-drinking Los Angeleans who found protest songs an aid to digestion and the folk circuit boomed. Herb Cohen took an interest in several other coffee houses and also a night club, Cosmo's Alley, which later became Bido Lito's, and helped to launch Arthur Lee's group, Love. In 1959 Cohen was busted on an obscenity charge after booking comedian Lenny Bruce. He'd had frequent run-ins with the Hollywood police department, who were suspicious of 'un-American activities' like drinking alcohol in a coffee house. This time he beat the rap but soon had occasion to take an extended holiday to Europe, the Middle East and Africa.

While he was away, his attorney brother Martin (also known as Mutt) Cohen managed the Unicorn. When Herb returned in 1963, he sold up and moved back briefly to New York, where he picked up the management of the Modern Folk Quartet (including the photographer Henry Diltz) and Judy Henske. Before long, he moved his operations back to Los Angeles, where 'folk-rock' was emerging. The new style took its lead from the Byrds, young ex-folkies who'd graduated from groups such as the Limeliters and the New Christy Minstrels. Their first name, the Jet Set, came from leader Roger McGuinn's fascination with airplanes. But, taking their lead from the Beatles (as who didn't then?), they metamorphosed into the Byrds.

They quickly became the group to see on the Sunset Strip, the winding, mile-long stretch of Sunset Boulevard between Doheny Drive in the west and La Cienaga Boulevard in the east. Their appearances at Ciro's, a rundown joint once the hangout of film stars that now looked, in David Crosby's words, like 'a Fifties Las Vegas showroom that had been done *cheaply*', and their hit version of Bob Dylan's 'Mr Tambourine Man', heralded folk-rock, the new trend in music.

Accompanying the band to their gigs was a rag-tag army of dancers and 'freaks' led by beat artist Vito Paulekas and his dionysian friend, Carl Franzoni, whose perennial costume was black tights, leopard-skin leotards and a cape with an 'F' emblazoned on its back. Most took it to represent his surname but, as far as he was concerned, it identified him as 'Captain Fuck'. He and Vito indulged that particular pastime whenever possible, even though Vito, in his mid-50s, was married to Sue, an ex-cheerleader more than 30 years his junior. They had a young son named Godot, who died aged three and a half when he fell through a skylight. Sue then produced a daughter called, at least for a while, Groovee Nipple.

Vito had 'long straggly white hair', Zappa told Andy Gill, 'used to wear tights all the time and part of a tablecloth taped over his chest. Sue used to wear basically just doily-type tablecloths and sandals.' Their entourage he dubbed a 'Bohemian bizarro group, and every night they'd go out dancing, and as soon as they arrived, they would make things happen, because they were dancing in a way that nobody had seen before.'[8]

Los Angeles freaks were different from the hippies congregating in the Haight-Ashbury district of San Francisco. Hippies preached tolerance and love, fostered a herd instinct when it came to modes of dress and vocabulary, and turned begging (in the name of self-help) into a community service. Down in mercenary L.A., where they emphasised the second word of 'show business', freaks were more individualistic and ego-driven, taking 'love' where they found it and equating 'tolerance' with 'every man for himself'. Frank had his own ideas about the differences. 'Hippies don't really care what they look like,' he told Jerry Hopkins, 'and the freaks care an awful lot. Their packaging and image construction is a very important part of their life style.'[9] Expressed in those terms, it was obviously an environment for an entrepreneur like Frank Zappa to thrive - if he ever got the chance.

TOO UGLY FOR SHOW BUSINESS

Despite his plans and projects, Frank was starving. If his band had a reputation it was for being unemployable and through that, it was hard to keep a stable personnel. The first addition to the band was folk singer/guitarist Alice Stuart, 'who played guitar very well and she sang well'. But - 'she couldn't play 'Louie Louie', so I fired her'.[10] For her part, Stuart claimed that she left after three months because she'd grown tired of Frank 'doing his Chicano rap'. 'I had an idea for combining certain modal influences into our basically country blues sound,' he said, ' . . . we were playing a lot of Muddy Waters, Howlin' Wolf-type stuff around that time.'[11] That suited Stuart's replacement, Henry Vestine.

Frank continued to write songs, most of which turned up on the Mothers' first three albums. Increasingly, they reflected his antipathy towards both his peers and the authorities opposed to them. Social unrest was rife in Los Angeles in 1965, in both the youth and black communities. In August of that year, racial tension in the Watts district finally provoked a riot that gained worldwide attention. At 1819 Bellevue, Frank wrote 'Trouble Every Day', initially referred to as 'The Watts Riot Song', along with 'Oh No, Bowtie

Daddy' and 'Hungry Freaks, Daddy'.

With his limited resources, he hung out whenever he could at Canter's, a delicatessen on Fairfax Avenue that had become what Frank later termed 'The Top Freako Watering Hole and Social HQ'. Denny Bruce put it more succinctly: 'Canter's was the only place longhairs could go and not get the shit kicked out of them by the suburbanites.'[12] It was also where Lenny Bruce, Tim Hardin and Phil Spector held their respective courts. Vito's *atelier* was just three blocks away on North Laurel Avenue, a store/studio where Sue sold bric-a-brac and Vito taught clay sculpture on Tuesday nights and dancing on Thursdays. The Byrds used the basement as a rehearsal room and storage facility.

It was around this time that Mark Cheka arranged for the Mothers to play at a party where they would be filmed as an example of musical outrage for *Mondo Hollywood*, an exploitation flick written, produced and directed by Carl Cohen (a coincidence?). Shot in the form of a semi-documentary, it featured Rudi Gernreich, designer of topless dresses, and Richard Alpert, sent down from Harvard for his LSD experiments, among a herd of hippies and wannabes.

Love guitarist Bryan Maclean attended the party: 'I stood near the band in rapture for the entire evening. I couldn't believe my eyes, I thought (Frank) was the greatest.'[13] *Party Scene From Mondo Hollywood*, on the *Mystery Disc*, captures the event at which 'freaks and maniacs cavort licentiously'. In his notes, Frank went on, 'The equipment we are playing on was lent to us by Jim Guercio. Thanks again, Jim. In the background, listening to this spewage, was Herb Cohen.'[14]

Even though he didn't understand their music, Cohen liked what he heard: 'They had enough things going on to make it obvious there was a viable commodity'. He and Mark Cheka were acquainted and introductions were made. In subsequent meetings, Frank explained his aims and Cohen was impressed that here was a musician who actually could explain himself. 'Not only did he know what he was talking about,' he said, 'but he had a good background and was an excellent musician.'[15]

Zappa and Cohen may have recognised the manipulator in one another. Neither was distracted by the 'enthusiasm' that was so much a part of the 'freak' scene and both liked to confront authority. Years later, long after artist and management had parted company, the 'real' Frank Zappa noted, 'Almost overnight we had jumped from starvation level to poverty level.'[16] When interviewed for BBC2's *Late Show*, he was asked how significant Cohen was to the original success of the band; he answered, 'I would say that he was of major significance. He helped us get work.'[17]

One of Cohen's first moves was to get the band an audition at The Action on Santa Monica Boulevard, which was 'kind of a entry level establishment.

Their clientele was prostitutes, underworld figures and television actors. There were some movie people too.'[18] Six months previously they'd been turned down by the management because their hair wasn't long enough. 'It still wasn't very long, so we went in wearing purple shirts and black hats,' Frank told Jerry Hopkins. 'We looked like Mafia undertakers. The management of this establishment responded on a visceral level to this packaging and hired us for a four-week tour of duty.'[19]

Cohen's next move, to get the Mothers paid for appearing in *Mondo Hollywood*, was not so successful. Their sequence was deleted from the film. The next practical steps to stardom were bookings at the Whisky A Go Go, on the corner of Sunset and San Vicente, and The Trip, east on Sunset. 'All the industrial types would spend their time at The Trip,' Frank told me, 'because that's where the "better class of people" were.' At The Trip, the Mothers got frequent requests for 'Help I'm A Rock' and 'Memories Of El Monte'; both songs contained talking passages and this encouraged listening rather than dancing. This was acceptable at The Trip but not good policy for playing the Whisky.

The Whisky was the almost exclusive preserve of Johnny Rivers, whose 1964 debut album, *Live At The Whisky A Go Go*, yielded his number 2 hit, 'Memphis'. From time to time, Rivers would go off on tour and some lucky group got to fill in. When their turn arrived, Frank was disgusted to discover that their name was not advertised outside the club until they payed for a sign to be made. 'The audience wasn't anything to brag about, they were just a bunch of drunk people in go go boots. But the money was a lot better than the Broadside, because we were actually making union scale.'[20]

Elmer Valentine, owner of the Whisky and The Trip, insisted that bands played music for dancing. After all, that's why the 'A Go Go' was there. But Frank had other ideas. On one occasion, the group played a medley of 'Help I'm A Rock' and 'El Monte' for a solid hour and nobody danced. 'Immediately after that we were selling pop bottles for cigarettes and bologna.'[21]

SUZY CREAMCHEESE

Although Frank held himself somewhat aloof from the 'freak' community, he understood the importance of being associated with the movement. He hadn't failed to notice the 'folk legend' that Vito and his harem/troupe had already become. But wearing floral-print stage clothes, as he and the band began to do (audiences saw the flowers, he saw the irony), and inviting Vito to sanction his gigs was not enough. There must be a Mothers mythology, a plot and cast of characters for impressionable minds to absorb and identify with.

He cast his net with analytical skill for what was to be one of the first 'bonus statistical improbabilities'. The band had to blend in chameleon-like with its surroundings. 'Now I didn't tell the guys what to wear; I merely suggested their mode of dress conform to what they were doing.'[22] They were still in the throes of changing from an R&B bar band into something a whole lot different. 'The appearance of a group is linked to the music the same way an album cover is linked to the record. It gives a clue to what's inside. And the better the packaging, the more the person who picked up that package will enjoy it.'[23]

There were others like him who inhabited the periphery of the 'scene' and Pamela Zarubica was one of them. Drawn to the Strip from her home in Inglewood, she hung out at The Trip, trying to convince Phil Spector, already with most of his hits behind him, of her love. Disabused of her dreams in that direction, she befriended Frank at a time when he still had to pay admission to the club when he wasn't playing there.

She first saw Frank at The Trip when he sat in one night with the Grass Roots, who would soon change their name to Love in order not to clash with the pop singles band created by P.F. Sloan and Steve Barri. Pam nicknamed him Omar, since Frank was wearing a fur coat making him resemble Omar Sharif's character in the recently-released film *Doctor Zhivago*. She was also present at the Mothers' first gigs at the club. 'They played 'Help I'm A Rock' for 20 minutes and everyone went *Ugh*,' she told David Walley. 'I loved it.'[24]

With their similar views on the world, a friendship struck up between them. There was a practical side to their alliance as well. For a nominal fee, Pamela agreed to clean his wretched apartment, in return for which Frank became her mentor and moral guardian while using her Kirkwood Drive apartment as a staging post for his forays onto the Strip. They would sit in Canter's together: 'I would stare at Phil Spector and he would look at all the girls but none of them would have anything to do with him 'cause he just wasn't getting any action.'[25]

That wasn't the action he was looking for. What he wanted most was a recording contract. That would legitimise his music, give him some standing amongst his peers but more importantly, would open up a work circuit at present denied to the band, and put up their price. Herb Cohen justified his 15 per cent by dragging record producer Tom Wilson along to see them.

The Mothers had recorded some demos at Original Sound Studios which had been sent to a number of record companies. Everyone turned them down; Clive Davis, then head of Columbia Records, declared that the band 'had no commercial potential', a resonant phrase that went straight into the Zappa artillery. MGM didn't turn them down, they just never replied. But Herb Cohen read the music press and knew that Wilson had been hired by the company and was the man to impress.

Wilson was a Harvard graduate with a degree in economics. As a producer at Columbia, he made Simon & Garfunkel's first album, *Wednesday Morning, 3AM*, as well as Bob Dylan's *Another Side Of Bob Dylan* and *Bringing It All Back Home*. In June 1965, he produced the ground-breaking six-minute single, 'Like A Rolling Stone'. In November he accepted the post of East Coast Director of A&R with MGM/Verve and took the first opportunity to travel west to check out the developing music scene.

HUNGRY FREAKS, DADDY

Cohen tracked Wilson down at The Trip on an evening when the Mothers were filling in at the Whisky. By whatever means, he convinced the producer to walk the four blocks to see his band. 'It was under duress,' Frank said to me. 'Herb Cohen dragged him away from a girl he had sitting on his lap.' They arrived while the Mothers were giving 'The Watts Riot Song' an extended boogie workout with Henry Vestine on guitar. 'He only stayed for a few minutes after which he came backstage, slapped me on the back and said, "Wonderful - we're gonna make a record of you . . . goodbye."'[26] 'He must have walked away saying, "Hey, a white rhythm and blues band,"' Frank told Jim Smith in 1974. '"We've got the Righteous Brothers, now we're getting the Mothers."'[27]

By this time, he and Henry Vestine had moved into a 'gingerbread' cottage on Formosa Avenue, just south of Sunset. It was one in a complex of four that fronted onto a central courtyard. Another was occupied by singer Victoria Winston, who'd attended the same high school as Phil Spector and dated fellow Teddy Bear Marshall Lieb. 'At the time, the area was filled with musicians. Members of Steppenwolf lived across the street and there were country players down the block.'[28]

Winston befriended her new neighbour and found him 'serious-minded, intelligent and focused. He knew where he wanted to go with his music. We spoke about composers like Edgar Varèse, who we both idolised. He told me, "Someday I'll get there. I'll be producing, writing and performing this sort of music."' In the few months that he lived there, Frank wrote several songs for Winston and her partner Curt Boettcher, who as Simon's Children had a contract with Columbia Records. 'I liked what he was writing, I wanted to do something that had a political message or statement in it. But our producer didn't like the material, so we didn't record it.'[29]

It took another four months, until March 1966, for the Mothers' contract to be drawn up and the band to be paid a $2,500 advance. Henry Vestine left: 'As our music got progressively stranger, Henry found he couldn't identify with what we were doing.'[30] Steve Mann and James Guercio (later producer of Blood, Sweat And Tears and Chicago) were temporary replacements who made way for Elliott Ingber. The band rehearsed on a Hollywood sound stage on Seward Street with an Akai tape recorder running. In his *Mystery Disc* notes accompanying 'Original Mothers Rehearsal', Frank reveals, 'We were completely broke and the (Laurentide) finance company was coming after Jimmy Carl Black's drum set.' The building was occupied by Tim Sullivan, the producer of *Run Home Slow*, who loaned the stage to Frank in lieu of the money still owed on the film score.

Eventually, the day of the first session, at TT&G Studios on the corner of Sunset and Highland, arrived. As always, the band was starving and Frank had to hit on Jesse Kaye, MGM's tight-fisted accounts director, for ten dollars. Kaye was present to ensure that the three-hour session didn't overrun. There were strict Musicians Union rules about session fees, which went to an overtime rate if the session exceeded its limit, and the number of songs that could be laid down in any one session. Having ingested ten dollars' worth of calories, the Mothers set about 'Anyway The Wind Blows'.

Over the years, Zappa mythologised this day, implying that Tom Wilson knew nothing about the Mothers' music until they set about their second song, 'Who Are The Brain Police?'. He painted a picture of a disconcerted Wilson phoning New York in something of a panic. But in 1968 his memory was clearer: 'He came back to town just before we were going to do our first recording session. We had a little chat in his room and that was when he first discovered that R&B wasn't all we played. Things started to change: we decided not to make a single, but an album instead.'[31]

Wilson and Frank entered into some sort of collusion; Frank talked of orchestrations, so Wilson was aware of his intentions and may only have been surprised by their scale. Far from panicking after two songs, Wilson 'was so impressed that he got on the phone to New York - and as a result, I got more or less (an) unlimited budget to do this monstrosity.'[32] David Walley quotes Wilson: 'Somehow I suggested we should do something big.'[33] 'The next day,' Frank went on, 'I had whipped up the arrangements for a 22-piece orchestra - not just a straight orchestra but the Mothers plus 17 pieces . . . we all worked together. The editing took a long time, which really ran the cost up - and Wilson was really sticking his neck out . . . he laid his job on the line by producing a whole double album.'[34]

The second disc of what became *Freak Out!* was devoted to longer, more impressionistic pieces than two-minute satires of teenage angst like 'Anyway The Wind Blows', 'Go Cry On Somebody Else's Shoulder', 'I Ain't Got No Heart' or 'How Could I Be Such A Fool'. The budget became $21,000, a considerable investment in an unknown group, even when a proven hit producer like Tom Wilson says, 'Trust me'. MGM/Verve executives must have felt that trust usurped when they heard 'Trouble Comin' Every Day' (a retitling of 'The Watts Riot Song'), 'Help I'm A Rock' and 'The Return Of The Son Of Monster Magnet', their confidence already undermined by the subversion of the first disc's 11 tracks.

'All the songs on it were *about* something,' Frank wrote in his 'real' book. 'It wasn't as if we had a hit single and we needed to build some filler around it. Each tune had a function within an overall satirical concept.'[35] Many, like 'Any Way The Wind Blows', 'I Ain't Got No Heart' and 'I'm Not Satisfied', sprang from his own experiences and hovered between cynicism, anger and self-pity. There were evocations of doo-wop in 'Go Cry On Somebody Else's Shoulder', leering sleaze in 'Motherly Love' and bubblegum in 'Wowie Zowie', all delivered in vocal timbres that conveyed an imminent threat to the 'Great Society' that Frank was satirising. 'Wowie Zowie' was one of Pamela Zarubica's mordant pronouncements and she was credited as the inspiration for 'You Didn't Try To Call Me'.

Frank threw down the 'freak' gauntlet with the first disc's opening track, 'Hungry Freaks, Daddy', written for Carl Franzoni but criticising the inadequate education system as well as 'the left-behinds of the Great Society', 'Who Are The Brain Police?', his first heavily-coded attack on institutionalised religion, and 'You're Probably Wondering Why I'm Here'. Unlike the songs that parodied lyrics and melodies of established pop fodder, music that in Frank's opinion conditioned and anaesthetised young record buyers, these three plus 'Trouble Comin' Every Day' (its full title only appearing on the record label) commented directly upon what he saw as the debased quality of life in contemporary America.

If the MGM executives were expecting Frank's 'protest' song to contain the poetic imagery of Bob Dylan's stock-in-trade, 'Trouble Comin' Every Day' disabused them of the fantasy. The Watts riot is captured in stark images that evoke the violence committed by both the police and the mob. Then he turned his basilisk stare on the news media, 'Take your TV tube and eat it', questioning the voyeurism of filming as 'another woman driver gets machine-gunned from her seat' and concluding, 'Our country isn't free'. Nor was he afraid to bite the hand that was feeding him: 'I shopped (the song) briefly all over Hollywood but no one would touch it,' he wrote in the album notes, ' . . . everybody worries so much about not getting any air play. My, my.'

'Help I'm A Rock' was in three movements; the first entitled 'Okay To Tap Dance', established the title chant; in the second, 'In Memoriam, Edgar Varèse', Frank developed a monologue which began 'It's a drag being a rock', and progressed to 'Maybe if I passed my driving test, I could get a gig driving a bus and pick up some freaks in front of Ben Frank's' before a sudden butt-edit into the third movement, 'It Can't Happen Here', a disjointed a cappella chant enumerating 'freak outs' in various parts of America. At its end, Suzy Creamcheese is addressed; Frank's comment, 'We've been very interested in your (pause for lubricious swallow) development' is countered with a firm 'Ferget it' delivered by Jeannie Vassoir.

For the climax of the project, Frank asked for $500 worth of percussion equipment, 'all the freaks from Sunset Boulevard' and sundry name guests like Les McCann, Paul Butterfield and Kim Fowley for the late-night session booked at the end of a week's recording. Victoria Winston reckoned, 'It was wall-to-wall people in there. From what I could see from the control room, it was a well-orchestrated freak out. I was there for the whole album recording, day after day, and Frank was always organised. He always appeared to be in control.'[36] Kim Fowley was *Featured on hypophone* on the album sleeve, a double-edged comment that acknowledged Fowley's self-promotion and signalled disapproval. Decades later, Fowley returned the compliment: noting Frank's dry humour, he called him 'a snob' and 'vicious'. 'For all his alleged humanity, there was a "chitlin'" streak in him. He liked to "keep the niggers down" - other white jerks, screwballs he could exploit. Like people who contributed to the first Mothers album.'[37]

In its final state, 'The Return Of The Son Of Monster Magnet', while a notable achievement for its time, palled on repeated listening. Deliberately provocative in its formlessness, it allowed Vito's troupe, already parodied in 'Help I'm A Rock', to 'freak out' in the recording studio. At the time, the result had a decided effect on some of his contemporaries. As his contribution to Jefferson Airplane's *After Bathing At Baxter's*, drummer Spencer Dryden came up with an instrumental, 'A Small Package of Value Will Come to You, Shortly'. He admitted his debt to Frank Zappa: 'Frank said that he hopes other bands will use his work as a point of departure to kill Ugly Radio. So do I.'[38]

Thirty years later, 'Magnet' sounds leaden; there's little impression of a hoard of celebrants cavorting in a confined space. And that may well have been down to Tom Wilson. In conversation with Frank in 1991, I commented that Wilson seemed to have been rather a passive element in the production. 'On the contrary,' he replied, 'he was enthusiastic to the point that on the night that we recorded 'It Can't Happen Here' and Side Four, with all the screaming and wailing and yowling and carrying on, he'd taken *acid* so that he could 'get into it' more. So, if you can imagine *your* producer on LSD, sitting in the control room giving the engineer instructions on what to turn up and turn down . . . In mitigation', he added, 'But we have to be appreciative of Tom. He's passed away now [after a heart attack in 1978] but he was visionary. He signed the Velvet Underground, he signed a number of other really obscure groups at that time. And we were just another of his obscure groups that he was producing.'

For his part, Wilson appreciated Frank's evident talent and regretted the inadequate means of portraying it: 'Zappa's a painstaking craftsman, and in some ways it's a pity that the art of recordings is not developed to the extent where you can really hear completely all the things he's doing because sometimes one guitar part is buried and he might have three different-sounding guitars overdubbed, all playing the same thing.'[39]

In all, the Mothers' first album took three weeks to complete at a time when most albums were made in three days - if not in one. Faced with a huge production bill, MGM/Verve were expected to invest a significant amount in promotion. Fat chance.

Two weeks after the *Freak Out!* tapes were finally edited and sequenced, Herb Cohen sent the band to work in Hawaii for most of April, where they could starve in more exotic climes. Subsisting on cigarettes and coffee, Frank devoted his time to writing. 'Call Any Vegetable' was one of the songs completed there in preparation for the next album.

Returning to the mainland, they discovered that there was a problem with their name at MGM/Verve. 'Some pinhead there had decided that this was a bad name for a group and that no radio station would ever play our records because the name was too risqué.' And, so the deathless cliché goes, of necessity they became the Mothers of Invention. 'But naturally, the radio stations didn't play the music anyway, because it wasn't about the name of the band. It was what we were singing and the way the music sounded.'[40]

Pretentious or not, *Freak Out!* was intended as a statement. As rock music's first double album, it was bound to be regarded as significant or preposterous, depending on the age and outlook of the listener. The colour photographs on the outer sleeve used a 'solarisation' process to emphasise the implied threat of the band's name and the album title. Elliott Ingber looked almost cherubic alongside Frank's shaggy mane, moustache and 'imperial' beard that Pamela Zarubica likened to an inverted anchor. He also wore his 'Omar Sharif' fur coat; the Egyptian actor would've had to be severely traumatised to look like Frank Zappa, 1966. Roy Estrada, Ray Collins and Jimmy Carl Black resembled lapsed beatniks rather than freaks.

The photographs were taken in the courtyard of the 'gingerbread' cottages on Formosa and Victoria Winston assisted photographer Ray Leong. 'We were dressing them for the shoot and we said, "Oh, it would be nice if they were wearing necklaces". Because they were all deciding what they were going to wear for the album cover. So I brought out a bunch of my necklaces and Ray Collins and Roy Estrada chose the ones they wanted to wear.'[41]

The world was introduced to Suzy Creamcheese on the back cover. Her letter, written by Frank, was composed of sentences designed to attract the album's potential 'freak' audience and repulse symbols of authority. 'These Mothers is crazy,' it began. More than the dadaist concept of Suzy Creamcheese herself, the letter seemed to have a profound impact on lonely 'individualists' in hick-towns and red-neck fortresses across America, who sent fan mail to the band. 'We're getting letters from very strange places,' Frank told Frank Kofsky. 'These are really the cream of the weirdos of each town, and they're coming from all over. Some of them think just in terms of like, "I feel funny because people think I'm strange." And, "Say that you like me, please, Mothers of Invention, so that I'll keep being strange and I'll stay alive in my small town.'"[42]

In contrast to the outer design's simplicity, the inner surfaces were packed with information; there were 179 names of people who had 'contributed materially in many ways to make our music what it is', with Pamela Zarubica at the head of the list; Frank's sardonic notes to the individual tracks; 'biographical trivia' on the members of the band; sundry relevant quotes and a mini-manifesto, 'What is 'Freaking Out'?', ending with an invitation to join the 'United Mutations', a fan club in all but name.

The manifesto encouraged like-minded 'freaks' to band together, giving them status by labelling those who disapproved as 'less perceptive individuals'. 'The participants, already emancipated from our national *social slavery*, dressed in their most inspired apparel, realise as a group whatever potential they possess for '*free expression*'. Rather than releasing them from the tyranny of being told what to think and how to behave, Zappa was merely issuing fresh instructions without delineating their consequences. He plainly doubted that they could apply the same intellectual rigour to their lives as he already did to his own. For several years during the 70s, there was a graffito on a wall in London's Earls Court: 'Do you do as you're told? Revolt!'

The problems with MGM/Verve didn't end with their name. 'They figured we were *odd-ball*, 'he told Jerry Hopkins. '*One shot novelty a-go-go*. But we weren't. We had to show them ways that they could make money on the product. From the beginning it was hard to convince them of what we were talking about.

'Another thing . . . the interior of the *Freak Out!* album made me vomit. The exterior packaging was pretty much under our control. That was all carefully planned merchandising there. At the time the packaging was being completed on that record I was in Hawaii. I didn't give it to an expert. The result was a really ugly piece of graphic art. Some of the worst reproduction work I have ever seen. The picture in the lower right-hand corner - it is a great panorama of all those people. They shrank it down and stuck it in a corner. I screamed all over the place.'[43]

As he railed against his record company, an auspicious gig was arranged at The Trip which underlined disparities within the youth movements of the East and West coasts. The Mothers, self-styled darlings of the LA 'freak' community, were to appear alongside Andy Warhol's Exploding Plastic Inevitable, which featured the Velvet Underground and Nico, darlings of the New York scene and yet another of Tom Wilson's MGM/Verve signings.

The projected month-long engagement, beginning on May 3, brought together two of rock's great sneerers, Lou Reed and Frank Zappa. While Frank was able to confine his principal emotion to disdain, Reed appears to have broken out in full-blown hatred. He was quoted as saying that Zappa was the single most untalented person he'd ever met in his life. Apparently, their limited acquaintance convinced Reed that Frank was two-bit, pretentious and academic (now there's a put down!). He was also incapable of playing rock 'n' roll because he was a loser and that was why he dressed funny. Of course, the Velvets didn't dress funny and appearing all in black could in no way be construed as a posture. Frank barely strained a brain-cell with his reply from the stage: 'These guys really suck.'

The Sheriff's Office closed the club after three days, helping to exacerbate the tension between young people and officialdom. But neither band was to escape, for they were jointly booked to appear May 27-29 at San Francisco's Fillmore Auditorium. This would be the Mothers' first gig at the Fillmore but they'd played the city's Longshoreman's Hall the previous November on a gig promoted by the Family Dog.

The first gigs at the Fillmore had been benefit nights for the San Francisco Mime Troupe, who'd been busted in Lafayette Park for performing without a permit. The first benefit took place on November 6, 1965, the same night that the Mothers played the Longshoreman's Hall, at the Troupe's loft on Fifth and Howard. Such was the response that a larger venue had to be found. The Fillmore was located on Fillmore and Geary and in its time had seen artists like Duke Ellington, James Brown, Bobby Bland and the Temptations on its stage. Further benefits were held at the Fillmore on December 10 and January 14, 1966, with Jefferson Airplane, the Great Society and the Grateful Dead performing. The first gigs took place on the weekend of February 4-6, with Jefferson Airplane topping the bill. Thereafter, gigs took place every weekend; apart from two appearances by the Butterfield Blues Band, the Mothers and the Velvets were the first out-of-towners to perform there.

The Velvets fell foul of promoter Bill Graham. 'When we went to Frisco,' Reed told Bruce Pollock, 'Bill Graham was doing his Fillmore, and he had a light show, right? So we walked in and we saw a slide of the Buddha and we said, "That's gotta go!" He hated us, said we were the lowest trash ever to hit Frisco.'[44] Graham exacted his revenge. Without warning, guitarist Sterling Morrison was ejected from the building. 'So I'm freezing my ass off on the kerb feeling sorry for myself,' he told Mat Snow, 'and all these cars come sweeping up: it's Andy and all his creeps who'd been to some glamourous cocktail party to which they'd somehow neglected to invite Bill Graham.' Nor did it stop there. 'Right before we went on, [Graham] looks at us and says, "You motherfuckers, I hope you bomb."'[45]

The Mothers returned to the Fillmore on June 24/5, sharing the bill with Lenny Bruce, one of Bruce's last gigs. Peter Berg, a member of the Mime Troupe, was present: 'I remember the horrified look on Graham's face when Lenny Bruce did that last pathetic performance, incredibly whacked out on amphetamine.'[46] 'It was the living death of a genius,' Graham said in his autobiography, *Bill Graham Presents*. 'Really, the Mothers saved the shows. It was really sad. He was a beaten soul and he was naked on stage. About six weeks later [August 3, 1966], he was dead.'[47]

In his *On The Town* column for the *San Francisco Chronicle*, Ralph Gleason was a little less melodramatic: 'It was something of a tribute to him since the hall is not really the best site for his performances. He could not work effectively with the noisy rock dancers waiting for the music and his own fans were uncomfortable from the heat and the chairs.' But then he turned on the music makers, dismissing their show with some perception. 'The Mothers, the rock band which followed Bruce, and played for dancing, are Hollywood hippies full of contrivance, tricks and packaging; a kind of Sunset Boulevard version of the Fugs. They are really indoor Muscle Beach habitués whose idea of a hip lyric is to mention 'LSD' or 'pot' three times in eight bars.'[48]

CHAPTER FOUR
FREAK OUT!

Freak Out! was released at the beginning of July 1966. Reaction was understandably mixed, little of it uncommitted to an extreme point of view. Only *Cash Box* hedged its bets: 'A powerful rock outing on which the Mothers of Invention live up to their name by using such instruments as finger cymbals, bobby pins & tweezers and guitarron . . . The album is colorfully packaged and contains extensive liner notes. 'Hungry Freaks, Daddy', 'Who Are The Brain Police?' and 'Motherly Love' are among the better tracks.'[1]

Others had more scope for invective: 'A new "singing group", the Mothers of Invention, have recently released their first album, entitled *Friek Out*.' Was the misspelling deliberate? 'They needn't have bothered,' the outraged scribe continued. 'With voices that should put an alley cat on a fence at midnight to shame, these 'mothers' have wasted two records and an album cover of indescribably (sic) poor taste recording 80 minutes of pure trash.' There was more in the same vein before an anti-climactic conclusion: 'This horror is obviously a satire of today's longmopped singing groups, but it has failed. It is in a class by itself - if it can be classified.'[2]

In the *Los Angeles Times*, Pete Johnson tempered his disdain with humour: 'The Mothers of Invention, a talented but warped quintet, have fathered an album poetically titled *Freak Out!*, which could be the greatest stimulus to the aspirin industry since the income tax.' Johnson concluded, 'There are a few tunes which sound as if they might be semi-serious rock 'n' roll, 'I Ain't Got No Heart' and 'How Could I Be Such A Fool', for instance, but most of the tunes are very experimental and are hard on the eardrums and the patience.'[3]

Bob Levinson in the *Herald Examiner* wrote under the headline, 'Mothers Invent Sounds Worse Than Music'. He interviewed Frank, whom he likened to 'an emaciated John Carradine', at a sidewalk table at Canters. 'Our whole bag is outrage,' Frank intoned. He'd tried to make the album as gross as possible: 'Even when it's supposedly serious, the whole thing is a satire. It satirises all those groups that cut stuff that oozes. It's satirising every puker rock-and-roll group and all that teenage nonsense with oversimplified lyrics, ooh-wah, falsetto and mumbling business.' Explaining how to 'freak out', Levinson concluded, 'The Mothers do it on their records and, one infers, the delicatessen delegation on their rye bread. Those who obtain the album may do it by discarding the records and playing the cover.'[4]

Not only were reviewers dismissing Frank's sardonic humour, they were ignoring the intention it masked. 'If you were to graphically analyse the different types of directions of all the songs in the *Freak Out!* album,' he told Frank Kofksy, 'there's a little something in there for everybody. At least one piece of material is slanted for every type of social orientation within our consumer group, which happens to be six to eighty. That whole *Freak Out!* album is to be accessible as possible to the people who (want) to take the time to make it accessible.'[5]

More in keeping with the spirit of its creator's intentions was Lorraine Alterman's piece in the *Los Angeles Free Press*. The *Freep* had started life on May 23, 1964 as the *Faire Free Press*, when ex-New Yorker Art Kunkin sold his eight-page broadsheet at a Renaissance Pleasure Faire. Cannily, he also included a *Los Angeles Free Press* logo so that he could turn the paper inside out after the fair was over. He'd worked on various Leftist and radical newspapers before setting up his own publication along the lines of New York's *Village Voice*. Some attributed the origins of the underground press to that organ but Underground Press Syndicate coordinator Tom Forcade averred, 'That history began with the founding of the *Los Angeles Free Press* in 1964.'[6] 'I wanted a paper that would draw together all the diverse elements in the community,' Kunkin said, 'and that would be not only political, but cultural as well.'[7]

Two years later, Lorraine Alterman was the *Freep* 'Teen Writer', from her photograph a conventional soul but with a wry sense of humour, as her opening sentences in the July 15 edition show. 'Mothers and fathers, you thought the Beatles were bad. You got up in arms about the Rolling Stones. Sonny and Cher made you cringe. Well, as the man said, you ain't seen nothing yet.

'The Mothers of Invention are here with an album called *Freak Out!* (someone suggested it should have been called *Flake Out*). They come from Hollywood. Their clothes are dreadful – and I dig mod clothes.' She went on to mention the band's July 12 appearance on Robin Seymour's *Swingin' Time*: the show's talent coordinator, Art Cervi, confessed, 'We've never had anyone on the show that brought anything near the controversy they caused. The switchboard was flooded with viewers either saying the Mothers were great or awful.'[8] Any readers who'd missed the band's appearance could watch the following week's edition of *Dave Prince's Club 1270* on Saturday, July 23.

The Alterman column also devoted several paragraphs to Frank's pronouncements. 'We play the new free music,' he declaimed, 'music as absolutely free (another resonant phrase), unencumbered by American cultural suppression. We are systematically trying to do away with the creative roadblocks that our helpful American educational system has installed to make sure nothing creative leaks through to mass audiences.'[9] Unfortunately, the Freep didn't reach a mass audience either. Even so, large campaigns start with small battles and Frank made extensive use of the paper's pages in later issues, devoting whole sections to mostly negative critical reaction to the band, advertising upcoming gigs and vilifying their detractors.

Immediately after appearing on *Swingin' Time*, the band went on a brief promotional tour set up by MGM/Verve. The first date was in Washington, DC, where they appeared on the *Kerby Scott Dance Party* on WDCA and went on to make a surprise appearance at Georgetown's Roundtable nightclub. Frank was interviewed by Ronnie Oberman of the *Washington Star*. After explaining how to 'freak out', the social makeup of Sunset Strip youth and their tribal dances, Frank made one of his earliest denouncements of drugs, already prevalent among the 'freak' fraternity. 'I don't use any and I've never encouraged it,' he said. 'The same state of psychedelic happiness can be induced through dancing, listening to music, holding your breath and spinning around, and any number of the old, easy to perform and 100 percent legal means – all of which I endorse.'[10] He was far more pithy years later when asked by Kurt Loder what he thought of the groups that got stoned and claimed to play far-out music: 'Well, basically, I saw assholes in action.'[11]

Next stop was Detroit and another television show, where the Mothers were expected to lip-sync their 'hit'. Frank used the opportunity to deliver what he later called, 'Detroit's first whiff of homemade prime-time Dada'.[12] He also spoke to Reb Foster of the *Detroit Free Press:* 'We consider ourselves therapeutic workers massaging the brains of people dancing to our music with the lyrics to our songs.' The Mothers regarded most people as 'Plastics', people with no soul. 'We get so tired of playing for these phoney people in blue Velour shirts and Poor Boy sweaters.'[13] Only a short time previously, the Mothers would have welcomed an audience of any kind. But the ponies didn't know that.

The final stop was Dallas where they played live on yet another television teenage dance show. Frank's lasting memory from the occasion was the look on the innocent children's faces as they watched the contortions of the band's 'go-go boy' Carl Franzoni's awesome testicles, struggling in the confinement of his ballet tights.

BARKING PUMPKIN (1)

Before he left Dallas, Frank rang Pamela and asked her to pick him up from the airport. She took a new friend along with her. While finishing off her schooling, Pamela worked evenings and weekends at the Whisky and had got to know one of the secretaries there. Adelaide Gail Sloatman had been born on the first day of 1945. Her father, a Navy scientist and nuclear physicist, was posted to London in 1959. Gail was placed in 'a severely Catholic all-girls school', which she left to work as a secretary at the Office of Naval Research and Development. It was the height of the Beatles era and she spent her nights clubbing. Her father was transferred back to America in 1965 and Gail lost her work permit. Returning to New York, she briefly attended the Fashion Institute of Technology before hitch-hiking to Los Angeles with her former London flat-mate, Anya Butler.

Once there, her previous lifestyle meant that she naturally gravitated towards the 'freak' community. 'Anya and I didn't even bring a brassiere with us to California,' she told Victoria Balfour. 'I don't remember if we were the first, but I certainly remember bothering a lot of people.'[14] Joining the crowd that followed Vito and Carl Franzoni around, Gail became by her own admission, something of a groupie. 'It was almost religious with the girls. They were the worshippers and those guys were like priests on the altar.'[15]

Nevertheless, that experience in no way prepared her for Frank Zappa. He and Pamela led something of a communal lifestyle at the Kirkwood apartment, where most things were shared amongst a floating population of musicians and groupies, including social diseases. At the time, Frank was playing host to a thriving crab colony. 'He was infested, and so was his hair. He hadn't taken a bath for months. Or combed his hair. I think it was not so much rock and roll and not so much the road as it is that nobody was taking care of him.'[16]

The attraction when they first met at the airport was clearly mutual and immediate - with reservations on Gail's part. 'I thought he was probably one of the grubbiest creatures I'd ever seen,' she told Drew Wheeler, 'but he was compelling. He had a compelling glare. He had major magnetic charm, I would say.'[17] In his autobiography, Frank refers to her as 'a fascinating little vixen'; and from the photograph which is reproduced three times at the head of the page, Gail had eyes to die for. It's easy to believe it didn't take her long to find the 'real' Frank Zappa. In a short space of time, a deep bond was forged between the two, one that survived everything that they and the world outside could throw at it. In 1989, Frank had to admit, 'It took a couple of minutes, but I fell (don't laugh) in love.'[18]

This reticence to reveal feelings and emotions was noticed by others. Ian Whitcomb, the English singer who had a 1965 hit with 'You Turn Me On', met Zappa the following year and found him 'heavily intellectual, rather withdrawn, and curiously ambivalent about his family memories. He showed us some slides of suburban housewives in curlers with their pot-bellied men, which we were all supposed to laugh at. But then, accidentally, he threw some shots of his family taken in the fifties onto the screen and he fell into a loving, nostalgic silence.'[19] Within a year, the Mothers would record 'Mom & Dad', asking the question, 'Ever take a minute just to show a real emotion?'

The Kirkwood apartment had now become the centre of Frank's own troupe of followers. He'd moved in when the Mothers returned from their

November San Francisco gig and almost immediately surrounded himself with band members and sundry visitors such as the members of Them and the Animals. The latter were in Los Angeles at the beginning of July 1966 to make their next album with Tom Wilson. Wilson invited Frank to participate but the group's enthusiastic drug consumption earned his displeasure.

'I found out that not only were they not particularly original,' he said later, 'but were hung up in that R&B bag, which is deadening when you get little white boys trying to be little black boys, screaming the blues and being funky and all - that's shitty.'[20] No mention of the Soul Giants/Mothers stock-in-trade before their recording contract, perhaps because it had only been a means to an end - or was it a case of 'don't do as I do, do as I say'?

Eric Burdon got his own back the following year; 'Frank Zappa - the Hitler of song, says Eric' was the eye-catching title to a *Record Mirror* piece that detailed his reactions to America. The erstwhile gun collector reckoned he wanted to spread peace through music but Frank 'excites violence as a reaction from the audience'.[21] In the end, Frank wrote the arrangements for 'All Night Long' and 'The Other Side Of This Life', for the Animals' American album, *Animalism*. Around this time, he also recorded a single with actor Burt Ward, who played Robin to Adam West's Batman in the television series; Frank wrote 'Boy Wonder I Love You' and arranged the b-side, 'Orange Colored Sky'.

With Gail's arrival, things began to change. One consequence was an inevitable rift between Frank and Pamela Zarubica, even though theirs was not a sexual relationship. Her biggest grievance seems to have been the loss of intimate contact with a man she regarded as something of a guru. But Frank could be ruthlessly self-oriented and dealt summarily with anything or anyone that diverted him from his intended course. In 1974, he referred to the girl who had befriended and housed him in these terms: 'So I procured the services of another girl named Pamela Zarubica who was hired to be the Suzy Creamcheese of the European tour. And so she maintained the reputation of being Suzy Creamcheese after 1967.'[22]

GUAMBO

In Issue 105 of the *Los Angeles Free Press* the 'Great Underground Arts Masked Ball and Orgy' (Guambo for short), given to celebrate the paper's second birthday, was advertised. It was set to take place between 9.00 pm and 2.00 am on Saturday, July 23 at the Aerospace Hall, 7660 Beverly Boulevard. Groups scheduled to appear were the Sound Machine, the Factory and the Mothers. Filmmakers were exhorted 'Bring your own film and show it yourself'.

Two days before the event the management of the Aerospace Hall cancelled the booking; they'd received phone calls claiming that 'the monster junk sculpture' to be erected in their parking lot was part of a narcotics 'scene' and complaints from missile bases around the state that their hall was to be used for an orgy. In the end, the principal factor in the cancellation was that the hall couldn't accommodate the expected attendance. At short notice, the Danish Center agreed to stage the event. The groups would appear in the upstairs ballroom and rooms on the floor below would be used for 'happenings' and screenings of Gary Taylor's film of the Pleasure Faire and 'Teague's footage of the Canter bust'.

Jerry Hopkins reported on the evening in *Freep*'s next issue, under the title, 'Guambo Is An Act Of Love'. 'Flickering and flashing at both sides of the stage, strobe lights and op art patterns [were] projected on the ceiling and musicians.' First on was 'Clem Floyd's newly reorganised Sound Machine', followed by the Factory, led by Lowell George, a multi-instrumentalist who as a child had appeared on talent shows, played flute in the Hollywood High School orchestra and oboe and baritone sax on Frank Sinatra sessions. The rest of the band consisted of Warren Klein on lead guitar, Martin Kibbee on bass and Dallas Taylor on drums.

The dancing intensified when the Factory took the stage. 'Vito and his acolytes are here,' Hopkins notes. When the Mothers go on, 'This is one of the truly wild scenes of the evening. Frank Zappa in his suit of flowers. His sidemen are garbed similarly and, behind them are five other musicians augmenting the group. Five short-haired American Federation of Musicians types in black suits, white shirts and black ties. Just sitting there, reading charts, blowing with the Mothers' sound. And the Mothers Auxiliary dancing, dancing, dancing . . .' Carl Franzoni led the pack. 'He is wearing what looks like zebra-skinned longjohns with a pop art All-American Superman bib. Two nice ladies are dancing with him, alternating with some of Vito's group . . . and from the dance floor comes a man in a mummy suit to join in.'[23]

With a legal capacity of 1,500 for the two floors, police and fire marshalls kept an anxious eye on things. Roads were blocked for miles around. Fire exits too were blocked and the ticket desk was closed, allowing some 500 people to gatecrash through an unsecured door. Police began to appear amongst the crowd, the amps were turned down and shortly before 1.00 am, a claim that illegal drinking was taking place was used as a pretext to end the evening. Hopkins concluded, 'Guambo was an act of love and not every act of love is perfect.' There were acts of larceny though, including the theft of some light show equipment and slides and 'One brand new suit owned by Herb Cohen'.[24]

Lenny Bruce died of a morphine overdose on Wednesday, August 3, at the apartment he shared with John Judnich. His funeral took place two days later, on the same day that Pamela Zarubica graduated from Pepperdine College. Frank didn't want to attend the funeral but Judnich, from whom the band rented their stage equipment, rang to request their presence. That day's issue of the *Freep* carried a four-stanza 'Tribute To Lenny' written by Animal J. Huxley (daughter of Aldous and girlfriend of soon-to-be Factory drummer, Richie Hayward). In his *Making It* column in *Freep*, Hopkins quoted Frank's 'ad-lib-pop-art-gut-eulogy' to Bruce: 'They dug a hole in the ground and they put a box in it. Then a little dump truck filled in the hole and these cowboy-dudes started flattening the dirt with a trip-hammer. The grave is in the [San Fernando] Valley and the Valley is a lousy place for Lenny to sleep.'

'Freak Out! Son of Guambo', the next Mothers' gig, would take place at Santa Monica's Shrine Exposition Hall on Saturday, August 13, where once again Factory were part of the supporting bill. The next *Freep* noted Carl Franzoni had been spotted distributing leaflets for the gig on Venice Beach. Once again, the gig drew widely varying responses. Hopkins reported that Frank was unhappy about nearly everything, the sound system was terrible and no one paid any attention to the music. 'He is at least partially wrong,' he wrote, 'because a lot of us heard what he was laying down and it was some of the grooviest music ever splashed across the consciousness of man.'[25]

Stan Bernstein of the *Los Angeles Times* was less cosmically impressed: 'P.T. Barnum said there's a sucker born every minute and about 500 wandered into the Shrine and found boredom. The show lacked direction and there was little or no supervision. What was supposed to be entertaining happened to be monotonous.' After likening the audience to domestic animals 'just mooing and bleating', Bernstein lashed into the band, the light show and the lack of ventilation before ending, 'After an hour of having the eardrums punctured beyond repair, it was time to fight off ennui. A guard warned at the exit that readmittance was not possible. It was the most welcome news of the night.'[26]

There was no mention of the Factory's performance in either review but Frank and Herb Cohen were taking an interest in the group. On August 18, the band recorded three demos with Cary Slavin on drums. 'Hey Girl!', 'Changes' and 'Candy Corn Madness' were frantic and disjointed with an uneasy juxtaposition of ideas that didn't really jell. Nevertheless, it was arranged that Frank would produce a single with them.

'Lightnin' Rod Man', with Lowell strumming a dulcimer and Frank contributing slowed-down Pachuco doo-wops, almost emulates Don Vliet's ramshackle blues. Frank's slowed-down voice is heard on the fade asking, 'Why didn't you sing on the last bridge?' George told Andy Childs he thought Frank had done a fantastic job. 'It's a cross between 'They're Coming To Take Me Away' and Ian & Sylvia - somewhere in the middle there.'[27] 'The Loved One' resembles Jagger and Richard's songs of the era, a two-chord vamp with a psychedelic chorus and lyrics about butterflies and 'a big black helicopter'.

The tracks weren't legally released until 1993, although 'Lightnin' Rod Man' turned up on Zappa bootlegs over the years. The band got a deal with

UNI Records and a single, UNI 55005, was released, coupling 'Smile, Let Your Life Begin' and 'When I Was An Apple'. These and four other titles were produced by Marshall Lieb, who in 1958 had been a Teddy Bear, recording 'To Know Him Is To Love Him' with Phil Spector and Annette Kleinbard. Lieb also produced Timi Yuro and others before moving into films.

There was a memorial 'Freak In' for Lenny Bruce on Sunday, August 21, at the Eden Memorial Park on Sepulveda Boulevard in Mission Hills. The notice in *Freep* added, 'Those planning to come should bring box lunches and noise makers'. Frank, in flowered bell-bottoms and sneakers, was one of the 200-strong crowd that attended and of a smaller group that walked to KDAY disc jockey Tom Clay's house, where Phil Spector and Dennis Hopper spoke their eulogies.

The Mothers returned to the Fillmore on the weekend of September 9/10, sharing the bill with Oxford Circle. Because of a ceremony at the synagogue next door, the venue was changed to the Scottish Rites Temple across town. That week's *Freep* carried advance notice of the band's next LA gig: 'Pat Morgan, Dallas producer, is presenting one of the wildest light shows and dance freak out performances at the Shrine Exposition Hall, Saturday night, September 17. The show will feature the Mothers of Invention, Little Gary Ferguson (seven years old and a star!), along with the West Coast Pop Art Experimental Band, Count Five, Kenny Dino, and the Factory.'[28] Another 'Freak Out' was scheduled for October 15 at the Earl Warren Showground in Santa Barbara.

The next two issues carried several pages of Mothers advertising ('Published when we can afford it. Mostly for fun.') along with a hectoring letter from Suzy Creamcheese/Frank Zappa:

This is about the Mothers of Invention. We have watched them grow, and with their growth, we hopefully have grown. Their honesty has offended some and been provocative to many, but in any case, their performances have had a real effect on their audiences.

The Mothers' music is very new, and as their music is new, so is the intention of their music. As much as the Mothers put into their music, we must bring to it. The Mothers and what they represent as a group has attracted all of the outcasts, the pariahs, the people who are angry and afraid and contemptuous of the existing social structure. The danger lies in the 'Freak Out' becoming an excuse instead of a reason. An excuse implies an end, a reason a beginning. Being that the easiest way is consistently more attractive than the harder way, the essential thing that makes the 'Freak Out' audiences different constitutes their sameness. A freak is not a freak if ALL are freaks. 'Freaking Out' should presuppose an active freedom, freedom meaning a liberation from the control of some other person or persons. Unfortunately, reaction seems to have taken place of action. We SHOULD be as satisfied listening to the Mothers perform from a concert stage. If we could channel the energy expended in 'Freaking Out' physically into 'Freaking Out' intellectually, we might possibly be able to create something concrete out of the ideological twilight of bizarre costumes and being seen being bizarre. Do we really listen? And if we really listen, do we really think? Freedom of thought, conversely, brings an awesome responsibility. Looking and acting eccentric IS NOT ENOUGH.

A mad tea party is valid only as satire, commenting ironically, and ending in its beginning, in that it is only a trick of interpretation. It is not creation, and it IS NOT ENOUGH.

What WE must try to do then, is not only comment satirically on what's wrong, but try to CHANGE what's wrong. The Mothers are trying.

Very trying indeed. Whatever the cost of a whole page ad in the *Freep*, of which this letter formed a small island in the centre, what did Frank expect to achieve? Did he really believe that audiences, already required to listen to his music rather than dance to it, would also think about his message and act upon it? There's no mistaking the earnestness in his sentences or the sententiousness in his call to arms. Not for the first time, he was preaching to deaf and distracted ears. But someone was taking note: McCarthyism had faded but Richard Nixon's Amerika was just around the corner and bridging the gap, J. Edgar Hoover, who also wore the odd floral number, had his brain police on alert.

There were sound problems for all the acts that performed at the Shrine on September 17. They were bad enough for the Mothers to announce later in *Freep* that the October 15 gig had been cancelled 'due to a critical acoustic problem & virtually non-existent P.A. facilities'. Even so, 'the multitude roared their bliss to those upon the platform,' as Sean McGregor reported in his *Tinsel Town* column. 'A horny hand of sound layed its black shadow over the evening,' he went on, 'and this would seem to be a problem that just can not be beat by producer Morgan and Company.'

McGregor's comments were not published until the October 21 issue, by which time the Mothers and the Factory had played the Whisky on September 27 and October 2. Most of McGregor's column was devoted to a rare attack on the Mothers in the pages of *Freep*. His prime target was Herb Cohen, 'a buddha-framed male attired in his bushy black face-piece and running mouth'. Applying his sarcasm like stucco, he went on: 'It is understood throughout Tinseled City that Mr C is of the total 'in' and lays artistic claim to a monstrous hate. He and his 'Mothers' shun the limelight like clean tubwater. During the night, Mr C barred film makers from shooting his

'Mothers', though he found heart later on, after all acts had retired, to having his group painted on 16mm film.

'So great is Mr C's anger at any who'd impose upon real Freaks that he and his 'Mothers' shelled out their hard-earned coin for two full Free Press pages and condemned those who'd take out full pages expounding their own virtues.'[29] McGregor's tortuous grammar hammered out a few more insults but there seemed to be a basis for his 'freakier-than-thou' criticism.

Frank's reply, in *Freep*, was swift and scathing. It seemed that McGregor was in the employ of Pat Morgan, promoter of the ill-fated Shrine gig, and his column's invective stemmed from an argument between Morgan and Cohen which had ended in a scuffle outside the offices of the *Hollywood Reporter*. Frank's densely-worded rebuttal strained for effect: 'SEAN McGREGOR took it upon himself to SUBVERT a QUASI-LEGITIMATE VEHICLE (his little column) in order to hurl a few cardboard thunderbolts at a quiet & peace-loving group of local lads whose only offense was having HERB COHEN for a MANAGER.'[30] About a quarter of the page was devoted to an ad for the rescheduled gig at the Earl Warren Show Grounds on October 29, with the headline 'Legalize Therapeutic Abortion with The Mothers'. It was a conjunction of commercialism and controversy that epitomised Frank's complex thought processes.

UNDERGROUND ORATORIOS

The volatile situation between the police and the kids on the Strip, which had already led to a 10.00 pm curfew imposed on under-18s, boiled over during November. A near-riot took place on November 12, when a demonstration got out of hand, street signs were torn up, buses attacked and dozens of young people clubbed and arrested outside Pandora's Box, a popular alternative to Canters located on Sunset at Crescent Heights Boulevard. A picket fence was placed around the coffee house and the two sides glowered at one another across it. Eventually, the police attacked and the 'hot-bed of insurrection' was razed to the ground. Stephen Stills wrote 'For What It's Worth' for Buffalo Springfield, Frank Zappa wrote 'Plastic People'.

Al Mitchell, owner of the Fifth Estate Coffee House, set up the Right of Assembly and Movement Committee the day after the first protest and took a leading role in setting up further protests on November 26 and December 10. Another group, which included Beatles publicist Derek Taylor, set up Community Action for Facts and Freedom. Interviewed by Raymond Gruenther in *Freep*, Mitchell didn't mince words: 'It was in part the frank and open use of police power on the part of one Strip economic group to suppress another economic group - the heavy real estate people against the places which cater to the young.

'The real estate people told the police, "We don't care how you get them off the Strip . . . just get them off." And the kids began to experience the same kind of police fascism which was in the past directed against minority groups in Watts and East Los Angeles . . . They may be stopped at any time, searched at any time, arrested at any time and slapped around during interrogation.'[31]

Two issues earlier, Frank had said much the same thing in an interview: 'The problem is not the police, 'cause they're only taking orders,' he said. 'The problem is the merchants and the money interests who are influencing the people who give orders to the cops. If it's as simple as money, the way to take over would be to have a few of the kids who are making bread from having long hair pay their own cops off.

'The people in L.A. haven't realised yet that this is where it's going to happen, the whole major breakthrough from a society controlled by the youth, will occur here. It looks like a revolution, it's got all the hallmarks of a popular revolt, but it's so small that it can't succeed and it's just like they've almost shot their wad. Leadership? I think any leadership that announced itself from that mass would be swiftly shot secretly someplace in these streets.

'I think that if there were ever one rallying point, something real that the kids could identify with, that they could focus their patriotism on and you know, really go for, you'd have a force in the United States that nobody would believe - it would really come back to life. Right now it's pretty hard to even walk in the woods and say, "Hey, this is nature and it's beautiful and I dig it", without remembering everything else that surrounds you that is nothing but a big lie. The whole system has unfortunately got down to a state where you can't believe anything anymore.'[32]

The conversation touched upon the clubs and the quality of music presented in them. By his answers, Frank indicated that he was ready to move on to the next stage of his master plan. When asked if he thought light shows and 'freakouts' would die out, he replied, 'Yeah. I hope it does, dies tomorrow.'[33]

It was against this background that the Mothers returned to TT&G during November to record their second album.

ABSOLUTELY FREE

The band had changed during the summer. Elliott Ingber had gone off to form the Fraternity of Man with Richie Hayward. He was replaced for a short period by Jim Fielder, before he left to join Buffalo Springfield. Given his love of percussion, it was no surprise when Frank added a second drummer; Billy Mundi had been in a San Francisco band, Lamp of Childhood, and would leave in January 1968 to join the Elektra band, Rhinoceros. The other new members, Don Preston and Bunk Gardner, stayed until Frank disbanded the Mothers in 1969. 'I'd known Don and Bunk several years before I met the other guys,' Frank said in 1968, 'we used to play experimental music a long time ago - we got together in garages and went through some very abstract charts.'[34]

Preston and Gardner added a dimension that had been lacking in *Freak Out!*. Frank could now add fresh tonal colours to his musical palette: 'When we became an eight-piece, we finally had a very workable ensemble.'[35] One element was the insertion of classical quotes in certain of the tunes that made up *Absolutely Free*. 'I think that the Stravinskian influence probably popped up on the second album,' he told Nigel Leigh (in 'Amnesia Vivace' and a musical interlude in 'Status Back Baby' that reproduces 'The Shrovetide Fair' introduction from *Petrushka*). 'But I'd say there's a certain Varèsian aroma to the introduction of 'Who Are The Brain Police?'"[36] And this time, each side of the album was edited into a continuous performance that reflected the group's live appearances.

Frank was also compounding the rhythmic complexity of his music, as he explained to Frank Kofsky that it had taken a year to learn to play 'Call Any Vegetable': 'Can you tell why? The time, the time - it's fantastic. It's four bars of 4/4, one bar of 8/8, one bar of 9/8 - OK? And then it goes 8/8, 9/8, 8/8, 9/8, 8/8, 9/8 and then it goes 8/8, 4/8, 5/8, 6/8 and back into 4/4 again.' When Kofsky asked him about the significance of the symbolism in 'Call Any Vegetable' and 'Duke Of Prunes', Frank's reply was succinct: 'Dada dynamite.'[37]

At the other extreme were songs like 'Plastic People' and 'Son of Suzy Creamcheese', both based on Richard Berry's 'Louie Louie'. 'Status Back Baby' was a refurbished version of a song from 'I Was A Teenage Maltshop', while 'Duke Of Prunes' had less to do with Gene Chandler's 1962 hit, 'Duke Of Earl', than it did with guying the nonsense of love lyrics in general. There were two extended performances, one instrumental, the other vocal. 'Invocation & Ritual Dance Of The Young Pumpkin' opens with a quote from 'Jupiter, The Bringer Of Jollity', part of Gustav Holst's suite, *The Planets*. The tune, a feature for Frank's guitar and Bunk Gardner's soprano sax, was dedicated to Gail, who appears in the front cover's main photograph taken by Alice Ochs, peering over Frank's shoulder and labeled 'My Pumpkin' on its reproduction inside.

The other extended track was a major composition and the album's highlight. 'Brown Shoes Don't Make It', a scathing attack on those, high and low, who formed America's government, was a complicated piece made up of several sections, with frequent tempo changes and numerous edits. It contrasted the average American family's humdrum existence ('do you love it, do you hate it, there it is the way you made it'), their limited expectations ('TV dinner by the pool, I'm so glad I've finished school'), the corrupt minds of politicians ('a world of secret hungers perverting the men who make your laws') and their triumphalism ('life is such a ball, I run the world from City Hall').

'These unfortunate people manufacture inequitable laws and ordinances,' Frank told London's *International Times*, 'perhaps unaware of the fact that the restrictions they place on the young people in a society are a result of their own hidden sexual frustrations.'[38] 'Brown Shoes' formed part of the album's second side, sub-titled 'The M.O.I. American Pageant'. Versions of the same song, with contrasting arrangements, opened and closed the side; 'America Drinks' is a deconstructed stumbling parody of a cocktail lounge love song; when it returns in jaunty 4/4 as 'America Drinks & Goes Home', it's performed over a cacophony of ringing tills, angry brawls, drunken revelry and seductions. Does this kind of life look interesting to you?

'The one thing that I think is really good about our music,' Frank said in September 1967, 'is that the setting for the lyrics are so carefully designed. Those things are so carefully constructed that it breaks my heart when people don't dig into them and see all the levels that I put in them.'[39] Once again, he wanted to have his cake and eat it too. It was impossible for listeners to dissect such a deliberately complex sound collage; nor could they be expected to divine the reasons for his methods of composition.

This was one of the fundamental conceits by which Frank would separate himself from his audience and which would allow him to reject or bypass all criticism. He was saying, in effect, 'If you don't understand musical theory (or the precise origin of a song's theme), then you are not competent to comment.' By 1972, he'd altered his stance: 'All I'm interested in doing is writing music that I want to hear,' he said in a radio interview.[40]

Throughout the album, Frank delivered snippets of dialogue, which sometimes provided specific instances of a song's subject and at others a counterpoint. 'Plastic People' began with a cryptic reference, 'There's this guy from the CIA and he's creeping around Laurel Canyon.' Later, he intoned, 'I hear the sound of marching feet down Sunset Boulevard to Crescent Heights and there at Pandora's Box, we are confronted with a vast quantity of plastic people.' While Stephen Stills' lyric about young people being attacked by 'the heat' fudged the issue, Frank called the police Nazis and criticised the conduct of those that allowed themselves to be manipulated.

MGM/Verve had placed a restriction on the amount of recording time available for this second album and so its recording was completed in four double sessions, totalling 24 hours. But the mixing was done at MGM's own studios in New York City, because the band had got its first East Coast engagement.

CITY OF TINY LIGHTS
The Mothers had been booked to play in New York the week beginning

November 26, Thanksgiving Day, at The Balloon Farm ('sort of a grubby location') at 23 St Marks Place, the building which house 'The Dom', where the Velvet Underground had made their name. Reaction was such that they were retained until New Year's Day. One review stated, 'The Balloon Farm became much more than a discotheque last weekend, and the resident combo became much more than a pop-music ensemble.' The Mothers were from 'deepest, freakiest L.A. They are a perfect embodiment of all that is super-hyped and stunningly creative about West Coast rock.'

'R.G.' went on: 'These eight musicians made the Balloon Farm a concert hall. They seized the stage and belted the world's first rock 'n' roll oratorio to an audience that was either too engrossed or too confused to do anything but sit and listen. The show was a single extended number, broken into movements by patter, and fused by repeated melody-themes. Especially notable was the use, as leitmotif, of music from *Boris Godunov*, sewn into the fabric of the song so that it became an integral part of the melody and not a sequin pasted on for class.' The review ended: 'The Mothers of Invention haven't arrived yet, but they strive with outstretched fingers towards something perceptively unique. Their first album, *Freak Out!*, is the most poorly produced package since the Hindenburg Zeppelin but don't let this baby-dribble fool you. The Mothers of Invention are to be watched, and leader Frank Zappa deserves your attention, and your three bucks.'[41]

Not that their money was worth much on the city's streets, as Frank recounted to a Dallas radio interviewer: 'We were grubby and long-haired and stuff – that sort of thing hadn't really taken over in New York – and it was the middle of winter and we were warm-blooded. It was freezing there, snow and everything, and we'd had to go to a used clothes store in Los Angeles before we left Los Angeles to get some old overcoats to wear. We looked like a bunch of immigrants standing out there in the streets, you know, and the cabs wouldn't pick us up to take us home. We had to walk home in the snow every night after the job.'

Their month-long tenure also drew an appreciative article in the Christmas Day edition of the *New York Times* by Robert Shelton. Declaring them 'The most original new group to simmer out of the rock 'n' roll underground in the last hour-and-one-half,' Shelton called Frank the 'Dada' of the Mothers, as well as 'a spindly-framed, sharp-nosed gamester whose appearance suggests some of the more sinister aspects of Edgar Allen Poe, John Carradine (him again!) and Rasputin.'[42]

Frank was on good form for the interview. 'I am trying to use the weapons of a disoriented and unhappy society against itself,' he said. 'The Mothers of Invention are designed to come in the back door and kill you while you're sleeping.' He identified one of the band's short-range objectives as doing away with the Top 40 broadcasting format because it was 'basically wrong, unethical and un-musical'. Shelton also commented on the use of classical elements in the band's arrangements, to which Frank replied, 'Stravinsky in rock 'n' roll is like a get-acquainted offer, a loss-leader. It's a gradual progression to bring in my own 'serious' music.'[43]

Another progression was taking place on the other side of the Atlantic. In November, 'It Can't Happen Here' had been issued as a single in England. It was reviewed on the November 12 edition of *Juke Box Jury*, a staid BBC television programme that voted the week's releases 'hits' or 'misses'. The guests on that week's show, presided over by disc jockey David Jacobs, were singers Bobby Goldsboro, Carole Carr and Susan Maugham, and comedian Ted Rogers, with audience member Robert Stringer as the casting voter. 'It Can't Happen Here' was played between the Small Faces' 'My Mind's Eye' and Jonathan King's 'Icicles'. No prizes for guessing how it fared. Other records reviewed that night included 'La-La-La-Lies' by The Who, 'Willow Weep For Me' by the Alan Price Set, 'Pamela' by Wayne Fontana and Sandie Shaw's 'Think Sometimes About Me'.

Writing in the December issue of *Queen*, Nik Cohn dismissed the Mothers' music as 'revamped Dada, souped-up Ginsberg and warmed-over Dylan. The only thing new about the Mothers is the speed and glibness with which they've become successful.' Comparing the Mothers to those he called 'the precursors', Cohn found the Mothers 'plain dull. This record is meant to be a brainstorm, a wild fit, and it should be monstrous or lovely, obscene or apocalyptic. Instead, it sounds tentative and self-conscious, painfully aware of how naughty it's being.' English pop intellectuals were already running round with their tongues hanging out over the Mothers apparently, but Cohn didn't intend to join them. 'The only thing that depresses me is that I'd like pop to be genuinely progressive and alive, and I hate a supposedly new sound to come out as tired and old-hat as the Mothers.'

CHAPTER FIVE
LUMPY GRAVY

The Mothers needed more than hats when they travelled from New York to Montreal for two weeks of gigs. 'We played a club called the New Penelope,' Frank told David Sheff, 'and it was twenty degrees below zero. We walked from our hotel to the club and the snot had literally frozen in our noses by the time we got to work. The wind instruments got so cold that if you tried to play them, your lips and fingers would freeze to them. The instruments couldn't even be played until they were warmed up.'[1]

Back in Los Angeles, work was still scarce and some of the band had families to feed. Frank, as usual, had work to do. He'd been commissioned by Nick Venet, the Capitol A&R man who'd signed the Beach Boys and produced their first albums, to compose and conduct an original orchestral work. Venet assumed that, even though Frank was signed to MGM/Verve as a member of the Mothers of Invention, the contract did not cover either of the roles expected of him by Capitol. Unfortunately, he thought wrong.

Lumpy Gravy was conceived as a roughly half-hour oratorio that combined the elements of rock band and orchestra, interspersed with idiosyncratic dialogue, percussion interludes and musique concrete. It's said that it took Frank 11 days to write but the finished work was plainly created in the studio, for it's a dazzling combination of the above forces, edited with humour and often with rapid precision. Much of Part One consists of different arrangements of 'Oh No', following one upon the other, sometimes at double speed. A vocal version of 'Oh No' was later issued on *Weasels Ripped My Flesh*, and the tune, with or without words, became a staple in the repertoire of successive Zappa bands. All this is punctuated by Varèse- and Stravinsky-like orchestral interludes, Motorhead monologues about girlfriends and their cars, and conversations by various individuals with their heads in a grand piano, the strings resonating to their voices.

This last was a typically contrived Zappa 'event', in which he placed people in a controlled environment, suggested their topics of conversation and recorded the outcome. In no time, people were competing for the privilege of going in the piano. 'The cast of characters that wandered in and out of the piano covered everybody from Motorhead and Roy Estrada to the sister of the guy who owned the (Apostolic) recording studio (Gilly Townley) to Monica the Albanian receptionist to bunches of people whose names I can't even remember.'[2] These last included Spider Barbour, All-Night John the studio manager and Louis Cuneo, responsible for the 'psychotic turkey' laughter. Over the course of three days, eight or nine hours of bizarre conversations were recorded.

Part Two continued in the same vein and included the theme of another Zappa mainstay, 'King Kong', before Zappa himself intones, 'Cos round things are (pause), are boring' and a perky version of 'Take Your Clothes Off When You Dance' fades into the ether. Some of the orchestral sessions, including woodwind players breaking down in humorous frustration, took place in Los Angeles before the tapes were taken back to New York for completion at Apostolic during February.

Capitol had invested some $40,000 before MGM/Verve got wind of what was happening and threatened a lawsuit. The matter went unresolved for over a year until Verve eventually bought the finished masters at cost and released *Lumpy Gravy* after *We're Only In It For The Money*, which had been recorded in the meantime. An acetate exists of two titles, 'Gypsy Airs' and 'Sink Trap', which Capitol may have considered releasing as a single.

While the first *Gravy* sessions were planned and recorded, a 'return' gig was arranged at the Lindy Opera House, 5214 Wilshire for February 3/4 and advertised in *Freep*. 'Yes, Ladies and Gentlemen, Boys and Girls, Policemen and Tourists . . . ! The MOTHERS return to play for what's left of the L.A. underground. We'll mention the Police and Gov't and we can all nod our heads together while we all cop out. We've been rehearsing a whole bunch of new numbers like 'BROWN SHOES DON'T MAKE IT', 'I'M LOSING STATUS AT THE HIGH SCHOOL', and a new Funset Strip version of 'WHO ARE THE BRAIN POLICE?' that is guaranteed to titillate your Liberal backgrounds.'

Another, this time full-page, ad appeared in the next issue with the headline, 'HEAR THE NEW M.O.I. SONGBOOK'. The 'Songs Of Love' were 'Duke Of Prunes' and 'Memories Of El Monte'; 'Songs Of Spiritual Significance', The Original 'Electric Banana' – 'At last you too can know what Donovan picked up on . . . , and 'Call Any Vegetable'; 'Songs We're Sick Of Playing' included almost all of Freak Out!; and 'Songs We Just Learned This Week That Will Sound Crappy' were 'Agency Man' – 'Wherein RONALD REAGAN is elected to the PRESIDENCY because nobody took the time to stop him' and 'Archie's Home' – 'What if Archie Shepp could play an ELECTRIC BASSOON?' In 1967, Frank must have regarded the idea of Reagan being elected President as outlandish rather than prophetic. But he under-estimated 'the great communicator', if not the power of the business interests who wrote his scripts.

Nat Freedland reviewed the evening in *Freep* 134: 'Frizz-pated, evil-goateed, wraithlike and stocking-less, Frank Zappa is – among many more other things than anybody else in the pop explosion – the Brecht and Weill of rock music. Much of his melodic approach could be an electronic 'Son Of Threepenny Opera'. Marching quarter-note melodies, one note per word, the magnificently precise Mother drummer accenting each word.

'Zappa is also the most avant-garde arranger in rock 'n' roll. His 'Archie's Home' number interpolated the incredibly complex New Jazz sound of Archie Shepp's style into a series of nonsense word turns . . . Sure, the Mothers run in a little protest and satire to keep up the far-outnik image. But it's pretty much kiddie boo-hooing. 'SELL US A PRESIDENT, AGENCY MAN' . . . 'NAZIS ARE RUNNING THIS TOWN' . . . It's gutsier than the run of the Top 40, but Dylan, Ochs, or the Fugs it is not. Why don't you take on some of these cats' groovier art-rock, Zappa?'[3] How about that 'groovier'? The final third of the review went into a Jack Kerouac stream-of-consciousness vision of the extended improvisation section of the programme and ended, 'Welcome home, Mothers.'

TREACHEROUS CRETINS

How the Mothers came to be invited to play at the ceremony for the ninth Grammy awards in New York's Waldorf-Astoria Hotel is lost to posterity. The blame for initiating the awards can be laid at the door of the Hollywood Beautification Committee. In 1955, this august body was planning the Hollywood Walk of Fame, a sequence of stars to be set in the concrete of Hollywood Boulevard going west from the junction with Vine Street, in an attempt to halt the area's slide into sleaze. As the film *Pretty Woman* illustrates, they failed signally in their endeavour; even in daylight it's the seediest part of town, pimps and hookers of all faiths commandeering the star-set sidewalk after dark.

The Committee asked the five gnomes of the music business – Jesse Kaye of MGM, Lloyd Dunn of Capitol, Sonny Burke of Decca, Paul Weston of Columbia and Dennis Farnon of RCA – to suggest a list of names for the 1,200 stars planned. The gnomes did what was asked of them but then began to consider an award that would be presented for artistic merit rather than commerciality. The National Academy of Recording Arts & Sciences (NARAS) was duly formed on May 29, 1957 in the back room of the Brown Derby restaurant. The Grammy was named after the statuette of a wind-up gramophone with its amplifying horn, a composite design based on Edison, Victor and Columbia originals.

The award ceremony for the 1966 awards took place on February 14, 1967. The programme read 'Music by Woody Herman; Entertainment by the Mothers of Invention'. NARAS was looking for credibility; Frank didn't intend to give it to them. His resolve hardened when he read the otherwise hilarious Stan Freberg's pompous Credo that NARAS judged records 'on the basis of sheer artistry and artistry alone'.

When the Mothers took the stage, Frank went for the fat cat's throats: 'All year long you people manufactured this crap, and one night a year you've got to listen to it! Your whole affair is nothing more than a lot of pompous hokum, and we're going to approach you on your own level.'[4] The band then proceeded to ravish 'Satin Doll', the tune with which the Woody Herman band had opened the evening, dismembering dolls and handing the limbs out to the stunned audience. The only bright note in an ugly evening was when John McClure, head of Classical A&R for Columbia Masterworks, approached Frank to say, 'When you get tired of that dipshit label you're on, why don't you come and make a deal with (us)?'[5]

The New York chapter of NARAS met the following Monday and told one another how disgusting it had been. 'Everyone rolled their eyes in the back of their heads and said, "What a schmuck, what a tasteless dope",' said Nick Perito. 'The idea [in inviting Zappa] had been to lend some energy to a prestigious affair. He turned it into a bar-room.'[6]

Frank may have regarded the band's performance as prestigious, too. If *Absolutely Free* had been in the shops, it would undoubtedly have sold in greater quantities. But, once again, MGM were complaining about the album artwork. Frank's vertical design for the gatefold sleeve incorporated a photographic collage and a brightly coloured cartoon representation of brown-shoed America's typical habitat. The word 'buy' appears frequently, most notably on a flag that says, 'BUY America' and 'Move Your Goods With Patriotic Sell!'. Another message read 'You must BUY this album now. Top 40 radio will never ever play it'. 'KILL UGLY RADIO', in large letters, appeared on the inside sleeve. What MGM's legal department objected to was the phrase that ran along the top edge of the American flag: 'WAR means WORK for all'. This was not included in the truths that Americans held to be self-evident and MGM refused to print it. Eventually a compromise was reached whereby the phrase remained but printed in a light grey rather than 100% black.

No compromise could be reached on Frank's intention to include a libretto of the album's lyrics. On that, MGM were not to be moved; customers could listen to the 'naughty' words but they couldn't see them in print. 'Brown Shoes' in particular posed them many problems: in a bizarre list of suggested changes, 'I'd like to make her do her nasty on the White House lawn' would have become 'I'd like to make her do the crossword puzzle on the back of *TV Guide*'. To paraphrase the well-known saw: 'when truth and euphemism exist, print the euphemism'.

In the end, Frank Zappa Music printed the libretto and the inner sleeve directed those interested in receiving one to send their money to 'The Mothers Idea Fund'.

Nigel Leigh asked Frank, 'Did the record company by that time have any idea of re-packaging you into something more commercial?' 'Oh, I don't think they ever thought for a minute that that could be successfully accomplished. I think that their attitude was that they were involved in a contract which had a certain number of years to run and they were obliged to put out a certain amount of product. And they were just going to hold their nose and go through with it.'[7]

Nor was the meddling at an end. On March 1, 1967, *Freak Out!* was issued in England – as a single album. Curiously enough, the tracks omitted were not the extended strangeness of the second album but three of the pastiche pop songs, 'How Could I Be Such A Fool', 'Any Way The Wind Blows' and 'Go Cry On Somebody Else's Shoulder'. A press release was issued by EMI the day before, with the impenetrable headline, 'The Mothers' Mind-Manifesting Music'. The single page began, 'A lot of interest has been aroused lately over the 'Freak Out' form of music' and went on to quote Frank's definition of 'freaking out'. It concluded, 'Their musical style is a mixture of solid rock 'n' roll and weird noises – except the last two tracks on side two, 'Help I'm A Rock' and 'The Return Of The Son Of Monster Magnet' which have paved the way for a whole new concept in popular music.'

The press release was written by Nick Massey, who went on to become an independent publicist with clients that included Tom Jones, Rod Stewart, the Moody Blues, Bucks Fizz and Bill Wyman. Twenty-three years later, having adopted the expensive lifestyle of the people he represented, he committed suicide in a hired Daimler while facing investigation for embezzling KA Publicity, the PR company he shared with Keith Altham. 'I was thrilled to bits for him when he died,' his first wife said. 'In the end he got what he wanted. If one of his artists had got so much publicity, it would have been unbelievable.'[8]

PIGS AND REPUGNANT

In the Mothers' absence, the L.A. authorities had clamped down on the clubs on the Strip and discouraged owners of larger venues from staging 'freak' events, be they 'in', 'on' or 'out'. Work had temporarily dried up for many bands and the Mothers had never averaged more than a couple of gigs a week. Apart from the Lindy Opera House, their only other notable gigs were two weekends at the Fillmore, February 17-19, with Blues Project and Canned Heat, and March 3-5, with Otis Rush and Morning Glory. 'We were never that popular in Los Angeles,' Frank told Nigel Leigh. 'In fact, if we hadn't left, we never would have gone anywhere. We would have just evaporated after the first album.'[9]

Lucky then that the success of their Balloon Farm residency led to an Easter weekend booking at the Garrick Theater, a 300-seater on Bleecker Street in New York's Greenwich Village. The weather was terrible, freezing cold and driving snow, but there were queues around the block for their two shows a night. 'We thought: Oh, this is it, this is the big one,' Frank told Kurt Loder. 'We're in New York City, and there's lines around the block.'[10] As soon as their audiences went back to school, there were as few as three to five people attending each night.

Even so, the theatre management were sufficiently encouraged by Easter's business to book the band for six nights a week for the rest of the summer. Their five month tenure grossed $103,000, which, after deductions for overheads, left each man with about $200 a week. Not a lot, when you have to live in New York. When they first arrived, Frank and a pregnant Gail lived at the Hotel Van Rensslaer on Eleventh Street. 'It was dreadful,' Gail told Drew Wheeler. 'We were living in a horrible hotel, sharing it with very large cockroaches. I think I lived off grapefruit and Frank lived off peanut butter. And coffee - we made coffee from the bathtub because the water that came into the bathtub was so hot you could really scorch yourself. You did not need to boil it. It was frightening, instant coffee.'[11] After awhile, they were able to rent a $200-a-month apartment at 180 Thompson Street, conveniently close to the Garrick.

The engagement began on Wednesday, May 24, and was reviewed the following day in the *New York Times* by Dan Sullivan. 'Their music is . . . more often than not, frankly hostile - both in its headachy volume and in those lyrics that you can make out amid the roar . . . As pure sound, though, some of this approaches genius. From an electrified kitchen [would that be a dangerous kitchen?] of percussion, saxes, guitars, flutes, etc., they produce a thick black sound shot through with odd treble sunbursts and pinwheels - the exact aural equivalent of the nervous, ever-changing abstract projections flashing on the screen behind them.'

'The Mothers of Invention are seven young men of saturnine, malevolent and hairy aspect,' wrote Jerry Tallmer in his *Across The Footlights* column in the *New York Post*. 'They . . . put on an air of having as much nonchalant contempt for their audiences as for society in general.' He went on about 'defecatory and expectorant humor, animus toward Ronald Reagan', 'the chewing of turnips' and 'an interestingly profane romance between a plastic doll and a common tropical fruit', but the music remained 'brilliant verging on great'.

Diane Fisher wrote her review for *The Village Voice*, finding herself liking the music and noting that the band's 'scandalously unrespectable appearance' couldn't disguise the fact that they were a generation older than their audience: 'Their attitude hasn't much to do with age. It might be called surrealistic enlightened.'

Eric Clapton, in town with Cream to record *Disraeli Gears*, was an enthusiastic visitor: 'The Mothers were at the Garrick Theater and there would be nobody in the audience - nobody! They were experimenting every night . . . Frank would come off and sit in the audience and talk to someone while the band played. It was madness! He took me home one night to his house and he made me play into a Revox and told me to play all the licks I knew . . . He was very manipulative and knew how to appeal to my ego and my vanity and I put everything on this tape. I think he just had files and files of tapes of people and I was in there somewhere.'[12]

Regular work, the first that the Mothers had had, improved their proficiency at playing Frank's progressively complicated songs. As *Absolutely Free* showed, he was developing material that reflected the quirkiness of speech patterns and their rhythms. Writing in *Downbeat*, Larry Kart noted, 'In the pieces with lyrics the often elaborate rhythmic and melodic patterns are tied directly to the words (one beat and one note to each syllable, with few large melodic intervals). This effect carries over into the instrumental pieces, where the tight rhythmic-melodic motifs expand and contract as if they had a life of their own.'[13]

Speaking at the end of their first Garrick run, Frank explained, 'The spoken word is differentiated from the sung word, in its rhythmic sense, as in poetry. But even normal speech patterns are beautiful in themselves. Because the way people talk, it doesn't make a shit what they're saying; in fact, most of the time what they're saying is really ugly. But when you think about the rhythm, or the way certain gas-station attendants might speak, you know, what they're saying is useless; but if you listen to it as a piece of music . . . I like to simulate things like that.'[14]

Many things were simulated on the Garrick stage that summer. Many times, the shows were not concerts but events. At least two marriages were performed on stage. Members of the audience were co-opted into taking part in the mayhem, to perform songs with the group or take over their instruments, subject themselves to ritual humiliation with varieties of foodstuffs, both solid and liquid, or assist in whatever spontaneous or planned 'dada' happenings that evolved. 'You could do anything,' Frank admitted. 'And because they were New Yorkers, they would at least consider it. You couldn't do that in Hollywood.'[15]

Doon Arbus and Valerie Wilmer reported on their visits to the Garrick. Arbus described the band: 'Frank Zappa ambles on stage. He is wearing a purple, high-school cardigan, knit pants, and butterscotch-colored shoes with pointy, turned-up toes. His face is made of planes and angles, like a house of cards, and is framed by a mantle of squiggly, black curls. He is like a wild, woodsy hermit, either very benign or very ferocious.'[16] The other Mothers each resembled a distinct character: Billy Mundi, 'a baker from the French

Revolution'; Roy Estrada looked 'perplexed and determined, like a Polish anarchist'; Don Preston, 'well-intentioned and vague, a Don Quixote before the windmill encounter'; Bunk Gardner exuded 'the unruffled elegance of a riverboat gambler'; Jimmy Carl Black, 'a Mexican bandido'; and Ray Collins, 'a high-browed Viking'.

Zappa ignores the audience as he tunes his guitar and adjusts the amplifier controls. 'His nonchalance is, of itself, a kind of frenzy. Finally he approaches the centre microphone and peers past the lights, scanning rows like a surveyor.

'"Hello, pigs." A few people giggle briefly.'[17]

Wilmer described how the show began with a medley of classic, tacky pop songs such as 'My Boyfriend's Back' ('a rock 'n' roll song which some of you may have gotten pregnant to'), 'Hanky Panky' and '96 Tears'. '"Soft and shitty, soft and shitty," whispers Zappa into the mike, sobbing gently as he falls down on to one knee. "Give it to 'em soft and shitty because Young America wants it that way and Young America doesn't know any better."'[18]

At that time, it didn't. 'When we moved to New York,' Frank later reminisced, 'there was virtually no scene at all. There was no long-haired anything there. People looked at us like we were from Venus.'[19] 'Our market was middle-class Jewish boys from Long Island with hair that was just growing out. That's where the line (in 'Who Needs The Peace Corps') came from: "Oh, my hair's getting good in the back". You used to hear these kids coming in from Long Island with little rags around their heads; that's an actual quote from one of them.'[20]

'In the middle of the show,' Arbus went on, 'Zappa introduces "this strange little person in her mod clothes", who is called Uncle Meat. She is a very young, expressionless girl with silky hair, who sings, sometimes in duet with Ray. They stand with their arms around each other rubbing chests and looking tender and mournful. They even dance with each other, separated by a century of style. Uncle Meat also gazes through a kaleidoscope or rattles a hypnotic rhythm on the tambourine or parries Ray's carrot swordplay using a lettuce leaf for a shield.'[21]

Uncle Meat was actually the folk singer Essra Mohawk, who'd had a single released on Liberty, 'The Boy With The Way', under the name Jamie Carter. Just for good measure, her real name was Sandra Hurvitz, born on Long Island and a student at Philadelphia Community College before arriving in New York via California. As well as opening the act and becoming an auxiliary Mother, Mohawk performed with flautist Jeremy Steig & The Satyrs, who also opened at the Garrick for part of the Mothers' stay.

'After a couple of months of it,' Sandra told Bruce Pollock, 'I said, "Hey, I really don't want to be Uncle Meat" and Frank said, "I'm sorry, but I must insist you are." And I said, "Well, excuse me. Here I thought you were Frank Zappa, the wonderful musician, and now I find out you're God and you're going to tell me who I am." So a few days went by and he said, "Okay, you don't have to be Uncle Meat. If you don't want to make money out of the name, I will."'[22] Despite that, she was the first artist to record for Frank's Bizarre Productions and her album, *Sandy's Album Is Here At Last*, was released on Verve the following year.

Amongst the Mothers' more pointed satires were ragged versions of songs like 'Big Leg Emma', 'Call Any Vegetable', 'Brown Shoes Don't Make It', 'Hungry Freaks Daddy', 'Status Back Baby' and 'America Drinks And Goes Home' and then the band would stretch out on an extended version of 'King Kong'. 'The only part of the show that's planned is the building blocks,' Frank told Jerry Hopkins, 'certain items, the noises, the songs, the cues for the songs and noises. The sequence is the most important part of the show and it will tell you how to listen to the music. It's all controlled by signals.'[23]

The band would rehearse during the afternoons and that led to one of the most bizarre evenings of the whole engagement, the story of which Frank told many times but most fully to Frank Kofsky in August 1967. 'A Marine was killed in the Village, remember? And there was a rumour that every Marine within shooting distance was coming down to beat up everybody they found with long hair. The week following that rumour, we're rehearsing in the theatre and in walk three full-dress Marines. So I said, "Oh, hello there, why don't you come in and sit down." I just went on with our rehearsal; we didn't pay any attention to them. When we were done, they said, "We just bought your album and we really like it." These kids, nineteen years old, stationed on the carrier Wasp at shore here, clean, you know? I said, "Well I'm glad yo do. Hey, listen, how would you guys like to work with us tonight?" They were really turned on. I said, "Can you sing?" They said, "Yeah". "What do you know?" "Well, I know 'Everybody Must Get Stoned' (Dylan's 'Rainy Day Women Nos. 12 & 35') and 'House Of The Rising Sun'. So we went across the street to have dinner; I ate and they practised their songs. Come back, we do this number. I said, "Now look, there's one little thing I want you to do. When I give you the signal, I want all three of you guys to lunge for the microphone and start screaming, 'Kill!'" So we played like that 'Archie' [Shepp] weirdness, with the dissonant chords and all that, and on cue they ran right to the mikes, started screaming "Kill!" The audience just went – they couldn't handle it. Then when it was over, they clapped. So I said to the audience, "Thank you"; and then Ray says to the audience, "Thank you"; and then when I pointed to the Marines to have them say "Thank you", the first one walks up to the mike and says: "Eat the apple, fuck the corps". And everybody went, "Whew!" (The second man repeats the phrase.) Point to the third one; he goes up, he says, "Hey, you know, I feel the same way as my other two buddies: Eat the apple, fuck the corps. Some of us love our mothers more."

'Court-martial city, all right? So then, we took an intermission and they stuck around. I said, "Do you guys know . . . ?" "I don't care, man. They can only get you once." All right, [we] go back on. I told Gail to get the doll. This is the first time we ever used the doll. We had this doll that somebody gave us, it was really shitty - big plastic doll. Bring it down and I say, "Hey, ladies an' gennlemen, the guys are, uh, gonna sing 'Everybody Must Get Stoned'". They go through all that shit and I says, "Now, we're gonna have basic training. Uh, ladies an' gennlemen, this is a gook baby; and the Marines are going to mutilate it before your very eyes. Kill it!" Tossed it to them, they ripped the arms off, beat it up, stomped on it, and just completely tore it apart. After they're all done, the music got real quiet, the lights went down, and I held it by the hair and showed the audience all the damaged parts of the doll's body, pretending . . . There was one guy in the front row, a Negro cat just come back from Vietnam, was crying. It was awful and I ended the show there.'[24]

The conflict of emotions can be sensed, both that night and in the recounting; satisfaction at proving the inhumanity of war, the men who perpetrate it and those who train them; and the discomfort of realising that, for the sake of satire, a line has been overstepped, that the shock tactics have rebounded on their instigator, that the surreal and the real have somehow merged and engulfed everyone present. That, in the end, the portrayal was as savage and implacable as the deed. As Frank admitted, 'It was an atrocity...'[25] He'd evidently forgotten the strength of feeling evoked that night when he said later, 'Music always is a commentary on society, and certainly the atrocities on stage are quite mild compared to those conducted in our behalf by our government.'[26]

Not every night produced such dramatic results but after that, dolls and toy animals became an integral part of the act. 'We had a system rigged with a wire running from the light booth at the back of the theatre to the stage and the lighting guy would send stuff down the wire. First, maybe a spread-eagled doll . . . followed by a salami, that would ram the baby doll in the ass. Our big attraction was the soft giraffe. We had this big stuffed giraffe on stage, with a hose running up to a spot between the rear legs. Ray Collins would go up to the giraffe and massage it with a frog hand puppet . . . and then the giraffe's tail would stiffen and the first three rows of the audience would get sprayed with whipped cream shooting out of the hose. All with musical accompaniment, of course. It was the most popular feature of our show. People would request it all the time.'[27]

Because of this interest, Frank wanted to do some live recording. 'We had a deal with Wally Heider who at that time had a recording truck in New York City,' he told William Ruhlmann. 'He had all this gear in a van and he needed a place to park his van. And I wanted to make a deal with him that we'd give him parking space for the van outside of (the Garrick). All he had to do was just turn the tape on every night. And we could have had it. Verve wouldn't do it.'[28]

FLOWER POWER SUCKS!

When the band weren't rehearsing or performing, Frank was writing material for the next album. His first intention, as he told Frank Kofsky during August, was for the album to combine his songs with tapes of a Lenny Bruce performance and be called *Our Man In Nirvana*. 'We have some material that's going into the next album about the concentration camps in California - you're seeing this before the world even knows what the tune is because I turned these out the other day.'[29]

The project never came to fruition, probably because Herb Cohen and Frank, already dissatisfied with MGM/Verve, were in the process of creating Bizarre Productions, which along with Nifty, Tough & Bitchen, Youth Market Consultants, which with Frank Zappa Music Co. Inc., would handle Frank's multifarious enterprises. The Lenny Bruce tapes were released (on Bizarre) in 1969 as *The Berkeley Concert* and the Mothers songs went into *We're Only In It For The Money*, Frank's jibe at other musicians that many critics took at face value.

The basic sessions took place during August and September 1967 at Mayfair Studios, with Gary Kellgren engineering. Further dubbing and the final mix were done at Apostolic Studios on East 10th Street, with Dick Kunc driving the desk. The songs were recorded on eight-track but, despite the scope for overdubbing, the system had its drawbacks. 'We were working in a studio in New York that had one speaker for every track,' Frank told William Ruhlmann. 'You sat in front of eight speakers. And you couldn't punch in and out without leaving an enormous click on the tape. It was living hell to mix something from that machine because every time you had punched in to add a part, in advance of pushing that part up in the mix, you had to first duck it out to get rid of the click.'[30]

1967 was The Summer of Love and the targets for Frank's acerbic wit were plentiful. 'Flower power' was at its commercial height, unaffected by his suggestion of vegetables as substitutes, and the Beatles had finally delivered themselves of *Sgt Pepper's Lonely Hearts Club Band* on June 1 in England, a day later in America - a week after *Absolutely Free*. *Sgt Pepper* was hailed as innovative and the 'very zenith of rock 'n' roll', perhaps the first 'concept' album, even though the songs were unrelated.

By coincidence, both albums made extensive use of the segue; the songs on each side ran in unbroken sequence. But while Frank relied on sudden changes of tempo and precise editing to create his effect, the Beatles used cross-fades and bits of 'business' like the laughter at the end of 'Within You Without You' to make the transitions between songs. Frank was punctilious when he called his sides 'oratorios'; his was very much a concept album but the Beatles effortlessly stole his thunder.

Because of its combination of melodic appeal and imaginative production, *Sgt Pepper* became a symbol of the mood of the time, encouraging both radicals and hippies to see it as an affirmation of their cause. *Absolutely Free* had a harder lesson to teach; it also spoke to the imagination but its purpose was a call to action, not euphoria. Under the circumstances, it fared considerably well in the *Billboard* album charts, reaching number 41.

Frank had seen the San Francisco hippie movement for himself and had been scathing of its banal conformity, its opting out of responsibility. Now its apparent ethos had been cosmeticised and sold to the world. On June 16-18, the Monterey Pop Festival took place, with Paul McCartney on its board of governors and a massive cast list including Big Brother and the Holding Company, Buffalo Springfield, the Byrds, Canned Heat, the Grateful Dead, Jimi Hendrix, Jefferson Airplane, Otis Redding, Ravi Shankar and the Who. As Ralph Gleason wrote in his *San Francisco Chronicle* review on June 19, 'The *Sgt Pepper* buttons set the theme.'

While the world swooned in cosmic brotherhood and groups rushed to emulate the Beatles' studio-craft, Frank Zappa used *Sgt Pepper* as a catalyst for a swingeing attack on the meretriciousness and self-deception that he felt it embodied. On *We're Only In It For The Money* he brought together a sequence of songs that punctured the blissful bubble all those around him were trying to inflate. Hippies had to be a prime target; 'Who Needs The Peace Corps?', with Frank reciting a diary of hippy aspirations, 'Absolutely Free' and 'Flower Punk', the latter a wicked piss-take of Jimi Hendrix' recent hit, 'Hey Joe' (which he'd also performed at Monterey), were new but the old 'Cucamonga' tune, 'Take Your Clothes Off When You Dance', also on *Lumpy Gravy*, took on fresh ironic significance.

'Concentration Moon', based on rumours that camps used to intern Japanese-American citizens during the Second World War were being readied to receive hippies and drop-outs, was the song shown to Frank Kofksy. The attitudes and ignorance of their parents were incisively captured in the sequence of 'Mom & Dad', 'Bow Tie Daddy', 'Harry, You're A Beast' (whose chorus, 'Don't come in me, in me' had to be aurally distorted on the original release) and 'What's The Ugliest Part Of Your Body?'. 'Mom & Dad', with its story of a daughter 'shot by the cops as she quietly lay by the side of the creep she knew', was grimly prophetic. On May 4, 1970, four students were killed on the campus of Kent State University by the National Guard, part of a nationwide protest against America's invasion of Cambodia. President Nixon called the protesters 'bums'; 'Dickie's Such An Asshole', though not intended as one, would never be an adequate response.

'What's The Ugliest Part Of Your Body' was reprised on Side Two of the finished album, in imitation of *Sgt Pepper*, and 'The Chrome Plated Megaphone Of Destiny' reversed the long die-away piano chord of 'A Day In The Life' before becoming a collage of twisted percussion, prepared piano, panting woodwind and hysterical laughter. 'The percussive-type noises,' Frank told Rick Davies, 'the thing that sounds like little squirts and explosions, was done by using a box that we built at the studio called the Apostolic Vlorch Injector. It was a little box with three buttons on it. The console at the studio had three master faders - a separate fader for the left, the centre and the right. So these three buttons corresponded to inputs to the three master faders, and you could play it rhythmically. There's a tambora in there, a koto in there someplace. Some filtered tapes of industrial noises, horses, all collaged together.'[31]

Frank advised listeners to read Franz Kafka's *In The Penal Colony* and imagine themselves in 'Camp Reagan' before playing this track. He explained the title to Kurt Loder: 'Before they started making dolls with sexual organs, the only data you could get from your doll was looking between its legs and seeing that little chrome nozzle - if you squeezed the doll, it made a kind of whistling sound. That was the chrome plated megaphone of destiny.'[32]

Each side opened with sound collages, speech (in both cases featuring Eric Clapton) and snatches of music. Clapton remembered being told, '"I want you to pretend to be Eric Burdon on acid". And that's what I did - I was just saying, "I can see God", and all this stuff, and it was just funny to be involved with these people.'[33] 'Are You Hung Up' also featured the whispers of engineer Gary Kellgren, threatening to erase all the Frank Zappa tapes. He returns in 'Concentration Moon'; when the album was remixed for CD, the sentence 'And the day after that', cut off at that point on the original issue, goes on to say, 'I get to work with the Velvet Underground, which is as shitty a group as Frank Zappa's group'.

'Nasal Retentive Calliope Music' was a more imaginative creation, even featuring a snatch of 'Heavies', one side of the Rotations single that Frank had produced in 1963. That was followed by songs 'about people with strange personal habits . . . many of which happen to be my dearest friends.' 'Let's Make The Water Turn Black' and 'The Idiot Bastard Son' entered the strange world of Kenny and Ronnie Williams, the latter of whom introduced Frank to Paul Buff in Cucamonga. The unreality of the situations the songs describe is enhanced by the fact that the lead vocals, like many on the album, have been recorded with the tape machine slowed down by a semi-tone. When played at normal speed, the voices sound speeded-up, making them more 'bizarre'.

The Williams brothers were experts at what Frank called 'The Manly Art of Fart-Burning' and more besides. When Kenny was sent to reform school, Ronnie and his friend Dwight Bement played poker in Ronnie's bedroom, smearing their bogies (or boogers, if you're American) on the window, until his mother, disapproving of the dense green light, screamed for their removal. Kenny returned from what he called 'boarding school' and took up residence in the garage, where he was joined by Motorhead Sherwood for a while. During the poker sessions that followed, they and their friends relieved themselves in the mason jars that Ronnie used to make raisin wine. Saved as 'trophies', the jars were examined months later, by which time they were populated by creatures resembling tadpoles which had to be consigned to the Ontario sewage system.

'Mother People', a self-proclaiming threat to 'normal' America, contained an orchestral sequence from *Lumpy Gravy* 'conducted by Sid Sharpe under the supervision of the composer'. The sleeve also noted that a verse had been censored out, recorded backwards and placed at the end of Side One, identified as 'Hot Poop'. This was done on purpose, Frank anticipating MGM/Verve's reaction to the line, 'Shut your fucking mouth about the length of my hair'. It wasn't until 1969, when Jefferson Airplane strong-armed RCA Victor about the lyrics of 'We Can Be Together', which opened the album *Volunteers*, that 'fuck' was heard in a pop lyric. Even so, the songsheet in the album reproduced the offending word as 'fred' on the two occasions it appeared.

FOR CALVIN

The cramped Zappa apartment on Thompson Street was playing host to a number of people. There was Bobby Zappa, Dick Barber the 'Snorker' and Bill Harris camped out in their sleeping bags in the living room. And then Cal Schenkel arrived. Frank needed an artist capable of creating a parody of the *Sgt Pepper* cover. Sandra Hurvitz suggested an ex-boyfriend of hers in Philadelphia. Schenkel came to New York, flourished his portfolio and got the commission.

The result was a faithful but satiric recreation of Peter Blake's original design. Where the Beatles' name was set out in a neat suburban herbaceous border, the Mothers' was spelt in vegetables. Instead of brightly coloured bandsmens' uniforms, the Mothers, never known for their physical beauty, wore dresses. As well as the band, Tom Wilson, a very pregnant Gail, Jimi Hendrix (who'd jammed with them at the Garrick) and Cal Schenkel, crouching with a carton of eggs (his favourite food) in his hands, were also present. Ray Collins was nowhere to be seen and a fresh-faced Ian Underwood stood diffidently at the rear. An accomplished musician and Yale graduate with a masters degree in music from Berkeley, he'd joined the band after seeing one of their shows, accosting Frank in the Apostolic control room and auditioning on the spot.

Where the Beatles had amassed portraits of their heroes, Frank was far more pointed in his choices, which ranged from Lyndon Johnson (twice) and Lee Harvey Oswald to Galileo, Beethoven and Herb Cohen. Some, including the Statue of Liberty, Jimmy Reed, James Brown, Nancy Sinatra and Eric Burdon had their eyes blacked out – to protect their identities.

The initial pressings also contained an insert with cut-outs of the grinning band, Frank's moustache combination, a bunch of his hair, a nipple badge, a School Safety Patrol Lieutenant's badge containing Gary Kellgren's photograph and half of a United Mutations One Navel note with Billy Mundi's pouting ditto in its centre.

For the centre spread photograph, most of the band managed to keep their faces expressionless but Frank, his hair in bunches, looked quizzical, as though in the presence of an objectionable odour. Motorhead got to face the camera on the rear sleeve, which also featured the first appearance of the Bizarre logo and Frank's hectoring note: 'THIS WHOLE MONSTROSITY WAS CONCEIVED & EXECUTED BY FRANK ZAPPA AS A RESULT OF SOME UNPLEASANT PREMONITIONS, AUGUST THROUGH OCTOBER 1967.'

CHAPTER SIX
DEAD GIRLS IN LONDON

Frank set off across the Atlantic in the middle of August 1967 to talk to the press about the Mothers' British debut at the Royal Albert Hall on September 23, the first date on a brief European tour that would also visit Holland, Sweden and Denmark. Earlier in the year, it had been announced that the band would be part of the original line-up for the '14-Hour Technicolor Dream' to take place at Alexandra Palace on April 29. The April 2 edition of *New Musical Express* noted that they would be flying in specially for the show to perform alongside Pink Floyd, Soft Machine, the Move and the Pretty Things. Presumably their success at the Garrick had caused a change of plan.

Both *NME* and *Melody Maker* announced in June that the Mothers would be coming to Britain in October as part of an exchange deal with the Move. At the time, the local Musicians Union would only allow American artists to tour if such a deal could be struck. Move manager Tony Secunda said, 'We are looking for one really big venue for the Mothers. We're also looking for genuinely interested people to help us set the whole thing up.'[1]

By the end of July, both papers reported the Albert Hall booking, adding that the band would be backed by a 15-piece orchestra. The August *Music Maker* announced the band had 'a reputation for incredible behaviour on stage during their Stateside gigs. One reliable observer tells us that they often harangue the audience, insult them mightily and even resort to mild profanities. It would therefore be keenly intriguing to book them in an East End hostelry where reciprocal badinage from the crowd might add spice to the occasion and give the Mothers something more to invent - such as a good reason not to be clobbered.'

After a day of interviews and discussions on August 18, Frank renewed his acquaintance with Eric Clapton, Jack Bruce and Ginger Baker, who were playing at the Speakeasy, a members-only basement club popular with musicians and record business 'heads'. Nick Jones reviewed the night in the August 26 *Melody Maker.* 'The late-night looners have favoured the Speak's environment because as boss Mother Frank Zappa so quickly realised, "the vibrations are groovy". And that's how Zappa introduced "this dandy little combo", otherwise known as the Cream, to a club full of Speak-goers last Thursday.'

Frank stared balefully from the front cover of that edition; beside the headline 'Meet A Mother!', he sat in a chair thrusting his falsies out in a floral mini-dress and fishnet stockings, his hair once again in bunches. Inside, the breathlessly groovy Nick Jones interviewed him. 'Frank Zappa is 26 years old. He is a very beautiful person, very aware of everything going on all around. Zappa is very aware of the "crumbling society" and "environment" that the American lives in. What Zappa and the Mothers are trying to do - through their incredible gestures, through the freaking pastures of the mind, through their music - is to stir the young American into action.' Gosh.

Wading knee-deep in Jones' hyperbole, Frank speculated on how his band would be received in Britain. 'Generally we seem to thrive in areas where there is unrest between the generations, because we tend to pep things up!' After acknowledging that few Britons knew about the Mothers, he continued: 'From what I can see so far, people in Britain have no idea what a real San Francisco love-in is like. There is a popularisation of the Flower Power movement. Everybody seems to have an idealised image that love must be good, and, you know, flowers must be OK, but you don't have the tension between the cops and the kids.' Rather than aping what they'd heard about the 'hippy' movement, British youth should be working out how to supplant the society created by their parents. 'We're the ways and means committee. I'm not talking about hot teenage blood in the street, bashing society over the head. It's just a matter of phasing them out.'[2]

The following edition's letters page quaked with outrage: E.H. Tull of Abingdon, Berks reckoned Frank must be joking. 'Lipstick and a handbag were all that were missing, or do MM readers fancy him as he is?', was the question. The answer?: 'Thank God for Tom Jones.' 'Own up Zappa!' wrote Londoner, Paul St Claire Johnson, 'You are part of that rotten, commercial and crumbling society in America.' Mike Wade, another Londoner, had never in his life seen such a horrid, vile and disgusting picture. 'Effeminate flower power has turned our pop scene into a charade of rubbish.' Jeff Cooke from Derby thought that groups like the Mothers and the Crazy World of Arthur Brown were 'degrading pop to the level of animals.'[3] Tucked away in The Raver column was a short paragraph: 'Our front page picture of Frank Zappa was nothing, folks. You should have seen Bobby Davison's tasteful study of Zappa - in a loo. But our lips are sealed.'[4] Not for long, it turned out.

Anne Nightingale in her 'My World of Pop' column in the Daily Sketch revealed 'Why this bearded Mother isn't flower powered.' Frank was blunt: 'A lot of nonsense, this love thing. How can you love complete strangers when a lot of them are unpleasant people? I want nothing to do with flower power. If people try to put beads round my neck, I just tell them to get lost.'[5] The Observer reporter, after noting Frank's past in advertising, went on, 'Even now he has the Mothers ploughing all their earnings back into an agency that advertises themselves and other youth products. Zappa sees no contradiction between being an adman and a hippy. "Advertising is beautiful," he says.'6

Intro magazine reckoned that Frank basically saw himself as a businessman. 'If the hippie movement's idea of changing the world is to sit around the parks smoking pot and getting beaten by the cops, they're welcome,' he told them. The Mothers' act was 'a type of entertainment, seeking out other levels of human endurance.'7

While being interviewed by David Griffiths of *Record Mirror*, Paul McCartney came on the phone to talk about the Mothers' spoof of the *Sgt Pepper* sleeve. McCartney said he'd have to refer the matter to the Beatles' business managers, to which Frank replied that business managers were there to be told what to do by their artists. When he returned, Frank told Griffiths that McCartney was 'disturbed that I could refer to what we do as a product but I'm dealing with businessmen who care nothing about music, or art, or me personally. They want to make money and I relate to them on that level or they'd regard me as just another rock 'n' roll fool'.8 Frank returned to America with the problem unresolved.

The long run at the Garrick ended in the first week of September. Work continued on *We're Only In It For The Money* and there were gigs in Detroit, Cincinnati and Miami. Preparations for the European tour included summoning Pamela Zarubica, herself just back from her prolonged stay in Europe during which she'd become pregnant, to look after Gail while Frank was away. By now, the Zappas, along with Cal Schenkel, lived in a floor-through basement apartment of a brownstone on Charles Street with Beatles posters on the walls. A life-size doll with a bayonet through its stomach occupied a chair in the living room. The room between the kitchen and the garden was used as the office for Nifty, Tough & Bitchen.

When Pamela learned that Frank had been asked to bring along Suzy Creamcheese on the tour, she made it very plain that the role was hers. Herb Cohen didn't like the idea much but Pamela, and thus also Frank, was adamant. Pamela went to the studio and added her contributions to the album tapes, singing back-up on 'Absolutely Free' and some spoken segments, delivered in a deadpan monotone, including a phone conversation with her friend Vicky, back in California.

A few days before he was due to fly to England, Frank married Gail at the New York City Hall, using the ten-cent ball-point pen he'd had to buy to fill out the licence form as a substitute for a wedding ring. Having punched their form in a machine that resembled a time clock, the official watched as Frank pinned the pen on her bulging maternity dress. His last words to Gail as he left for Europe were, 'If it's a girl, call it Moon and if it's a boy, call it Motorhead.' Two weeks later, Moon was born.

BRIXTON STILL LIFE

A motley crew posed for photographs on the tarmac at Heathrow Airport on Monday, September 18. *Melody Maker* was confused; there were two Suzy Creamcheeses. Other newspapers contented themselves with identifying her as just 'a girlfriend' but it was in fact Sandra Hurvitz. Back in August, Tony Secunda had said that the band might bring along 'another chick called Mother Meat'.[9]

The *Daily Sketch*, with a style of prose that surely helped to bring about its demise, said, 'They are, we understand, an American pop group. Or dealing as we are in a contradiction of terms, a beat group. There is of course no biological accuracy in their choice of title; at least as far as is visually determinable.'[10] The piece ended with a dictionary definition of 'freak': 'A product of sportive fancy; monstrosity; abnormally developed specimen.'

The *Sun*, some way from locating its lowest common denominator, reported, 'Frank Zappa, their leader, is an anarchist whose incredible clothes and haircuts (sic) make normal hippies look as respectable as bank clerks. He and Herbie Cohen, the group's manager, will stay at the Royal Garden Hotel, Kensington. The rest will be salted away in a secret suburban hotel, to keep them away from metropolitan temptation. The Royal Garden seem to be awaiting Zappa with fortitude. Last time he stayed there he felt warm in the restaurant, so he stripped off first his jacket, then his shirt, then his vest, to finish lunch half-naked. The staff, who would normally turn you away if you arrived without a tie, turned not a hair.'[11] Perhaps little has changed at the *Sun*, after all.

That evening, Frank and Pamela caused heads to turn at the Marquee, where The Crazy World Of Arthur Brown were playing, and at the Speakeasy. The *Evening News* located the band the following day rehearsing at a bingo hall in Brixton. The reporter found Frank drinking tea in a nearby cafe and declared his hair to be 'long, very long'. Frank played along: 'The only trouble with it this length is it gets in your mouth when you eat. So I use elastic bands.' While they talked, a waitress came over. '"Can I settle a dare?" she said. "Is your hair real?" Frank took off his cap and allowed her to pull it. It was.'[12]

Frank was also tentative in his curiosity about the English and their habits. When we talked, I asked for his first impressions. 'One of my major recollections of that trip was Tom Wilson, who had been there several times before, was showing me around London and took me to a pub and introduced me to a pork pie. I took this thing and, wisely, opened it to see what was inside it before I ate it. And when I saw that grey, melted wax-like who-knows-what-the-fuck-it-is? squatting in the bottom of this pastry shell – and realised that people around me were eating them – you think, who are these people? How did they come to this?

'Because in 1967, Britain was quite a different place. I thought the atmosphere was pleasant. I thought the attitude of the people on the street was positive. I thought that there was something creative going on there. I thought it was a positive thing for the young people in the country at the time to see the Beatles and the Rolling Stones being successful and all the other people in the British Invasion that had gone to foreign shores and made a lot of money. And now they could come back and live a lifestyle that a guy in a poor part of town could only dream about in his wildest fantasies. And here were these guys living like kings, which has a "trickle down" psychological effect. Like, "He did it. I went to school with him, why not me?"'

While rehearsing, Frank hung out with Hendrix and Jeff Beck and visited other 'psychedelic dungeons' like Middle Earth at the Roundhouse, where he disconcerted a hobbit or two when presented with a nugget of hash by not only not wanting it but having to ask what it was first. A large proportion of his Albert Hall audience would have been similarly disappointed. But some of us there attended out of curiosity. I'd watched *Juke Box Jury* and been intrigued but it was a matter of chance that a ticket came my way. Like most of those around me, I sat stunned by the evening's events. My musical background was Buddy Holly and R&B; I'd never encountered satire in music, nor a band that could encompass 'Baby Love' and contemporary classical music, which that night was played by ten members of the London Philharmonic Orchestra.

Bernard McElwaine gave his impressions in the following day's *Sunday Mirror*: 'It was probably the weirdest, hippiest, most psychedelic – frankly, way out – happening that London has endured since it started swinging. Peeps, pauses, scratches, bops, hisses and shrill, sharp noises belted out from a frightening assortment of electronic gear as coloured spotlights swept the stage. The Chief Mother is a gentleman called Mr Frank Zappa. He speaks in a pleasant, well-modulated voice, softer and more soothing than some of his music. Dressed like his colleagues in clothes apparently grabbed from a burning warehouse, his profuse hair flowing in Biblical style, Mr Zappa did not pull any punches. He told the audience, who unlike the music, did not fill the hall: "I will recite the lyrics of this song before the band starts because you won't be able to hear them when they do. You will hate it."

'Sometimes the music built up a mental picture of a tin convenience being attacked by whistling banshees armed with rubber hammers. It seems that Mr Zappa was right. His reception was less than rapturous. Then he said: "You will find it repugnant." Right again. Perhaps the bombardment just stunned the audience into silence. Or, as Miss Creamcheese rather aptly put it: "Perhaps you are not ready for this kind of music yet." Not that audience reaction really worries the Mothers. Mr Zappa's associates send out photographs of him sitting nude on a lavatory. This may be a subtle comment on what he thinks of those who come to hear him.'[13] And those that wrote about it.

I told Frank that I had never before seen anyone on stage with such apparent indifference for his audience. 'Well, I don't think you can really ask for much more than that,' he replied. 'Unless you're one of these ass-licking pop performers that must always do a song that people must enjoy in the traditional sense of enjoyment. If that's your job, to provide traditional enjoyment, then you really have to be a lot more pandering to an audience. But if you're doing something - I hate to use the word "experimental", but it was at the time - if you're doing something experimental then you have to take the attitude that the audience is part of the experiment; and they're not necessarily there to engage in the same sort of "enjoyment" exercise that they would be getting from something from *Top Of The Pops*.'

The most notable *event-structure* of the evening was Don Preston's assault on the Albert Hall pipe organ, commemorated on *Uncle Meat*. Far from being stunned into McElwaine's silence, the tape shows that we were very much into the iconoclasm that the Mothers seemed to represent; the strains of 'Louie Louie' invading the hallowed portals of the Albert Hall tickled our Carnaby Street consciousness. Nick Jones couldn't restrain himself: 'Without doubt, this the debut of the Mothers in England, was one of the greatest live performances to have shaken this earth on this side of the Atlantic for a long, long time.' But he got it right when he ended his *Melody Maker* review: 'As a colleague said, "They're about two years too early."'[14]

By contrast, the *NME* reviewer struggled to get his mind out of neutral: 'This was the greatest send-up (or down) of pop music, of the audience, America and the group themselves I've ever witnessed. As musicians they were fantastically good and the entire act was unbelievably professionally presented. But, frankly, what was the point of it all? An entire concert of biting ridicule, both verbal and musical - however well done - is just a bore.'[15] Londoner Tony Kerpel's letter in the October 7 *MM* spoke for some of us: 'Out of sheer curiosity I decided to go to the Mothers of Invention concert at the Albert Hall, fully expecting an evening of meaningless noise. I could not have been more wrong. The Mothers produced the most original music that I have heard from a pop group. They managed to fuse pop music, modern jazz, fragments of modern classical music and music concrete. Surely this is an achievement which must give them much wider recognition. Here, at last, is one American group that really lives up to its name.'

The tour moved on into Europe, playing concerts in Amsterdam, Copenhagen (after which Frank got the news that Gail had given birth to a girl), Gothenburg (where Frank developed what was later diagnosed as food poisoning), Stockholm (Frank had to leave the stage half-way through the show), a return visit to Copenhagen, where they had to use John Mayall's gear because their own failed to arrive, and a final gig in Lund.

Despite the overall success of the tour, Frank was unnerved by the attitude of those he had met and been interviewed by, many of whom regarded him with something approaching messianic fervour. He was expected to behave like a leader of youth opinion and instruct his followers on how to overthrow the system, whatever that system was. It was the same undirected revolutionary urge that he'd dissociated himself from in America. But while he liked to provoke and declaim from the stage, Zappa had no pretensions to real power. He may have believed the polemics he delivered but his audiences failed to realise it was part of the show, just as his songs were but one aspect of his musical output. Whatever he said by way of observation on the inequities he saw were almost a by-product of a mind that was dedicated to music – and nothing else.

STINKFOOT

That dedication continued when he returned to New York and set to work on the next album. And, as the October 28 edition of *Intro* reported, the band returned to the Garrick to revive the *Absolutely Free* concerts. 'The evening opens with a spot from a duo calling themselves The Times Square Two. After having sung, crooned and screeched their way through a series of parodies of old vaudeville numbers, the Mothers themselves come on. The sax player looks like an escaped Beach Boy. The vocalists (all with below shoulder-length hair) look like left-overs from the court of Charles 1. Highlight of the evening for many people was a handout of pizza and beer.'

In November, Frank flew back to Los Angeles to perform a walk-on part in The Monkees film, *Head*, written by Jack Nicholson and Bob Rafelson, who also directed. Frank played 'The Critic', who led a prize bull out of the studio after witnessing Davy Jones perform Harry Nilsson's 'Daddy's Song'. With his unruly hair draped over the collar of his blue blazer, he instructs Jones in a tone of increasing irony to spend more time on his music 'because the youth of America depends on you to show the way'. By a long coincidence –or was it conceptual continuity? - Timothy Carey, 'The World's Greatest Sinner', also appeared in the film as 'Lord High'n'Low'.

Drummer Billy Mundi left the band in December. The Mothers were winning acceptance but the musicians were still on salary; for someone like Jimmy Carl Black, with five children, it was hard to understand that greater popularity didn't bring automatic benefits. 'I think they liked the idea that they were in a group that had a certain amount of notoriety,' Frank said later, 'and they liked the fact that they got a regular pay cheque. But other than that, if anybody had come along and said, "I'll pay you more money to be in this group over here", they would jump.

'That's borne out by the fact that Billy Mundi was hired away by Elektra.

When Elektra decided to put together this supergroup called Rhinoceros, they went shopping for band members throughout the New York area . . . and gave them a bunch of money ($80,000) and locked them away for months on end so they could develop fresh new vibrant material.'[16] In the event, Rhinoceros made three albums before becoming extinct in 1970.

Luckily, a replacement was quickly found. Dick Kunc's wife knew Art Tripp's wife and in Arthur Dyer Tripp III, Frank acquired a classically trained percussionist who'd spent two years with the Cincinnati Symphony Orchestra and had given solo concerts of music by John Cage and Karlheinz Stockhausen. His arrival made the recording of what was to be a predominantly instrumental set that much easier. At the same time, Frank was also recording an album of original songs that on the surface would be his tribute to 50s doo-wop.

Cruising With Ruben & The Jets sounded deceptively simple in its execution but in fact the banality of the lyrics and the absence of more typical Zappa flourishes disguised some complex arrangements. 'Actually, what it is a mutated version of Stravinsky's neo-classic period,' Frank told Nigel Leigh, 'where in his writing he took the norms and traditions of the classical period and then he did it in his own style and created a body of work in that vein. And I thought, Well, that's an interesting concept. So I would take music from a certain classical period in US musical history and perform my own personal tweeze on it.

'I think that if you look at some of the neo-classic writing of Stravinsky, there's just a certain amount of irony in there in the way that they handle the classical traditions. So, to the same degree that it exists in Stravinsky, it happens in *Ruben & The Jets*. The music of the early 50s was characterised in that harmony group vocal stuff, themes that went on in the background, the so-called words which were usually quite limited in scope.'[17] As an instance, 'Fountain Of Love' combined a Moonglows background chant with the opening theme of Stravinsky's *Rite Of Spring*. 'There's all these different vocal parts and they're all clichés and they're carefully chosen for nostalgic value and then built into this song with the most imbecile words in the world.'[18]

Apostolic Studios was booked for the entire month of January; 180 hours, made up of 30 double sessions. Sally Kempton wrote a piece for *The Village Voice* entitled 'Ugly Can Be Beautiful', part of which detailed a visit to the studio while Ian Underwood on harpsichord and Bunk Gardner on flute were recording an insert for the instrumental album. Frank explained that this was to be the soundtrack of a movie, shot in 'hand-held Pennebaker bullshit' style. 'Then we're going to do a monster movie in Japan - Japan is where they do the best monster work. And we're starting our own record company. We'll record our own stuff and also some obscure new groups.'[19]

After her time with Frank, Sally Kempton wrote: 'Frank Zappa is an ironist. He is also a serious composer, a social satirist, a promoter, a recording genius but his most striking characteristic is his irony. (It) arises from an immense self-consciousness, a distrust of one's own seriousness. It is the most modernist of defence mechanisms, and Zappa is an almost prototypically modernist figure; there are moments when he seems to be living out a parody of the contemporary sensibility.'[20]

W.H. Manville reported on a different Frank Zappa in the January 13 *Saturday Evening Post*. In an article headlined 'Does This Mother Know Best?' he described his encounter with Frank and Herb Cohen at the offices of Unicord, Inc., encapsulating the Zappa business style. 'They were lying on the rug. It was clear that they had carefully, with great artistry and the utmost contempt, constructed of themselves everything that the businessman at the conference table would find most objectionable; they were the standard figures of protest of our time. The first one had long, thick ringlets of hair hanging down below his shoulders, plus an evil, black-pointed beard and heavy moustache. He was wearing skinny Yale 1912 football pants with no padding or color, and a child's sweatshirt that did not come down far enough to cover his bare belly. His shoes were broken at the toes, which, incidentally, peeped out through the crack since he wore no socks. The second figure was similarly decorated, and he seemed sound asleep, his head pillowed on the rug.'

Frank's photo was helping to advertise the company's amplifiers. They'd advertised on FM radio, offering a photograph of Frank and the Mothers if kids wrote in for a catalogue. '"We got 14,000 requests," Mr Mersky (company vice-president) sounded awed.'

'Most music companies,' Frank told Manville, 'they hype the kids. Our ads are true. There's nothing wrong with advertising, only with liars. I hate liars.'

'Why should I believe that?' Manville asked. 'Why should I believe anything you say? For instance, here you are - a businessman talking to his clients. Why are you wearing those ridiculous clothes? Isn't it a pose?'

Manville noticed Frank's charming wolfish smile, almost of complicity. 'I dress like this, half because I like it, half because it's my trademark.' Frank paused. 'And mostly to put you on.' Manville liked Frank all the better.

Frank took Manville on a tour of the factory, explaining that kids didn't want pretty, distortion-free amplifiers. 'The amplifier is their weapon of destruction.' After the meeting, Frank took him to the Charles Street apartment, where *Freak Out!* was played. Before they left for the Garrick, Herb Cohen arrived to accompany them.

'As we walked,' Manville's article continued, 'the business manager told me about the new, powerful amplifiers that Zappa was recommending that Unicord build.

'"Frank thinks that they should call them, literally, 'Weapons of

Destruction'." "Or maybe just 'Death'," Zappa said.'[21]

The article was accompanied by a photograph of Frank in jeans and braces with no shirt, seated with right ankle on left knee, a wrinkled foot thrust at the photographer. Grimacing through tobacco smoke, he was holding a sock in the direction of a speaker cabinet.

This was not the only adventure into advertising pursued while Frank was in New York. He'd done one commercial for Luden's Cough Drops, which won an award for 'Best Music In A Commercial' in 1967. He then got a request from Remington Razor to put music to one of their ads. With assistance from Ian Underwood and a vocal by Linda Ronstadt, then managed by Herb Cohen, he produced a demo for which Remington paid $1,000 and never used.

UNCLE MEAT

After the basic backing tracks had been recorded, most of the work was completed by the four band members who could read music, Frank, Art, Bunk and Ian. As the sleevenote indicated, some sections contained as many as 40 overdubs. This sort of manic profusion was only possible because Apostolic had a prototype Scully 12-track tape machine. Even so, it required a very quiet desk to ensure that excessive tape hiss didn't build up during the frequent mix-downs.

'There was this music left over from ['Run Home Slow'],' Frank told me. 'What we tried to do was play all the individual lines in this orchestral score. We had two wind players who could read, that was Ian and Bunk. And so they would be playing these parts two at a time, and we'd be stacking them and bouncing them together. And then we added the percussion and the woodwind and the other stuff. It took days just to do a few seconds of music that way. But it was an experiment that needed to be done.'

It was to be a pivotal album. In it, Zappa deliberately moved away from the confrontational stance that gave *Freak Out!*, *Absolutely Free* and *We're Only It In For The Money* their abrasive identity. He announced on the inner sleeve: 'The words to the songs on this album were scientifically prepared from a random series of syllables, dreams, neuroses & private jokes that nobody except the members of the band ever laugh at, and other irrelevant material. They are all very serious & loaded with secret underground candy-rock psychedelic profundities.'

Uh huh. That certainly applies to 'Dog Breath', 'In The Year Of The Plague' and 'The Uncle Meat Variations', but there's some continuity of sense in 'The Air' and 'Cruising For Burgers'; 'Electric Aunt Jemima' (written about an amplifier) and 'Mr Green Genes' fall somewhere in between. Live, 'A Pound For A Brown On The Bus' and 'Sleeping In A Jar' were usually performed together under the title 'The String Quartet', since they originated in a string quartet that Frank had written in high school. Spoken interludes on *Uncle Meat* were rationed to interjections by Suzy Creamcheese, Jimmy Carl Black complaining 'this fuckin' band's starving' and Ian Underwood explaining his arrival in the band.

For the first time, live recordings were interlaced among the studio tracks. The most celebrated was the moment when Don Preston assaulted the Albert Hall organ; there was also a brief satirical rendering of 'God Bless America', recorded at the Whisky A Go Go, 'Ian Underwood Whips It Out', from Copenhagen, and the final segment of 'King Kong', recorded in March at the Miami Pop Festival. The latter, lasting 18 minutes, took up the album's fourth side, skilfully spliced together from a number of takes.

The album's main themes, like 'King Kong', would become concert favourites; 'Uncle Meat' and 'The Dog Breath Variations' were often combined on stage, and 'A Pound For A Brown On The Bus' launched many extended solos. By contrast, 'Nine Types Of Industrial Pollution', its title inspired by a drive through New Jersey, was created in the studio, a guitar solo which quickly freed itself of rhythmic and tonal constraints as it developed against a backdrop of spluttering percussion. 'Zolar Czakl' was a brief reversal of the main theme, a dazzling patchwork quilt of different musical fragments edited together as one continuous performance. 'We Can Shoot You' and 'Project X' both stretched Ian Underwood and Bunk Gardner's breath control as they alternated between dense harmonic clusters and sustained slurred notes. Once in a while, speeded up woodwinds and keyboards skittered across the aural picture.

Another fresh feature throughout these tunes was the precision of the percussion overdubs, for which Art Tripp was joined by Ruth Komanoff, later to become Mrs Underwood. She had been a regular at the Garrick: 'One night my brother and I went to the Village Gate to hear Miles Davis. We were standing around waiting for show time and Frank was just walking down Bleecker Street. This was before bodyguards; he was just a guy on his way to work. My brother accosted him and said, "You should hear my sister play! She's a great marimbist!" I was totally embarrassed. Frank turned to me and said, "Fine. Bring your marimba backstage and we'll check ya out." The next thing I knew I was recording *Uncle Meat* at Apostolic Studios on East 10th Street.'[22] Interviewed for BBC2's *Late Show*, she admitted, 'I remember being very upset when they finally finished their stint at the Garrick Theatre and went back to LA. I felt as though the real heart had gone out of New York City and I had to get back on with my conservatory music training life, which seemed very dull after this.'[23]

Bizarre Records commenced operations in March with offices at 5455 Wilshire Boulevard; as with all of Frank's enterprises, it was a division of Intercontinental Absurdities. The Bizarre logo, an arcane Victorian stirrup pump, appeared on what should have been the outer sleeve of *We're Only In It For The Money*, which finally escaped Paul McCartney's clutches that month. Frank's visual satire remained but MGM/Verve's craven lawyers had forced him to invert the artwork, so that the front and back covers now formed the inside spread. The company had also finally bought the *Lumpy Gravy* tapes, thus allowing Frank to add a speech bubble by his grimacing face - 'Is this Phase One of *Lumpy Gravy*?'.

Eighteen months after suggesting in the *Los Angeles Times* that aspirin should be taken before listening to *Freak Out!*, Pete Johnson evinced more respect than enthusiasm in his review. 'Zappa is a brilliant musician with a flair for satire,' he wrote. 'Unfortunately, he tends to do things a couple of years before people are ready for them and often crowds so many ideas into such brief musical space that they get lost in the confusion.' He concluded: 'The record is largely a series of polemics but Zappa's barbs are witty enough to make his messages entertaining. Zappa is pop music's bravest iconoclast and perhaps its brightest.'[24]

Melody Maker reviewed the album in June, although its release was held until October, when the Mothers played at the Royal Festival Hall. Under the headline, 'Zappa masterminds a Mothers' masterpiece', reviewer Bob Houston wrote. 'Musically, the Mothers are streets ahead of most pop groups. The send-ups of various styles, from Jimi Hendrix, the Kinks, New Vaudeville Band(!) to Beatles' neo-Indian are brought off brilliantly and incorporated into the overall scheme of the album.'[25]

THE HANDSOME CABIN BOY

By the time that review was published, everyone had been back in Los Angeles for a month. Frank had sent Gail and Moon on ahead in April to scout out fit living accommodation for the rock star he was becoming. Frank's brother Carl described her eventual choice: 'The house she selected is a stunning early American dwelling right in the heart of Hollywood (on the corner of Laurel Canyon Boulevard and Lookout Mountain Avenue). The exterior is tastefully done in scrub pine and eucalyptus bark. To enhance this rugged façade, clumps of moss treated with Karo syrup are neatly ticked into delicate crevices. This unusual effect gives the house the appearance of a blighted avocado.'

Inside, the decor was 'cheerful Ruinic, done in malaga, mauve, gold ochre and muted khaki cream . . . On one of the living room walls are mounted two mahogany-stained shadow boxes. Each contains a ceramic duck, a miniature storm lamp and tiny dolls dressed in colorful Japanese, Scandinavian and Latin-American costumes. The clever blend of warm decorating techniques and zany originality on the part of the designer was scarcely noticed by Frank when he arrived. What he was most interested in was the seemingly endless room the house afforded.'[26]

This was the Log Cabin, once reputedly owned by Tom Mix, set in several acres, with caves, a stream and a small lake in the grounds, which also contained the remains of his beloved horse, Tony. When Gail signed for the $700-a-month lease, the cabin already housed a commune of freaks, presided over by Carl Franzoni, who lived in the one-lane bowling alley at the back of the premises. In the vault next door lived two girls, Lucy and Sandra; a large closet opposite was occupied by Christine Frka. They, along with Sparky and Pamela (Miller), were members of Vito's dance troupe; they referred to themselves as the Laurel Canyon Ballet Company but would soon become Girls Together Outrageously.

Frank flew in on Sunday, May 5, and was still investigating his new home when Carl came to visit two days later. The pair went through a door in the foyer and down a stone staircase into a cave which was actually the entrance to a tunnel that led to Harry Houdini's house opposite. The tunnel was sealed with concrete and stone, the reason for its excavation long forgotten. Back above ground, Carl met Frank's secretary, Pauline Butcher, who was to help prepare an encyclopaedia of 'useless information' to be published by Stein and Day in New York.

Carl borrowed a few Johnny Otis albums and left so that Frank could get ready for his appearance on the Les Crane Show that evening. 'On my way home I couldn't help thinking that what Frank does and how he does it has become a recognisable phenomenon,' he wrote. 'As a composer and performer, he's amazingly proficient. As a creative person, I know he has all the qualifications. As my brother, he's really a mother.'[27]

The Log Cabin became the home of Frank's commune, which included Pamela Zarubica, Cal Schenkel, Christine Frka, who'd been hired to be Moon's nanny, not to mention sundry Mothers, road managers and the almost constant presence of the LCBC. One evening the girls turned up in plastic baby bibs and oversized nappies, their hair in pigtails. Frank was so impressed, he invited them to dance on stage with the Mothers at their Orange County gig that night. He wanted them to call them Girls Together Only but after some discussion, Outrageously was settled on. However, the Orange County coneheads wouldn't allow half-naked girls on stage and their only audience that night were the men detailed (but not de-sexed) to prevent their appearance.

The final element of the GTOs persona was bestowed upon them by Herbert Khaury. Before coming to Los Angeles, he'd performed Twenties Rudy Vallee songs in Greenwich Village, where he called himself Darry Dover and Larry Love. As Tiny Tim, he'd become a frequent celebrity guest on the *Johnny Carson Show*, made an album, *God Bless Tiny Tim* and a hit single, 'Tiptoe Through The Tulips', for Reprise. The girls went to see him at the Sunset Marquee and his quaint punctiliousness in calling them Miss Lucy, Miss Pamela, etc. completed the image that the GTOs would present to the world.

The momentum of the Mothers' career was mounting. Gigs in larger halls for more money were becoming more frequent, and even though radio exposure was unthinkable, the press were beginning to pay more than sneering lip service to the music. *Jazz & Pop* voted Frank 'Pop Musician of the Year' and *Newsweek* ran a feature in their June 3 issue, in which he was ranked second behind John Lennon as the 'leading creative talent in pop music'. The Mothers were 'missionaries with a message, first-line musicians using their gifts to reshape the minds of America's teen-agers'. A 'hawk-nosed, spectral Frank Zappa' explained their show as 'the sound of your transistor radio burped back at you, a panorama of American life'. With the memory of his near-deification in Europe in mind, Frank stated, 'Half of America is under 25, yet there is no real youth representation in government. It's not my job to organise then. The best I can get them to do is ask a few questions. If we reach a million, maybe 500 will become active and get out and influence the opinion of others. But those 500 could be dynamite. I'd be happy to have that.'[28]

On June 5, Frank and some of the Mothers went into RCA's Hollywood studios to work on a collaboration with Jefferson Airplane's Grace Slick. A largely improvised piece, 'Would You Like A Snack' bore little resemblance to the song that would later be part of *200 Motels*. In fact, it languished in the RCA vaults for 25 years before being included in the box-set retrospective *Jefferson Airplane Loves You*.

The June 1968 issue of *Life* contained Frank's article, 'The Oracle Has It All Psyched Out', in which the genesis of rock 'n' roll and its effects on society and business was filtered through his own experiences as a 50s teenager. He concluded with a teasing nod to brainwashing techniques already featured in films like John Frankenheimer's *The Manchurian Candidate*, planting the disturbing thought (for *Life*-enhanced parents) that loud noises and flashing lights might be used as tools for the indoctrination of innocent American youth. The seed of this conclusion had been sown in an earlier digression about 'The Big Note' and its theory that the universe was made up of vibrations.

It was his way of advertising the release of *Lumpy Gravy*, which was reviewed in the June 22 *Rolling Stone*. Jim Miller found the music 'strangely sterile' but called Frank a 'protean' talent (twice) and concluded: 'It might be said that Zappa makes mistakes other rock composers would be proud to call their own best music; *Lumpy Gravy* is an idiosyncratic musical faux pas that is worth listening to for that reason alone.'[29] Not too many agreed with him and the album spent just five weeks in the charts, peaking at number 159.

Two issues later, Frank was the subject of the *Rolling Stone* interview, conducted by Jerry Hopkins, now graduated from the *Freep*. Hopkins asked how Frank looked back on his albums. 'It's all one album. All the material in the albums is organically related and if I had all the master tapes and I could take a razor blade and cut them apart and put it together again in a different order, it still would make one piece of music you can listen to.'[30] He also previewed his next two releases; *Whatever Happened to Ruben and the Jets?* was referred to as 'a secret project', the other would be a three-record set, *No Commercial Potential*. The latter had 'such eight-minute tidbits as police busting our recording session. New York cops! Live! In person!' 'The Bust' was never to be released, as the set shrank to two records and became *Uncle Meat*; similarly discarded were 'Agency Man', 'Randomonium', 'All The Way Down To The Tonsils', 'Get A Little II', 'Wedding Dress Song' and 'Handsome Cabin Boy'.

Also from this period was a proposed live album, culled from the tapes of the Mothers' July 18 gig at The Ark in Boston. Frank took a set of rough mixes home from TT&G but someone absconded with the master tapes. Some time later, a bootleg album appeared with artwork imitating Cal Schenkel's *Uncle Meat* dental frenzy. After the 'warm-up trash' of 'Big Leg Emma', 'Some Ballet Music' was a six-minute piece for flute, clarinet, klaxon, car horn and drums, elements of which turned up later in *Greggary Peccary*. 'Valarie' and 'My Guitar' completed Side One, while Side Two comprised a medley of 'Uncle Meat' and 'King Kong'. 'I know (they're good),' Frank told *Black Page*, 'because the tapes were made on a 4-track machine and they've been stolen from me: so that's the worst kind of bootlegging.'[31]

CHAPTER SEVEN
OUR BIZARRE RELATIONSHIP

Frank had Bizarre business on his mind. The MGM/Verve contract had been due for renewal in March 1968 but someone in the legal department neglected to take up the company's option. With Herb Cohen, he'd negotiated the release of *Cruising with Ruben & The Jets* and a 'best of' compilation, *Mothermania*. But that wasn't all. 'I filed suit against them right around the time that the deal was lapsing,' Frank told me. 'There'd been a certain boost in sales right around that period with *We're Only In It For The Money*, which did a lot better than the first two albums. They didn't really want to let us go but they were fucking around with accounting procedure. The royalty statements were in the realms of science fiction.' The situation would not be resolved until 1976.

Now that they were free to seek another distributor, Herb met with Mo Austin at Warner Brothers and convinced him that Frank's projects were exciting enough for Warners to provide finance. There would be two labels; Bizarre, already incorporated, would be for Frank's projects, while Straight, as a division of Bizarre, would release more diverse material principally from artists also managed by Herb Cohen. The initial Bizarre releases would both be double albums: *Lenny Bruce - The Berkeley Concert* and *An Evening With Wild Man Fischer*.

Larry Fischer was one of life's casualties; committed to mental institutions twice by his mother, he sang for dimes outside the Whisky and other establishments. As well as street recordings, his album consisted of songs and monologues recorded at Sunset Sound and in the basement of the Log Cabin. Some tracks featured percussion overdubs by Art Tripp, Frank constructed backings for 'The Taster' and 'Circle', and Strip personalities Kim Fowley and Rodney Bingenheimer cried up Fischer's talents on a meandering monologue, 'The Madness & The Ecstasy'. 'In The Wild Man Fischer Story', Larry conducted a Norman Bates dialogue with his mother. Finally, 'Larry Under Pressure' revealed the vertiginous panic underlying Fischer's 'wildness'; the listener becomes an unwanted intruder in a private hell.

'I don't know if people will enjoy him,' Frank told Chris Welch, 'but for the first time in recording history you will have a chance to hear a man's thoughts as they happen. You'll be laughing at home and saying, "He's out of his mind", but he's not out of his mind. You will be hearing a person who has been stuck in an institution and told he is insane.'[1] Frank talked about recording another character, Crazy Jerry, with a craving for electricity, who made Larry Fischer look like 'a mere buffoon'.

At the end of July 1968, the Mothers played the Whisky and the GTOs performed 'Getting To Know You' and danced with the group. Before leaving on a short summer tour, Frank told the girls to write songs with a view to making an album of their own. He also launched the idea of *The Groupie Papers*, which if they'd ever been published would have created the sub-genre of 'fuction' 25 years before it was applied to UK MP Edwina Currie's Westminster bodice-ripper, *A Parliamentary Affair*. The principal contents would be Pamela Miller's diary and the extensive notes of Cynthia, one of the Plaster Casters of Chicago.

AHEAD OF THEIR TIME

Frank had been introduced to Cynthia and Dianne by Eric Clapton, when the Mothers had opened for Cream at Chicago's International Amphitheatre. Characteristically declining their attentions, he was fascinated by their method of making plaster casts of group members' members. Dianne (who'd taken over from Cynthia's friend Barbara) was the 'plater' or oral exciter while Cynthia, with her sometime assistant Marilyn, prepared a vessel of alginate. This was a powder used by dentists to take casts of patients' teeth; when mixed with water, it first became rubbery and then hardened to make an exact mould. The vessel, varying in size from a vase to a plastic coffee cup (sorry, boys), was plunged over the fully-excited 'rig'. When the alginate had hardened it was removed, along with any ancillary foliage; small talk (or larger) and energetic pastimes ensued while the resulting mould was filled with plaster and a triumphant 'statuette' ultimately emerged.

Interviewed for the 'Groupies' issue of *Rolling Stone*, the girls reckoned they'd approached 150 to 200 groups, although most times the band had chickened out, to be enthusiastically replaced by their roadies. The girls wore logo-ed T-shirts and toted their equipment around in a similarly emblazoned suitcase. 'Eventually, I'd like to get other types of people,' Cynthia told the magazine. 'You know, have a whole museum of casts. Wouldn't that be nice? A whole room of pedestals and these things on them! I'd like to get a common laborer. I'd love to get the President. Maybe a Zulu chief, too.'[2]

This was the sort of social phenomenon that Frank loved. 'It was the most fantastic thing I ever heard,' he told *RS*. 'I appreciate what they're doing, both artistically and sociologically. I want to make one thing clear. The girls don't think this is the least bit creepy and neither do I. Pop stars are idolised the same way General Grant was. People put up statues to honour war heroes.

The Plaster Casters do the same thing for pop stars. What they're doing is making statues of the essential part of the stars. It's the same motivation as making statues of Grant.'[3]

He encouraged Cynthia and Pamela to correspond and eventually Pamela flew to spend two weeks in Chicago, during which they compared notes on Noel Redding, who had flunked his cast but passed his 'fuction' test with Pam. Frank asked Cynthia to join the GTOs but she was fundamentally shy and preferred building alginate mountains (and foothills) in the privacy of hotel rooms to making records and cavorting on stage.

The Mothers took off on another European tour during September and October. Frank flew into London on September 24 for a press conference. The *Evening News* thought him 'the scruffiest pop singer around - blue jeans, brown shoes, long black hair knotted into a gipsy pony tail behind his head', clearly offended that he didn't sound as stupid as they thought he looked. The *Evening Standard* plainly wanted a fashion review: 'First impressions of a close-up of Mr Zappa are brain-curdling. He's an amazingly thin man and when I saw him, he appeared to be wearing a kind of buttonless, cream liberty bodice, with long black sleeves, half-mast black bell-bottoms, pea-green wool socks and brilliantly shiny cow-brown brogues - a sort of out-of-office-hours look.'[4] Hidden within the piece was the news that the Mothers would be at the Festival Hall on October 25.

His best coverage was in *The Guardian*, where Stacy Waddy gave Frank three columns to express his views on flower-power, protest, and pop music. 'I feel bad about the words sometimes. I enjoy writing the music more. Unfortunately, the level on which an artist communicates with the audience is still pretty much limited to the verbal. Instrumental music is a coming thing in pop, but for years if you didn't sing a song, you didn't make a record. I'm forced to write words to put on a piece of music in order to make it accessible for an audience. I'm not going to deny anything I've said in my songs, but my main interest is in composing music. If I wanted to be a lyricist, I'd write books.'[5]

Starting in Germany, the tour progressed through Denmark, Holland, France and Austria before finishing in London. The summer of 1968 had seen near-revolution in Paris and the students at the Berlin Sportpalast on October 16 pined for the barricades. Their leaders demanded Frank should show support for their cause by inciting the audience to set fire to a nearby Allied fuel dump. What followed was reported with Germanic precision in *Der Abend* the next day by Helmut Kopetzky, under the headline, 'The Toys Are All Broken'.

'The first missile, something green, buzzed through the air at 20.40; for the moment unconcerned, the Mothers carried on removing sundry toys from a hatbox and symbolically destroying them. Then the first (rotten?) egg smashed to pieces on Zappa's yellow (Les Paul) guitar. The Mother Superior opined, "You people act like pigs!" Battle lines were drawn: "Evolution versus Revolution".

'At 12 minutes past nine the stage hangings were in tatters; "Evolution" left the stage. There was a feeling of helplessness everywhere. Mothers manager (Dick) Barber, only outwardly calm himself, groaned, "No, no - this can't be happening."

'The forces of "revolution" created havoc on stage and made it plain that worse would happen if the band didn't return. After telling the crowd that the band was there to play music, Frank said, "Your situation in Berlin has got to be desperate for you to behave like this. You're behaving like Americans."'

Kopetzky continued, 'The band, with damaged equipment, hammered out the "Ho-Ho-Ho-Chi-Minh" chant of the stage occupiers, making it sound like the martial rhythm of a Nazi parade. Organiser (Fritz) Rau threw himself forlornly between the two camps, hoarse from imploring, "Friends, let's talk.." But nothing came of it. The police, who up until then had stayed discreetly in the background, gave both friend and foe ten minutes to leave the battlefield. The evacuation took place without any clashes. Frank Zappa pondered: "It was a very enlightening experience."'6

Footage of the gig appears in the *Uncle Meat* film; even without sound, the sense of menace is evident. Nevertheless, 'conceptual continuity' was observed; 'Holiday In Berlin' became Frank's ironic response. And he gave everyone in the band a medal, 'The Berlin Survival Award, 1968'.

The Mothers arrived in London three days before their Festival Hall gig. For almost two months, Frank had spent his daylight hours in various hotel rooms, writing music. He'd had an idea for a playlet that would take up the first half of the London concert requiring the services of 14 members of the BBC Symphony Orchestra. It would be recorded for a possible 'European Album' and filmed for inclusion in the on-going *Uncle Meat* chronicles. In the event, just two excerpts found their way onto record; 'Prelude To The Afternoon Of A Sexually Aroused Gas Mask' (which cocked a snork at Debussy's faun) and part of 'The Orange County Lumber Truck' appeared on 1970's *Weasels Ripped My Flesh*. Twenty sundry minutes made up the first side of the 'Mystery Disc' in *The Old Masters Box Two*; but it wasn't until the 1993 release of *Ahead Of Their Time* that those of us present could relive the evening.

Frank's original title for what he'd written was 'Music For The Queen's Circus'. The initial piece for piano, clarinet and percussion would become 'This Town Is A Sealed Tuna Sandwich' in *200 Motels* and ultimately a component of 'Bogus Pomp'. The play, directed through a bull-horn by Frank in plus fours, outsize jacket, dark glasses and beret, depicted the clash between the 'talented' members of the 'rocking teenage combo' (Ian, Bunk and Art) and Don Preston, who advocated macrobiotic food and the death of diatonic music.

The subsequent mayhem included the BBC Symphony orchestra members joining the 'talented' boys' 'band with a lot of discipline'; Jimmy Carl Black donning Hendrix fright-wig and Regency jacket to score some 'pussy' in the audience; and Roy Estrada as the Mexican Pope, in chain-mail, metal tits and bishop's mitre, distributing 'birth pills' from a bucket. We laughed a lot but Frank told Dick Lawson a year later that we'd 'missed the whole point of it'. Our lack of apparent appreciation was somehow connected with the fact that 'that show cost us $5,000 just to get those musicians to record it, film it, get the costumes, make arrangements with the Hall itself to put on that kind of show. But I thought it was worth it.'[7]

The *Daily Sketch* didn't. 'Having watched them at the Festival Hall the only "invention" they seem to have developed is how to make boredom a paying proposition. The most extraordinary thing about their performance was that they were allowed to get away with it. Their leader, Frank Zappa, publicises himself as guitarist by appointment to the world. I'd put Eric Clapton against him any day.'[8] For what purpose?

The band stayed on to appear on BBC2's *Colour Me Pop*, taking over the 25-minute show to play 'In The Sky' and an extended 'King Kong'. While the band played, the director and his cameramen played their usual game of 'spot-the-soloist', made harder for them by Frank keeping his back to the cameras as they improvised with solarisation and fast zooms. In a brief interview, Frank was his usual scathing self: 'We're involved in a low-key war against apathy. I don't know how you're doin' on apathy over (here) but we got a lot of it, boys and girls. A lot of what we do is designed to annoy people to the point where they might just for a second question enough of their environment to do something about it. As long as they don't feel their environment, they don't worry about it, they're not going to do anything to change it. And something's got to be done before America scarfs up the world and shits on it.'

THE STRING QUARTET

Cruising With Ruben & The Jets, the last album for MGM/Verve was released in November. Cal Schenkel's cartoon cover of dog-faced Mothers set an appropriate tone. 'When we were still in New York,' he said, 'I started working on the Ruben & The Jets story, which is connected with the Uncle Meat story in which this old guy turns this teenage band into these dog-snout people. That came out of my love for comics and anthropomorphic animals.'[9]

Billboard thought it, 'One of the great put-on records of our time'; *Record World* called Frank, 'more a parodist than anything else,' but redeemed itself by rating it, 'One of the highpoints of the rock and roll revival.' Early copies of the album included leaflets with helpful diagrams on 'How To Comb & Set A Jellyroll' and how to dance the 'Bop'. Despite a speech-bubble on the front cover – 'Is this the Mothers of Invention recording under a different name in a last ditch attempt to get their cruddy music on the radio?' – potential customers were put off by the concept, which required an interest in original doo-wop, and the music, which subverted it, so it only reached number 110 in the album charts.

Back at the Log Cabin, Frank perused the GTOs lyrics, found them 'inspiring' and suggested that the newest Mother help them with their melodies. This was Lowell George, the late Factory hand who'd spent time with the Standells and helped the Fraternity of Man to make their second album, *Get It On*. He'd been hired as a replacement for Ray Collins, but he spent most of his time in the Mothers playing rhythm guitar, making pronouncements in a stereotyped German accent and singing pachuco falsetto harmonies with Roy Estrada.

Preparations were also made for a pair of gigs at the Shrine Exposition Hall in Santa Monica on December 6/7. As well as the Mothers, the GTOs and Wild Man Fischer, the bill promised two other bands, Easy Chair and Alice Cooper. Easy Chair had supported the Mothers at the Sky River Rock Festival in August and moved to Los Angeles after Frank offered them an audition. While they waited to go into the studio, they changed their name to Ethiopia but split up before they'd recorded a note. Their bass player, Jeff Simmons, stayed on to work on soundtrack music for a biker film, *Naked Angels*.

The story was Alice Cooper was a 17th-century witch who'd been reincarnated in the body of Vincent Furnier, the group's lead singer. He was from Detroit but had formed the band, called at various times the Earwigs, the Spiders and the Nazz, in Phoenix, Arizona. They'd come to California earlier that year and had established a reputation as being the worst band on the LA bar circuit. Frank can't have thought so, because Alice Cooper had opened for the Mothers (and Wild Man Fischer) on November 8 at Cal State in Fullerton. Miss Christine was smitten with Vince but that had no bearing on the band being signed to Bizarre Productions.

Before the Shrine gigs, the Mothers went north to play two nights at the Berkeley Community Centre on November 30/1. San Francisco had taken to the band, helped by Ralph Gleason's review of their previous appearance. 'Those Mothers Can Really Play' headed his *On The Town* column. In it, he called them 'brilliant satirists and absolutely unique and first rate musically as well'. Gleason also appreciated Frank's audience control. 'He explained his hand signals for the orchestra's vocal effects and then directed the audience to stand and make the indicated vocal sounds while the two side sections waved their arms and the center section grasped its crotch. And it did!

'"Don't we look foolish with the lights on?" he remarked and then told the people they were an audience again and would respond en masse to "hootenannies, politicians" promises and Madison Avenue, as well as instructions like this.' A more devastating demonstration of his point could not have been made.'[10]

Another time, as reported by Larry Kart, an audience was offered the chance to hear the band play 'Caravan' with a drum solo, an offer they declined. Frank then instructed the band to play 'Wipeout', which they did – in three tempos at once. 'The mindless riff of 'Wipeout' melts like plastic.'[11]

Warner Brothers' money was now supporting Frank's extended family of musicians; even the GTOs were receiving $35 a week. Mercy Fontenot, a migrant from San Francisco, had joined the girls and she in turn introduced Cinderella as the last, and at 17, the youngest GTO. One of the songs they rehearsed for the Shrine Christmas concert was 'The Captain's Fat Theresa Shoes', about an outsize pair of women's shoes worn by Captain Beefheart. Another was 'I'm In Love With The Ooo Ooo Man', Miss Pamela's paen of love for Nick St Nicholas of Steppenwolf. Don Preston was brought in to help them with arrangements for their recording debut. As Miss Pamela noted, 'We had serious trouble harmonising, so we all sang together like a grade-school choir, which didn't faze Frank – he thought of us as a living, breathing documentary.'[12]

The Mothers rhythm section provided backing tracks for the GTOs album, which got its title, *Permanent Damage*, from Miss Mercy's physical status. She and Miss Christine and Miss Cinderella had taken up residence at the Landmark Hotel and were shooting heroin in Room 229. When Frank found out, he put their album on indefinite hold. The girls featured in the centre spread of the February 15 *Rolling Stone* – 'The Groupies' issue. 'The act they debuted at the Shrine Exposition Hall here a few weeks ago was beautifully choreographed,' the article ended, 'and so what if one of the Mothers thinks they're astonishingly flat, can't carry a tune in a bucket.'[13]

Elsewhere in the issue, Frank gave his assessment of road ladies: 'New York groupies are basically New York chicks. They're snobbish and uptight – they think they're big. San Francisco groupies are okay, but they think there's nothing happening outside San Francisco. LA groupies are without doubt the best – the most aggressive and the best fucks, and the only drawback is the incredibly high rate of venereal disease.' Bands travelled with the necessary preventive medicines. 'It's sort of take your choice,' Frank instructed. 'Cuprex burns something awful; it'll take the skin right off. But A-200 smells something fierce.'[14]

The magazine noted that Frank had presented *The Groupie Papers* to Stein & Day. 'They asked me to write a political book,' he said. 'I couldn't get into that, and I had a January 1 deadline. So I did the groupie book. I wonder what their first impression was.' He also expressed the opinion that pop music had done more for oral intercourse than anything else that had ever happened, 'and vice versa'.[15]

RIGHT THERE

The Mothers put that proposition to the test in February, with an East Coast tour from The Ark in Boston down to Thee Image in Miami and recording sessions at Miami's Criteria Studios and A&R Studios in New York. 'My Guitar Wants To Kill Your Mama' was cut at both locations and 'Eric Dolphy Memorial Barbecue', later released on *Weasels Ripped My Flesh*, came from the New York session.

On the road, sets contained staples such as 'Trouble Every Day', 'Let's Make The Water Turn Black', 'Oh No', and 'Plastic People', as well as 'Charles Ives' (of which more anon) and themes from Frank's score for *Run Home Slow*. Lowell George got to sing oldies like 'Here Lies Love' – 'a minor-key blues on which we did basically the same arrangement as the record'. The original by Mr Undertaker was one side of the Music City single that featured 'WPLJ' by the Four Deuces. Sometimes Frank would leap on a drumkit to do battle with Art Tripp while Jimmy Carl Black kept time.

Every night, he'd conduct spontaneous improvisations, sometimes, as on 'Right There', to the accompanying gasps of one of Bunk Gardner's night partners. Years later, with titles such as 'You Call That Music', 'Proto-Minimalism', 'Chocolate Halvah' and 'Underground Freak-Out Music', these would turn up on various volumes of *You Can't Do That On Stage Anymore*, a prophetic title whose significance only became clear when the series was almost over. Then again, a concert might start with what Frank called 'a chamber piece for electric piano and drums' like that on *YCDTOSA 5*, based on a 'module' of 'Bogus Pomp'. Or Ian Underwood might sit down to play Mozart's Piano Sonata in B flat.

Relatively little of releaseable quality exists from this period. 'There wasn't that much recording going on at that time,' Frank told me. 'Today, you take it for granted that you can take a little pocket cassette machine with you and bootleg yourself anyplace. But portable recording gear at that time didn't exist. So, if you were going to make a recording someplace, you really had to make some special arrangements to do it.'

All this was abstruse fare for the Mothers' audiences, whacked out and weaned on Cream, Hendrix and Vanilla Fudge. Although band members appeared to be cranking up for standard rock emotion overload, their playing never succumbed to Pied Piper simplicity. Larry Kart witnessed the phenomenon: 'Zappa would stomp off a number that had "Watch Out! Explosion Ahead!" written all over it, and the people around me would murmur "yeah", and a blank look of anticipated ecstasy would settle on their faces. By the end of the piece no explosion had occurred and they looked vaguely bewildered, although they applauded, of course.'16

Uncle Meat was issued in April 1969 in a lavish package, including a 12-page booklet with Cal Schenkel cartoons on the front and back covers. On the front, a cherry-flavoured jelly in the shape of a roadster was chasing the Mothers, while on the back in a rear-view, the roadster, incorporating the Mt. Rushmore monument, was attacking the Vatican. Inside was a scenario for an Uncle Meat film that never got made, lead scores for 'Uncle Meat' and 'King Kong', and story-boards of government troops opening fire on a mutant monster vegetable. There was a diagram of a 'Doll Foot As Young Rifle Showing Mu Meson Voluptuizer' and of its application to the rear end of a startled giraffe while it was singing lines from Captain Beefheart's 'Moonlight On Vermont'. Two photographs portrayed the same utensil deputising for a vibrator, nuzzling the chin of an appreciative female. A speech bubble introduced the immortal words, 'Zorch stroking Fast N' Bulbous'.

MGM/Verve chose the same month to release *Mothermania*, the first and only anthology prepared by Frank. Once again, conceptual continuity was served; Schenkel's gruesome dentistry on *Meat* 's cover was echoed by the inside spread of dubious embouchures in *Mothermania* 's gatefold sleeve. The record became collectable since Frank had slipped in an uncensored version of 'Mother People' while no one was listening and 'Idiot Bastard Son' was a radically different mix.

The first Straight albums also began to appear: Alice Cooper's *Pretties For You*, its cover a painting by Ed Beardsley; *Farewell Aldebaran* by Judy Henske and husband Jerry Yester (late of the Modern Folk Quartet); and *Trout Mask Replica*, the brilliant double album by Captain Beefheart & His Magic Band. During the album, Don Vliet satisfied those of an analytical bent: 'A squid eating dough in a polyethylene bag is fast n' bulbous. Got me?'

FROWNLAND

Since collaborating in the Soots and other Cucamonga confections, Beefheart had recorded for A&M, Buddha and Blue Thumb, been hailed as a true original and sold fewer records because of it. General opinion was that his previous album, *Strictly Personal*, recorded in the last week of April 1968 at Sunset Sound, had been violated by producer Bob Krasnow, who reacted to the Captain's surreal word pictures by twirling every knob on the mixing desk he could reach. Protectors of Beefheart's Grail pronounced it shoddy goods but some liked it. One thing was certain, its creator, away on tour, had had no control over the presentation of his work. The capper came when the money ran out and his band deserted him in the middle of the European leg of the tour.

Beefheart returned to Lancaster to start again. He and Frank are supposed to have run across one another at a Kentucky Fried Chicken stand soon after Straight's inception. They reached an agreement and Beefheart set about putting together a new Magic Band. 'He told me that he would give me complete freedom, as far as freedom goes,' Beefheart told Ben Edmunds. 'When another man tells me that he'll give me complete freedom, all I can think is that he's in a cage. But since he was in a cage, I thought maybe I could run around the outside and play a little bit.'[17]

Over the years, legends have left their accretions on the truth of what happened next. Beefheart said that he wrote almost all of *Trout Mask*'s 28 songs in one eight-hour stint with a piano and a tape recorder - and it wouldn't have taken that long if he'd been able to play the piano. Then followed some six months while every note of every arrangement was taught to his musicians, Zoot Horn Rollo (Bill Harkleroad), Antennae Jimmy Semens (Jeff Cotton), The Mascara Snake (his cousin, Victor Haydon), Rockette Morton (Mark Boston) and Drumbo (John French).

In a suspicious echo of their composition, the songs are said to have been recorded in another eight-hour session. 'Dick Kunc (the engineer) wasn't happy with the fact that we weren't given enough time,' Beefheart said. 'He did the majority of the producing and everything. I think that Frank was actually trying to stay out of my way, actually. The band played straight through on all the cuts in one night. It took them four hours to do the entire album. We didn't use overdubs or anything.'[18]

Frank's memories of the experience, however long it took, were substantially different. 'The original plan for the album was to do it like an ethnic field recording,' he told Matt Groening. 'He and his group lived in a house out in (San Fernando) Valley, so I wanted to take a portable rig and record the band in the house, and use the different rooms in the house as isolation - very slight. The vocals get done in the bathroom. The drums are set up in the living room. The horn gets played in the garden, all this stuff. And we went over there and set it up, and did tracks that way. I thought they sounded good but suddenly he was of the opinion that I was just trying to be a cheapskate producer, and not do any studio time.'[19]

When Nigel Leigh asked what he thought he'd brought to the album, Frank's reply was initially succinct: 'Tolerance.' Pressed for further comment, he continued, 'That was difficult to produce because you couldn't explain, from a technical standpoint, anything to Don. You couldn't tell him why things ought to be such and such a way. And it seemed to me that if he was going to create a unique object, that the easiest thing for me to do was keep my mouth shut as much as possible, and just let him do whatever he wanted to do, whether I thought it was wrong or not. Like covering the cymbals and drums with cardboard and overdubbing his vocals with no ear phones, hearing only vague leakage through the studio window, rendering him only slightly in sync with the actual track that he's singing on. That's the way he wanted it.

'I think that if he had been produced by any professional famous producer, that there could have been a number of suicides involved. I remember that I finished editing the album, it was Easter Sunday. I called him up and I said, "The album's done," and he made all the guys in the band get dressed up and they came over here early in the morning and sat in this (living) room and listened to it. And loved it.'[20]

Interviewed in November 1969, Beefheart reckoned that the album had 'a natural sound – as natural as you can get from amplifiers'.[21] Frank saw the roots of Beefheart's music in Delta blues and avant garde jazz. 'You can really hear that influence,' he said, 'and it's perfectly blended into a new musical language. It's all his. And it bears no resemblance to anything anybody else is doing.'[22]

Some of the field recordings made it onto the finished tapes, including 'China Pig', 'The Dust Blows Forward 'N The Dust Blows Back' and 'Orange Claw Hammer'. 'The Blimp' was the only track that didn't feature the Magic Band. It was one of the clearest examples of Frank's capacity for spontaneous creation. He was working on some Mothers tapes at Whitney Studios in Glendale when a call came in from Beefheart, eager for the lyrics of his latest composition to be recited over the phone. Before this was done, Zappa lined up a take of 'Charles Ives' and gave Antennae Jimmy Semens his cue to start. The random combination was completely successful, even down to the conversation with Beefheart at the song's end.

Trout Mask Replica was perhaps the most celebrated Straight release but, of course, it didn't sell. Only critics, fanatics and the terminally curious were prepared to shell out for a double album of such dizzying originality. It didn't take long for the ultra-suspicious Beefheart to fall out with his friend/producer. 'I was told by Frank that I would have, if you want to call it, special treatment, that I would not be advertised or promoted with any of the other groups on the label. But somehow, I guess he got hard-pressed for cash, and decided that he'd round me up and sell me as one of the animal crackers. I didn't like the idea of being labeled and put aside as just another freak.'[23]

Given the costumes that his quaintly-named crew adopted, this was a rather disingenuous statement. No one could doubt the seriousness of the endeavour on Beefheart's part but, as Frank obviously realised, audiences reacted to surfaces not contents, and if the music wasn't labelled, they would invent one for themselves. The Magic Band looked like freaks, whatever your interpretation of the word, and the music could hardly be said to sound normal. And then there was the celebrated front cover photograph. 'The original concept came from Don's title,' Cal Schenkel revealed, 'then I decided, "Well, why don't we get a real fish head?" We went to the farmers' market and got this actual fish head, a real fish and rigged it up for a prop. It was just an amazing session.'[24]

I'M NOT SATISFIED

At the end of May, the Mothers set off on another European tour. For the first time, there was a tour of England, with gigs in Birmingham, Newcastle, Manchester, Bristol and Portsmouth before a return engagement at the Royal Albert Hall. Needless to say, there was the usual amount of negative publicity. Worst of all was that Pye Records, distributors of Warner Brothers at the time, had refused to issue *Uncle Meat* and the Lenny Bruce album for their use of what they considered bad language. The baton eventually passed to Transatlantic Records but they didn't put the album out until September, three months after the tour, and their poor distribution didn't help sales.

Even before the first gig in Birmingham on Friday, May 30, Frank had got himself into the newspapers. On Tuesday, May 27, he talked to students at the London School of Economics. It turned out to be a rerun of the Berlin Sportpalast without the music. The LSE that year was rife with -ists and -isms, the Paris revolt was still fresh in the angry young men's minds and they were eager to import anybody else's social outrage as an excuse to be seen holding a demonstration or sit-in.

'The bar was a very good place, very political,' David Widgery reckoned. 'Constant arguments with people always trying to convert each other. Odd Situationists knocking around being rude to everyone, a few proper Anarchists arguing with the Trotskyists, all the Trotskyists would be arguing with each other, and occasionally the Labour Party emerged and everyone howled them down.'[25]

The *Daily Sketch* reported on the event, with a photograph of Frank seated on stage with microphone in hand. 'The students, who for once put down their protest-daubing paint-brushes and sandwich-boards to crowd into the assembly hall, heard the articulate promoter of "underground socialism" pronounce on extra-curricular subjects. But they didn't like all they heard. Zappa was predictably pro-youth, but anti-drug and, horror of student horrors, he worked in ADVERTISING before making it in pop.'[26] The *Daily Mirror* had an acerbic comment: 'America's explosive pop man Frank Zappa lectures on evolution to London School of Economics students. I don't like the Zappa image. I like less the LSE students. They deserve each other.'[27]

Virginia Ironside's *Daily Mail* article was more clear-sighted. 'Zappa talks sense,' she stated, 'and in the States, the Mothers, for all their freakishness, are dug by middle-class kids with short hair who rebel against their parents. Here, misled by their appearance and their music which is definitely in the progressive pop bag, they're heroes of the Underground who are fast getting confused where their loyalties lie.'[28] Frank, as usual, knew where he stood: 'I am a composer but I happen to care enough about politics to talk to people about it.'[29]

On the day, the students watched 18 minutes of film, which the UK edition of *Rolling Stone* identified as *Intercontinental Absurdities* but was in fact *Burnt Weeny Sandwich*, before Frank took the stage to answer questions. The students expected to hear inflammatory rhetoric and wanted to know about the recent Berkeley campus riots. 'I got the feeling from the audience there that they thought of me as a political candidate,' he said.[30] 'I told them that what they were into was just the equivalent of this year's flower power,' he told Larry Kart. 'It's really depressing to sit in front of a large number of people and have them all be that stupid, all at once. And they're in college.'[31]

'They are not, as they imagine themselves to be, the spearhead of some fantastic revolution that's going to turn the planet into some kind of Garden of Eden after they're done,' he told Dick Lawson. 'They're into revolution on a carnival level and they aren't thinking in terms of the best things for the most amount of people.'[32] He told *Beat Instrumental*, 'The same kids who a year ago were wandering round with beads and all that gear are now yelling "Kick out the jams". They are at the mercy of the establishment when they act like that. The establishment looks at these kids and sees they are not going to do anything, but if a guy comes into the office and acts on his choice to try and change it, they are going to be hard-pressed to stop it.'[33]

No wonder that Frank reacted as he did at the Albert Hall, with a rejoinder that found its way onto *Burnt Weeny Sandwich* and into Zappa folklore. When attendants hustled fans invading the stage at the end of the performance back to their seats, bovine voices from the back of the hall shouted, amongst other things, 'Get the uniforms off the stage, Frank!' His reply, 'Everybody in this room is wearing a uniform and don't kid yourself,' drew applause but didn't silence the lowing cattle.

Talking with Lawson before the gig, Frank defined the band's music as 'electric chamber music' and revealed that five of the pieces to be played that night had been written on the plane. 'We've been rehearsing them in our hotel with just the bassoon and the flugelhorn and the clarinet.' Later, Frank told us that one of these pieces was going to be recorded on stage and that if the band didn't get it right the first time, we'd sit quietly while they played it again. They didn't and we did.

Now that Frank had moved into more instrumental music, it was difficult for interviewers to identify his intentions. Music without words was one of two things, serious or jazz, and Lawson opted for the latter. 'It's foolish to, every time you hear someone improvise, to assume that it's jazz,' Frank scolded. 'One of the main problems we've had all along is making people realise that you can improvise in any given set of themes or chords or basic rules. I mean, is John Cage's music jazz? – much of it is improvised.'[34] 'The kids are going to be confused by what we are moving on to,' he told *Beat Instrumental*, 'because people don't know how to listen to music.'

Not only that, he felt that few were actually interested in his music, 'which is one of the Mothers' great failings. No one bothers to listen to the music and I rarely get asked about the music. I think it's likely that the Mothers will fail and this year is a crucial point because we are breaking out to music with less commercial potential – concert music.'[35]

There was more evidence that Frank was dissatisfied with the position he found himself in. Larry Kart noticed divisions within the band. He saw Frank as basically pessimistic and the group as good-naturedly optimistic and illustrated it with a conversation between Frank and Don Preston. Frank didn't think the typical rock fan smart enough to know when he'd been dumped upon. 'The best responses we get from an audience are when we do our worst material.' Don Preston didn't agree but Frank pressed on. 'I think most of the members of the group are very optimistic that everybody hears and adores what they do on stage. I can't take that point of view. I get really bummed out about it. Because I've talked to (audiences) and I know how dumb they are. It's pathetic.'[36]

The summer of '69 had little to do with love. Frank had choices to make and no room for sentiment. The Mothers in their current form could hardly continue; there were now ten musicians on the payroll, each receiving $250 a week, irrespective of the gig sheet. That money came out of Frank's rapidly diminishing publishing royalties. 'We'd been touring such an awful lot and sustaining huge financial losses,' he told Richard Green. 'One of the other problems, my attitude was getting very sour because we were working in places where it just seemed like I was banging my head against the wall.'

Part of that 'wall' was the widening gulf between their audiences' expectations and what he was attempting to achieve with the band. 'We had developed the music of the group to a stage where it had really evolved. We would go on stage and we didn't need to play any specific repertoire. I could just conduct the group and we could make up an hour's worth of music that I thought was valid. On the spot it would be spontaneous and new and interesting. It would be creative because the personalities of the people in the group were contributing just as much as their musicianship.' But 'nobody knew how to take the band, they didn't know if we were Spike Jones with electronic music or whether it was serious or what it was. I just got tired of it.'[37] There was also the matter of band members' attitude: 'most of the people in the band didn't want to rehearse,' he told William Ruhlmann. 'It was just a job to them. You couldn't get them to put in extra effort to make the group move forward to do anything spectacular. They didn't have any faith in it, it was their gig.'[38]

At the beginning of the last tour, Frank took $400 from his bank account to cover his food costs. By its end, he was $10,000 in debt. The end of the Mothers as a working unit was plainly in sight. It wasn't a matter of how, but when.

CHAPTER EIGHT
SHUT UP 'N PLAY YOUR GUITAR

The discontent within the band was later voiced by Lowell George: 'The band at that time was very much like the Lawrence Welk of rock 'n' roll. Frank wrote all the charts. Everything was very prescribed. There was no room at all for any emotion. The band felt very hurt and ripped off because Frank was living in a $100,000 house in Beverly Hills and they were all still down in he valley. Frank would write piece after piece after piece and they would all have to play it exact. They were hurt by the fact that he was making more money, but more than that they became more alienated by the fact that he would overwork and become totally inhuman.'[1]

Frank and Gail had left the Log Cabin, moving further up Laurel Canyon to a large house cut into the hillside on Woodrow Wilson Drive. Their entourage moved with them, including Carl Zappa, Janet Ferguson, who'd taken over as nanny to Moon Unit and her new baby brother, Dweezil (named after one of his mother's toes, his birth certificate read Ian Donald Calvin Euclid), the GTOs, retrieved from limbo to finish their album, and the usual band members and roadies. When he was at home, Frank slept through the day and spent his nights in his still-underequipped basement studio, editing tapes and writing scores by night, surrounded by his record collection and the burgeoning tape vault.

In April 1969 the band took part in the fourth Boston Globe Jazz Festival, a two-day event which also featured Roland Kirk, B.B. King, Nina Simone and Sun Ra. Kirk and the Mothers played on the first night, sandwiched between the Newport All-Stars and the Dave Brubeck Quartet. 'I met (Kirk) after he had done his part,' Frank told Dick Lawson, 'and I said, "Would you be interested in playing with us?" He said he didn't know. And I said, "Well, you've never heard the group before – you don't know what we do. If you like it – come on out on stage and start playing, and we'll back you up." So we'd played for about five or ten minutes and he came wheeling out there with horns hanging all over him and blew his brains out.'[2]

The *Downbeat* reviewer found it 'quite literally indescribable' before making a brave attempt to do so. He thought the Mothers 'make the East Village look like a Brooks Brothers showroom' but he acknowledged that they could play .

. . 'and then pandemonium broke out as Kirk wandered out and jammed with them for the rest of the night. All stops were out; Kirk wailed, the Mothers dug it and responded with uncanny support . . . Kirk sounding as raspy and earthy as he ever has. Zappa instantly picking up Kirk's concepts and playing telepathic guitar counterpoint . . . the audience was close to berserk. Wein had to close the curtains, turn up the house lights and beg them to leave, which they ultimately, happy-sadly did.' He concluded, 'That particular set is lost forever, but Kirk and Zappa are crazy if they don't make a record together.'[3]

Wein put together a short East Coast tour, teaming Kirk and the Mothers with Gary Burton and Duke Ellington. Frank thought they were there 'as bait to get the teenaged audience'. But, on a sultry day in July in Charlotte, North Carolina, the most significant nail was driven into the Mothers' coffin. 'We went into a 30,000 capacity auditorium with a 30-watt public address system. It was 95 degrees and 200% humidity, with a thunderstorm threatening.'[4] Worse still, Frank witnessed a pathetic vignette. There was still bitterness in his voice when Frank recounted the story to me more than 20 years later. 'Here's Duke Ellington, after all these years in the business, on the same tour with us, begging the road manager of the tour for a $10 advance. And the guy wouldn't give it to him. That's like a glimpse into your future.' After that, there was a band meeting where he told them of his attitude towards 'grinding it out on the road'.

On his return to LA, he went back to working on a solo album with Ian Underwood and sessionmen John Guerin, Paul Humphrey and Max Bennett. Working with musicians who were undaunted by elaborate arrangements and could improvise creatively in any time signature reminded him yet again of the shortcomings of his own group. I asked him if this had been in part an opportunity to jam in the studio. 'I don't like playing in the studio. I hate it. The real reason for *Hot Rats* was to do the overdubbing. Because I don't think there'd been anything outside the early experiments of Les Paul where there was that much overdubbage applied to a piece of tape. We were using a primitive, maybe even a prototype 16-track recorder for that. So it was the first time we could really pile on tracks. I think that that album is more about overdubbing than it is about anything else.'

Interviewed in November 1969, Frank was a little more frivolous. 'It's surprisingly easy to listen to. Some people have even been known to tap their feet to it. The emphasis is split between the composing, arranging and playing. I play guitar and Ian Underwood plays all the reeds and all the keyboards on it – including a real pipe organ [referred to on the sleeve as 'organus maximus'], with a lot of special effects like percussion sounds and tin whistles, which was in the studio.'[5]

The result was a masterful combination of tautly conceived and arranged themes and extensive improvisation. Ian Underwood built up whole saxophone sections and multiple keyboard parts. 'Peaches En Regalia', the album's enduring opening track, and 'Little Umbrellas' (the latter basically an Underwood feature) were short and accessible to ears unaccustomed to Frank's music; 'Son Of Mr Green Genes' and 'It Must Be A Camel', though still intricately scored, gave more scope for soloing; while *Willie The Pimp* and *The Gumbo Variations* were vamps for extended improvisation, the first for Frank's guitar, the latter for Ian Underwood's sax and Sugarcane Harris' violin.

Don Harris, one half of the 50s rock duo, Don & Dewey, was one of two violinists of widely divergent styles featured. He played amplified alley fiddle, its whining discordant wail the perfect foil for Frank's effect-laden guitar. He played a backing role on 'Willie The Pimp', which also featured Captain Beefheart's appropriately salacious vocal, and took his fair share of 'The Gumbo Variations'. Years later, when compiling the *Mystery Disc* for the second *Old Masters* box, Frank included 'The Story Of Willie The Pimp', a short interview with Annie Zannas and Cynthia Dobson from Coney Island, talking about one girl's father and referring to him as Willie the Pimp, from the Lido Hotel. 'You can see where the song came from,' Frank told Rick Davies.[6]

The other violinist, present on 'It Must Be A Camel', was Jean Luc Ponty, a French classical musician who had made the transition to jazz during the early 60s. Ponty had already recorded two albums for World Pacific Jazz. His producer, Richard Bock, had played an acetate of Jean Luc's music to Frank, bringing about the violinist's inclusion in the *Hot Rats* cast list. Their interest in each other's music led in September to Ponty recording an album of Frank's compositions, and his own *How Would You Like To Have A Head Like That*. The album took its title from a succinct reading of 'King Kong', one of three vintage Zappa tunes, the others being 'Idiot Bastard Son' and 'America Drinks And Goes Home'. 'Twenty Small Cigars' had been part of the *Hot Rats* sessions but that version was issued later on *Chunga's Revenge*.

The principal focus of the album was an extended orchestral piece Frank had developed, incorporating 'The Duke Of Prunes' and 'A Pound For A Brown On The Bus'. Frank asked for a 97-piece orchestra but the budget could only stretch to 11 musicians, explaining its eventual title, 'Music For Electric Violin And Low Budget Orchestra'. Sleevewriter Leonard Feather waxed eloquent in its description: 'It emerges not as a segmented series of ideas arbitrarily linked together, but as a securely integrated whole that moves with almost subliminal subtlety from one tempo, metre, mood or idiom to another, and from reading to blowing; from the opening bassoon figure to the demonic closing violin passages in 7/8, it sustains this validity throughout its multi-textured duration.'

Ian Underwood conducted the 19-minute piece and played tenor sax on 'King Kong'; both tracks also featured Art Tripp, the only other Mother involved. The other significant musician present was pianist George Duke, then working with Ponty after a stint with trumpeter Don Ellis' big band. Before that, he had worked in the house band at San Francisco's Half Note jazz club, while still studying at the city's Conservatory of Music. He combined formidable technique with a sense of humour that erupted in 'America Drinks'; Feather quoted Frank's assessment, 'I'm only surprised that he didn't happen sooner.' Frank confined himself to writing arrangements, only getting his guitar out for a short solo on Ponty's composition.

Hot Rats (a pithy phrase first seen in an advert for a Mothers gig with the Doors and Tim Buckley at the Hollywood Bowl on Sunday, September 10, 1967) was released on Friday, October 10, 1969 and failed almost immediately, barely entering the album charts. Lester Bang's *Rolling Stone* review was enthusiastic but misguided: 'The new Zappa has dumped both his Frankensteinian classicism and his pachuco-rock. He's into the new jazz heavily . . . and applying all his technical savvy until the music sounds a far and purposely ragged cry from the self-indulgence of the current crop of young white John Coltranes.' While he thought the 'mostly little-known talents' came up with some interesting ideas, Bangs concluded the album was 'a good stepping stone to folks like (Albert) Ayler, Don Cherry and Cecil Taylor - the real titans these cats learned it from.'[7]

When the album was released in Europe in February 1970, it was a hit in both Britain and Holland. Its British success, Frank told me, was 'partly because it was useful to many British shop-owners'. He was in England during the Spring 'and every boutique that you'd go into on Kings Road was playing *Hot Rats* in the background. It was like the muzak of Boutique Row at the time.' He told Nigel Leigh, 'Compared to other things that were being done at the time, I don't think that it sounds like a commercial record at all.'[8]

Concurrent with the album's American release the end of the Mothers of Invention, 'infamous & repulsive rocking teen combo', was announced. Setting aside any personal differences, Frank also dispensed with modesty. 'The Mothers set new standards for performance,' he wrote. 'In terms of pure musicianship, theatrical presentation, formal concept and sheer absurdity, this one ugly band demonstrated to the music industry that it was indeed possible to make the performance of electric music a valid artistic expression . . . The Mothers managed to perform in alien time signatures and bizarre harmonic climates with a subtle ease that led many to believe it was all happening in 4-4 with a teenage back-beat.'

In the October 18 *Rolling Stone*, he gave Jerry Hopkins his reasons for the break-up, citing the North Carolina gig as the principal instigation. 'The last live Mothers performance was in Montreal. The last "otherwise" performance was a television show in Ottawa the following night - August 18th and 19th.' 'I got tired of playing for people who clap for the wrong reasons,' he said. 'I thought it time to give the people a chance to figure out what we've done already before we do any more.'

While in print he held out the vague chance that the group might reform, in reality he'd put a definite end to this stage of his career. For their part, band members felt exploited. 'Frank borrow(ed) a lot of music from a lot of players that are in the group,' Lowell George, who played uncredited on *Hot Rats* but had left before the band's dissolution, told David Walley. 'Don Preston has been ripped off all along. A lot of chord passages are Donny's concepts that Frank borrowed. Frank's attitude is, "The guy plays in my band. I pay him $250 a week, sure I can borrow anything from him'.'9 Art Tripp and Don Vliet made similar comments. 'If he does make some money, I hope he does look back at some of those people like Jimmy Carl Black and Roy Estrada,' the Captain said, 'and slips them a parcel of loot under their doors, because he's used those people to get as far as he got.'10

For his part, Frank was unrepentant. Had he felt that the band wasn't able to perform his music effectively, I asked him. 'They could barely perform it at all. Not only that, when they did perform it, they didn't want to perform it.' Later he added, 'Musicians left to their own devices are incredibly lazy. Outside of sea slugs, I don't think there's any species less oriented toward punctuality.' But bitter reactions from both sides didn't hide the fact that lack of money was the fundamental reason for the band's demise. 'I'd done everything that I could but there's no logical way you can expect any employer to just keep shoveling out money for no services rendered.'11

For years thereafter, Frank had to counteract nostalgia for the 'original' Mothers. 'I don't share the enthusiasm,' he told me. 'I think that, in an ideal way, the nostalgia for that band is for the concept of the band – and also for the fact that such a thing could exist as a touring musical entity in spite of everything that was going on. You really have to put your mind back to what else was on the road at that period of time. It's quite unbelievable that a band like that could get work anywhere for a period of years. I think that what it represented to a lot of people was the idea that there's a certain type of freedom that's involved in doing weird stuff just because you feel like it, and getting paid to do it.'

In the *Rolling Stone* article, Hopkins enumerated projects upon which Frank was engaged. These included the GTOs, Beefheart and Ponty albums; the resurrection of *Captain Beefheart vs The Grunt People*, now a 92-page shooting script with parts for the members of the Magic Band, Bob Guy, Motorhead Sherwood, Grace Slick and Howlin' Wolf, which had offers from three major film studios (never taken up); and a weekly television show for which a deal was imminent (which again never transpired). He also announced that he was talking to *Playboy* magazine about the creation of a Mothers of Invention Record Club, which would release 12 albums of material recorded live and in various studios over the group's five-year lifespan. These even had titles: *Before The Beginning, The Cucamonga Era, Show And Tell, What Does It All Mean, Rustic*

Protrusion, Several Boogie, The Merely Entertaining Mothers of Invention Record, The Heavy Business Record, Soup and Old Clothes, Hotel Dixie, The Orange County Lumber Truck and *The Weasel Music.*

There was one other project that would occupy Frank's time during October 1969, a European tour by Captain Beefheart and his Magic Band, which he would accompany in the role of road manager.

DAMP ANKLES

Most noteworthy of the gigs the Magic Band and their roadie played in Europe was the Paris Actuel Music Festival. By the time it took place at the end of October, the site had been changed a number of times, ending up in a large marquee in a turnip field near Amougies, just across the border in Belgium. It was an ambitious three-day event, involving a unique blend of musicians from America and Europe, including Archie Shepp, the Art Ensemble of Chicago, proto-minimalist Terry Riley and a host of British bands of every kidney, from Soft Machine, Colosseum, the Nice and Pink Floyd to Caravan, East of Eden, Aynsley Dunbar's Retaliation and Black Cat Bones.

I was present as a representative of The Decca Record Company's A&R department; Caravan and Black Cat Bones were on the label and I and fellow producer David Hitchcock were there to try and convince Soft Machine to join the Decca subsidiary label. The whole weekend was a nightmare, our hotel was in Lille, multi-kilometres away, and each night's drive was a voyage of discovery through freezing fog that never seemed to dissipate. Once there, unlike the audience that resembled a peasant army on winter manoeuvres, we could at least stand close to the industrial heaters that failed to warm the backstage area. Several times, Frank's path and mine crossed. As I told him later, I very much wanted to speak with him but his basilisk stare warned me off. I apparently did the right thing.

In the course of the weekend, he acted as MC and stood up with a surprising mixture of bands, with Archie Shepp, Retaliation, Pink Floyd, Caravan and Black Cat Bones as well as the Magic Band. 'What else was I going to do? You had your choice at Amougie: you could either watch the green weenies bobbing up and down in the tank; you could eat the Belgian waffle wrapped in cellophane; you could freeze to death out in the secondary tent; or you could go in the main tent and freeze to death if you didn't stand next to the jet-blast furnace that they had backstage. It was that horrible. You remember?'

We both remembered the Art Ensemble's attention-grabbing ploy. 'Everybody was in the big tent in their sleeping bags and they were asleep. Here comes the Art Ensemble of Chicago, the guy lights a highway flare, they start playing and he throws it into the middle of these sleeping people. And a few of them woke up because their things were on fire.' I said I didn't know if that was dumb or creative. 'Both.' Frank hesitated and then added, 'I think that the real reason that I ended up going there in a cosmic sense was to finally wind up with Aynsley Dunbar in the band.'

Aynsley remembered the circumstances of their meeting later. 'He was compering, linking the groups, but it was so cold that he wanted to do something. He wanted to sit in with (the band) and we did about two numbers together. We chatted about a few things in the beer tent later when we left for another gig.'[12]

Highlight of my weekend was probably standing right behind the Magic Band for their set. Since *Trout Mask Replica* had yet to arrive in Europe, the glorious cacophony sounded more akin to avant garde jazz than anything else. There was a ramshackle genius to it all, epitomised by Drumbo's bass drum skin, which had a large hole in it, held together with gaffer tape. The ensemble were all dressed in the costumes they wore for the *Trout Mask* sleeve photographs. Earlier that afternoon, I'd had a brief word with the Captain, along with East of Eden's alto player, Ron Gaines. Ron introduced himself and announced with a total absence of humility that his band sort of played the same type of music, which from the look on his face Beefheart doubted absolutely. The Magic Band were standing about 30 feet away, in their sundry capes, kaftans and twin sets. We looked in their direction. 'What's it like being on the road with those guys?' Ron asked. We all looked again. 'What do you think?' the Captain replied.

When interviewed in London the following week, Frank had recovered sufficiently to pass judgement on the event. 'I guess it was more of a political than a musical success. The festival was moved around so much that it was a triumph to get it on at all. It was so disorganised that when all the lights and amplification worked on the first night, the organisers looked at each other in amazement. They couldn't believe that it was really going to happen. But I was there. Six to 12 hours a night, I was there.' He was asked if any groups impressed him. 'Yeah, I really liked the Nice. They were good musically and they've got a very exciting stage act, too. And I dug Colosseum - particularly Dick (Heckstall-Smith), the guy who plays tenor and soprano. Does he do sessions in London? He ought to - he's really a bitch.'[13]

In the meantime, the various Mothers had instigated projects of their own. Jimmy Carl Black and Bunk Gardner formed Geronimo Black, named after Jimmy's youngest son and featuring Denny Walley on guitar. Don Preston went to New York to work with Meredith Monk's multi-media musical theatre. For a while, Ian Underwood contemplated forming his own jazz group with wife Ruth (née Komanoff) on drums but continued to work with Frank on various recording projects. Roy Estrada joined Lowell George's band, Little Feat, which took its name from Jimmy Carl Black's remark about the size of Lowell's pedal extremities. Negotiations for the band to sign with Straight fell through, which may in turn have sharpened George's opinions of Frank and Herb Cohen, and they went with Warner Brothers instead.

Two months after their demise, the Mothers' latest album, *Burnt Weeny Sandwich*, was released. More tightly organised than *Uncle Meat*, it took the previous album's emphasis on instrumental music to a formal extreme while offering fresh interpretations of older themes. The album was topped and tailed by straight renditions of two doo-wop gems, 'WPLJ' by The Four Deuces and 'Valarie' by Jackie & The Starlites. In between was a rich filling which again benefited from Ian Underwood's versatility. 'Holiday In Berlin', its theme less turbulent than the event it referred to, had been developed from 'Run Home Slow', and the extended version of 'Little House I Used To Live In', featuring solos by Sugarcane Harris on violin, Don Preston on piano and Frank on organ, had grown out of a 'module' that had been previously known as 'The Return Of The Hunch-Back Duke'. 'Theme from Burnt Weeny Sandwich' was a random skirmish between a wah-wah guitar solo and invading war-parties of percussion. 'Igor's Boogie', a piece for formal and informal wind instruments, existed in two brief 'phases'.

With the New Year, Frank took a break from public performance. He concentrated on his writing and finding the finance to finish the film of *Uncle Meat*. As would happen again, the original script had gone by the board. Frank had several hours of film that documented real and staged craziness by members of the band and scenes of the reluctant mutant Dom De Wild, personated by Don Preston, drinking from foaming cloudy beakers and turning into the hunch-back duke. Preston clawed at the camera over a hunched shoulder while squinting and sticking his tongue in his cheek, which was an appropriate place for it.

Frank had secured the services of cameraman Haskell Wexler, who donated a week of his time. They had already collaborated on Wexler's directorial debut, *Medium Cool*, which used the violence of the 1968 Democratic National Convention in Chicago as the backdrop for a story about a dispassionate TV newsreel cameraman's discovery of political and personal awareness. Wexler filmed his principals, Robert Foster and Verna Bloom, wandering through the crowds as they were set upon by Mayor Daley's goon squad and the National Guard. Frank's 'Oh No', heard for the first time with lyrics, played over these scenes and 'Who Needs The Peace Corps' turned up in another sequence.

It was a far cry from that to be filming Don Preston and Phyllis Altenhaus (once Tom Wilson's assistant and now *Uncle Meat*'s film editor) standing in a shower rubbing raw hamburger on each other. The vagaries of scenes like this and Cal Schenkel (as 'Zolar Czakl') and Motorhead attempting music in the Hollywood Ranch Market, and the refusal of the original Mothers to be interviewed on film, led to what financing that Frank could find being withdrawn. He was left with 40 minutes of edited film that would not be completed until the mid-80s.

HOT RATS

Meanwhile, there were unpublicised screenings of *Burnt Weeny Sandwich*. Kathy Orloff from *The Hollywood Reporter* attended a showing in the second week of January at San Fernando Valley State College. The film had to be screened five times for the 2,000 students that turned up in pouring rain when only 200 had been expected. In the following question-and-answer session, Frank stressed that the film would 'hold relevance for anyone who is concerned with social change at it applies to the period in which we now find ourselves'. Orloff ended, 'With narration by Zappa, the film just may unlock some of the mysteries which have been plaguing Motherophiles and pop culture historians ever since a doll's foot and a giraffe first came together at the Garrick Theatre.'[14]

There was no such aberrant behaviour at two gigs performed with the Hot Rats line-up, including Ian Underwood, Sugarcane Harris, Max Bennett and Aynsley Dunbar. 'I wanted not just to play more guitar,' Frank told Richard Green, 'but play it in the context of a stronger rhythmic feeling, 'cause if there was one weak point of the old Mothers it was the rhythm section because it was too static. In order to synchronise both drummers they had to be limited in the types of things they could play so that the beat stayed pretty monotonous.'[15]

He'd been impressed by Aynsley when they jammed at Amougies; he reckoned his own playing 'took off within a couple of bars'.[16] When Frank had been in London around Christmas-time, he'd tried to make contact with Aynsley, leaving messages for him at the Speakeasy. 'When I rang him up, he offered me the job of playing with him,' Aynsley said. 'I turned it down because I had just formed Blue Whale but I thought about it and a week later accepted. It was only after very careful consideration and thought that I decided to join.'[17]

Frank was considering a follow-up album to *Hot Rats* and he needed a drummer that would do for him at live gigs what Ralph Humphrey and John Guerin had done in the studio. 'The first day he arrived,' said Frank, 'we got to work in my basement studio. Aynsley has a rhythmic concept that none of my other drummers have had. If I get it off then he's with me and the others just stand there.'[18] The gigs at San Diego's Sports Arena (February 28, 1970) and LA's Olympic Auditorium (March 7) confirmed the viability of Frank's fresh approach. Inevitably, a bootlegger was present at the latter venue and an album containing 'Sharleena', 'Twinkle Tits', 'Directly From My Heart To You' and 'Chunga's Revenge' was soon available. But using studio musicians already in demand restricted the possibility of gigs further afield. So in April, Bennett was replaced by Jeff Simmons, who joined Ray Collins, Billy Mundi, George Duke and Aynsley Dunbar for a short US tour which ended at the Fillmore on April 19. After that, Frank disbanded them.

The following month, Frank was able to realise something he'd wanted for almost 15 years, to have an established symphony orchestra play his music. The opportunity had come about through talking with KPFK's David Raksin earlier in the year. Frank had been bemoaning the difficulty of getting his scores played and Raksin invited him to sit in on an interview with Zubin Mehta, conductor of the Los Angeles Philharmonic Orchestra. After the interview, Mehta informally commissioned him to write a piece for the LAPO's 1971 season. Frank said he already had something written and negotiations were eventually concluded for *200 Motels* to be performed on May 15 at UCLA's Pauley Pavilion. However, 'they wouldn't play my music unless there was a rock group on the bill called the Mothers of Invention,' he told Richard Green.[19]

The Pauley Pavilion was a vast basketball dome with horrendous acoustics. Two of the six rehearsals were taken up with attempts to balance the sound. The evening, part of Mehta's Contempo '70 series of concerts, was also scheduled to include Mel Powell's *Immobiles 1-4* and Frank's interpretation of Varèse's *Integrales*. Powell, dean of the California Institute of the Arts' School of Music, disapproved of the attempted fusion of rock 'n' roll and symphonic music. He chose to demonstrate his antipathy by withdrawing his composition while the concert was in progress.

Frank sounded almost awed when he addressed the 11,000-strong audience about what the Los Angeles Philharmonic was going to 'crank off'. He described *200 Motels* as 'a collection of sketches that was orchestrated recently, the sketches having been written over a period of years when I thought it would be fun to be a composer. And then, during the last week, I got to hear 'em playing this stuff at rehearsals and I saw all the horrible errors that I'd made. Too late to change 'em. You get to hear all the mistakes too! It's not really a great piece of music but we might be able to get off a couple of times in it. All right, Zubin, hit it!'

Zubin and the boys didn't hit anything until some way through 'A Pound For A Brown On The Bus', which then segued into a version of 'Bogus Pomp'. The suite continued with 'Holiday In Berlin', 'Duke Of Prunes', 'Who Needs The Peace Corps' and a convoluted piece that bootlegs have identified as the 'Eric Dolphy Memorial Barbecue'. The rest of the evening became increasingly anarchic as Frank subjected orchestra members to his spontaneous whims. During the encore of 'King Kong', clarinettist Michele Zurkovski had a toy giraffe, minus the doll's foot, inserted under her dress. Her reaction went undocumented.

There was implicit sympathy for the orchestra in *Time* magazine's report on the evening, but, it indicated, this was balanced by the box office takings of $33,000. It noted that Mehta had excised Part Two from the four-part score, which Frank had completed during the last three months of 1969. *Rolling Stone* looked down its nose at rock/symphonic collaborations in general, dismissing Deep Purple's *Concerto for Group and Orchestra* as a 'pompous bit of crap'. But David Felton obviously revelled in what he saw as the LAPO's humiliation. 'It took Zappa to break fresh wind among those suffocating old toads.' Felton continued: 'Mehta and the Philharmonic were simply new lab toys for his mad genius and they became better people for it.'[20]

Once again, Frank had cause to regret his own pretension. He'd had to hastily reconvene an ersatz Mothers, including Collins, Mundi and Motorhead, in preparation for the concert. The band toured briefly, playing two nights at the Fillmore East in New York and Philadelphia's Academy of Music to get ready. He'd paid a team of copyists some $7,000 to prepare the orchestral parts. 'I'll guarantee you I didn't make anything like that from the concert,' he told Don Menn.[21] And he'd fought the local Musicians Union, who refused to allow him to tape the resulting performance, even when he assured them it was for his sole use as a composer. 'They told me that if I turned the tape on, I would have to pay the whole orchestra Musicians' Union scale.'[22] In the event, the bootleggers did what Frank couldn't and none of the musicians benefited.

FLO & EDDIE

In the audience that evening were Howard Kaylan and Mark Volman, until very recently lead singers of the Turtles. Along with Al Nichol, the pair had formed the group, originally called the Crossfires, soon after leaving Westchester High School. By 1965, they were working a weekend residency at the Revelaire Club in Redondo Beach. They were on the point of breaking up when they were signed up by White Whale Records on the recommendation of the club's owner, who quickly became the Turtles' manager, ex-DJ Reb Foster.

As the Turtles, their debut single, Dylan's 'It Ain't Me Babe', became a hit, to be followed in the next year by no less than four others, 'Let Me Be', 'You Baby', 'Grim Reaper Of Love' and 'Can I Get To Know You Better'. As a prime instance of Frank's conceptual continuity, Foster's comment that 'I'd like to clean you boys up a bit and mould you. I believe I could make you as big as the Turtles', had been a 'relevant quote' on the inside sleeve of *Freak Out!*.

1967's 'Happy Together' was their biggest hit, ending up as the eighth best-selling song of the year. The same issue of *Melody Maker* (May 17) that announced the Mothers' first Albert Hall gig had also carried details of the Turtles' UK tour in June, during which they also appeared on UK television and radio, notably *Saturday Club*, *Dee Time*, *Easy Beat* and *Top Of The Pops*. Their success put paid to the break-up of the band that was imminent even then, and two other hits followed that year, 'She'd Rather Be With Me' and 'You Know What I Mean'.

Internal divisions within the band, which operated on a notional co-operative basis, led to bizarre gigs and publicity, including a naked photo session with strategically-placed fig-leaves that adorned a November 1968 *NME* article. Ann Moses' piece was a preview the band's latest album, *Battle Of The Bands*, in which each track was meant to sound like a different group. Among the names they used were the Crossfires, the Fabulous Dawgs and the Atomic Enchilada. But what was intended as versatility merely emphasised the chameleon-like character of a band that had no discernable identity.

Dissension intensified through 1969, despite moderate hits like 'You Showed Me' and an album, *Turtle Soup*, produced by Ray Davies of the Kinks. In May, they played alongside the Temptations at a White House party for Tricia, daughter of Richard Nixon, during which cocaine was hoovered up from Abraham Lincoln's desk. 'We weren't having any fun anymore,' Howard told *Rolling Stone*, 'and one evening everybody came to my house and we said fuck it and we broke up.'[23]

Howard, Mark and Frank were not unknown to one another. They'd worked at the Whisky and the Trip, they'd gone to the Garrick Theatre shows and visited Frank's Thompson Street apartment at a time when Joni Mitchell was sleeping on his floor – with or without Cal Schenkel. Howard Kaylan was a distant cousin of Herb Cohen's and he and Mark went to see him for advice. Herb gave them tickets for the Pauley gig and may well have told Frank of their circumstances. After the concert, they went backstage to congratulate him and Frank told them of an upcoming European tour, including an open-air festival in England, a Dutch television special and the filming of *200 Motels*, and asked if they were interested. Two days later, they went to Frank's house and auditioned, proving that their prowess on saxophones didn't match their tonsils.

'It seemed like a good idea,' Frank said to me years later. 'We'd worked some gig with them when they'd been the opening act as The Turtles. We had a lot of laughs backstage, so it wasn't inconceivable that I could imagine going on the road with them. They had the "road rat" mentality. In order to tour, you really have to have a special mentality. No matter how good a player is, if he doesn't have that "road rat" sense, he'll die out there. I've learned the hard way about a few guys that I thought could play the parts but they just weren't "roadable". They couldn't stand the pressure and the isolation and they cracked up and I had to send them home.'

Since the Turtles were being sued, individually and collectively, by their record company, Howard and Mark were unable to work under their own names, so Frank's offer represented a very acceptable compromise. Even so, they weren't exactly prepared for the difficulty of the task they took on. Both were more or less pitch-perfect singers but they weren't accustomed to the precision required by Frank's arrangements. 'Frank demanded something of us that we had never really experienced in rock 'n' roll,' Mark told Co de Kloet, 'which was fitting ourselves into a band, not just as singers, but as musicians using our voices as musical instruments.

'This was a process that took hours and hours and hours of rehearsal time, and that was something that Frank never had any problem with . . . it demanded learning notes, and singing those exact notes, or they wouldn't fit with single notes being hit by a piano, a saxophone, a guitar and a bass . . . Those were notes that we had to sing out of our mouths the same way every time or it would sound wrong, because of what everybody else was playing.'[24]

The intensively-rehearsed group flew to Europe and recorded the Dutch TV documentary on Thursday, June 18. Two days later, they arrived in London and played what *Friends* magazine described as 'a late and somewhat unsatisfactory set' at the Speakeasy. For what Frank must have regarded as a public rehearsal, George Duke and Aynsley Dunbar had to use the equipment of the band booked that night, Aquila. The reporter was impressed by Aynsley's dramatic improvement as a drummer. 'His work is more fluid and he is to a large extent the sweaty driving force of the band, while Zappa is the delicate fingertipped dictator.

'The set began with what is basically the Rats, without Sugarcane Harris' lunatic violin . . . and later they were joined by the two ex-Turtles. Instead of getting lighter the music became more intense and strained as they searched for the right combinations.'[25] Some of these were obviously found, for the band spent most of the following week recording in Trident Studios with engineer Roy Thomas Baker. From these sessions and others at The Record Plant in Hollywood came six of the ten tracks that made up *Chunga's Revenge*.

The Bath Festival of Blues & Progressive Music was held at the Bath & West Showground in Shepton Mallet. Eleven acts, including Fairport Convention, Colosseum, Johnny Winter, Steppenwolf, John Mayall, Canned Heat and Pink Floyd, were to perform during 12 hours of Saturday June 27, with a further ten, the Mothers, the Moody Blues, Jefferson Airplane, Led Zeppelin, Santana and the Byrds among them, on Sunday. One of the acts I was producing, the Keef Hartley Band, played early on the first day and I took up position in the stockade built behind the stage.

Things rapidly got out of hand. There was a carnival atmosphere in the stockade that sunny Saturday afternoon; the members of Fleetwood Mac, Peter Green with flowing beard and floor-length kaftan, processed across the greensward and 'an awful lot of dope' was smoked. On stage, road crews struggled to break down and build each group's gear and the timetable was abandoned sometime after dark. I woke from a cramped sleep in my hired station wagon to hear Canned Heat performing at four o'clock in the morning. The Mothers were scheduled to play at 6.40 pm Sunday but appeared somewhat earlier. My chemically-jostled brain took in little of their set, beyond recognising 'Holiday In Berlin' in its vocal version and being unaccustomed to the air of vaudeville that clung to many of the songs. This was a new Zappa for whom most of us were unprepared.

'When we played the Bath Festival the group had been together about 20 days,' Frank said six months later, 'ten days of which was rehearsal, and the group hadn't really got together psychologically and the personalities still hadn't meshed in.'[26]

Even so, Peter Cole of the *Evening News* thought the Mothers were 'one of the few bands which really brought (the Festival) to life. The reformed Mothers, which include the British drummer Aynsley Dunbar, have a more direct sound now. It is still very complex in structure but its appeal must be wider because of its more commercial sound.' Cole asked Frank about his work producing other artists. 'In general I've had really horrible personal experiences producing other acts,' he said. 'You try to do the best thing you can in a very difficult situation. If the artist has his own creative talent, the best thing you can do is stay right out of his way and let his music get on to the record the way he wants it to be.

'In which case, the artist takes 100% responsibility for the success or failure of his music. So it's distressing when they come back to you saying, "WHY didn't I make $200 million dollars from that record? You produced it."'[27] The unnamed subject of this statement was Captain Beefheart, as became clear in the conversation he then had with Richard Green and Allan McDougall. 'I'm now Beefheart's biggest enemy, it seems. He just don't talk to me anymore . . . (He) asked me to assemble a bluesy, commercial album because he wanted to earn some money. So, I got a whole set together for him, and the next thing I know he hates me for selling-out to commerciality or something . . . I think Don is fantastic but he's un-marketable.' He was in better humour when asked about *200 Motels* and Zubin Mehta: 'Oh, that went along just fine, but Zubin is really the publicity-seeking, would-be playboy image. Wants to be a big star with all the kids.'[28]

His orchestra had its eye on the main chance, too. 'About a year after I did that concert with the L.A. Philharmonic,' Frank later told Matt Resnicoff, 'they said they would like to have me write a two-piano concerto and they would give it the world premiere. I said, "Oh, that's really very nice of you." They said, "Yeah, but we want you to buy us two grand pianos." And that was the last thing I had to do with the L.A. Phil, okay? Why pick on me? 'Cause I'm in rock 'n' roll? What, you think I should go out and spend $100,000 to get you a pair of Bosendorfers, so that you'll do two rehearsals and play my two-piano concerto? Go fuck yourself.'[29]

CHAPTER NINE
WEASELS RIPPED MY FLESH

The original Mothers' swan-song, *Weasels Ripped My Flesh*, was released in August. 1970 This was yet another compilation from the unrealised 12-record set, consisting of both studio and live recordings. Some titles, like 'Oh No' and 'The Orange County Lumber Truck', were familiar, as was the improvised texture of 'Didja Get Any Onya' and 'Prelude To The Afternoon Of A Sexually Aroused Gas Mask'. In this context, the exposed blues roots of 'Directly From My Heart To You', sung and scraped by Sugarcane Harris, portrayed stark simplicity when placed alongside 'Dwarf Nebula Processional March & Dwarf Nebula' and 'Eric Dolphy Memorial Barbecue'. The album title proved apposite for what was two minutes of glorious undigested feedback from the end of the Mothers' Birmingham gig on May 30, 1969.

It also gave aural enhancement to a cover illustration that alienated and amused in equal measure. It had been painted by Neon Park (real name, Martin Muller), a poster artist working with the Family Dog in San Francisco. The inspiration came from the cover of the September 1956 edition of *Man's Life*, which depicted a man naked to the waist and standing in a river, being attacked by a number of small reddish-brown flesh-eating mammals. Frank's challenge was to come up with an even more gruesome picture, for which Park would be paid $250.

Twenty-one years later, *Rolling Stone* chose it as number 30 in its special issue devoted to The 100 Greatest Album Covers Of All Time. It seems no one at Warner Brothers liked it, although they were finally convinced that their corporate image wouldn't suffer. But that wasn't the end of it. 'The printer was greatly offended,' Park revealed. 'The girl who worked for him, his assistant, she wouldn't touch the painting. She wouldn't pick it up with her hands.' Both he and Frank had no such qualms. 'I was greatly amused by the cover, and so was Frank. I mean, we giggled a lot. It was an infamous cover, although I guess by today's standards, it's pretty tame. It's not like eating liver in Milwaukee.'[1]

The release of an album that for some celebrated the definitive Mothers union didn't help to ease the acceptance of the latest incarnation. Part of the problem was that the new musicians had a considerable amount of material to master and they were being judged by their performance of what audiences saw as others' repertoire. There were gigs in San Rafael in August and at the Hollywood Bowl in September and rehearsals continued through the autumn.

Chunga's Revenge was issued towards the end of October as a Frank Zappa release. But it wasn't the *Hot Rats* sequel that was the general expectation. Rather, it was an uneasy amalgam of material drawn from at least three musical aggregations. 'Twenty Small Cigars' was a remnant from the *Rats* sessions with Max Bennett and John Guerin, while 'Transylvania Boogie' and 'Chunga's Revenge' documented Aynsley Dunbar's arrival. As the sleeve noted, six of the vocal tracks that had been recorded in England represented a preview of *200 Motels*. The seventh was 'The Nancy & Mary Music', recorded live at Minneapolis' Tyrone Guthrie Theater in the summer.

There was an air of haste about the tracks cut in London; the vocals were buried in the welter of over-dynamic bass and drums that typified English engineering of the period. 'Road Ladies', 'Tell Me You Love Me', 'Would You Go All The Way' and 'Sharleena' were quickly incorporated into the stage show. Because of their legal problems, Howard and Mark became The Phlorescent Leech & Eddie, named after two members of the Turtles' road crew.

The inside spread of the gatefold sleeve featured a Cal Schenkel cartoon which was explained on the front cover. 'A Gypsy mutant industrial vacuum cleaner dances about a mysterious night time camp fire. Festoons. Dozens of imported castanets, clutched by the horrible suction of its heavy duty hose, waving with marginal erotic abandon in the midnight autumn air.' Chunga had one wheel on a wah-wah pedal and the whole scene was viewed through the control room window of a recording studio.

In November, the winter tour schedule began with four days at the Fillmore West, followed by two at the Fillmore East with Sha-Na-Na also on the bill. Lisa Mehlman, American correspondent for *Disc*, typified prevailing opinion with her piece, 'Why I'm Sick Of Zappa': 'The music was done extremely well but some of the visual excitement is gone. I for one am getting a bit tired of Frank Zappa's cynicism and put-downs of the audience.'[2]

She evidently wasn't present at the show when the Mothers were joined by Joni Mitchell. 'She is very shy and we had to lead her on eventually,' Frank told *NME*, 'then I said to her, "Look, we don't play any of your songs and you don't sing any of ours, so just make up some lyrics and we'll follow you".' Timid Joni stepped up to the mike and sang, 'Penelope wants to fuck the sea . . .' 'When she sang that first line, she blew all the kids' minds. They couldn't believe it was coming from her. She did another song that sounded a bit like 'Duke Of Earl' and we finished up doing that song.'[3]

Bootlegs from the shows appeared (none featuring Miss Mitchell's contributions) and *Freaks & Motherfuckers* and *Tengo Na' Minchia Tanta* were eventually included in Frank's two box-sets, *Beat The Boots*, released through Rhino Records. No reasons were given for why particular bootlegs were chosen for the series, although documentary value came into it. It's intriguing to recognise future songs amid certain arrangements; the coda of 'Holiday In Berlin' at this time contained a riff that would become 'Easy Meat', and 'Inca Roads' was in there, too.

The band arrived in England at the end of the month and there were gigs in Liverpool and Manchester before they played the London Coliseum on November 29. This show began with a stage full of performing dogs, midget tap dancers and jugglers before Frank and the band arrived. 'Call Any Vegetable' now contained a monologue by Frank that was the basis for what would become known as 'The Groupie Routine'. It heralded the arrival of the '200 Motels' suite which combined new songs with adaptations of older material such as 'Little House I Used To Live In', that now became 'Penis Dimension'. Roy Carr thought the evening was 'Zappa at his bizarre best', although the music 'fluctuated between sheer brilliance and naughty schoolboy pornography'.⁴ He singled out Howard and Mark and Aynsley (called 'The Silver Rivet' by the band for his extra-curricular activities on this night and at every other opportunity) for particular praise.

Frank was content; 'The essential thing I like in a band is now present in this group - there's a group spirit that transcends just friendship among the members of the group and there is now a certain devotion to some mythological cause and I think it comes across on stage.' He felt that band members knew that they had 'their whole musical world within which they can operate and anything they do in there is fine by me as long as they play the songs. They have freedom to express themselves in a number of different ways . . . even the old Mothers of Invention numbers that we play in our repertoire have been re-arranged to the point where it's not even the same song anymore, for instance we do 'Who Are The Brain Police?' but it sounds like Canned Heat.'⁵

The tour continued into Scandinavia and Europe during December. When they played the Palais Gaumont in Paris on December 15, they were joined on stage by Jean-Luc Ponty, who took control of a half-hour version of 'King Kong' during which he took two extended solos, the latter turning into a free improvisation with George Duke. Aynsley Dunbar also got a chance to batter his kit into submission before Frank announced 'the George Wein variations', which included a manic version of 'Ain't She Sweet' and Crosby, Stills and Nash harmonies. The bootleg that emerged from the evening, *Disconnected Synapses*, became part of *Beat The Boots, Box 2*.

DANCE OF THE ROCK 'N' ROLL INTERVIEWERS

On Monday, January 11, 1971, reporters assembled at Nash House in Carlton House Terrace, London, for the press launch of *200 Motels*. Frank was there to explain the film's story and to announce that live excerpts from the film score would be performed at the Royal Albert Hall in four weeks time, with the Royal Philharmonic Orchestra in attendance. Before the conference could get under way, he had to apologise for the fact that the previous day's *Sunday Mirror* had already run a feature in which he was quoted extensively on the film and the resources being used to make it. After all, this was the first time that a film would be made with video equipment, at that time the sole preserve of television.

'After nine days' rehearsal, the whole cast go into the studios, where there are four video cameras running all the time,' he'd said. 'Then we let it all happen and afterwards it's transferred to film. All that hanging around, waiting for a dozen technical prima donnas to do their pieces, is eliminated.' That left a shooting schedule of five days. The *Mirror* noted, 'As this is the time it takes for many stars to get their dressing rooms re-decorated, it's a schedule that would appear to be little short of a miracle.'[6]

Given the truculence of Fleet Street's finest in those days, it would've been a miracle if they'd accepted Frank's apology with the same good grace with which it was offered. They didn't and the tone of the meeting was set. At one point, one reporter called Frank 'luv'. 'Don't call me "luv", buddy boy,' came the retort. The *Daily Sketch* wanted to know if there'd be any nudity and sex. 'Well,' Frank pondered, 'I don't know if you'll be turned on by any of the actual hairs between the legs. I don't know what you like.'

On a more serious note, he explained, 'We're working to a basic 180-page script. Improvisation will be limited basically because all the musical material and dialogue is going to be rehearsed in advance, so that when the cameras are pointed at the artists, they are going to perform it just like it was a concert.' The budget had been set at $630,000 and *200 Motels* would be shot and edited on video before being transferred to 35mm film stock.

After 40 minutes of sniping and sneering, Frank fired a final broadside: 'There's one sequence in the movie where a girl journalist in a stereotyped reporter's outfit . . . comes on to the stage and sits in a chair and begins asking me a series of really banal questions. At one point, I get up and from behind an amplifier place a rubber dummy of myself in the chair. Without looking up, she continues to interview the dummy. After a time, I pick up the dummy and cast it into the screaming mass of dancers who proceed to kick it to death until the stuffing comes out of its head. The reporter jumps down off the stage and begins to play with the rubber hand, still asking questions.'[7] With that, he left the room.

200 MOTELS

This was but a prelude to the actual filming, which proceeded in the first week of February in an atmosphere of chaos not helped by the reluctant co-operation of most of the forces marshalled at Pinewood. The Royal

Philharmonic, the Top Score Singers, the Classical Guitar Ensemble supervised by John Williams, Theodore Bikel and Gillian Lynne's dancers had little idea of what *200 Motels* was about. How could they? You had to have been on the road with a rock band to respond to the craziness of the real thing or the fantasies that Frank meant to depict. Ringo Starr (as Larry the Dwarf/Frank Zappa) and Keith Moon (as a groupie nun) had no such problems. Why couldn't a newt rancher fall in love with a gypsy mutant industrial vacuum cleaner? How many towns had they been in that resembled a sealed tuna sandwich? And didn't everyone steal the hotel towels?

Nor did Frank make life easy for himself when he engaged Tony Palmer as assistant director. Palmer had filmed Cream's Albert Hall farewell concert and promotional films for Colosseum and Juicy Lucy. He'd made *All My Loving* for the BBC, a film combining pop music with (often violent) documentary footage, which had been greeted by the press as 'magnificent', 'brilliant', 'hypnotic' and 'overwhelming'. He'd also written *Born Under A Bad Sign*, a slim volume with collage illustrations by Ralph Steadman and a foreword by John Lennon. It was Palmer's personal view of pop music in which he included interviews with various music personalities, including Frank. In his preface, Palmer wrote, 'I do not know whether pop music is good or bad and I'm not concerned with its musical stature or social significance. Such conclusions as might become evident in the course of the book, therefore, are yours and not mine.'[8] The description of the 'grotesque ugly and grisly' Janis Joplin as 'King Kong in drag', therefore, must have been somebody else's.

Palmer took himself (perhaps too) seriously; his determined clutch on reality may have begun to slip at a script conference where Frank asked Art Director Leo Austin for 'a Newt Ranch complete with newts, a rancid boutique, a Cheesy Motel, a bank, a fake nightclub, a Redneck Eats Restaurant, a theatre groupies' room, a liquor store, four houses, Main Street, a concentration camp, a crashed Spitfire, the Ku Klux Klan, a Pan-Am Jumbo and something called a Tinsel Cock Car'. Hearing Frank's score, Palmer pronounced, 'Some of it was overwritten and overscored but it had pretty tunes.' 'Occasionally,' he added, in a barely tolerant tone, 'rock musicians imitate classical music lest they be thought musically illiterate.'

When he discovered that Frank intended to direct his actors from the floor, Palmer offered to leave the premises but was persuaded by producer Jerry Good to stay and supervise the technical side of things. 'Maybe this was the role of the electronic director of the future,' he wrote later, 'happy enough to point the electronic cameras in the right direction and push the buttons. I was persuaded that this was a sufficiently complicated job to warrant my staying with the picture and who was I to complain?'

Miffed at being merely an assistant director, 'pushing the buttons proved to be quite as hazardous as trying to direct the actors,' he said, 'the whole operation threatened to descend into chaos. Still, I needn't have worried nor under-estimated the infinite talents of Zappa, because when we finally got to the editing stage, he decided to take over that too.'[9] The words 'Do you know who I am?' hovered in the ether.

Hadn't he seen eye-to-eye with maestro Palmer? I asked Frank. 'Well, I'm the one who hired him,' he replied. 'He had a lot of problems during the making of the film. He was on the verge of a divorce, he had the 'flu and he seemed to be a fairly ill-tempered individual even on a good day. I don't want to be unkind to him but on the production of the film, he did two things which I will always remember. One: at the completion of principal photography, he had demanded of the producer that his name be left off the credits for fear that it would harm his career. And then, once the editing was started on the film, he decided he did want to have his name on the credits. And the other thing was, in a little fit of pique in the middle of production, Gail happened to be walking by and overheard him saying that he was threatening to erase all of the master tapes of the movie if something wasn't done to his satisfaction. So it was not easy working with him.

'I had a certain amount of control over what got done and actually it would have been quite a different movie if he hadn't decided that he didn't want to have his name on the credits. Because at that point he refused to even go into the editing suite. And I'd never edited video. Now, remember, they did not have computers then. All editing was done by using a felt pen and making a mark on the edge of the tape, reeling it back ten seconds, playing it in, waiting for it to lock and then your edit would roll. And it was all manual and it was unbelievably primitive. And to edit you stood in an ice-cold room for ten hours a day. That's a far cry from today's video editing suites. It was like guerrilla warfare to put this film together.'

And what about the Royal Philharmonic, had they been reluctant? 'That would be the nicest way to put it. I think that there's always been, since the invention of rock'n'roll, anytime that somebody from that other musical world walked into their musical world, it would be regarded as an intrusion or an inconvenience.' What happened when they discovered that what he'd written was quite demanding? 'Well, that's adding insult to injury. It's one thing to say, "Oh, look at this weird guy and what does he want now? 'Course, he's paying us to do this." Then suddenly, they get a piece of paper that they can't really play. And then you compound that with the fact that there was never enough rehearsal time to teach them how to play it to make it sound right. So the level of commitment to a proper musical performance simply wasn't there.

'I know that there are some parts in it that are pretty hilarious. This is musical jokes, the whole thing is a musical joke. They could have gone on shooting for a few more days but they refused to. And at the end of 56 hours, only one third of the shooting script had been shot. So, in order to make any kind of a story out of it at all, I had to invent the thing in the editing room. So what you see on the screen is the result of the people at United Artists saying, "Well, why did we do this at all? We're not going to spend another penny on this."'

'There originally was a story and it involved the groupie routine from the *Fillmore East* album and a whole bunch of other stuff that was really supposed to be about going on the road and how it makes you crazy. But there was no way to tell the story with the chunks at different points of the script that had been shot and all the continuity pieces had not been shot. Jeff Simmons disappeared just before the film was to be shot. His girlfriend convinced him that he should be a blues musician. She told him that he was too heavy to be in this group and he went for it and on the evening of the second script reading at the hotel, he announced that he was resigning from the band. He had the best part in the movie. So, in order to replace him, we went through all kinds of weird shit and we ended up with Martin Lickert, who was Ringo's driver.'

Howard Kaylan took up the story when he spoke with Harold Bronson: 'Now we're thinking, not only do we need a bass player who has to learn some complicated shit, but he had to act. The next day, Frank shows up at Pinewood Studios with Wilfrid Brambell. It was gonna be real cute and we'd just have to overdub the bass later – we were gonna play with the Philharmonic live, so it was gonna be difficult at that. So he got his lines, rehearsed with us, even hung out with us to get to know us.'

Brambell had trouble with lines like, 'Zappa's fucked'. 'Finally, on the last day of rehearsal, he just went screaming down the yellow halls at Pinewood Studios yelling "aaugh . . . this is crazy". We started shooting the next day and we were just fucking panic-struck. Then Frank said, "Look, the next person who walks in is it - what the fuck." The next guy who walked through the door was Ringo's chauffeur, Martin Lickert, a pretty-boy type of about 21 with a psychedelic Chelsea shirt on, and everybody went, "Hmmm". He read the lines in a cute Liverpudlian accent, and not only that but Ringo said that he could play bass.'[10]

Miss Pamela was recruited for the part of the reporter, while Miss Lucy Offerall and Janet Ferguson were groupies. The GTOs had moved into history and Pamela Miller had gone through such luminaries as Jimmy Page and Mick Jagger before ending up in London with Duncan (Sandy) Sanderson of the Pink Fairies. Jimmy Carl Black was Bertram Redneck, Motorhead was the hare-lipped newt rancher and Dick Barber was the embodiment of an impassioned industrial vacuum cleaner.

Keith Moon seems to have been another last-minute recruit. 'I was at the Speakeasy with Pete [Townshend],' he told Jerry Hopkins, 'and Frank happened to be at the next table. He overheard some of our conversation and leaned over and said, "How'd you guys like to be in a film?" We said, "OK, Frank." And he said, "OK, be at the Kensington Palace Hotel at seven o'clock tomorrow morning." I was the one who turned up. Pete was writing and sent his apologies, and I was given the part Mick Jagger was to play - that of a nun. Mick didn't want to do it.'[11]

There's a desperate sense of mix and match about the finished film. Groundbreaking it may be in its use of video techniques, now long superseded, but what was already an elliptical flight of the imagination was rendered incomprehensible by the compromised nature of the final edit. 'I want to get 'em out there and make 'em know that they went someplace and then get 'em back again,' Frank had told Miles the previous November. 'And that ain't easy to do.'[12] In the end, it proved impossible.

Years later, Frank released a Honker Home Video, *The True Story of 200 Motels*.

THE LEGEND OF THE GOLDEN ARCHES

The same forces that had struggled through the previous week arrived at the stage door of the Albert Hall on Monday, February 8 1971, for a lunchtime rehearsal of that evening's concert. They found the doors locked against them and the gig cancelled. It must have been a surprise to Herb and Frank but they weren't unaware of the management's caution over what had been scheduled to happen within their hallowed portals.

On January 18, Marion Herrod, secretary and lettings manager, had requested a copy of what *The Times* termed the 'libretto'. But despite further requests, samples of the lyrics didn't turn up until Friday, February 5. 'We read it, decided that many people would be offended, and because time was so short asked for a revised version by the next morning,' Miss Herrod was quoted. 'This was not forthcoming, so we had no alternative but to cancel the concert.' She declined to specify what they'd found objectionable but said, 'there were words I did not want to be spoken in the Albert Hall'.[13]

The *Daily Telegraph* quoted Sir Louis Gluckstein, president of the Royal Albert Hall, who reckoned that the Mothers had used the Royal Philharmonic Orchestra as 'a cover for the undiluted filth' they planned to perform that night. 'If people were going to produce a lot of filth, as appeared likely according to the unamended script, our officials were perfectly right to cancel the concert,' he thundered.[14] A few days later, he wrote a rallying cry for the paper's letters page: 'It is time that a stand was taken against the production of what many regard as dreary and inartistic filth for money.'[15] That's an awful lot of filth.

A spokesman for the RPO said that they'd accepted the film and concert deal, worth £20,000, purely to play the music. If the orchestra had been required to do anything obscene, they wouldn't have taken part. Trumpeters John Wilbraham and Ray Allen didn't take part anyway; they withdrew their services at the first rehearsal. 'The whole thing revolted me,' Wilbraham told

The Times. 'I am a person pretty much in the public eye and I did not think I could play a trumpet concerto one night and do this the next.'[16]

More than 4,000 tickets had been sold and the event had cost £5,000 to mount. Herb Cohen told the press that he intended to take legal action to recover the money. Not to be outdone, promoter Harold Davison took out a High Court writ against him, seeking damages for the cancellation and claiming that he was liable to indemnify Davison's company against all claims by the Albert Hall.

Many of the ticket-holders turned up and were given their money back. They also received personal apologies from Frank and the group who turned up for the purpose. 'It's ridiculous,' Frank said. 'We are all very upset. It was all right for us to appear at the Albert Hall in 1968, when the place was black and dirty. Now they've had the place cleaned up, they don't want to know us.'[17]

Most of the band went straight back to California, Frank stayed on to edit his footage and Aynsley spent some time at his Essex home. The *NME* asked for his thoughts on recent events. 'The Albert Hall is behind the times,' he said. 'The woman who decided to ban us is a very weird person, she picked out words that are in everyday use and said we couldn't use them there.' He had fulsome praise for his employer: 'You just have to put Frank out on his own. He is helping people to listen to other aspects of music they've never heard. Frank's just taken the plunge. If people don't appreciate it, they don't, so he'll keep on doing it until they do.'[18]

Frank worked on the music tapes for the United Artists soundtrack double album back at Whitney Studios in Glendale during April and early May. George Duke went off to work with Cannonball Adderley, so Bob Harris came in on keyboards with Ian Underwood and another ex-Turtle, Jim Pons, came in on bass for a tour which started at Bridges Auditorium at Pomona College, Claremont on May 18. This tour saw the premier of another magnum opus, 'Billy The Mountain'. It moved east during the rest of the month, including Chicago, Detroit and Columbus, Ohio. They were booked into the Fillmore East on June 4/5 as part of the venue's closing series of gigs.

Bill Graham, tired of coast-to-coast commuting, had decided that the Fillmore East was no longer the white man's Apollo Theatre. So between May 20 and June 27, he put on ten separate shows that began with Leon Russell and Taj Mahal, included Humble Pie, Laura Nyro, Alice Cooper, B.B. King and Johnny Winter before finishing with the J. Geils Band and the Allman Brothers. Support for the Mothers' gigs was provided by Head Over Heels.

SCUMBAG

Saturday night's two performances were recorded for a live album. *Fillmore East, June 1971*, released just two months later, had a deliberately rushed air about it, prompted by Cal Schenkel's scrawled artwork (referred to by the band as 'the pencil front cover') with its bracketed caveat, 'he made me do it'. Its contents juxtaposed recognised favourites such as 'Little House I Used To Live In', 'Willie The Pimp' and 'Peaches En Regalia' with the 'groupie' routines that had evolved from band members' encounters.

'The reason we were performing that is because it was a true story,' Frank told Martin Perlich. 'It actually happened to Howard Kaylan. It was just a process of commemorating a piece of folklore that was peculiar to the group. I think that other groups that ignore the folklore that happens to the members of that group a missing a good shot for preserving a little history. Because I also take the position that contemporary history is going to be retained on records more accurately than it's going to be within history books.'[19]

'What Kind Of Girl Do You Think We Are', 'Bwana Dik' (adapted from the opening theme from *Lumpy Gravy*), 'Latex Solar Beef' and 'Do You Like My New Car?' (the latter dialogue taking place in the Tinsel Cock Car was never filmed for *200 Motels*) were tightly structured but also called for a high degree of spontaneity from Flo and Eddie. There were other aspects of their 'vaudeville' act whose visual elements precluded their inclusion. 'The Sanzini Brothers' was eventually included on *Playground Psychotics*, its sodomy trick lost on those that never witnessed it. Likewise 'Little Carl', the subject of 'Penguin In Bondage', an inflatable penguin that was launched through 'a hoopa real fire', consisting of a pair of coat-hangers wrapped in burning toilet paper.

At the end of the second show, which ran into the small hours of Sunday, an extended encore brought John Lennon and Yoko Ono on stage to a rapturous greeting from the crowd. They had met the Mothers earlier in the day after Howard Smith, whose *Scenes* column appeared in *The Village Voice*, had told Lennon he was interviewing Frank that afternoon. Smith reckoned that Lennon acted deferential at their meeting, while Yoko Ono asserted herself to all those present. Smith was also the one to propose that the Lennons join the Mothers on stage that night.

Lennon launched into a song he remembered from his days at the Liverpool Cavern, 'Well (Baby Please Don't Go)', which without his wife's caterwauling would have been moderately successful. After that, things got out of hand. 'King Kong' degenerated into a duel between the band and Yoko Ono's tonsils before Frank led them through a series of falsetto punctuations of her noises. By the audience's laughter, someone should have felt foolish, but then, true art must expect ridicule. 'Scumbag was a fast vamp over which Lennon and Flo & Eddie chanted the title. Mid-way, Frank broke in to inform the audience that they should join in: 'Right on, brothers and sisters! Let's hear it for the Scumbag!' As interest in the puerile goings-on waned on stage, a bag was dropped over Yoko Ono's head. Lennon set his guitar to feedback and everyone else left the stage while the bag-lady evoked the sodomisation of birds and small animals. By their applause, the audience was plainly enthralled.

Over lunch the following day, it was decided that the Lennons would be given copies of the 16-track masters for their own use. The possibility of further live concerts was discussed but neither party pursued the idea. 'It may have been a lot of pleasant thoughts in an Italian restaurant,' Frank said in an interview six months later.[20]

'We wanted to make the Mothers Fillmore East album a double one,' Howard Kaylan told *Rolling Stone*, 'shove 'Billy The Mountain' on one side and put the Lennon stuff on the other. Unfortunately Allen Klein (Lennon's manager) doesn't move as fast as Lennon does.'[21] The Lennons released their version of the tapes on June 12, 1972, as part of a bonus album released with *Some Time In New York City* that also contained their 'War Is Over' gig at London's Lyceum Theatre on December 15, 1969. This was the epitome of their revolutionary phase, combining paeans to Angela Davis and John Sinclair with Ono's 'Woman Is The Nigger Of The World' and Lennon's 'Sunday Bloody Sunday'. Despite Frank's injunction that everything should be properly credited and paid for, 'King Kong' was renamed 'Jamrag'. No doubt Lennon expected the British slang word for a tampon to go unnoticed in the land he was trying to make his home.

Frank's version of the tapes eventually surfaced in 1992. His sequence on 'Playground Psychotics' was shorter than the Lennons' but better mixed. They had overdubbed Klaus Voorman's bass on 'Well (Baby Please Don't Go)', edited out band solos and swamped everything in cavernous sub-Spector echo. The band tracks were poorly balanced and Flo & Eddie's improvised humour in 'Scumbag' was missing. Frank restored the edits (but deleted 'King Kong'), redressed the balance and also nailed the final soliloquy by naming it 'A Small Eternity With Yoko Ono'.

Fillmore East didn't get a good press. Frank's year-long obsession with *200 Motels* and its depiction of life on the road had crafted a piece of theatre that was self-referential and full of in-jokes. Other rock musicians got the point but the attitudes displayed in the 'groupie' routines offended many who would never be 'jooked by a baby octopus' or 'spewed upon with cream corn'. *Rolling Stone* gave the lead: 'It may seem a quaint notion now, but there actually was a time when Frank Zappa was considered one of the prime geniuses of rock.' With swipes at his 'arrogance' and the 'steady downward curve in quality' of his albums, Fillmore East apparently represented 'a real nadir. The sometime ribaldry of the early albums has finally been allowed to bloom like a Clearasil jackoff fantasy, resulting in two sides mostly filled with a lot of inanity about groupies and exotic fuck-props.'[22]

Don Preston had joined the Mothers on the Fillmore stage for 'Lonesome Electric Turkey', an encore excerpt from 'King Kong'. He now returned to the band after Bob Harris's brief tenure as another gig was recorded for future issue. The return to UCLA's Pauley Pavilion on Saturday, August 7 included another stab at 'Billy The Mountain', which occupied Side One of *Just Another Band From L.A.*, when Zubin Mehta's name was substituted for Felix Pappalardi in the New York version. Cal Schenkel's poster for the show contained a thumb-nail sketch of said mountain and his wife Ethel, 'a tree growing off of his shoulder'; more than 20 years later, he plagiarised his own work to make it the cover art of *Playground Psychotics*. It had already been lifted for the cover of *Safe Muffinz*, a bootleg issue of the band's appearance at El Monte Legion Stadium that summer.

Like most of Frank's film scripts, *Billy The Mountain* went through several changes; the central plot devices remained the same while the incidental details changed. As he revealed to Roy Carr, 'In the opening part, God decides to make a home movie with a sofa, a short girl and a squat magic pig. Then he gives the film to winged holy children who take it to a lab where they don't ask any questions. While he's waiting for his dailies to come back from the lab he lays down on the sofa, crashes out and he dreameth a great dream.'[23] This dream involves Old Zircon, a 'phased-out Byzantine Devil', whose dancing cloven hooves strike sparks and smoke which congeal into a number of lumpy mountains, one of which can talk.

As recorded in New York and Los Angeles, Billy gets a royalty cheque for all the postcards he'd posed for and decides to take Ethel on a walking holiday across America. Since Edwards Air Force Base gets destroyed on the first day's journey, informed sources in Washington call in special agent Studebaker Hoch to put a stop to the devastation by serving Billy with his induction papers for the Army. To locate Billy, Hoch has a unique mode of transport involving Aunt Jemima Syrup, sundry flies and a phone booth. The performance ended with Hoch being destroyed in the avalanche caused by Billy's laughter. Later episodes from the script involving a Government agent called Little Emil, who is later revealed to be the head of the Electric Mafia, don't seem to have been performed.

'What a lot of people wouldn't realise,' said Dick Barber, 'is that each night they did that show, Mark and Howard and sometimes Jim Pons would alter the lyrics slightly to tie them in more with the local area . . . They'd just doctor the lyrics up, and change 'em around, partly to amuse themselves, and also to amuse Frank, because if Frank was in a good mood, it made it easier for everybody.'[24] It also got them taken to jail in Virginia Beach, after they forgot that the local chief of police had warned them not to say 'fuck' on stage.

The rest of *Just Another Band* contained up-to-the-minute retreads of 'Call Any Vegetable' and 'Dog Breath', 'Eddie, Are You Kidding?', a Kaylan/Volman/Zappa collaboration about tailoring double-knits for the portly, and 'Magdalena', a tale of prospective incest conceived by Howard and Frank. This gig was also the last time that Jimmy Carl Black appeared on a Mothers' stage. His guest appearance on 'Lonesome Cowboy Burt' later appeared on *YCDTOSA 6*, in a 'mutant blend' of this and a performance from Genoa during Frank's final 1988 tour, at which the song became 'Lonesome Cowboy Nando'.

Howard Kaylan talked about being a Mother in the September 16 edition of *Rolling Stone*. 'Zappa has the last word – don't get me wrong, it's definitely Frank's group. I don't believe it's any more oppressive than working in (John) Mayall's group, or anybody else's band. Except for the last musical say and how the thing is brought to the stage, it's fairly open. It's a well-known fact that if anybody brought a song to the group, and if it fit in with what we were doing, we'd do it. It's hard to do that though.' Was there a contrast between being a Turtle and being a Mother? 'If you think it takes some heavy acid flash or a change in intelligence to go from singing 'Happy Together' to a song like 'Mudshark', you're wrong. Outside of the fact that this is Frank's group, the road's the road, getting high has always been neat, money's good when it's here, groupies are fantastic. It's all the same.'[25] The road rat's charter had never been put so succinctly.

STRICTLY GENTEEL

200 Motels, as a film and a double album, was released in October 1971. The film began an exclusive run at the Doheny Plaza in Beverley Hills on Friday, October 29. Writing in the *Los Angeles Times*, Robert Hilburn found it 'a stunning achievement'. 'It is at its best when it seems off-balance,' he continued, 'giving a glimpse of the way time, space, sanity, get confused during a long rock tour . . . Some of the film's best sequences are those which show all the energy devoted by musicians and the groupies to getting together.' Despite its evident flaws, Hilburn thought that the film had 'a sense of vitality and excitement akin to some of the feelings generated by the early rock records' and that, in the final analysis, 'Zappa has come up with a minor classic'.[26]

It opened at New York's Plaza Theater on November 10. The following day in the *New York Times*, Vincent Canby thought that it was 'not all bad' but 'a movie with so many things going on simultaneously, it becomes too quickly exhausting – in actual effect, soporific'. There were 'several dozen potentially funny ideas that are never developed, since the movie has the attention span of a speed freak'. Ultimately, though, *200 Motels* was 'an anthology of poor jokes and spectacular audio-visual effects, a few of which might expand the mind, but of which, taken together, are like an overdose of Novocain'.[27]

Over in England, the 'celebrated' film director Tony Palmer was busy dissociating himself from his work. He told the *NME* that in his estimation, *200 Motels* was the worst film in the history of Western cinema. 'I've been trying to get my name removed from the credits for months,' he expostulated.

'The story behind the film is horrific, but the picture itself is a complete abuse of technique and ideas and, in my opinion, is a total waste of half-a-million dollars.'[28]

There was a special preview at the London Pavilion on Wednesday, November 17, after which Frank and the band hosted a party at the Hard Rock Cafe. Two days later, the latest European tour began in Stockholm and was scheduled to continue through Denmark, Germany, Holland, Austria, Switzerland and France, before they returned to England to appear at London's Rainbow Theatre on Friday, December 10 and Saturday, December 11.

Frank talked to *NME's* Roy Carr about his film, parts of which Carr thought were an expensive in-joke which placed the audience in the position of eavesdropper. 'Well, the film was designed for people who already know something about the legend and lore of the Mothers of Invention,' Frank replied. 'I would say that the hard-core Mothers of Invention freaks are gonna get off on it probably more so than those people who dislike the group or don't know anything about it.'[29]

The conversation moved on to how the Mothers reproduced the complexity of the records on stage. 'I was interested in the juxtaposition of various musical textures – pieces of recordings from different times – one from now, one from a few years ago. At the same time, I got interested in the editing technique. All the albums were heavily edited to make abrupt changes, then we were faced with the problems of duplicating that on stage. So I devised the hand signals that would allow things to change, and so we rehearsed in such a way that it was a question of . . . keep your eyes open for a signal every once in a while . . . so that when it comes it will sound just like an edit on stage.'[30]

Did this mean that every gig was recorded? 'No, but this formula allows us to do so if required.' Frank then revealed that the Rainbow gigs would be recorded for a possible album. Mark Volman, also present, described what would soon become standard procedure for Frank's recordings. 'For me that's the greatest way to get the best recordings. (Frank) is very smart, he tapes just the tracks in a lot of cases, so you've got something that's being played in front of people and generally when you play in front of people they performance of any tune exceeds itself, 'cause you've got something really happening. So we get just the band track and then go back into the studio, change it from four- to 16-track and you've got endless amounts of room to do something.'[28]

He didn't know it but soon Frank would have what must have seemed endless amounts of time to do anything but pursue a normal life.

CHAPTER TEN
SMOKE ON THE WATER

The European tour was nearing its end when the band arrived in Switzerland to play in the Montreux Casino on Saturday, December 4. The ballroom of this aged and elegant edifice was also the venue for the annual Golden Rose TV awards ceremony, and this was to be the last gig of the season before the Casino shut for the winter.

As documented by two bootlegs, *Swiss Cheese* and *Fire!*, that subsequently became part of *Beat The Boots 2*, the gig was slow to take off. For 14 minutes, a synthesiser drones on as the various members of the band take their places on stage and begin to play. Frank tunes up after ten minutes and solos until, four minutes later, the band moves into a pedestrian version of 'Peaches En Regalia'. 'Call Any Vegetable', during which it is made plain that the secret word for the night is 'fondue', and 'Anyway The Wind Blows' are most notable for Aynsley Dunbar's energy. The rest of the band begins to hit its marks during an 18-minute version of 'Sofa', with all its variations, in German and English.

'The translation was done by a girl who used to be our babysitter,' Frank told Matt Groening. 'That particular tour, I tried to convince Mark and Howard that it was a good idea to learn these things phonetically, because most American groups, if they go and play in another country, make no attempt to communicate in the native language, and I thought it would be a worthwhile gesture and probably a ground-breaking thing to do.'[1]

'Sofa' formed the prelude to 'Billy The Mountain', during which God, along with his faithful St Bernard, Wendell, decides to make a raunchy home movie with an un-named small girl, Squat the Magic Pig and a fat, floating sofa. Sung by Flo & Eddie in German and spoken in English by Frank, the everyday story of a girl and a magic pig sharing an intimate experience on a sofa – without soiling it – has its moments. Though never committed to record in its complete form, the section describing the action, 'Stick It Out', eventually turned up on Volume Two of *Joe's Garage*, by which time the protagonists were the eponymous guitar playing Joe and a chrome-plated kitchen appliance adorned with marital aids that merely looked like a magical pig.

Since this film is directed by God, the special effects have to be just that.

Just over 14 minutes in, as the lyrics depict sparks shooting out and nebulas being revealed, Frank intones, 'Sheets of fire, ladies and gentlemen. Sheets of real fire.' After 'A Pound For A Brown On The Bus' and a medley of 'Wonderful Wino', 'Sharleena' and 'Cruisin' For Burgers', the band is just a minute into 'King Kong' and Don Preston is winding his moog up to sound like a siren, when someone fires a Very pistol and the flare lodges itself in the ceiling's electrical wiring. Soon, Frank's words appeared to have been an omen. Mark Volman thought that Frank felt 'his anti-Christianity stance . . . might have played a little role in the negative things that happened in Montreux.'[2] In the light of 'Dumb All Over', recorded in 1980, it's unlikely that Frank's Catholic upbringing caused him a moment's doubt, either then or later.

The members of Deep Purple, who had booked the ballroom for the next three weeks to record their next album, were in the audience that night. 'Within seconds,' said Ian Gillan, 'the whole thing was really sparking and the room filled with smoke. Zappa was great - he stayed very calm.'[3] Having told the audience to calmly go towards the exits, he and the band left their gear onstage and were led through an underground tunnel from the back of the stage into the parking area outside. 'Everyone was a bit dazed,' Gillan continued, 'and we went back to the hotel and sat in the restaurant watching this beautiful building blaze. Flames were shooting two, three hundred feet, and the wind coming down the mountains blew the smoke across Lake Geneva - an incredible sight, I shall never forget it. And Roger Glover came up with the idea of 'Smoke On The Water' and scribbled it down on a napkin.'[4]

Twenty years after the event, Frank was stoic in his assessment of the hit record that emerged from his misfortune: 'It's too bad there had to be a fire in order to produce the song.'[5] Frank watched the Casino burn from the veranda of his hotel and said to Dick Barber, 'Get me on the first plane back to the US'. 'Prior to that, we had blown up two or three trucks,' Barber said, 'including one big semi tractor-trailer on the Autobahn in East Germany . . . because a week before, it had frozen up in Malmo, Sweden.' The crew had managed to fix it but were a day late getting to Odense in Denmark, forcing the band to use a local band's equipment, 'a couple of stacks of Marshalls and a little P.A. and borrowed instruments'.[6]

The whole tour, in Dick Barber's words, 'was a disaster'. Now, with all their equipment destroyed, some of it customised to the music's demands, Frank's desire to cut the group's losses, cancel the remaining gigs and return to America was strong. But, according to Mark Volman, 'The band felt we needed to make the money, and it was Christmas time. So Frank went along with it.'[7]

The gigs in Paris, Lyons and Brussels were cancelled but the four

Rainbow shows in London went ahead, using yet more borrowed gear. After two days rehearsals with unfamiliar equipment that also proved to be unreliable, the first show on Friday, December 10 went well enough. As previously agreed, the band's first encore was the Beatles' 'I Want To Hold Your Hand'.

Howard Thompson, a long-time fan of Zappa's music seeing his hero for the very first time, was sitting in the front row. 'After 'I Want To Hold Your Hand', everyone left the stage again and then Frank came out to announce the next encore. Suddenly, out of the corner of my eye, I saw this guy run down to the orchestra pit, leap over it onto stage right, run across about five feet to where Zappa was standing and just shove him. And Zappa tumbled into the orchestra pit, right in front of me. I leaned over the barrier and looked down into the pit, which was about 15 feet below the stage. Zappa was just lying there, prone. The kid continued running across the front of the stage and got collared by some roadies. And then the band started coming out to do the next encore. Mark and Howard were looking around for Frank and then they looked to where we were all pointing.'[8]

'I remember looking down at him from the top of the pit,' said Mark Volman, 'and his leg was bent underneath him like a Barbie doll; his eyes were open but there was no life in them. Two or three of us were cradling him in the pit and the blood was running from his head to his knees. We weren't sure if he would live through the night.'[9]

Luckily, Frank's injuries looked worse than they were - but not by much. He had a fractured ankle, at least one broken rib, a temporarily paralysed arm and a number of contusions and gashes to his head. In addition, his head had been forced round over his shoulder, which resulted in a crushed larynx. An ambulance took him to the Royal Northern Hospital, where he was kept overnight in considerable pain, since his head injuries precluded the use of painkillers.

Saturday's press identified Frank's assailant as Trevor Charles Howell, a 24-year-old labourer of Hatherly Road, Walthamstow, London E17. The *Daily Express* quoted the Rainbow's business manager, Michael Jaffe: 'The audience went absolutely mad. They all rushed towards the stage. The man ran off across the side of the stage but he was quickly caught. He said he was upset because his girl friend (Susan North) had a crush on Zappa.'[10] Howell appeared at North London Court, accused of causing grievous bodily harm, and was remanded on £100 bail.

At much the same time, Frank was transferred to the Weymouth Street Clinic. Herb Cohen was involved in a scuffle with a press photographer, grabbing the man's camera and dashing it to the ground. John Morris, managing director of the company that leased the Rainbow, intervened and later presented Stuart Goodman with a cheque for £100, as compensation for the loss of his camera.

Two days later, the *Daily Mirror* reported that Frank would be in hospital for at least a month. Herb Cohen said, 'I'm not able to say when Frank will be able to go back to work. He has received a compound fracture to his ankle. His foot should be in a cast for about eight weeks.'[11] Howard Kaylan and Mark Volman later claimed the band had been approached to continue the tour without him. 'I can't even imagine what would have happened if we would have showed up at some of these shows as the Mothers of Invention without Frank,' Kaylan said.[12]

The band got to see Frank a few days after the incident. 'We went in and there was Frank on his back, arm in a sling, one leg in a cast on a sling in the air,' said Mark Volman. 'His head was bandaged like a mummy. You couldn't see his hair or his moustache – just his lips where they had cut a hole in the bandages, and his eyes, which followed us to the foot of the bed. And then he said, "'Peaches En Regalia' - one, two, three . . ." We died laughing. It was the sorriest of jokes. But it was his way of saying, "It's okay".'[13]

But it wasn't okay. On January 7, 1972, the *Daily Mail* reported that Frank would be in plaster up to his hip for the next four months and that he had to stay at the Clinic for at least another ten days. 'Things can hardly get any worse,' said Herb. 'I don't know how long it will be before he will be able to perform again. He's very depressed about it.'[14]

ANY KIND OF PAIN

1971 had been Frank's annus horribilis, a burnt weeny sandwich with a filling of hard work encased in two slices of misfortune, both of them at the hands of the British. Because of it, as he says in his autobiography, the nation earned a special place in his heart.

While he convalesced before returning to America, Frank was interviewed by Keith Altham for a two-part feature in *NME*. In the February 5 edition, a compassionate sub-editor headlined the first part, 'Forget The Leg A While. It's ZAPPA on rock, porn and blues'. Altham persisted in trying to find ways of bringing John Sebastian into the conversation until the subject was summarily dismissed by Frank. The journalist also found it odd that Frank should be 'an extremely astute business man', since 'one of the "cutest" features of the deal he negotiated with Warner Records is that at the end of their five-year contract, the group get their masters back.' 'That's what I call a good deal,' said Frank. 'You make a record, and what normally happens is that the record company owns the tapes for ever – it's not your music anymore. I happen to like the idea of retaining my so-called works of art.'

Enforced rest had apparently turned his mind to some of his musical roots, R&B in particular. 'I still enjoy that music,' he said, 'and it may seem absurd – but if I were in the proper circumstances, and I told the guys in the band this,

I would be just as happy playing R&B. That's because I love it, it sounds good to me. It has definite musical merit. The emotional quality of the music of the 50s, and the feel of those performances – everything they have is cheap. But the sound that comes out is just great, it inspires you. When they have the cheapest stuff they come out with a piece of art at the end.'[15]

In the second instalment, Frank had a tilt at rock journalists: 'The level of pop journalism in the UK seems to be superior to that of the US, although it may be an illusion. However, neither are good.' Asked if there was an age limit to being a musician, Frank replied, 'No. I hope I will still be on stage playing the guitar when I'm 50. I love to play the guitar. It's one of the great physical sensations of all time.'[16]

A less welcome sensation was provoked by another article in the same issue, 'Svengali Zappa and a horrible freak called Beefheart'. On the eve of a British tour, the Captain was in an unforgiving mood. 'Zappa is an oaf,' he boomed. 'It was disgusting and totally degrading that Zappa should do this to me. The trouble with Frank Zappa is that he's not a good artist or a writer and by surrounding himself with good musicians and exploiting them he boosts his own image.'[17]

By now, Beefheart had three ex-Mothers in his band, Elliott Ingber, Roy Estrada and Art Tripp, each of whom had reason to be discontented with their ex-boss; they each took their turn to run with the ball. Beefheart expressed disappointment at Ringo Starr's involvement with Frank: 'I'm not into pornography and so I wouldn't look at *200 Motels* but from what I hear, it's nothing more than cheap smut. It's not worth getting into the bullshit to see what the bull ate.'[18]

Trevor Howell had his day in court when his case was heard at the Old Bailey on Wednesday, March 8. Judge Rigg sentenced him to 12 months imprisonment when he admitted maliciously inflicting grievous bodily harm on Mr Zappa. His reason for the assault was that he thought 'Mr Zappa was not giving value for money', *The Times* reported the following day. No doubt he'd been advised that his girlfriend's crush would not be seen as a viable defence. Eleven days later, the *Daily Telegraph* announced that Frank had begun a High Court action for damages against Howell. 'Mr Zappa, leaders of the 'Mothers of Invention' group, and his company, Bizarre Productions, are also suing the theatre owners, Sundancer Theatre Co., of Oxford Street, claiming damages for alleged negligence and breach of duty and contract.'[19]

THE GRAND WAZOO

After spending a short while recuperating in Hawaii, Frank was at home but still confined to a wheelchair. Some time later, he learned to walk on crutches but his leg refused to heal. Doctors wanted to break it and reset it but Frank opted to take his chances. Eventually the cast was removed and his leg was put into a brace. When it finally healed, the leg was slightly crooked and shorter than the other. Luckily, he never wanted to be a Dancin' Fool.

Now, instead of directing enforced recreation live on stage, Frank had some of his own. It was time to take stock of the situation. Even without the climactic events of one week in December, this tour had been only a conditional success. There was more than enough justification to regard this particular phase of his career as at an end. *200 Motels* had monopolised his attention for the best part of 18 months. The compromised film he'd ended up with, confusing to fan and foe alike, fell short of their and his intentions. The stage repertoire he'd developed from its elements, though undoubtedly entertaining, had had a trivialising affect on audience perception of the instrumental expertise supporting it.

Limited mobility gave him the time to do what he often stated he liked best, compose music, but inevitably that wasn't all. Between February and August, he worked on a number of projects, some of which, like an album project for Jeff Beck, never came to fruition. One that did was to oversee the creation of an actual Ruben and The Jets. The band consisted of Ruben Ladron De Guevara, rhythm guitarist Robert 'Frog' Camarena, Johnny Martinez on bass and keyboards, and guitarist Tony Duran, all of whom shared vocals, Robert 'Buffalo' Roberts on tenor sax, bassist Bill Wild and drummer Bob Zamora. Motorhead Sherwood also came in on baritone sax and tambourine. A deal was secured with Mercury Records and Frank produced the album, writing and arranging 'If I Could Only Be Your Love Again' and co-arranging 'Mah Man Flash' and 'Santa Kari' with Ruben Guevara.

As for his own work, he conceived *Hunchentoot*, a science fiction musical of which only fragments were ever released. The story concerns an evil alien female, Drakma, who means to invade Earth. The final 72-page script, including stage directions and costume designs, called for a cast of 42, of which 31 were musicians. In the end, only small group versions of three songs, 'Time Is Money', 'Spider Of Destiny' and 'Flambay', were issued on Sleep Dirt, one of the three shoddily presented albums with which Warner Brothers said goodbye to Frank seven years later. The 1979 vinyl issue used the instrumental tracks but the 1991 CD reissue featured vocals by Thana Harris.

The Adventures Of Greggery Peccary is the tale of a nocturnal gregarious wild swine who one day invents the calendar and the consequences thereto. Though written during the summer of 1972, it was not recorded until at least two years later and then not released until September 1978. Originally conceived as a ballet with recitation, the recorded version is dotted with references to 'Billy The Mountain', 'Big Swifty' and 'Toads Of The Short Forest'. The music is as complex as the story is bizarre, fragmented with sequences for percussion and frenzied brass and passing gibes at the hip (a snatch of Herbie Hancock's 'Chameleon' from his 1973 album, *Headhunters*) and the hairy (Elmore James' 'Dust My Broom').

Greggery worked for Big Swifty & Associates - Trendmongers. With his habitually mordant eye, Frank concentrated his scorn on merchandisers and advertising agencies, investing them with 'the frightening little skills that science has made available'. No doubt he chose to ignore the irony implicit in criticising others for utilising the very methods he'd used to promote the Mothers (and thus himself). When he hijacked the freak banner, he'd attracted a following not, as many thought, to formulate the strategy of an alternative lifestyle but for them to buy his product.

The latest piece of product, the last Mothers' swan song, *Just Another Band From L.A.*, was released in May. Because of the lop-sided nature of its contents, with one side devoted to 'Billy The Mountain' and rearrangements of 'Call Any Vegetable' and 'Dog Breath' on the other, critical reaction was wary and mixed. Since the magnum opus relied upon local detail every time it was performed, references to L.A. districts were incomprehensible to New Yorkers, let alone Europeans. One reviewer thought it 'very simply the best thing Frank Zappa and his resident crazies have ever done', but his was a lone voice. Writing two years later, Charles Shaar Murray, long a Zappa zealot, thought it 'the total triumph of style and technique over content'. 'Technically,' he went on, 'it's extraordinary, and it contains some staggeringly funny moments, but it has no real content - presumably because Zappa has absolutely nothing to say and was therefore content to experiment with style.'[20]

By setting high standards and creating high expectations, Frank had made a rod for his own back. Apparently, musical complexity and wit were no longer enough, Zappa compositions also had to mean something. More than that, the meaning had to be comprehensible to critics and journalists who increasingly were becoming the protagonists in their work, at the expense of their interviewees. By simultaneously courting and disparaging the press, Frank laid himself open to adverse comment anytime his motives were misunderstood or fell short of the precarious regard in which he was held. He had not lost the guru's cloak that so many still wanted to drape about his shoulders and any perceived lapse of divinity called down censure.

As Frank told Martin Perlich, 'All I'm interested in doing is writing music that I want to hear. If I'm going into an area that you're not interested in going, fine, you stay home. I'll tell you what happened when I get back. I'll do you a public service, I'll find out what's out there. The only problem is, if you don't go there with me, you're gonna have to take my word for it when I give you my report. Now that's not too smart. You should at least come along for the ride and find out what's happening out there.'

While on the subject, he couldn't resist a tilt at a favourite windmill.

'Judging from the quality of the rock 'n' roll writers that are appearing in rock 'n' roll publications, I would say they're not doing quite as good as the people who're actually making the records. Therefore, if in a hundred years, people want to find out what was going on during this period of time, they'd be better off listening to the source rather than to read the thing in print.'

In another part of the conversation, Frank gave an indication of the direction that his current writing was taking when he was asked whether he would return to satire. 'I think that satirical content in music does not necessarily have to lean on the verbal aspect. There are plenty of satirical things that you can do with a mere note or a mere inflection and never say a word. It's unfortunate that the audience that thought that the satirical aspect . . . had vanished from the Mothers of Invention music was insensitive to the other aspects that remained in the music. In other words, they were so verbally oriented that by the time we'd progressed into other forms of commentary, they didn't go along. You missed the road, boys and girls.'[21]

In late spring 1972, still confined to a wheelchair, Frank booked sessions at Paramount Studios in Hollywood from which two albums would emerge. First was his solo follow-up to *Hot Rats*, taking its title from one of the tunes, *Waka/Jawaka*. The basic rhythm section consisted of George Duke, Alex Dmochowski, bass player in Aynsley Dunbar's Retaliation, and Aynsley himself. Don Preston contributed to the title track and a pardoned Jeff Simmons played Hawaiian guitar on 'It Just Might Be A One-Shot Deal'. 'Sneaky Pete' Kleinow took a pedal steel solo on the same number and Tony Duran added slide guitar to it and 'Big Swifty'. Brass and woodwind players Sal Marquez, Joel Peskin, Mike Altschul, Bill Byers and Ken Shroyer in a variety of combinations, added tonal colour.

Despite a close identification with the original *Hot Rats*, this music had less of Frank's heretofore characteristic stamp to it. 'Big Swifty' was a side-long extravaganza with extended solo space for George Duke, Sal Marquez and Tony Duran as well as Frank's guitar. After a series of opening variations which put complex melodies to Aynsley's drum patterns, the piece slid into a medium-paced shuffle that required a lighter touch than Dunbar gave it. Though plainly holding back, his rock 'n' roll roots lent a weight and deliberation to his continual excursions around the kit, distracting attention from the soloists he was meant to underscore. Frank's solo indulged in pyrotechnical phrasing that suggested he'd been listening to John McLaughlin, the British guitarist who'd worked with Miles Davis and Tony Williams' Lifetime before forming the Mahavishnu Orchestra with ex-Flock violinist Jerry Goodman, Jan Hammer and Billy Cobham. Their first album, *The Inner Mounting Flame* had just been issued.

'Waka/Jawaka' itself was another blowing vehicle with solos by Marquez, Don Preston, Frank and Aynsley. It also called for more complicated playing from the brass and woodwind contingent as layers of intricate overdubs provided the piece with a lush climax. Sandwiched between these instrumentals, 'Your Mouth' and 'It Just Might Be A One-Shot Deal' featured indistinct vocals by Chris Peterson, Sal Marquez and Janet Ferguson. She'd taken over as nanny to the Zappa children, a job which she no doubt performed with more confidence than she shows as a vocalist.

Other material from these sessions became *The Grand Wazoo*, a suite of tunes which made a coherent whole, even without the elaborate fiction which Frank wrote as a sleevenote. The story, which ties together the title track, 'Cletus Awreetus-Awrightus' and 'Eat That Question', concerns the Funky Emperor Cletus and his fight with the dastardly Mediocrates of Pedestrium. He also regularly deals with a 'grotesque cult of masochistic ascetic fanatics who don't like music' known as 'Questions'. 'The original name of that song was 'Eat That Christian',' Frank told Bob Marshall. 'I thought Question was better – it's a more twisted concept.'[22] Cletus allows the 'Questions' two chances to redeem themselves before they are pitched into tanks of 'Undifferentiated Tissue'. The Wazoo itself is the 'oversize primitive-but-effective megaphone' through which he addresses them.

'For Calvin (And His Next Two Hitch-Hikers)' is a dream-like piece with an almost sublimated pulse which regularly disintegrates into communal improvisation. During the burbling muted trumpet solo, first a trombone and then Frank's guitar play the theme of 'New Brown Clouds', the finale of *Greggery Peccary*. 'The Grand Wazoo' is another extended solo vehicle intercut with richly orchestrated themes. Cletus has a militarily strutting theme and terse sax solo by Ernie Watts, identified on the sleeve as the original Funky Emperor. 'Eat That Question' opens on a free improvisation by George Duke's electric piano before the staccato theme is established; it's repeated with massed overdubs at the piece's end. 'Blessed Relief' is the most overtly jazz-oriented tune present, as if Frank finally gave full rein to the direction in which the music had been leaning throughout the sessions.

FOR REAL

While these sessions took place, the other erstwhile Mothers pondered their future. 'For months and months and months, we had no contact with (Frank) whatsoever,' said Howard Kaylan, 'we had no contact with his office whatsoever . . . members of the band were sitting around their homes waiting for the phone to ring, wondering if they would ever work again, wondering if there would ever be another Mothers of Invention.'[23] In the absence of any hard information, Kaylan and Volman put together a demo tape of songs and began searching for a deal of their own. But when Roy Carr interviewed them for the June 3 *NME*, they were careful to leave the door open. 'Though we still work with Frank,' said Kaylan, 'we now have the freedom to do exactly as we please. This album that we're making has been born out of this new-found freedom.'[24]

The July 5, 1972, release of Frank's brand new solo album, *Waka/Jawaka*, dispelled any uncertainty about their future. They signed with Reprise and *Phlorescent Leech & Eddie*, on which they were joined by the other ex-Mothers including Aynsley Dunbar, was issued in August. Meanwhile, the success of the Wazoo sessions encouraged Frank to take a 20-piece orchestra on the road. He recruited many of the musicians who'd played on the album, adding a couple of familiar names and substituting others. It took three or four months to accomplish, because most had studio commitments.

'It came as a considerable surprise to them to learn that they were going on the road,' Frank told Charles Shaar Murray. 'They'd never experienced it before, and I'd never been out on the road with a group that large trying to perform electric music.'[25] The full run-down of the Grand Wazoo orchestra was: Sal Marquez, Malcolm McNabb and Tom Malone on trumpets; Glen Ferris and Ken Shroyer on trombones; Mike Altschul, Jay Migliori, Earl Dummler, Ray Reed and Charles Owens on various flutes, clarinets and saxophones; Joanne McNabb on bassoon; Ian Underwood on piano and synths; Tony Duran on slide guitar; Dave Parlato on bass; Jim Gordon on 'electric' drums; Jerry Kessler on electric cello; and Tom Raney and Ruth Underwood on sundry percussion.

Rehearsals took place in the Glendale Civic Auditorium, the repertoire consisting of 'New Brown Clouds', 'Big Swifty', 'For Calvin (and His Next Two Hitch-Hikers)', 'Approximate', 'Think It Over' (another *Hunchentoot* song), 'Low Budget Dog Meat' (a medley of themes from *Music For Low Budget Orchestra, The Dog Breath Variations* and *Uncle Meat*) and 'The Adventures Of Greggery Peccary'. The necessarily brief tour of what Frank called 'The Mothers Of Invention/Hot Rats/Grand Wazoo' began at the Hollywood Bowl on September 10 and moved to Europe for gigs at the Berlin Deutschlandhalle (15), the Oval Cricket Ground in London (16) and The Hague's Hourast Halle (17), before returning to America for gigs at New York's Felt Forum (23) and the Boston Music Hall (24).

News of the tour appeared in the British music press in the August 26 editions and Frank did telephone interviews for the following week's papers. 'I have mixed emotions about coming back,' he told Caroline Boucher of *Disc*. 'I'm still on a full leg-brace and walk on crutches. It was a terrible break and I've still got to wear this thing for another two months.'[26] From the size of the band, it was obvious that this music would be very much different from what Britain had heard before. 'What we really have here is an electric symphony orchestra,' he explained to *NME*'s Danny Holloway. 'Aside from the recognisable pieces which are rock-oriented, there are two or three semi-symphonic-type pieces which are of a humorous nature simply because of the subject matter. But we're not going to have people jumping around on stage or falling down with tambourines and saying zany stuff - we're not supplying that this season.'[27]

Both journalists asked for his reaction to comments made by Howard Kaylan and Mark Volman as part of the promotion for their new album. His comment to Boucher was succinct: 'I think it's highly unlikely that I'll be playing with Mark and Howard again.'[28] He was a bit more forthcoming with Holloway. 'I would say that the press releases they put out are involved with their own promo as a group and have been very unfair in terms of the conditions under which the group disbanded. The main thrust of all that press material is geared to exploiting them as new artists and partly due to the record company's interest in selling their records. Apparently, they believe it's ethical to do it at my expense. I'm extremely disappointed in their behaviour, because there was a time when I thought they were my friends.'[29]

Once again, it seemed that misunderstandings were rife on both sides. Flo & Eddie, like other Mothers before them, had ended up feeling exploited; Frank had assumed ownership of their contributions to the band's records and gigs. Frank's idea of friendship seemed to include the right to incorporate the bands' characteristics and adventures into his material, blurring the line between salaried employees and acknowledged collaborators. In an accompanying *NME* piece by Ian McDonald, even the mild Ruth Underwood was quoted to devastating effect: 'Frank Zappa is a cynic but totally destructive. He doesn't believe in anything, not even love. He's just empty inside.'[30]

Further justification for Frank's cynicism wasn't slow in making itself apparent. At the press conference held on the day before the Oval gig, he was presented with a £15 bouquet of flowers by Susan North, girlfriend of Trevor Howell, his Rainbow assailant. *The Evening News* reported her words to Frank: 'You don't know how sorry I am for what my boyfriend did. I hope this can go some way towards apologising.'[31]

Frank didn't know until later that North had been put up to the 'gift' by Ronnie and Ray Foulks, promoters of the next day's gig. 'I discovered the depths to which the British will sink in order to sell a concert ticket,' he said in his autobiography. Ah, the British again. The tilt was irresistible, even though by then he'd toured enough to know that promoters as a species, with some notable exceptions, shared characteristics that transcended nationality. But only in England . . .

It was lucky he wasn't aware of the original idea put forward by press officer Peter Harrigan that the Foulks had rejected. They had publicised their previous promotion, a rock 'n'roll festival at Wembley, by having a naked girl walk up Downing Street to knock on the Prime Minister's door. This time, the idea was to have a naked couple play the two-backed beast on the hallowed Oval turf. On a bed, of course. They'd even considered offering

Susan North £50 to be the female part of the equation.

Hawkwind had been engaged as a support band but on the eve of the concert, both bands' managements were still demanding to go on last. Originally scheduled to last from noon until 9.00 pm, the attendance had been limited to 15,000. Eventually, Frank agreed to go on first – but only if the second half of his 12,000 fee was paid in cash before the band went on stage. Having dealt with Chuck Berry at their rock 'n' roll festival, the Foulks should have been prepared for this demand. Unfortunately, insufficient gate receipts meant that there wasn't that much cash available. Tense moments passed until a cheque was reluctantly accepted. Frank struggled onto the stage and, in Philip Norman's words, 'delivered an electronic symphony, like the disputing of many xylophones, to a largely expressionless night'.[32]

By the time he finished at 10.00 pm, the Greater London Council licence had expired before Hawkwind had even taken the stage, let alone played a note. The atmosphere was tense. 'As Zappa left the backstage enclosure,' wrote Norman, 'a girl shrieked something at him and was pushed aside by his black bodyguard. An admirer of the girl started to attack the roof of Zappa's limousine with a wooden post. He was laid senseless by the black man. The same black man had also dealt with one of the West Ken Mob (a gang employed as 'Security') who now leaned at a drainpipe with a diagram in red where his lips ought to have been.'[33]

This was in marked contrast to what Frank had written in the intended tour programme, where he referred to the group's 'green limousine consciousness' and described their staid stage presence. 'The concert will be performed in a relaxed, tolerably direct and non-theatrical style. Only a few members of the Wazoo are used to playing popular music or are able to function safely if disguised by fringes, leaves and tinsel.'[34]

The MOI/HR/GW managed to function properly for the remaining dates in New York and Boston. And then they fulfilled their destiny, as prescribed by Frank: 'The Wazoo has probably earned its place in the Rock and Roll Hall Of Fame (something he never did in his lifetime), for the simple reason that it is the only 'new' group in rock history which has known from the start that it will not be as successful as the Beatles, and has also known throughout its history the exact time and place that it will split up: after the Boston show, in the dressing room, on September 24.'[35] In the same circular, Frank also announced his intention of immediately beginning rehearsals of another band, this time a ten-piece, and a new repertoire.

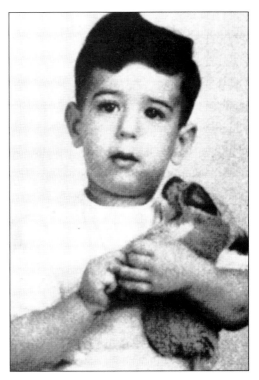

1941: Pancho Villa·or Viva Zapata!   c. 1943

The Mothers, 1967, l-r; Bunk Gardner, Art Tripp III, Don Preston, Motorhead Sherwood, FZ, Jimmy Carl
Black, Ian Underwood, Buzz Gardner. (LFI)

The mercurial Don Van Vleit (Captain Beefheart)

Outside the Albert Hall in February 1971. (LFI)

The committed and serious cigarette smoker onstage. (LFI)

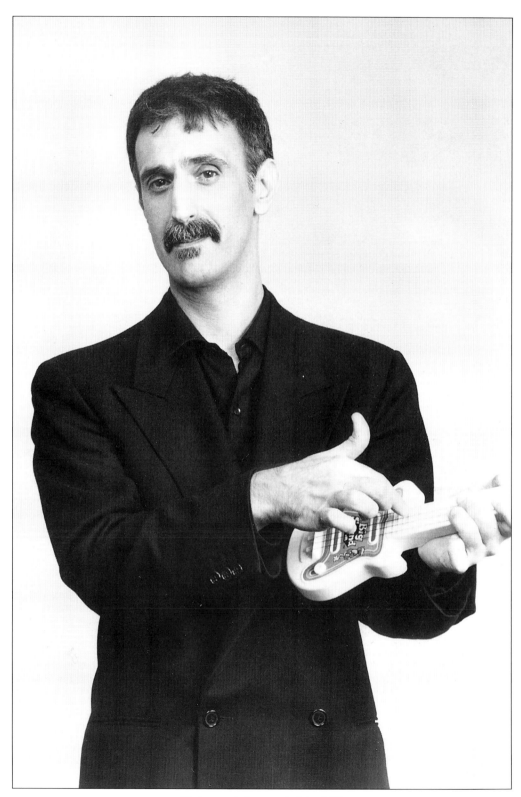

Shut up and play yer ukelele. (LFI)

The Mothers touring line-up from 1974 to 1976, l-r; Tom Fowler (bass), Napoleon Murphy Brock (sax and vocals), FZ, George Duke (keyboards and vocals), Ruth Underwood (percussion) and Chester Thompson (drums). (Redferns)

FZ in the mid-eighties. The serious composer twirls his baton. (LFI)

(LFI)

The entire Zappa family in the basement studio, early 80's.
l-r Dweezil, Gail, Ahmet, FZ, Moon. (LFI)

Greying, tired and unwell in the 90's. (LFI)

CHAPTER ELEVEN
OVERNITE SENSATION

'It was a worthwhile experience,' Frank commented after the Grand Wazoo tour. 'It only cost me $2,000. That's how much I lost on the tour. The tour grossed $97,000, and the expenses exceeded that by $2,000. A group that size, carrying that much equipment, going to Europe, playing that few jobs in that amount of time cannot make money at all.'[1]

Three years later, his attitude had changed: 'I think the overall impact of that group would be that it was between pseudo-jazzette and cranial. And the people who were in the band at the time - with a couple of exceptions - were genuinely boring people. I mean - I don't appreciate a band that likes to play chess in their off-stage hours. If you have to spend a lot of time with people who are interested in their chess-boards and little card games and shite like that, it can drive you nuts.'[2]

It didn't cross Frank's mind that drawing clefs and crotchets on manuscript paper, as he spent most of his time doing, wasn't a road rat's idea of how to spend time in a hotel room, either. But the tour had been a calculated risk that hadn't entirely failed, and one that had perhaps been anticipated by the creation of the streamlined ten-piece band that as previously announced now evolved from the larger group. At least the tour had enabled Frank to assess the practicality of the band arrangements and to consider ways of achieving comparable results from a more compact unit.

All but one of the musicians were retained from the Grand Wazoo, the exception being trumpeter Gary Barone, who replaced Marquez. Rehearsals by the Petit Wazoo took place during the first weeks of October and the tour, more specifically two groupings of gigs, began in Syracuse, New York on October 28. Although an entirely new repertoire had been promised, there was a judicious sprinkling of old favourites in new apparel. 'America Drinks', 'Duke Of Prunes', 'Chunga's Revenge', 'King Kong' and 'Willie The Pimp' paved the way for tunes such as 'Cosmic Debris' and 'Montana' that would soon turn up on the next couple of albums. There was also a medley of themes identified as 'Farther O'Blivion', beginning with an element of *Greggery Peccary* and containing other parts which would later become 'Cucamonga' and 'Be Bop Tango'. This medley was sometimes confused with the song 'Father O'Blivion', which formed part of a sequence that appeared on Frank's next solo excursion, *Apostrophe (')*.

The balance of the Petit Wazoo's live appearances ranged from Binghampton, NY to Portland, Oregon and finished on New Year's Eve 1972 at Washington DC's Constitution Hall. The latter was a return date, for they and Tim Buckley had played the hall on Saturday, November 11, when the evening had been reviewed for *The Star News* by Richard Harrington. He thought the Wazoo possessed 'one of the most dazzling, powerful and talented horn sections' he'd seen 'in all too long a time'. Picking out Bruce Fowler, Dave Parlato and drummer Jim Gordon for particular mention, Harrington saved his fullest praise for Frank: 'His guitar breaks reflect the general attitude of his music - jams built around a concrete concept, the development of a statement as opposed to mere technique. Zappa played long and well, and like a magician, left everyone filled, not with questions of how and why, but the knowledge of wonder.'[3]

Despite such praise, the New Year's Eve concert in Washington put an end for the time being to Frank's experiments with purely instrumental ensembles. Having taken his performance music from one extreme to the other, he now chose to combine instrumental and vocal dexterity. To achieve this, he assembled a group of musicians whose abilities, for the most part, were already known to him and each other.

Most important was the return of George Duke and Ian and Ruth Underwood, all dependable collaborators in the past, along with trumpeter Sal Marquez. Jean Luc Ponty's violin added a valuable solo voice, trombonist Bruce Fowler returned and brought along brother Tom on bass and the line-up was completed by drummer Ralph Humphrey. Rehearsals, as usual, were gruelling; 'You would go into the studio at noon or one o'clock,' said George Duke, 'and be there until seven or eight o'clock in the morning.'[4]

Barry Hansen described a rehearsal that he attended from this period: '(It) was devoted to the meticulous honing of several especially angular and asymmetrical instrumental passages. The musicians worked diligently, oblivious to the light crews who scurried about in their midst, setting up strobe lights and such. Except for the flashing lights, and the scarcity of music stands, the process resembled a symphony rehearsal far more than the usual loose rock session, with nary a beer bottle or joint to be seen. Zappa is a perfectionist, but what may be more remarkable is his prodigious energy level, which enables him to be a prolific writer/composer despite a heavy touring schedule.'[5]

That continued as the new band travelled to the East Coast for a series of gigs beginning on February 23 in Fayetteville, NC. Continuing through Durham, Atlanta and Athens, Georgia and three gigs in Florida, they returned via Arlington, Texas to L.A. where the now road-tested material was recorded for the next Mothers album.

After two predominantly instrumental releases, Frank opted for an album of songs where solos were kept to a strict minimum. Having stimulated his fans' heads, he would massage their other parts. It was also an opportunity for him to flex his own vocal chords. 'I'm back in the singing business again,' he announced to Charles Shaar Murray. 'For the kind of lyrics that I write, it's hard to get somebody else to identify with them to the extent that they express 'em properly.' He'd made a similar comment in the days immediately before he joined the Soul Agents. 'I have a pretty limited range - I can't sing very high, so there are certain things that have to be done by other people.'6

In terms of longevity, *Overnite Sensation* contributed a high proportion of future concert favourites. Whether it was because 'Camarillo Brillo', 'Dinah-Moe Humm' and 'Dirty Love', which Frank referred to as 'glandular epics', conjured up the perfumes and sauces of sexual encounters is debatable. As it was probably intended to do, 'Dinah-Moe' provoked extremes of reaction. Masturbation and 'coming from behind' were topics guaranteed to titillate young audiences and offend self-styled guardians of the nation's morals. In Frank's words, it became 'the one that really gets the most mongoloid audience glee-factor. They always demand it.'7

'Dirty Love; was less graphic but how explicit do you need to be when you write a song about a woman receiving oral gratification from a poodle? Frank kept a straight face when he explained, 'Poodles serve as a convenient mechanism for conveying certain philosophical ideas that might otherwise be more difficult.'8 When did bestiality become a philosophy? On the other hand, 'I'm The Slime', a warning about the insidious influence of television, and 'Montana', a bizarre fantasy about pygmy ponies and a dental floss farm, though devoid of sexual content, were equally popular. By comparison, 'Zomby Woof' and '50-50' made less frequent appearances over the years.

The album was released two months later, the first to be issued with the DiscReet logo. Bizarre and Straight had been wound up, 'partly for economic reasons' Herb Cohen told *Sounds*. Indeed, there had been no releases on the latter label for at least two years. 'Reet' was an important component in the 'vout' language invented by multi-instrumentalist Slim Gaillard during the 40s. By another fortuitous coincidence, the album was also issued in quadrophonic sound which was referred to as a 'discrete' system. It was a typical piece of Zappa opportunism, a label identity with more than one layer of meaning.

Critical opinion varied widely. Arthur Schmidt toed the usual *Rolling Stone* line; Frank Zappa was a spent force descending into obscene self-parody. He was 'tempted to compare Zappa to Henry Miller, with whom [he] shares a vision of sex as rancid, dumb and funny. Like Miller getting older, he is less shocking, tapeworming himself [what!] and overwriting.' Reserving what praise he could muster for 'Camarillo Brillo' and noting that 'Montana' 'could have been a great Mothers ditty'[9], Schmidt quoted a line from '50-50' and concluded that Frank had nothing to say.

Charles Shaar Murray thought it was 'a very relaxed album of slight-but-charming songs . . . decorated with all kinds of musical razzle-dazzle' but 'certainly not one of Frank's most outstanding efforts'.[10] Another reviewer, having expected further tales of the *Grand Wazoo*, thought that the album needed a smell sachet, because it was 'all about Buttons and Zips and the furry, vibrant wonders that lie beneath'. Overall, the album was a disappointment; 'most of the time we are obviously meant to be paying attention to the various and vile songs about all those lovely, soft, sticky, gooey, salt-smelling, strange-tasting plasms and secretions that the human body is just bursting with'.[11] Funny what crosses your mind when you listen to music.

Noe Goldwasser, writing in *Crawdaddy*, thought that 'Dinah-Moe Humm' was 'a seemingly misogynist work which, upon deeper inspection is just a funny, horny song . . . It is above (or below) feminist reproach; its comic tensions embody the textural psychosis of the supermusical vision, as it were.' Were it? Goldwasser saw the album as the beginning of a new chapter in Frank's career: 'It's as if he's finished having to proselytise and everybody's already been converted so there's nothing left to do but gird the loins, enter the breach and massage the musical clit.'[12]

Which Frank and the band proceeded to do. After ten American dates during May 1973, the Mothers spent three weeks in Australia, appearing in Brisbane on June 21 and then Sydney, Melbourne and Adelaide, before returning to Sydney for two more days at the Hordern Pavilion. Frank addressed a press conference in Melbourne, at which he floated the idea of a live album from their Australian gigs. It never happened but it could have, for he included a Sydney performance of 'Farther O'Blivion' on *YCDTOSA 6*.

For some time, he'd been recording most of the various bands' gigs. 'Starting in 1969,' he told Don Menn, 'Dick Kunc . . . built this little James Bond suitcase recording apparatus. He took a couple of Shure mixers, and packed it all in there, and we had a Uher (tape recorder). He accompanied us on part of the US tour that year, and would sit in the corner of the room with earphones on and try to do a mix on whatever we were doing. When we did the Pauley Pavilion recording (*Just Another Band From L.A.*), I had just bought this Scully four-track, and that was the first of the four-track recordings that we did. We recorded four-track for, I guess, ten years, nine years.'[13]

The band bid goodbye to Sal Marquez on its return to America. 'I felt bad about leaving the group,' he said later, 'but we were broke. One day I called Frank and tried to get him to give us a per diem. And he got all upset, claiming he never paid his groups that way. "Not even $15?" And he said, "No, man, I've never done it and I'm not going to start. You can hand in your music too." And that was it. I was shocked. I thought he liked me.'[14]

RUTHIE RUTHIE

By the time the Mothers set off to Europe in the middle of August 1973, their evident success on stage and with their audiences had sent Frank's creative muse into overdrive. As the tour progressed and the musicians developed an intuitive empathy, new material was continually added to the set. The individual dexterity of the Underwoods and George Duke made the complexities of 'Dupree's Paradise', 'Echidna's Arf (Of You)' and 'RDNZL' palatable to untrained ears more likely to respond to the 'Father O'Blivion' song cycle. For the first time, Frank had musicians around him who could realise both the humour and the technical brilliance of his writing. In particular, Ruth Underwood's phenomenal skill with vibes, marimba and other percussion brought a pointillistic exactitude to the jagged terrain of Frank's melodies.

'I was ready to dedicate myself completely to Frank's music,' she said later in tribute. 'He really knew what buttons to push, emotionally and musically. He was a remarkable referee. He knew how to synthesise people's personalities and talents. That's a very rare gift. He wasn't just a conductor standing there waving his arms; he was playing us as people! I became a perfectionist, I suppose because I had to be.'[15]

In a two-part interview that began in the August 25 *NME*, Frank was guardedly pleased with the band's success. 'Our audiences are generally larger than they've ever been before, but there's no guarantee that the understanding has increased proportionately.' Irrespective of their audiences' comprehension, he was well content with his musicians. 'You ought to hear the stuff we're playing now. It's hot sheeit ! Lemme tell ya - this band is playing the hardest repertoire you ever heard. They got some unbelievable things to do - from memory. With the Wazoo they were all playing off sheet music.'

And there was choreography 'of the most absurd variety'. 'We're playing songs like the 'Eric Dolphy Memorial Barbecue' now and it has choreography. We have a new song called 'Don't You Ever Wash That Thing?' which has some very mysterious choreography. You'll have to imagine . . . all the sheer hurt and anguish that went into 'Penguin In Bondage'. There is degradation; there's also perversion and hotness.'[16] Well, it made good copy; but all it proved was that Frank was 'a booga of a good talker', which was the gnomic headline of a dwarfish interview in the same week's *Record Mirror*.

The European tour was extensive; after dates in Scandinavia, the Mothers played four gigs in Italy and four more in Germany, with Zurich in between. Brussels, Amsterdam and Paris followed before they arrived at Liverpool on Tuesday, September 11. The city's Stadium was the venue for the world premiere of 'T'Mershi Duween', the latest fiendishly complicated module, written the week before in Frankfurt. Two days later, they played Birmingham and the next day, Wembley's Empire Pool.

Frank was in typical sardonic mood. The *NME* 's Charles Shaar Murray was present: 'He prefaced the performance with a short rap to the effect that "in accordance with our long established policy that 'the hits just keep on comin' atcha', we will be presenting material that you have never heard before [loud applause]. However, in the latter half of the programme we will be referring back to the first half. In fact, we'll leitmotif our fuckin' brains out up here" . . . One member of the audience compared the show to being "bludgeoned into catatonia", while another just thought it was "horrible". Me, I dug about half of it.'[17]

The music papers didn't mention the other member of the Mothers' entourage. 'He is Frank's bodyguard,' The *Sun* explained, 'a rugged, former Los Angeles policeman who will stick close to Frank on and off the stage. Frank is taking no more chances. He said: "Sure, that attack still bothers me. A thing like that makes you realise just how careful you have to be in this business. You get a lot of very strange people at any rock concert. And the drugs people use at the moment increase the risk of a crazy, violent attack."'[18]

The Mothers returned to America for a busy autumn schedule that began with Halloween concerts in Chicago. Most of November was spent in New York state, Canada and New England. When the band played two days at Toronto's Massey Hall, Frank was interviewed in bullish mood by Jim Smith for *NME*. 'Nobody has combined music and theatrics the way I have. I'm looking for scope in music. My problem is economics.

'A lot of people think I'm a millionaire, and I'd just like to say I'm not, nor is there any chance in the near future of me becoming a millionaire. The reason is that the largest percentage of my money has gone back into equipment. Then you have to hire the technical people to move it, plug it in, and repair it. For every person onstage, there's another person off-stage helping to make it happen.'

It was always difficult, he said, to find musicians with the right ability and character. 'There are plenty of people interested in playing with the group and there are good musicians among them. But the ones who are technically skilled don't have a sense of humour. And the ones who have a sense of humour usually don't have the mechanical chops. Whether it's easy or hard to play with me depends on the character of the person involved. Some people like a challenge and other people like it soft. For the second group, it can be a traumatic experience playing with me.'[19]

On their return to L.A., the band took up a week-long residence starting Friday, December 7 at The Roxy, the latest club on the Strip, located alongside The Rainbow Room. Half of the shows were recorded, at least one on video, for future release. The band was augmented on various nights; Jeff Simmons sang and played rhythm guitar, Don Preston drove a synthesiser and Walt Fowler came in on trumpet. Frank reverted to two drummers and brought in Chester Thompson on the second drumkit.

The most notable addition was the extrovert Napoleon Murphy Brock on tenor sax, flute and vocals. On his way back from Australia, Frank had found Brock leading a Top 40 soul band in a Hawaiian nightclub. Frank watched a set and then asked him to join the Mothers for the August 1973 European tour. Brock turned him down because his group was booked into the club for the next seven weeks, but told him to call after he got back. Which Frank duly did.

Brock's arrival brought important changes to the context of the group. He had a distinctive and flexible voice and struck up an immediate and overtly warm rapport with George Duke, sharing the broad and quick sense of humour that Frank had drawn out of the keyboard player. Their on-stage badinage, which both celebrated and satirised black consciousness, contrasted with Frank's own studied bizarre humour and there were moments when one sensed that he was happy and relieved to become a sideman in his own group. But these moments were no more than a fleeting relaxation of the rigid control which was the keynote of a Mothers gig.

Even though the evenings were recorded on Wally Heider's 16-track remote equipment, the number of musicians crowded onto the Roxy's stage made separation something of a problem. The final mixes on *Roxy & Elsewhere* lack the clarity that Frank would later achieve with digital equipment. Each side of the double album featured a 'Preamble' in which the origin of the following song was explained. Frank wouldn't always provide this service, thinking perhaps like Gustav Mahler that audiences shouldn't always have a safety net.

As it was, Frank's introduction to 'Penguin In Bondage' was vague and cryptic: 'This song suggests to the suggestible listener that the ordinary procedure that I am circumlocuting at the present time in order to get this text on television is that if you want to do something other than what you thought you were gonna do when you first took your clothes off – and you just happen to have some DEVICES! around, then it's not only OK to get into the Paraphernalia of it all but hey –.' The sexual connotations were deliberately mystifying; even the stage antics described in the notes of 1992's *Playground Psychotics* failed to equate with the events 'way over on the wet side of the bed' with which the song concerned itself.

Luckily, the introductions to 'Village Of The Sun', 'Cheepnis' and 'Be-Bop Tango (Of The Old Jazzmen's Church)' were confined to more literal terms. The latter's 'Preamble' ended with Frank's instruction: 'Not too fast, now, 'cos I want to get the right notes on the tape. This has to be the one . . . and this is a hard one to play.' But it was no harder than 'Echidna's Arf', a fiendishly tortuous theme that George Duke would record even faster the following year for his solo album, *The Aura Will Prevail*. 'Don't You Ever Wash That Thing' was similarly complex, with the added impediment of a series of staccato interjections between solos by trombone, electric piano, both drumkits and guitar before a marimba cadenza from Ruth Underwood.

One song performed during these gigs and often during this period was 'Dickie's Such An Asshole', Frank's acerbic commentary on the events that would eventually bring down Richard Nixon, the only American President forced to resign while still in office. It had received its 'world premiere' on October 26, 1973 at the Armadillo World Headquarters in Austin, Texas. The Nixon administration had been collapsing ever since the June 17 break-in at the Watergate offices of the Democratic National Committee. The subsequent trial had revealed a world of dirty tricks, slush funds, wiretapping and the clandestine recording of Nixon's Oval Room conversations. Wriggle as he might, Nixon could not avoid public revulsion at the machinations of his advisors, performed under his instruction, or the lengths to which he was prepared to go in order to conceal them.

Even so, the apparent ultimate purpose of the break-in didn't come to light until much later. 'Cointelpro was what they were trying to hide with Watergate,' Frank told Don Menn. 'It wasn't just breaking into the Democratic headquarters. What they're trying to cover up is the fact that Nixon had decided to create a secret police. There was no legal authority to spy on US citizens. He felt he had enemies everywhere, so he created a programme called Cointelpro. It was all the domestic spying on political groups, people he perceived as enemies. And since it couldn't exist under law, it had to be financed by a slush fund.'[20]

'The money to finance the dirty tricks and the spying on US citizens was coming from tangential sources,' Frank told me. 'From the minute that there was such a thing as a youth culture in the United States, when long hair first started appearing in Los Angeles, the people who were doing the spying were part of a special LAPD secret police unit. And then Cointelpro would be the national version of that. When Cointelpro was revealed, that it existed, everybody said, "Oh, we won't do it again." *Nobody proved it was ever dismantled.*

'All you gotta do is look at the way people were treated during the Reagan administration who supported Nicaragua, who didn't like the idea of the Contras going in there and having a private war. The same kind of break-ins occurred in their homes and their offices. And whether it was being done by the FBI, an offshoot of the FBI, the Cointelpro leftovers or something, there is a secret police in the United States that's got a name someplace and somebody tells them what to do. And they still work and they're still out there and they have better equipment than the KGB ever did.'

The shifty-eyed 'asshole' was still almost nine months from his resignation when this version of the song, released on *YCDTOSA 3*, was taped. Frank hadn't been this blunt for some time, first calling him 'a cocksucker by proxy' and noting 'the man in the White House has got a conscience black as sin'. It's little wonder that no performance of the song was made available until 1988's *Broadway The Hard Way*, but the Roxy recording benefits from its currency with unfolding events. Only a few days before, Nixon had announced on national television, 'I am not a crook' and Frank intoned those words during 'Son Of Orange County', one track that did get released.

There were favourable reviews of the gigs in the *Los Angeles Times*, the *Los Angeles Herald-Examiner* and even *Variety*. Ruth Underwood came in for particular praise; the Times thought her 'deft', but Robert A. Kemnitz in the *Herald-Examiner* wrote that she 'kept up with the band's frenetic pace without missing a single swat of the gong, and she was incredible'[21]. *Variety* was unequivocal: 'Highlight of the evening was the Ruth Underwood, Frank Zappa duo on vibes with double drum sets beating perfect rhythms while the other musicians supported. Underwood's striking performance was phenomenal as she rushed about the percussion section playing the various instruments.'[22]

EXCENTRIFUGAL FORZ

Recording sessions during the first two months of 1974 put the finishing touches to Frank's next solo album, *Apostrophe (')*, and material that appeared on *Bongo Fury* the following year. *Apostrophe (')* combined recent recordings with the current Mothers and others that went back to the *Hot Rats* sessions, involving past collaborators such as drummers John Guerin and Aynsley Dunbar, violinists Sugarcane Harris and Jean Luc Ponty and a final contribution from Ray Collins. The title track was a studio jam recorded the previous September in New York's Electric Lady studios between Frank, Jack Bruce and Jim Gordon, with Tony Duran on rhythm guitar.

'I found it very difficult to play with him,' Frank said in 1977, 'he's too busy. He doesn't really want to play the bass in terms of root functions; I think he has other things on his mind. But that's the way jam sessions go.'[23] As it went, it was atypical of the rest of the album, which combined humour and instrumental dexterity in equal measure. If there were serious subtexts, such as seal culling, mysticism ('Cosmik Debris') and black protest ('Uncle Remus'), they were viewed through the distorting prism of Frank's laconic wit. The marriage was particularly evident in the sequence of 'Don't Eat The Yellow Snow', 'Nanook Rubs It', 'St. Alfonso's Pancake Breakfast' and 'Father O'Blivion', which quickly vaulted into the surreal to the well-nigh impossible accompaniment of Ruth Underwood's dazzling mallets.

The lyrics of 'Excentrifugal Forz' were obscure beyond analysis but the title's image could have represented Frank himself, drawing influences and events into his creative vortex to emit them recast as original compositions.

Well, maybe. A case in point was 'Uncle Remus', which George Duke helped to compose and would also include, in a more gospel-based arrangement, on *The Aura Will Prevail*. The lyrics dealt with black fashion and styling ('can't wait 'til my 'fro is full-grown') before ending with the random destruction of jockey statues on rich peoples' lawns at the crack of dawn - your average association of ideas.

'Stink-Foot' made an equally bizarre shift, inspired by a Mennen foot spray commercial, from the subject of smelly feet to thoughts on conceptual continuity addressed to its master by a poodle puppy. In this case, appropriately enough, the crux of the biscuit was the apostrophe. Was this the puppy (first identified as Frenchie in 'Dirty Love') that grew into the giant Frunobulax who menaces the Power Plant in 'Cheepnis'? And to which breed did 'Evelyn, A Modified Dog' belong? Was there any significance to the fact that a poodle-faker was defined as someone who cultivated female society? The legend would grow and books would be written to plumb the mystery.

Apostrophe (') was released on April 22, 1974, and was an instant success. It was no doubt helped by the 'Tenth Anniversary' tour that began two days later and continued until mid-August. In that time, the album had gone gold and climbed the album charts, peaking after 11 weeks at number 10 in the week ending June 29. Belatedly realising the need to climb on the bandwagon, *Rolling Stone* reviewed it seven weeks after its release and found it 'Truly a mother of an album'.[24]

In a dramatically positive move, Warner Brothers sanctioned some television advertising; Frank and Cal Schenkel put together a 30-second commercial which they placed during the transmission of monster movies, figuring that their target audience would be watching. Frank was so pleased with the outcome that he ordered a celebration, described in *Rolling Stone*: 'Frank Zappa, happy that his *Apostrophe (')* album is in the Top Ten, hired a 50-piece marching band to thank Warner Brothers Records. They tootled past headquarters led by a sign-bearer with the message: "Anyone who can get Frank Zappa even to the bottom of the Top Ten is OK in my booklet".'[25]

Frank thought he knew why the album had been a success. 'That was an accident,' he told William Ruhlmann, 'because a radio station in Pittsburgh took 'Don't Eat The Yellow Snow', cut it down . . . to three minutes and put it on the station. The guy who did it heard the song, perceived it as a modern-day novelty record and put it on right alongside of 'Teeny Weeny Bikini' and it became a hit. But it was nothing that Warner Brothers ever foresaw, it was nothing that I could have foreseen as a guy at DiscReet Records, a subsidiary of a subsidiary of a subsidiary. Who knew? The credit goes to the DJ.'[26]

Reception in England was mixed. *Melody Maker* thought it showed 'a touch of genius' but *NME* had reviewed an advance copy in their April 6 issue, under the headline, 'The unsightly debris of Francis Vincent Zappa'. Ian MacDonald had a 'Z' in his bonnet; the last 'remotely listenable' album had been Fillmore East and subsequent releases were 'more or less grotesquely indulgent on the musical level and lyrically . . . despicably irresponsible'. This time, Frank had 'retreated into his studio with a bunch of faceless yes-men virtuosi and squandered two years of his life producing some of the most carefully-constructed redundant dreck ever to find its way into the record-racks of the Western world'. He saved his broadside for a direct remark: 'With *Apostrophe (')*, you've blotted your escrutcheon but *permanently*.'[27] Pity about the spelling.

MOTHERLY LOVE

There was much to celebrate in the summer of 1974. The seventh gig of the Anniversary tour was at Chicago's Auditorium Theater on May 11. At midnight, Frank announced to the sell-out crowd that it was now Mother's Day, the exact anniversary of the naming of the Mothers of Invention, and talked about the early days of the band. Then, with typical sentiment, he said, 'You're gonna hear *Freak Out!* 'til it's coming out of your ass', and led the present Mothers through a forty-minute medley of songs from his first album. The resulting bootleg of the event, *Unmitigated Audacity*, was later included in *Beat The Boots 1*. The most notable element in the proceedings was Frank's impromptu first verse of 'More Trouble Every Day' as feedback interrupted the opening words, which he instantly changed to, 'Well, I'm about to get sick of listening to this monitor system.'

'What I'm going to do is play twenty of those things in a row,' he told Barbara Charone before the gig, 'and I think the audience will love it. Those songs are all so easy compared to what we've been doing recently. In rehearsal we learned two and three of them in a day - which is sickening, because when we first put out *Freak Out!* it took weeks just to get one little song right. Today (it) sounds like a bunch of demos to me.' Charone's piece included a timely quote from the soon-to-be-ex-President: 'There is no undertaking more challenging, no responsibility more awesome than being a Mother.'[28]

Four days later, a new Zappa entered the world. Frank and Gail's second son was named Ahmet Rodan. His first name was that of an imaginary person 'we always had hanging around back when we had no one on our payroll,' Gail told Victoria Balfour. 'We'd snap our fingers and say, "Ahmet? Dishes. Coffee, please".'[29] He was also named after a giant pterodactyl that would have ravaged the world if the Japanese film director Ishiro Honda hadn't destroyed it in 1957. The proud parents could have carried on using names from the same source, Majin, Mothra, Gamera, Barugon and Ghidorah among them, but fortunately their next child was a daughter.

Frank stayed home during June, overdubbing and mixing *Roxy & Elsewhere*

(elsewhere being the May 8 gig at Edinboro, Pennsylvania and the Chicago Mother's Day bash), appreciating his new son and editing a film by Seattle animator, Bruce Bickford. Barry Hansen interviewed him during the process: 'As I was about to compliment Zappa on composing music that so perfectly fit the Hadesian mood of the film, he told me that the music had not been written for the film at all, but had been extracted from live recordings of Mothers concerts which took place before Frank had ever seen the movie.

'I got the work print,' Frank explained, 'and edited that without sound. Then, just last night . . . I put the (Mothers) tracks on, and it worked. It's so unbelievable . . . when you think what it would take to actually score a film like that, and last night I put on this music, which was something constructed for completely different purposes, spontaneously at another location and another time, and I put them together and they worked perfectly.'[30]

This was yet another opportunity for 'conceptual continuity' to be explained. Hansen thought that the chance matching of Mothers music, deliberately chosen, to Bickford's film was a rather more subtle manifestation of a haphazard phenomenon, and perhaps the product of Frank's single-minded dedication. 'Zappa is so absorbed in his work that he appears to need no other pleasures.

'When I'm home, I have a work schedule that goes like this. If I'm not rehearsing, I spend about 16, 18 hours a day down here (in the workroom) writing music, typing, working on film . . . and if I'm not here, I usually do about 10, 14 hours in the studio, seven days a week, until rehearsal schedule starts. The only thing I would see as a worthwhile interruption would be 100% concentration on a feature film.'"[31]

Hansen commented that few people were as thoroughly committed to their work, nor enjoyed it as much. In hindsight, Frank's reply supplied food for thought: 'What else you gonna do, work in a gas station?'[32] Instead, he went back on the road with a stripped-down sextet of himself, Brock, Duke, Underwood, Fowler and Thompson for July gigs in Arkansas, Florida, Arizona and California. The band spent two days in Culver City Studios, recording a television special. The following day, August 8, they were back in Hollywood for a gig at the Shrine Auditorium. There was more than just an anniversary to celebrate that night; Richard Nixon had resigned earlier in the day. His step, as he boarded his Presidential helicopter for the last time, was firmer than his successor Gerald Ford, whose ability to take prat-falls could have earned him a lifetime achievement award.

During the rest of the month there were rehearsals for the next European tour by a new, streamlined Mothers. The intensity of their workload reflected the intensity of the tour itself, 23 dates in 29 days, travelling through Italy, Sicily, Austria, Germany, Scandinavia, Holland, France, Belgium, Switzerland and Spain. But not to England.

An angry Frank held a press conference in the Sandringham Suite of Kensington's Royal Garden Hotel on September 5, the day before the tour's opening gig in Rome. 'Ordinarily, we come to England to play concerts, to promote an album,' he said. 'This time I have the unfortunate duty to announce that we can't play in this country. The reason for this is something that dates back to the case we have against the Albert Hall.'³³ The August 26 *Daily Telegraph* had announced that Bizarre Productions had taken out a High Court action over the concert ban three years earlier and were claiming damages for conspiracy against Marion Herrod, the lettings manager, and Frank Munday, the general manager, even though he'd died the previous February. There was also an action against the Rainbow, as well.

Fred Bannister, the promoter of the proposed UK tour which would have covered September 21-26, had met with 'unusual discrimination' in his dealings with controllers of the London halls. 'Certain halls were available,' Bannister explained, 'but they would not rent to me because of the Albert Hall thing. Two actually said that. We talked about getting the Drury Lane Theatre and the Palladium with a Mr Verner (of Moss Empires), and he told us that the halls were free but that he wouldn't be happy to let us use either of them in the light of the Albert Hall lawsuit. We then spoke to a Mr Fishman, on behalf of the New Victoria Theatre, the Odeon Hammersmith and the Kilburn State Theatre (all controlled by the Rank Organisation), who said much the same thing but in a more roundabout way.'

'We had to give a big concert in London to make our performances in the provinces financially viable,' Frank said. Herb Cohen reckoned that the cost of keeping the 21-piece entourage on the road for a day, including seven and a half tons of hired ELP pa (costing around £18,000 for the European tour), exceeded the estimated gross from the proposed Birmingham concert. A measure of Frank's desperation was evident in the dramatic offer he made at the end of the press conference. 'I would like to announce that I will pay for Ms Herrod to fly anywhere in Europe for any length of time to attend any of the concerts . . . I will even take her on the whole tour, *myself, personally*, just to show what a nice clean wholesome group we are – and I guarantee she'll have the best time of her life . . . '³⁴ Ms Herrod was not available for comment. A less convinced conspiracy-theorist than Frank would have found it hard not to feel victimised.

These were still the days when the British bulldog occasionally emitted a rheumy gruff at the influx of all things American, and it was Frank's turn in the barrel. Any doubt was dispelled when John Blake wrote his pop piece for the *Evening News*, after he'd travelled to Paris on September 27 to see the show and interview the aggrieved party. Under the headline, 'Zappa – is it goodbye for ever?', he described how Frank 'fixed me with a baleful stare and spelt out the news that will bring gloom to his fans – and cheer to everyone else. "It is possible I may never perform in London again," he said.'[35]

Smug antipathy suffused Blake's piece. 'I have two or three bad memories of London,' Frank told him. 'We have played there about six times and I haven't enjoyed myself most of the time. And I don't like the attitude London's pop Press have. The journalists are virtually unconcerned with what I am doing musically.' Blake thought his music 'a pain in the ear', having found the Grand Wazoo Oval concert 'spectacularly dreary'. His final thrust quoted an ex-Mother: 'It's so easy to convince yourself that he is the genius he thinks he is. But really he just bewilders the audience so much that some of them walk away believing that anyone that bad and that popular must be great beyond their comprehension.' The quote went unattributed, of course.

In fact, the music press gave ample space to this same Paris gig, at the Palais de Sport, and the 30,000 party (paid for by Warner Brothers) afterwards at the Alcazar nightclub. It was, in Charles Shaar Murray's words, 'a kind of acrobatic-musical-sexual-satirical cabaret with a cast of thousands'[36]. *Melody Maker*'s Allan Jones was also present: 'The climax is a real bazooka. Cecil B. De Mille meets Fellini in a head-on crash at a hundred miles an hour, with choreography by Busby Berkeley, out of his brain on bad acid.'[37]

The evening started badly when the gear, delayed by customs and a ferry, failed to arrive in time for the afternoon sound check. The previous gig, in Gothenburg on September 25, had been the second of two that replaced the British dates. And the first? What sort of conceptual continuity was it that caused Frank to choose the almost-complete September 22 Helsinki gig as Volume Two in the *You Can't Do That On Stage Anymore* series? It can only have been the long arm of coincidence that a concert that wouldn't have taken place without the cancelled British gigs was chosen.

Whatever the circumstances, the concert was very good indeed, in spite of Napoleon Murphy Brock having pneumonia and Coy Featherstone, the band's lighting director, being maced in the face by a guard at the Hotel Hesperia the night before. In his booklet notes, Frank pointed out, 'The repertoire is basically the same as the *Roxy* album, however, the ultra-fast tempos on the more difficult tunes demonstrates what happens when a band has played the material for a year, and is so comfortable with it they could probably perform it blindfolded.'

The other manifest quality is the good humour with which the music is performed, even when 'Montana' has to be begun three times before proceeding. As George Duke told *Keyboard*: 'If you didn't get it, Frank would know it. He would look around at you and make you do it again. On stage! He would make us go over one lick until there was no way we could forget it. That was some of the most difficult music I've ever played, partly because he composed a lot of it from the guitar. Frank's music was like organised chaos. That's exactly what it was.'[38] One listen to 'RDNZL' (during which

Frank takes a solo that includes part of the melody of 'Conehead'), 'Echidna's Arf', 'Approximate' (in its three guises) and 'T'Mershi Duween' bears out the truth of Duke's remark.

He had another reason for the release: 'One of the things that was good about that show was that there was a lot of improvised, funny talking and witty stuff in there. So it's got part of the attitude of the band and I think it's a good record. It's got some good spirit in it.'[39]

CHAPTER TWELVE
ONE SIZE FITS ALL

There was more good spirit on display when the Mothers played at New York's Felt Forum on Halloween Night, establishing a precedent for subsequent tours. The stage was littered with assorted theatrical props; a female dummy wearing a 'Don't Eat The Yellow Snow' T-shirt; a dangling skeleton; a rubber chicken suspended from an iron beam; and a lifebuoy liberated from a production of *HMS Pinafore* draped over a microphone. There was much for the audience to enjoy – but not for a reviewer anticipating the momentous and encountering the momentary.

Michael Watts typified the sense of betrayal felt by all his ilk who'd espoused Frank's music when it flattered their sense of their own radicalism. But now Frank was reneging on the contract they'd drawn up by apparently moving in a direction that trivialised their pretensions. Moreover, the spectacle of musicians who could not only play seriously difficult music but had fun doing it was confusing for journalists accustomed to trenchant postures and loaded statements. One critic thought *Roxy & Elsewhere* 'the lowest point in Zappa's career', asserting that too many artists were 'simply farting around instead of getting down and producing work of real importance or merit; to see Frank Zappa joining the legions of rock and roll suicides and producing dull, trivial work is nothing less than offensive'.[1]

Watts' review of the Halloween show, headlined 'Zany Zappa runs out of ideas . . .', acknowledged 'this is not Serious, there is Fun and much In-Joking up there onstage'. But while he joins in the audience's laughter, he hears 'alarm bells' as he watches Ruth Underwood 'laughing and waving her arms as if she's partaken of some vile, foamy liquid', aided and abetted by Napoleon Murphy Brock who's 'quite, quite daft'. He's left wondering 'what happened to the Great Satirist when I see the Zee now inflating into tomes one-liners about dental floss and other inconsequential paraphernalia'.[2]

Much of the current repertoire was recorded in KCET-TV studios in early December 1974, including an extended version of the 'Room Service' routine, during which Frank referred to 'that wretched state of Maryland', from where he, Chester Thompson, Napoleon Murphy Brock and their roadie and dog enthusiast, Marty Perellis, all came. The programme, A Token

Of His Extreme, was later used in *The Dub Room Special*, Frank's video combining live music from 1974 and 1981 with the convoluted clay animation of Bruce Bickford. The basic tracks of two 1974 titles, 'Inca Roads' and 'Florentine Pogen', were used in the next Mothers album, *One Size Fits All*. Frank spliced an edited version of his 'Inca Roads' guitar solo from the recent Helsinki concert into the finished master.

Further recording for the album took place during December at Jim Guercio's Caribou studio in Colorado, where basic tracks for songs from *Hunchentoot* were also laid down. Sessions also took place at the LA Record Plant and Paramount studios, although some material like 'The Adventures of Greggery Peccary', 'Revised Music For Guitar And Low-Budget Orchestra' and 'RDNZL' would not be released until 1978, and then in less than ideal circumstances. Another song, 'A Little Green Rosetta', didn't appear until a year after that on *Joe's Garage Acts 2 & 3*. Demo'ed in Studio D at the Record Plant, it was 'just George Duke playing a tack piano and me singing on top of it,' according to Frank. 'It was just a little stupid song.'[3]

The same combination also recorded 'Evelyn, A Modified Dog', the latest instance of canine conceptual continuity. 'It recurs on each record,' Frank said. 'It's an abstract concept, much in the way that Rembrandt added brown to all his colours. That's the level.'[4] Evelyn, her modifications unspecified, is the dog sitting in Apostolic Studios during the *Lumpy Gravy* sessions, bewildered by sounds emanating from the covered piano as strings resonate to the conversations taking place within.

Mark Volman's alter ego, the maroon sofa, adorned the cover of *One Size Fits All* along with other abstruse cosmology; more comfortable than a 2001 monolith, it sped through the heavens with a formica-topped aluminium table and chair as satellites. Its musical manifestation made two appearances on the album, one vocal, one instrumental, George Duke's moog bass adding a touch of funk to the original landler rhythm. 'San Ber'Dino', containing a verse that referred to Frank's brief incarceration in the city jail, featured harmonica by Don Vliet as 'Bloodshot Rollin' Red' and the flambe vocals of Frank's first guitar hero, Johnny 'Guitar' Watson. The latter also sang on 'Andy', which was alleged to be a veiled reference to one of Beefheart's erstwhile managers.

On both 'San Ber'Dino' and 'Can't Afford No Shoes', Frank played a fretless guitar. 'At one time Acoustic . . . made a prototype and tried to interest people in it,' he told Steve Rosen, 'but nobody wanted it. So the prototype ended up at Guitar Center. I walked in there one day and asked them if they had anything new, and they said, "Have we got one for you!" It's different than a regular guitar; you don't push the strings to bend then, you move them back and forth like violin-type vibrato, which is a funny movement to get used to.'[5]

Work on *One Size* and the television special carried on in the first months of 1975. At one point, Tom Fowler broke his left hand and James 'Bird Legs' Youmans came in to play bass. Tour dates had been scheduled for this period but they were cancelled, in order for the work to continue. Time was also needed for Frank and Herb Cohen to prepare for their High Court case against the Albert Hall management, which was due to be heard in London during the second week of April.

During the lull in group activity, George Duke spent time during January making *The Aura Will Prevail*, his fourth solo album for MPS, at Paramount Studios with regular Zappa engineer Kerry McNabb driving the desk. He was accompanied by Alphonso Johnson on bass and Leon 'Ndugu' Chancler on drums. Both were members of Weather Report, the fusion band formed in 1970 by Miles Davis alumni, Joe Zawinul and Wayne Shorter. In the ensuing weeks, Chancler would leave and be replaced by Chester Thompson. His tenure, including the sessions for *Black Market*, one of Weather Report's more successful albums, would be brief.

The drummer's departure brought to an end one of the most highly regarded incarnations of the Mothers. By the end of the year, only Napoleon Murphy Brock would remain in the band, which would be the last to tour as the Mothers. Most of the band had been with Frank for two years, during which shrinking numbers placed increasingly heavy workloads on the eventual sextet. 'Frank was the hardest worker I've ever played with, hands-down,' said George Duke. 'I never saw anyone work harder than he did. From the time he got up to the time he went to bed, he was thinking music.'[6]

'I've always thought the work ethic was one great thing about him,' added Bruce Fowler. 'He was completely tireless. In a sense, he never stopped. Also, he was really open-minded. He wanted to learn.'[7] 'It was the greatest experience of my life and the most difficult experience of my life,' Ruth Underwood averred. 'He just devoured music; that was all he thought about. We listened to his music on the bus; we rehearsed it at sound checks; we played it that night; we analysed it the next day. Everything was music.'[8]

Well, not quite everything. There was a court case looming. But in the meantime, Frank had to put a band together for two months of gigs booked through April and May. First, there had to be auditions for a new drummer. Having listened to *Roxy & Elsewhere* and *Apostrophe (')* for 48 hours, Terry Bozzio flew down from San Francisco and found himself in a rehearsal room with a crowd of hopefuls, playing by turns on two drumkits set up for the occasion. The failure rate was so high that he considered applying for the Weather Report job until he found out that Chester Thompson's departure to join them had brought about this audition.

'The one thing I'd noticed was that a lot of the drummers were sort of flaunting their chops,' he told Andy Greenaway. 'So I did the best I could: sight-reading a very difficult piece, memorising a very difficult piece, jamming in a very odd time signature - like 19/16 - and then playing a blues shuffle. At the end of that, Frank said, "You sound great; I'd like to hear you again after I hear the rest of the guys". I turned to his road manager, his road manager turned to the 20 or so guys that were hanging around and they're all shaking their heads, and the road manager turned around and said, "That's it, nobody else wants to play after Terry". So Frank turned to me and said, "Looks like you've got the gig if you want it".[9]

Napoleon Murphy Brock, George Duke and Tom Fowler retained their places in the band and Bruce Fowler returned on trombone. Denny Walley, an ex-member of Geronimo Black, the band that Jimmy Carl Black and Bunk Gardner had formed after the original Mothers had disbanded, came in on slide guitar and vocals. But the most noteworthy addition to the band was Don Vliet, his own career on temporary hold, stalled in a legal log-jam.

'Don had the ability and the inclination to sign any piece of contractual paper shoved under his nose at any time,' Frank explained, 'without comprehending what these papers said and how they interacted with each other. And so his career fell on evil days, because he had signed papers with companies all over the place that all had conflicting claims on his services. He was in a position where he couldn't tour and he couldn't record. It was at that time that I put him in the band to do the Bongo Fury tour. That was the only way he could make some money because he was just legally tied up all over the place.'[10]

'He called me up and asked for help,' Frank told *NME*. 'I told him that the Mothers were holding auditions on Tuesday and Thursday (just before their Halloween show), and that he should come along.'[11] 'He flunked,' he told Steve Weitzman. 'See, he had a problem with rhythm, and we were very rhythm oriented. Things have to happen on the beat. I had him come up on the bandstand at our rehearsal hall and try to sing 'Willie The Pimp' and he couldn't get through it. I figured if he couldn't get through that, I didn't stand much of a chance in teaching him the other stuff.'[12]

Things went better at the Spring 1975 rehearsals. 'Although he still has trouble remembering words and making things happen on the beat, he's better,' Frank said. 'Just before the tour, I tried him again and he squeaked by.'[13] He denied that there was animosity between them, even though the Captain had hardly wasted an opportunity to bad-mouth him over the last few years. 'Any idea of a feud between us is quite pointless.' But any affection he had for their almost 20-year friendship didn't prevent Frank from a stark assessment of Vliet's unique talents.

Speaking after the tour's first gig at Bridges Auditorium at Pomona College in Claremont on April 11, he said, 'The way he relates to language is unique, the way in which he brings my text to life. Of course, he has problems. His memory causes him trouble. He won't be separated from his sheets of paper that have his words written on. He clings to them for dear life. He also has a literacy problem. He can hardly read. He also has trouble staying on a beat. Captain Beefheart has no natural rhythm. He does have this thing inside him. It's dynamic and he wants to express it. In a voice like Howlin' Wolf.'[14]

SEXUAL HARASSMENT IN THE WORKPLACE

Frank had flown to London after the Friday night gig, where he took up residence at the Dorchester Hotel in Park Lane. His company's law suit against the Albert Hall management began at 10.30 on the morning of Monday, April 14 in Court No. 7 of the Strand Law Courts, presided over by Mr Justice Mocatta. What should have been a straightforward action for breach of contract was guided by Michael Ogden QC, on behalf of the Albert Hall, into the lurid realms of obscenity, the threat of which was the management's sole justification for cancelling the Mothers gig.

What transpired over the next three days was pure farce, with no attempt by either side to comprehend the other. The judge was a figure out of caricature, fit to have sat bewigged beside Sir John Willes when Hogarth painted The Bench in 1758. Willes had been a notorious lecher but Mocatta had little knowledge of and no inclination for the pneumatic world of sex that Frank's music delineated. There were other gaps in his experience, too.

'Is a groupie a girl who is a member of a group?' he asked Frank. 'No,' Frank replied, 'she is a girl who likes members of a rock-and-roll band.' Did any of the court staff note the use of the word 'member'? Sometime later, Mocatta made an admission: 'When I started this case, I knew very little about pop and beat music. I knew it was to do with rhythm, banging, and an infectious atmosphere. I didn't know it was anything to do with sex or drugs.'[15]

Ogden made sure the veil dropped from his eyes. When Frank took the stand on the second day, Ogden just had to produce the toilet poster for comment and then spent hours dissecting his songs, line by line, trying to find sexual references wherever he could. Even though that wasn't difficult to do with songs like 'Half A Dozen Provocative Squats' or 'Penis Dimension', Frank complained, 'You are attempting to direct my lyrics to sexual intercourse and I don't think that is accurate or fair.' At another point he protested, 'I don't think the reproductive process is to be feared. You are making it sound frightening and horrible.'[16]

With all the moral rectitude he could summon, Ogden descended through age groups to discover where Frank considered his lyrics to be inappropriate for children. Despite the QC's condescending tone throughout much of the questioning, Frank kept his emotions under control and answered in his customarily articulate manner; but sometimes, he bit back. 'Are you sure that "newts" just means newts? That there is nothing at all suggestive about that?'

Ogden fearlessly probed. 'Anyone who is disturbed by the idea of newts in a night club is potentially dangerous,' Frank retorted.

Alan Campbell, QC for Bizarre Productions, had some of the songs from *200 Motels* played in court. The judge held his head in his hands as he listened to 'Lonesome Cowboy Burt', 'She Painted Up Her Face' and 'Daddy, Daddy, Daddy'. As 'Penis Dimension' was about to be played, he asked Campbell if he had to listen to it. When Campbell said he didn't, Mocatta intoned, 'I do not think I want to hear this objectionable song.'[17]

It was Frank's contention that he'd offered to rewrite any lyrics that were deemed objectionable or even to perform the concert without vocals. As an example, Campbell got him to rewrite 'Half A Dozen Provocative Squats', which Frank did in just five minutes. The point was made but it had no bearing on a case that was already building to a foregone conclusion. When asked by Campbell to comment on Sir Louis Gluckstein's contention that he wrote 'filth for filth's sake', Frank replied, 'My only response to that is that if I were in his position, I would not make an irrational statement like that.'[18]

After a day and a half on the witness stand, Frank flew back to America on Thursday, April 17, to prepare for the next gig on the Mothers tour in New Haven, Connecticut. Herb Cohen took the stand and reckoned that up to 80% of pop music dealt with sex in one way or another. After further questioning, he said that anybody who got erotically stimulated by Frank's music was in serious need of treatment. Alan Campbell referred the judge to a James Brown concert that took place at the Albert Hall on March 10, 1971, for which Brown was described as 'Superking of Funk'. With a straight face, he informed Mocatta, 'Funk does not mean what it meant when we were at school – a coward. It means here a mood of idle depression.'[19] The depression in the Zappa camp got more active by the minute.

The following day, Tony Palmer spoke up on Frank's behalf. The judge asked him, 'Is this stuff about sex a necessary part of pop?' 'It is an essential ingredient,' Palmer replied, 'even if you are talking about music hall or opera. The entire history of pop music is the history of the way we express that sort of thing.'[20] He told the judge that none of Frank's songs, including 'Penis Dimension' and 'Bwana Dik', could reasonably be objected to as part of a pop concert. He described Frank's lyrics as 'feeble' compared to some other 1971 hit songs but didn't feel they would have caused offence at the time.

After the weekend recess, George Melly gave Frank another glowing character reference on Monday, April 21. The judge asked him to explain about girls 'who cannot manage a silicone beef-up'. Melly replied, 'Girls who feel that their "mammary glands" or "titties" are too small can have them injected with silicone to make them larger. It is what is known as vanity surgery and is common in the USA. I personally think it is absurd.' Commenting on 'Penis Dimension', he said, 'The myth is that pop stars are supermen. To show that a pop star can worry about the size of his penis takes away some of the mythology and can only create reassurance in the minds of the pop public.' Frank was turning 'the spotlight of his intelligence' on pop's more absurd aspects, Melly thought. 'Gilbert and Sullivan satirised the conventions of light opera in the 19th century,' he added, 'at the same time contributing considerably to the tradition. This applies to Zappa, I would say.'[21]

After 15 days, Mr Justice Mocatta reserved judgement in the case, which would be delivered on June 10. Frank gave his impression of the case to Robin Denselow: 'It was like a ritual oriental drama. They'd never believe it in LA. I tried to buy a wig as a souvenir.'[22]

Mocatta's decision when it came can hardly have been unexpected, but its ramifications were. Losing the claim for £8,000 was bad enough; paying the costs of the trial, estimated at £20,000, was the real blow. As reported in *The Times*, Mocatta 'made no ruling on allegations that Mr Zappa's songs were "obscene, objectionable or indecent", but based his decision on the fact that under the contract the Albert Hall management could cancel if it thought the concert was open to "reasonable objection".'[23] *The Daily Mirror* carried a further quote: 'What might be open to reasonable objection at a performance at the Albert Hall might not be open to such objection at a performance at, say, the Round House.'[24]

'Yeah, that was pretty weird,' Frank said to me years later. 'Expensive, too. But it's not every day that a guy like me gets to go to the High Court. Justice Mocatta was a unique individual. I'm sure the Crown was proud of him for what he did. He agreed that the contract had been breached. He agreed that the show was not obscene. But basically, they were royal and I wasn't and there was no way I was gonna win a lawsuit, so go fuck yourself.'

Would an American court of the time have been any better, I asked. 'I think so. One of the reasons I say that is that there's more of a tradition for awarding damages here. For one thing, in the United States it would have been a jury trial. And for another thing, the whole rules of evidence are different in court here. And I think that it's demonstrably ludicrous that this spinster closed the door on us because of words like "brassiere". And I think that, as long as you can point out to a jury that this is a breach of contract suit, not an obscenity trial, did she or did she not breach the contract?'

I thought that the trial showed hypocrisy on a grand scale.

'On a royal scale.'

BONGO FURY

The Spring 1975 tour continued after Frank's return from England. A curiously subdued Captain Beefheart was interviewed at the Capitol Theatre in Passaic, New Jersey, explaining the reconciliation between him and Frank.

'I said some silly things because I'm a spoiled brat and I don't understand business to the degree that Frank does. I probably felt neglected. I'll admit it . . . and I told him so. I said, "I'm sorry Frank and I don't mean that for an excuse." We shook hands and that was that.'[25] It was uncharacteristic behaviour, perhaps a measure of the bad situation in which he'd found himself before the tour started.

Maybe it was also because Beefheart wasn't used to being merely a band member. He got to do 'Willie The Pimp' and some of his own compositions like 'Orange Claw Hammer', 'Sam With The Showing Scalp Flat Top' and 'Man With The Woman Head', as well as things that Frank had written for him, such as 'Debra Kadabra', 'Poofter's Froth Wyoming Plans Ahead' and 'Why Doesn't Someone Get Him A Pepsi?'. When he wasn't singing, which was quite often, he'd sit on the side of the stage, jostling his song sheets.

Frank wanted him 'to relax to the point where he can improvise words. He can do really funny stuff when he's sitting around in a room. But he hasn't really gotten comfortable enough yet.' For his part, Beefheart was having 'an extreme amount of fun on this tour. They move awfully fast. I've never travelled this fast. With the Magic Band - turtles all the way down.' And he had a compliment for his leader: 'Frank is probably the most creative person on this planet. He writes things for instruments that haven't even been invented. He's another Harry Partch - only he hasn't dried up yet. Get it?'[26]

Years later, Frank told Nigel Leigh, 'Don is absent-minded and it was a great challenge for the road manager on this tour to try and keep him integrated with the rest of what was going on. All the other musicians in the band were well seasoned road rats. They knew how to pack up and get out of a motel; they knew how to show up at the sound check on time; they knew how to live that life on the road. They knew how to do it. Don carried his possessions in a shopping bag, including his soprano sax which stuck out the shopping bag, and was forever leaving it in hallways and not knowing where he was or what he was doing.

'He would forget the lyrics to the songs, requiring that large sheets of cardboard had to be provided that were lying on the stage, so that he could follow his own lyrics. He was always complaining about the monitor system never being loud enough for him to hear his own voice.' Beefheart sang so loud that the pressure caused his ears to close down. 'So the harder he sang, the more he would have to turn up the monitor system to the point where anybody in the vicinity with their clothes (on) would catch fire.'[27]

The tour schedule was fairly intense, with only nine days off between April 18 and the final two-day stint at the Armadillo World Headquarters in Austin, Texas on May 20/1. These gigs were recorded by the LA Record Plant's remote facilities for the requisite album release, augmented by '200 Years Old', 'Cucamonga' and the introductory passages of 'Muffin Man' from the

Record Plant sessions.

There's a formlessness about *Bongo Fury* which is engendered by the clash between Frank's precision and Beefheart's spontaneous effusion. Their only real collaboration is in Frank's 'Debra Kadabra', written about his and Don's love of third-rate Mexican horror films and isolated incidents from Don's colourful past. The complicated arrangement over which Beefheart hollers is not particularly well played. The band's involvement in 'Sam With The Showing Scalp Flat Top' is minimal, confined to a recap of 'Louie Louie' behind Don's chanting of 'Bongo Fury!'; 'Man With The Woman Head' is pure Beefheart recitative.

Frank's own material divides most of its attention between sex and the coming bicentennial, which he satirised in 'the cowboy song', 'Poofter's Froth Wyoming Plans Ahead'. He prefaced its performance with a warning: 'This is a song that warns you in advance that next year everybody is going to try and sell you things that maybe you shouldn't ought to buy.' The suggestion being that the political agenda behind the patriotism was just as tawdry as the merchandise with which the country would be regaled.

Beefheart sang '200 Years Old' after Franks' opening monologue about life on the road, but any relevance to forthcoming events is obscured by the Captain's diction. Cucamonga was a fragment that referred back to Studio Z days, while 'Muffin Man' contained the first reference to the Utility Muffin Research Kitchen. Accompanied by George Duke's piano, even Frank himself couldn't recite the bizarre scenario without laughing: 'Arrogantly twisting the sterile canvas snoot of a fully-charged icing-annointment utensil, he poots forth a quarter-ounce green rosette near the summit of a dense but radiant muffin of his own design.' After that, any song would be an anticlimax and this was. Even so, it became a concert favourite because of its simple repetitive melody line and the humorous put-down in the lyrics. Or, as Frank put it, 'The bigger the venue, the more need there is for 'Muffin Man'.'[28]

'Advance Romance', with a lead vocal by Napoleon Murphy Brock, was the longest track on the album, allowing extended solos by Denny Walley, Beefheart and Frank. The coda re-introduced a character first encountered in 'San Ber'Dino'; 'Potato-headed Bobby was a friend of mine . . .'. This potato fetish would culminate in *Thing-Fish*, where 'Sister Potato-Head Bobby Brown' would become a Mammy Nun and have a 'head like a potato . . . lips like a duck.' By that time, the tuber-pated Bobby Brown had also been a gender-bending record plugger with a hit in Scandinavia.

One significant song in the repertoire didn't make it onto the album. 'Why Doesn't Someone Get Him A Pepsi?' referred to high school days: 'When I used to go over to Vliet's house . . . the only thing you would ever hear him say was, "Sue! Get me a Pepsi!". He was always yelling at his mother to get him a Pepsi, and sometimes the Pepsi wouldn't arrive, so it was like "Please!

Somebody get him a Pepsi!'"[29] Sung by Beefheart over a metronomic riff played by Denny Walley that echoed Howlin' Wolf's 'Smokestack Lightning', a radically altered arrangement of the song appeared on Frank's next album, *Zoot Allures*, as 'The Torture Never Stops'. The original version was eventually released on *YCDTOSA 4*.

When the British press announced Mr Justice Mocatta's tortuously-reasoned decision on June 11, most indicated that there would be an appeal. The August 29 edition of the *Evening Standard* noted that one had been lodged by Bizarre Productions Inc., but this was subsequently withdrawn. During the same month, Frank's company also entered a $2 million suit against MGM-Verve, through which he hoped to regain possession of his master tapes.

One Size Fits All was released on June 25, to rather indifferent reviews. In *Melody Maker*, Michael Watts referred to the Felt Forum gig, at which a 'disappointingly inconsequential' Frank had acted 'like a snotty sixth former with a large IQ'. Proving that he knew what that meant, Watts noted that Frank's lyrics had 'an irrelevancy that's dadaist and a detachment that's Bunuelian'. Consequently, the album was 'daft but interesting and recognisably Frankie the Zee'[30] but broke no new ground.

Writing a week later in *NME*, Charles Shaar Murray managed to sit on the fence while at the same time voice his disapproval. Frank had 'consciously withdrawn something of himself from his music'; his guitar playing was merely 'consistently adequate' and there were only two acceptable songs ('Can't Afford No Shoes' and 'San Ber'Dino'). But, perched on his picket, Shaar Murray conceded, 'the thing is that these days Zappa has Commercial Potential . . . and all those early albums which us Zappa connoisseurs think are so great were commercial lead balloons by comparison, so who's the bozo?'[31]

ORCHESTRAL FAVORITES

During 1975, through circumstances not entirely under Frank's control, the Mothers went through three changes of personnel in which Napoleon Murphy Brock was the only constant. Each change led to fresh arrangements and new material. While that was the sort of challenge to which Frank could readily respond, it confounded the expectations of audiences. When unspecified contractual difficulties held up the release of *One Size Fits All* until after the *Bongo Fury* tour, the Commercial Potential that Shaar Murray identified was damaged and the album did not do as well as its predecessors.

Public perception of what Frank was doing was inevitably guided by his concerts and albums. Critics like Shaar Murray plainly cherished their own idea of what his work represented; by trying to identify a logical progression in a career remoulded as much by arbitrary necessity as choice, their observations were based on false criteria. The assumption that what was presented live or on record was the sum total of Frank's creativity fell far short of the reality, which was that it was merely the visible tip of a large floating mass of themes and variations undergoing constant change.

'The putting out of material is not the desired end result,' he told Tom Mulhern. 'I really don't care whether it comes out; I like to hear it. But I do it for my own amusement. The fact that it comes out is just something that has to do with the business world, rather than the artistic world. The composing actually takes up the smallest amount of my time. I've already written so much that hasn't gone through all those in-between steps before it turns into music on tape, or music in the air, or whatever, that I could sit still for five years and have tons of stuff coming out.'[32]

For all his compulsion to write music, Frank still fought shy of being regarded as a composer. 'I don't think a composer has any function in society at all,' he said in 1986, 'especially in an industrial society, unless it is to write movie scores, advertising jingles, or stuff that is consumed by industry. If you walk down the street and ask anybody if a composer is of any use to any society, what kind of answer do you think you would get? I mean, nobody gives a shit. If you decide to become a composer, you seriously run the risk of becoming less than a human being. Who the fuck needs you?'[33]

There was little awareness of the flow of compositions and scores that Frank wrote while on the road, notwithstanding the fact that *200 Motels* was known to have been produced in this manner. The opportunity to stage an orchestral concert presented itself very rarely. The Albert Hall debacle had frustrated his attempts to do so in England, but Frank now turned his attention to a pair of orchestral concerts, conducted by Michael Zearott, to be given at Royce Hall on the UCLA campus on September 17/8. For them, he assembled a 37-piece band, including Terry Bozzio, Dave Parlato, Emil Richards and others from Grand Wazoo days, which was christened the Abnuceals Emuukha Electric Orchestra.

The repertoire combined old and new and rearranged material: 'Duke Of Prunes', 'Dog Breath' and 'Uncle Meat' mutated afresh, as did 'Strictly Genteel', 'Rollo' (part of 'Farther O'Blivion'), 'Black Napkins' (first played at LA's Shrine Auditorium in August 1974) and 'Revised Music For Guitar & Low Budget Orchestra', while 'Pedro's Dowry', 'Naval Aviation In Art?' and 'Bogus Pomp' made their debuts. Parts of these performances, all of which were recorded, were subsequently released under contentious circumstances on *Orchestral Favorites*.

Bongo Fury, its artist credit a terse 'Zappa/Beefheart Mothers', its cover a glowering Zappa and a modest Beefheart with downcast head seated at a backstage table, was released in America on October 2 1975. It ran into trouble in England because of Don Vliet's contractual problems. In 1973, he'd signed a two-album deal with Mercury, while in England the rights were acquired by Richard Branson's Virgin label. The albums, *Unconditionally*

Guaranteed and *Bluejeans And Moonbeams*, were intended to broaden Beefheart's appeal but were poorly conceived and badly received by fans with no taste for the mundane nonsense that they contained. The consequences of this catalogue of disasters produced the morass from which Frank had saved him. Now it seemed that the respite was only temporary.

Virgin Records, who regarded Beefheart as their exclusive artist, took out an injunction against Warner Brothers issuing *Bongo Fury* in England. Neither company could agree on a suitable formula for its release and the album would not be officially issued in England until 1989. Meanwhile, Virgin were content to sell it as an expensive import in their record stores. Beefheart was on tour in England in November and protested the situation from the stage of London's New Victoria Theatre: 'They have no right to stop the world from hearing Frank and I having fun. Who are they kidding with a name like that? There are no more virgins, we all know that. The dance of the seven veils is over!'[34]

FILTHY HABITS

By this time, Frank had been back out on the road for a month with his third personnel of the year and the last to bear the name Mothers Of Invention, a stripped-down combo consisting of Napoleon Murphy Brock, Andre Lewis, Roy Estrada and Terry Bozzio. When the group played a Halloween concert at New York's Felt Forum, they were augmented on saxophone and vocals by Norma Jean Bell. She'd been suggested by Ralph Armstrong, bassist with the Mahavishnu Orchestra, and Frank invited her to accompany the tour. But, as Terry Bozzio explained, 'By the time we got back to LA at the end of the tour, she had pretty much succumbed to hanging out with the wrong people and doing a lot of drugs. So Frank said, "Forget this!"'[35]

She did, however, get to go to Yugoslavia on a two-concert trip officially sanctioned by the Yugoslav Tourist Board. The gigs took place in Zagreb and Ljubljana: 'I recall Zagreb was literally the smokiest gig I've ever played,' said Terry Bozzio. 'I had never been in a hockey rink with 10,000 people filled with so much smoke in my life. It was probably terribly unhealthy. But the gig went over great.'[36] 'It's my understanding,' Frank said later, 'that Yugoslavia was the most liberal of all the East Bloc countries (at that time). But lemme tell ya, if Yugoslavia was the most liberal of the "workers" paradises' of that era, the other places must have been pure hell.'[37]

For anything other than the road rats Frank liked to employ, the next three months would have been pure hell, too. Immediately after Christmas 1975, the band played Oakland and San Francisco before returning to LA to play The Forum in Inglewood on New Year's Eve, with Captain Beefheart and Todd Rundgren's Utopia also on the bill. At the end of January 1976, there was a tour of Australia followed by gigs in Japan, from which sundry recordings, including 'Black Napkins', 'Zoot Allures' and 'Ship Ahoy', turned up on later albums. With just a few days' break, the band (including sometime-engineer Davey Moire on vocals) continued to Europe for 23 dates that took in every country but Britain.

By now, Frank was being systematically bootlegged and at least six albums from the European tour were circulated, one three-LP set, *Good Evening Vienna*, even had individual air-brushed artwork for each of its 500 copies. From these, it can be gathered that the band's repertoire was fairly evenly drawn from most periods of the Mothers' 12-year existence. 'Stink Foot', 'Dinah-Moe Humm', 'Advance Romance' and 'The Torture Never Stops' were already concert favourites, and the nostalgia section included 'How Can I Be Such A Fool', 'I Ain't Got No Heart' and 'I'm Not Satisfied'. The new material comprised 'Trying To Grow A Chin', 'Wind Up Working In A Gas Station', 'Naval Aviation In Art?', 'Honey, Don't You Want A Man Like Me', 'Black Napkins', 'Filthy Habits' and 'The Illinois Enema Bandit'. Frank told Nigel Leigh how the latter came about: 'I actually heard about it on the radio. We were returning from a job in Normal, Illinois and had the radio on in the station wagon. The announcer said, "The Illinois Enema Bandit" has struck again', and I went, "What!" Apparently, this guy had been ravaging the area of Southern Illinois for a number of years. He would find a co-ed's apartment with the door unlocked and he would walk in with a ski mask on and I guess a revolver, and force the woman to experience a severe internal rinse at gunpoint.'[38]

Thirty-year-old Michael Kenyon was finally arrested and pled guilty in Urbana, Illinois to six counts of armed robbery and admitted to administering enemas to at least three of his victims. But, as Frank said, 'since there is no law against giving anyone an enema, he went to jail because he took money from the ugly ones'.

'Many of the things that I've written have been true stories in song about obscure people who did obscure things, and they function in the same folk music tradition except that it's been performed on electric instruments.' To Frank, Michael Kenyon's anal obsession was 'the chance to do a folk song, especially since we were playing a lot of jobs in the Midwest. He's like a household word here, he should have a song. It's not exactly John Henry and the steamhammer, but, you know, he needs to have a song.'[39]

Other tunes, like 'Black Napkins', had more prosaic origins. The composition had been around for a while but 'it was finally named last Thanksgiving when we were having this horrible Thanksgiving dinner in Milwaukee. Sliced turkey roll with the fucking preservatives just gleaming off of it, and this beat-up cranberry material. The final stroke to this ridiculous dinner was the black napkins, sitting next to the dishes. That really said the most about the dinner.'[40] 'Trying To Grow A Chin', which began life as a one-verse vocal by Frank over the 'Black Napkins', was 'constructed using every kind of cliché that folk-rock brought to the world – all those stupid bass lines. And it's sung by (Terry Bozzio) who has a squeaky little teenage voice.'[41]

The tour ended in Bilbao on March 17 and once back in LA, Frank turned his attention to a backlog of album projects that were at various stages of completion. 'There are three things that are important to me right now,' he said in April. 'The 40-piece orchestra album, the guitar album and the ten record set.'[42] The previous year, the latter had been a 12-piece set of previously unissued material documenting the history of the Mothers. Then he'd said, 'This is a very difficult and expensive project. We currently have someone canvassing retailers. If we can get orders for 5,000, the company will release it.'[43]

Now, he admitted, 'The problem with that – we got the 5,000 orders – is that if you deliver a double album, that still counts as one album. But if it's a ten record album? I don't feel that it's right to count that as one album. Warner Brothers aren't even sure they want to count it as a single album against my contract etcetera . . . that it's maybe not commercial.'[44]

That wasn't the only problem Frank faced in the summer of 1976.

CHAPTER THIRTEEN
ZOOT ALLURES

In addition to all the existing projects, there was the matter of a new album to be considered. For this, Frank block-booked the LA Record Plant and for the first time approached his task literally as a solo venture. He told Steve Rosen, 'I did a lot of tracks just starting with a Rhythm Ace and building all the stuff up from there'.[1] With the exception of a live version of 'Black Napkins', recorded in Osaka the previous February, and the title track, all nine tunes on *Zoot Allures* were basically duets between Frank and Terry Bozzio, with selected instrumental embellishment from Ruth Underwood, Don Vliet, Dave Parlato and harpist Louanne Neil, and vocal assistance by Roy Estrada, Davey Moire, Ruben Ladron de Guevara and Sparkie Parker.

Asked whether he'd ever consider using a producer again, Frank replied, 'I would if I thought I could find somebody who would produce things the way I want to hear them. But the details that I worry about when I go into a studio are how the board is laid out, what EQ is going to be on the stuff you're listening to in the headphones, what kind of echo you're going to be using, how long you should be taking to do such-and-such, because at $150 an hour you don't want to be wasting your time in there. It's hard once you've got all that stuff set up to just walk in and play and forget about it. I'll spend anywhere from three to nine hours just getting the sound on the rest of the band right before I'll record.'[2]

But, while this method of working eliminated some of the likely misunderstandings that take place when human beings congregate in a recording studio, Frank discovered, like Paul McCartney, Andrew Gold and Todd Rundgren before him, that the finished product lacked the warmth and accessibility that collaborative effort imparts. Solo albums can be flattering exhibitions of versatility, but they can also be cold and impersonal. And when the subject matter, including soft porn, leisure devices, dead-end jobs and dead-beats, is filtered through Frank's habitually cynical perspective, that can get pretty cold.

'Wind Up Workin' In A Gas Station', 'Wonderful Wino' (co-written with Jeff Simmons in 1970 and part of the Flo & Eddie band's repertoire), 'Find Her Finer' and 'Disco Boy' are repetitive and static, lacking the energy evident in stage versions. Neither the balance nor the sound of individual overdubs was particularly precise and Frank's double-tracked sleazoid vocals seldom varied. The latter song had the distinction of being a good enough parody of its genre to be mistaken for the real thing. Frank's opinion of it was typically scathing: 'Disco music makes it possible to have disco entertainment centres. Disco entertainment centres make it possible for mellow, laid-back kinds of people to meet each other and reproduce.'[3]

By comparison, a marathon version of 'The Torture Never Stops' is a complete success, Frank's quietly salivating vocal enhancing the ominous atmosphere of the arrangement and the lyrics. These conjure up the baroque black humour of The Pit And The Pendulum and The Fall Of The House Of Usher, two of film director Roger Corman's finest moments, although Frank's leering Evil Prince misses the camp elegance that Vincent Price brought to his characters. And throughout, females groan and squeal in a manner more appropriate to the (then double) album's original title, Night Of The Iron Sausage.

'The sound effects to 'The Torture Never Stops' were an evening's work,' he told Pauline McLeod. 'We did most of it in the bedroom of my house. There were two chicks there – one was my wife – plus myself. I think they enjoyed it very much. We got four hours on tape and then cut it down to just under ten minutes. My friend opens up with the first grunt and it carries on from there. Er, I don't think it's worth telling you precisely what went on . . . you wouldn't be allowed to publish it.'[4] From her photograph, McLeod didn't look gullible but unless she'd done her research, there was no way she'd have known about Frank's bust at Studio Z, otherwise the similarities would have been all too apparent.

Less epic but unrepentantly disgusting is 'Ms. Pinky', a lumbering and salacious paean of praise to a 'lonely person device'. Frank came across this one in a Finnish porno magazine. 'It was a head with its mouth wide open and its eyes shut and a short haircut.'[5] When the band reached Amsterdam, he sent bodyguard John Smothers out to buy one to use onstage. 'Sure enough, for $69.95, he came back with Ms. Pinky. It was even worse than I had imagined. Not only is it a head, it's the size of a child's head. The throat is sponge rubber and it's got a vibrator in it with a battery pack and a two-speed motor. Sticking out of its neck is a nozzle with a squeezebulb that makes the throat contract.'[6] 'Lonely Person Devices', recorded in Copenhagen the previous March and released on YCDTOSA 6, tells the story to the accompaniment of much Danish laughter.

Best of all were the instrumentals. 'Black Napkins' and 'Zoot Allures' are two of Frank's most distinctive themes, the first consisting of a terse introductory riff and a fleet-fingered extended solo of flashing brilliance, the second a measured, chord-based melody with precisely controlled feedback and poised harmonies over the drums' steady pulse and Ruth Underwood's burbling marimba. In fact, so mesmeric is the latter theme that there's an acute sense of regret when the track begins to fade after Frank's solo has only just begun.

'Friendly Little Finger' opens with a quasi-oriental theme on guitar and marimba and then becomes an extended improvisation on bass and guitar by Frank, with Terry Bozzio's drums shifting accents and tempos. Its principal interest lies in its being an early example of what Frank termed 'xenochrony', or strange synchronisations. Prior to this, the most striking instance of what he would develop as a full-blown technique was 'The Blimp' on Beefheart's *Trout Mask Replica*, when Antennae Jimmy Semens' lyric chant and Don Vliet's horn flourishes were randomly added to a Mothers master with an intriguing result.

On 'Friendly Little Finger', while the bass and guitar share the same tonality, the tempo and time signature of what they play are unrelated, creating a random but coherent whole. On later albums, Frank would combine instrumental tracks from different recordings to create the illusion of simultaneous improvisation and paste live guitar solos onto studio backing tracks.

He explained his attitude toward soloing on record: 'I try to have the event that's going on the record make musical sense and fit in with what's going on; because a record is a fixed object, it doesn't change. It's not a song anymore, it's an object. If you're playing a song on the road it can change every night. It can be something, it comes alive each time you play it, and it has its own existence. But once you've committed it to wax, it never changes. So if you're going to leave your guitar solo on, you're stuck with that for the life of the record.'[7]

To achieve satisfactory results with such precise criteria, he had to have reliable backing musicians. 'It's hard to explain to guys just coming into the band, the rhythmic concept I have about playing, because it's based on ideas of metrical balance, long, sustained events versus groupettoes that are happening with a lot of notes on one beat. This is sort of against the grain of rock 'n' roll, which likes to have everything in exactly duple or triple, straight up and down, so you can constantly tap your foot to it. But I prefer to have the rhythm section be aware of where the basic pulse of the time is and create a foundation that won't move, so I can flow over the top of it.

'It's hard to do, it's hard to get people to do that. And it's also hard to get them to leave some space for where the fast notes occur. Rhythm sections always have a tendency to copy; if they hear somebody else playing fast notes, they want to play fast notes too, and then you can't hear any fast notes any more. I've always had good rhythmic rapport with Aynsley Dunbar - I thought he was really good, drum-wise. And Terry Bozzio . . . is excellent.

He has a tendency to frenzy out a little bit, but I just figure that's because he's from San Francisco.'[8]

He elaborated on the subject in conversation with Nigel Leigh: 'I like to find players that have unique abilities that haven't been challenged on other types of music. I mean, a good example would be a guy like Bruce Fowler, who has an incredible range on the trombone. When he plays the trombone, you hardly recognise it as a trombone because his technique is so bizarre. Or Terry Bozzio, whose idea of constructions for drum solos was in a whole musical realm that nobody had touched before. And Tommy Mars, this is a guy that you could hold a conversation (with) and Tommy could harmonise it while you were talking. You would just follow dialogue with chords. How often do you get a chance to apply these unusual skills on other types of music.

'I could always make do. You can't always get what you want, so a lot of times I would be stuck with musicians that were merely competent. (I) would try and push the envelope and teach them new techniques and see whether they could adapt and grow into another style. But for me, it was always more interesting to encounter a musician who had a unique ability, find a way to showcase that and build that unusual skill into the composition. So that for ever afterward, that composition would be stamped with the personality of the person who was there when the composition was created.'[9]

ANY DOWNERS

It's surprising that Frank had any stamina left for recording during these summer months. After returning from Europe, Frank had gone to Michigan to record the basic tracks for the new album by Grand Funk Railroad. One of America's quintessential heavy metal bands, Grand Funk had received ten consecutive platinum albums but had intended to disband in 1975, after the release of *Born To Die*. But when Frank expressed an interest in producing them, they stayed together long enough to record *Good Singin', Good Playin'*. The album was completed at the LA Record Plant, with engineers Michael Braunstein and Davey Moire, the team he would use on *Zoot Allures*. As well as producing, Frank played guitar on 'Out To Get You'. The band broke up soon after the album's release in August.

But the most distracting event was the end of his partnership, after more than a decade, with Herb Cohen. Amidst the lawsuits and recriminations, there were two tangible consequences; both Frank's *Zoot Allures* and Captain Beefheart's new album, *Bat Chain Puller* were prevented from being released. 'Listen to this,' Frank told Miles, 'I am the chairman of the board of DiscReet and the president of the company – also those guys (at the Record Plant) are supposed to be my friends – but they wouldn't release the master tapes to me unless Warner Brothers indemnified the studio from any legal action that Herbie might take against them.'

Warners agreed to do that but insisted that Frank indemnified them. 'Can you believe it? An individual artist having to indemnify one of the biggest record companies in the world so that they can bring his record out?'[10] In the event, the album was mastered from Frank's own safety copies, and after several months delay, *Zoot Allures* was released on the Warner Brothers label on October 29.

As for Beefheart: Frank hadn't produced the album, but the master tapes of *Bat Chain Puller* were in his basement. Still, they couldn't be sent to Virgin in England while the Cohen/Zappa dispute continued. Miles' *NME* article implied that the Beefheart album had been financed with Frank's money, and both he and Herb Cohen were claiming the album advance. Beefheart had no choice but to be philosophical about his situation, but there was a note of sympathy in his comments in a phone interview with Miles. 'When Frankie left Herbie, he reckons (it) opened up a whole can of worms - a whole new can of worms he didn't even know was there. It seems that over the years Frank had signed these pieces of paper, you know, signed in order to be able to keep on with his art . . .'[11] If it was true, how ironic that Frank should be as susceptible as Beefheart to fine-print blindness; how different was his reaction.

In the wake of this flurry of legal action, Frank decided not to pursue his argument with the Albert Hall. 'It's cost me $50,000 so far,' he said to Miles, 'and the lawyers want another $8,000 to appeal. It's not worth it.' Even so, an appeal was eventually lodged. There was some good news: his lawsuit against MGM-Verve was settled: 'We made a settlement in which we get the masters back plus $100,000. But MGM gets a 3% production over-ride on all future use of them.'[12] Out of the five albums that the Mothers had recorded for them, the label had managed to repackage 11, an inventive abuse of creativity. Unfortunately, these funds too were tied up in Frank's action against Cohen. He wouldn't take physical possession of the master tapes until 1982.

With so much contention in the air, it was only common sense to dispense with the name, Mothers of Invention. Since the last Mothers had, by most people's reckoning been the twenty-fourth to bear that name, Frank had every justification in saying 'any resemblance between this group and the original Mothers of Invention is purely conceptual'. Not using the name would also prevent Herb Cohen from putting any restraint orders on Frank's work schedule and earnings.

The new group, which began yet another tour in mid-October, was just known as Zappa. It consisted of Terry Bozzio on drums, Ray White on guitar and lead vocals, Patrick O'Hearn on bass and Eddie Jobson on keyboards and vocals. In the early stages, Bianca Odin also played keyboards and sang. Like Bozzio, White and O'Hearn were both from the Bay area, with backgrounds in funk and jazz. O'Hearn was Bozzio's friend and earlier in the summer had been staying at his Los Angeles house while playing with saxophonist Joe Henderson at The Lighthouse. The Mothers had been disbanded and Frank and Terry were laying down tracks at the Record Plant. The drummer invited O'Hearn down to the studio to listen to what had been laid down.

'I stopped by at about 2.30 in the morning,' he told Robert L. Doerschuk. 'Not being one to leave my upright bass in the car, I carted it into the studio. Frank, upon seeing me with this bass, remarked, "Do you play that dog house, fella?" I said, "Sure do." Then, without even a formal introduction, he said, "Well, how would you like to put some acoustic bass on this track?" I said, "Let's do it". The cut was finally released as 'The Ocean Is The Ultimate Solution'.'[13] Frank liked O'Hearn's playing enough to invite him back the following night to play electric bass on another track. As they listened back to the first take, he offered O'Hearn a job in the new band.

'At one point, Frank, Terry and I were just a trio. We jammed and played throughout the summer as such. Frank was producing *Good Singin', Good Playin'* at the time, and those guys would come in and encourage Frank to 'revive the power trio'. This was before the Police; the last trios had been Hendrix and Cream. We thought about that and actually rehearsed it for a while. But eventually Frank felt that he needed at least five guys to make things interesting.'[14]

Eddie Jobson had replaced Darryl Way in Curved Air at the precocious age of 17, and then in the summer of 1973 joined Roxy Music as the replacement for the sacked Brian Eno. He was never a full member of the group, merely a salaried employee like the members of Frank's bands. He'd met Frank when Roxy Music supported the Mothers at a gig in Milwaukee in May 1974, when he'd sat in with one of his musical heroes. At the end of Roxy's American tour, he remained in Los Angeles and played with an early incarnation of Ritchie Blackmore's Rainbow. Then Frank invited him to accompany the Mothers on a week of Canadian gigs.

Jobson and Frank played together at sound checks and in dressing rooms as Frank assessed both his musical ability and his capacity to memorise arrangements. But he did get to play onstage at two shows. 'He'd sort of say maybe five minutes before he was due onstage, "It'd be nice if you played along tonight",' he told Chris Salewicz. 'You know, there's 10,000 people out there and he tells you like five minutes before and you just have to go onstage and jam, really. I mean, he goes into a riff that you've never heard before in your life and just points at you and you have to do a solo. It was really good for me . . . I mean, that's his strength. He stretches his musicians beyond their capabilities all the time. And then when it comes to a performance he'll just relax it slightly to the point where people can actually play what he wants.'[15]

With an open invitation to join the band whenever he could, Jobson returned to England, where he was offered gigs with Ian Gillan and Procol

Harum. Then he was told that Roxy Music were taking an indefinite break, during which he wouldn't be paid. He rang Frank, and Frank sent him a plane ticket. He'd passed the test but even so, the matter of his origin couldn't go unnoticed; the tour programme pointed out that Jobson brought to the band 'a sort of damp English charm, smothered in rosy-cheeked appeal'.

'I remember when Frank went through the law-suit,' said Terry Bozzio, 'he said he might not be able to pay us. We all said, "Well, we're willing to hang in there for a few months as long as the savings hold out", in the hopes that things would get better. Frank was really depressed at that time. It was just me and Patrick O'Hearn and Eddie Jobson. I was going to be the sort of lead singer, and do the stuff that Napoleon did. It was a very strange time, you know. Then he got Ray White.'16

Both O'Hearn and White would stay with Frank for some years, but Jobson left at the end of the tour and Biana Odin's tenure only lasted a few weeks. Her presence in the band is commemorated on *YCDTOSA 6* in her lusty singing on a version of 'Wind Up Workin' In A Gas Station' from the October 29 gig at The Spectrum in Philadelphia.

Despite little or no promotion by Warner Brothers, *Zoot Allures* (with cover photographs that featured Zappa, Bozzio, O'Hearn and Jobson, though the latter pair were not on the record) sold 117,000 copies in its first week of release. Speaking towards the end of November, Frank still wasn't particularly impressed with his record company. 'They've been giving me the shits on this new album. Normally you come into town and there's the local Warners representative to take you to the local radio station. Well, so far on this tour I've seen five guys . . . In New York we sold out three nights at the Felt Forum. Warner Brothers bought 15 tickets for the press.'17

Surprisingly, the song content was not preventing album tracks from being played on the radio. 'It's getting played everywhere,' Frank told *NME*, 'except oddly enough in Toronto, Canada. I was doing an interview on what used to be one of the most progressive stations there when I noticed that the album had white stickers on two of the tracks, 'Black Napkins' and 'The Torture Never Stops'. Frank proceeded to have an argument about censorship on air with the station manager. 'What it amounted to was that he didn't understand the lyrics. All he knew was that they made him hot so he thought they must be bad!'18 How an instrumental could arouse a station manager's ardour was never revealed.

At Cobo Hall in Detroit on November 19, Flo & Eddie appeared as the opening act and returned to jam with their old boss, along with bass player Ralph Armstrong from the Mahavishnu Orchestra and drummer Don Brewer from Grand Defunct Railroad. Flo & Eddie had auditioned for Frank's latest band and he'd wanted them but their record company, Columbia, wanted them to go on the road with their own group, which included Bruce and

Walt Fowler, to promote their new album, *Moving Targets*. When their guitarist, Phil Reed, fell to his death from a hotel window, Frank agreed to let them join his tour.

SUPERNAUT

Back in April 1975, while in London for the Albert Hall case, Frank had given journalist Giovanni Dadomo a list of 'faves, raves and composers in their graves'. At the head of the list, which also included *Abbey Road*, *The Best Of Muddy Waters*, *The Complete Works Of Edgard Varèse*, *The Story Of My Life* by Guitar Slim and 'anything by Richard Berry', was Black Sabbath's 'Supernaut'. 'I like it because I think it's prototypical of a certain musical style, and I think it's well done.' A couple of years later, he'd changed his mind. He told Hugh Fielder, "Iron Man'. Are you kidding me? 'Iron Man'! That's a work of art. I used to like 'Supernaut' but I think 'Iron Man' is the one now.'[19]

Now there were plans for Frank to learn three Black Sabbath numbers so that he could jam with them at New York's Madison Square Gardens on December 6. It didn't quite turn out that way. Frank had asked to go to their sound check but this never happened. When he turned up to the gig, he found a mini-wall of Marshalls set up for his use, but he refused to play without knowing what his sound would be like.

'What happened was that Tommy (Iommi) had some trouble with his guitar and decided to change his strings at the very last minute. The audience had already been sitting there waiting for an hour or so since Ted Nugent, and they wanted me to go out there and make an announcement and calm them down. So I did. And I introduced them and then sat by the side of the stage over by Ozzy's orange juice. I just sat there and marvelled at it. I think it's great. Especially in a place like Madison Square Gardens with 20,000 people grunting and wheezing and shoving each other.'[20]

Five days later, the Zappa band did a 15-minute live set on *Saturday Night Live*, the hugely successful satirical NBC television show that had begun back in October 1975, made media stars of Chevy Chase, Dan Aykroyd and John Belushi, and won four Emmys seven months later. As well as 'Peaches En Regalia' and 'Dancin' Fool', 'The Purple Lagoon' featured Belushi as a Samurai Be-Bop Musician and 'I'm The Slime' let veteran NBC announcer Don Pardo come in front of the cameras to assume the title role. Pardo enjoyed himself so much that Frank invited him to appear with the band during its four-day residence between Christmas and New Year at the Palladium in New York City.

'He's never been seen,' he told Tim Schneckloth. 'The man's been working (for NBC) for 30 years and nobody knows what he looks like. So I thought, fantastic, let's bring Don Pardo live out on stage and let the world see him. We got him a white tuxedo; he did some narration for some of the songs we were doing; we brought him out to sing 'I'm The Slime'. And the audience loved him . . . the highlight of his career.' Schneckloth tried to be facetious by asking how Frank had managed to get Pardo to debase himself. 'Debase himself? That's really not right. First of all, he has a good sense of humour. Second, he really enjoyed doing that. I don't think it was debasing at all. It was giving him an opportunity to expand into other realms.'[21]

For the Palladium gigs, Frank expanded the band to include a five-piece brass section of the Brecker Brothers, Randy and Mike, Lou Marini, Ronnie Cuber and Tom Malone. David Samuels played timpani and vibes and on assorted percussion was the indispensable Ruth Underwood. Along with John Bergamo and Ed Mann, she would also add 'various humanly impossible overdubs' to certain tracks, and Louanne Neil overdubbed 'osmotic harp' (absorbing stuff). The four nights were recorded as part of the package of albums with which Frank hoped to finish his Warner Brothers contract.

Once again, the set had changed to enhance both the vaudeville elements, with an emphasis on oral sex, and the fiendishly difficult instrumental themes. It reached back to 'Big Leg Emma', which at this stage had only appeared on a Verve single, 'Pound For A Brown' and 'Cruisin' For Burgers'. As well as 'Sofa' and 'The Purple Lagoon' (which also incorporated 'Approximate'), the band had to weave its tortuous way through 'I Promise Not To Come In Your Mouth', 'Manx Needs Women' and 'The Black Page'.

Of the latter, O'Hearn said, 'The toughest chart I ever had to play with Frank was the straight version of 'The Black Page'. It's mainly difficult for the drum chair, but it's a tough chart all around. We actually worked up two arrangements of it: the straight one and the disco arrangement, which was hilarious. Terry would slip into sort of a Latin hustle beat, and I did the ubiquitous bass octaves that had been made popular by God knows how many groups of the era.'[22]

Having thrilled to the legend of 'The Illinois Enema Bandit', the audience could revel in 'Titties & Beer', a mountain-top encounter between Frank as a rancid biker and Terry Bozzio as the Devil, 'Honey, Don't You Want A Man Like Me?', charting a couple's evening that climaxed in a blow-job, and 'Punky's Whips'. The latter came about, as Frank told it, when Terry Bozzio 'came into contact with a Japanese music magazine called Ongaku and saw in the middle of this magazine a large head shot of a guy named (Edwin) 'Punky' Meadows, who was the lead guitar player from a group called Angel, which was one of those manufactured supergroups from the people who brought you Kiss (Casablanca Records). Kiss wore black, Angel wore white.

'Again, nobody had ever heard of an Angel record, but here they were being promoted rather severely in Japan when we were there - and to Terry, Punky looked good. He had a nice hairdo, his lips were pooched out in this pose and Terry went for it. He thought that this was something pretty sensational, so it was like one of those revelation kind of things. We gave Terry a new direction and behaviour, clothing, comportment, the whole deal. So I wrote this song about what happened to Terry as a result of seeing this picture.'[23]

DONG WORK FOR YUDA

The British music press announced in December that Frank Zappa would be playing dates in England and Scotland for the first time since September 1973. As Frank commented to Miles, 'I have made statements in the past that I would not come back to England until I got a personal apology from the Queen. Well - one has not been forthcoming - and I figured I couldn't wait forever. But there is still time. She can repent. I'll even give her a backstage pass.'[24]

The six-week swing through Europe ignored the Mediterranean countries this time and concentrated on Scandinavia and Germany, with no less than eight gigs in the latter. As for Britain, gigs in Stafford, Glasgow and Edinburgh were sandwiched by two stints at London's Hammersmith Odeon on February 9/10 and 16/7. By now, Frank had trenchant views on European audiences: 'The audience in London is very similar to the audience in LA - which is to say, singularly boring and jaded. The audiences in some of the smaller places in Germany are more like East Coast or Midwest audiences - they have a good sense of humour, they like to make a lot of noise, but they're not obnoxious. And then you have your pseudo-intellectual audiences like in Denmark. Paris is a pretty good audience; I'd have to give Paris like a San Francisco rating.'[25]

The Times sent Clive Bennett along to the opening night at the Hammersmith Odeon. Although Frank had 'substantial musical virtues', Bennett questioned his self-discipline. 'He veers too haphazardly between unorthodox virtuosity and childlike, though not childish, silliness, and goes too far too often.' All in all, 'Zappa may represent a minor threat to entrenched values, but his concerts are a welcome breath of bad air.'[26]

Miles didn't have to stoop to enjoy himself; it was 'a real Zappa concert' for him. He attended both concerts and noted their differences. 'On the first night (Frank) played one totally misconceived solo - there was no way that anyone could have resolved it - though he did his best. The same solo spot on the second night he excelled himself, playing a solo so strong and inventive that the other guys were all laughing with him as more and more riffs appeared and were developed. Even Frank was smiling.'[27]

Some songs had undergone radical changes; 'Titties & Beer' had another verse augmenting the drug indulgence and regurgitation before he and his girl went on their ride 'up the Mountain of Mystery'. In London, it was also the occasion for a wicked imitation of Black Sabbath. 'Broken Hearts Are For

Assholes' now segued into 'Dong Work For Yuda', an affectionate tribute to Frank's bodyguard, John Smothers. As Frank told the Hammersmith audience, 'Mr Smothers purportedly speaks the English language but he speaks it in such a way as to add new dimensions to it.' Sung in the style of an a cappella vocal group, Terry Bozzio as 'Bald-headed John' referred to water as HtO and saliva as salima; 'Take me to the falcum 'was the order to a confused Danish cab-driver when Smothers had to get to Copenhagen's Falkoner Theatret.

Frank found it hard to overcome his prejudice about London. As Miles noted, 'He berates his audience. He called them 'stodgy, tense, neo-Victorian, hung-up, and more concerned with clothes than what's happening out in the world'. The ecstatic reception given him restored his confidence. He encored with 'Camarillo Brillo' and 'Muffin Man' on the first night, and spoke to the audience about his accident at the Rainbow and his law suit - he was genuinely moved.'[28]

The prejudice was fully operative once again when Chris Salewicz interviewed him for *NME*. It was a mean-spirited exchange which served to confirm the preconceptions of both parties. Salewicz expected 'Rent-a-Spiel' and said so; Frank shot back, 'I don't pretend that anyone who ever talked to me for any one minute of my life wanted to know anything about me.' When it resumed, the conversation inevitably came round to his record company.

'I've been associated with Warners for five years and I just think it's time to go someplace else. You know, I go in the studios and I really think I'm doing something wonderful. And there are people who think it's wonderful too. But there isn't anyone at the fuckin' record company who'd agree with that. As far as they're concerned it's a box of shoes.' To underline the message, he added, 'There's no way to do too many interviews when you're signed to a record company like Warners. Somebody's got to sell the records!'[29]

Soon after he got home, at the beginning of March Frank took several boxes of tapes to the Warners offices. 'The Discreet contract was coming to an end,' Frank said to me, 'and I owed them three or four albums. Whatever it was. I had a deadline to deliver these things and the fact of the matter was, the albums were in the can. So I walked into their office and handed the master tapes to this girl about three months ahead of the deadline. And I'd spent the money out of my own bank account to make those albums.'

The albums constituted the bulk of recordings made of material written since his enforced lay-off during 1972. Two were live recordings; *Live In New York* was a double album taken from the Palladium shows during Christmas week, 1976; *Orchestral Favorites* came from the September 1975 concerts recorded at Royce Hall, Los Angeles. *Studio Tan* and parts of *Sleep Dirt* used studio sessions from Spring 1974, with George Duke, Bruce and Tom Fowler, Ruth Underwood and Chester Thompson. The balance of *Sleep Dirt* consisted of hybrid tracks begun with the 1974 band and overdubbed later, with the afore-mentioned 'The Ocean Is The Only Solution' and 'Filthy Habits', an instrumental from the 1976 Record Plant sessions that Frank had originally intended to include on the double album version of *Zoot Allures*.

The contract stipulated that Frank should receive $60,000 advance for each album. No money was forthcoming and from that moment yet another law suit was inevitable. At this point, Frank had no effective management, the litigation with Herb Cohen was ongoing, with no resolution in sight, and his record company was refusing to release the albums he'd already made. Anyone of a nervous disposition would have become a Child of God or moved to Oregon and bought the Bhagwan Shree Rajneesh a couple of Rolls Royces. Instead, Frank embodied Hunter S. Thompson's dictum: 'When the going gets weird, the weird turn pro.'

No suit was left untended. The May 7 *NME* carried a news item: 'Zappa sues previous licensees of Rainbow'. Frank 'and two US companies' were claiming $250,000 damages from Sundancer, which might prove difficult to obtain since the company had gone into voluntary liquidation. 'Zappa and the two companies with exclusive rights to his services are now claiming for loss of earnings during that period. No date has been set for the hearing.'[30] It was also reported that he'd entered an appeal against the 1975 Albert Hall judgement, which was due to be heard shortly.

THE MEEK SHALL INHERIT NOTHING

Throughout the summer, Frank concentrated on assembling an almost totally new band, which would significantly increase the quality and extent of what could be realised on stage. Retaining Patrick O'Hearn and Terry Bozzio, he recruited percussionist Ed Mann, keyboard players Tommy Mars and Peter Wolf, and guitarist Adrian Belew. For what Frank wanted to achieve, it was important that as many of the band as possible could read music. Adrian Belew was the one exception.

Frank had seen Belew playing in a Top 40 cover band in Nashville the previous November. The band, Sweetheart, was the favourite of Frank's chauffeur that night, so when Frank asked to be taken to hear some music after his own show, he and John Smothers were driven down to Fanny's, the bar where Sweetheart were appearing. 'I saw him walk in from the back and just watch us, which made me a little nervous,' Belew told HP Newquist. 'In the middle of playing 'Gimme Shelter', he came up to the side of the stage and reached over and shook my hand. Later, he got my name and number from the chauffeur, and not too long after that he gave me a call to come audition for him.

'We began three months of rehearsal, and it was pretty tough. Ten hours a day, five days a week. I'd spend my weekends with Frank, and he'd prep me before the next week's rehearsals so that I was ready when we went to play with everybody else. During those weekends I'd watch him arrange pieces of music and it was just amazing. For those three months it was just a joy being around him because I picked up so many things.'[31]

Peter Wolf received a Conservatory training for ten years in his native Austria, before forming a rock band, Gypsy Love, with Carl Ratzer and Lalomie Washburn. He'd been in Los Angeles for two weeks, playing keyboards on Washburn's album sessions. Through her, he met Andre Lewis, who passed his phone number on to Frank. 'The next day at nine in the morning I got a call from Frank. "This is Frank Zappa; I'm looking for a keyboard player. Do you want to audition?"'

After listening to some tapes of *Zappa In New York*, Wolf was put through his sight-reading paces, after which Frank said, 'Play me something'. 'I took a piano solo. Patrick O'Hearn was there and he whipped out his acoustic bass. Finally, Frank said, "Well, what do you think, Pat, you want to play with this guy?" And Pat said, "Yeah". So Frank turned around and said, "You're hired". That was it.'[32]

Tommy Mars had had a more chequered career before becoming a band member. He graduated from Hart College of Music in West Hartford, Connecticut in 1972; by 1976, 'I was working in this revolving organ bar in Kodiak, Alaska, with Japanese and Russian fishermen kicking me in the back if I couldn't play an ethnic folk song to their drunken satisfaction.'[33] He was living in Santa Barbara, working as a choirmaster, organist and occasional jazz pianist, when he got a call from Ed Mann.

He'd known Ed Mann back in Connecticut and Ed told him, 'Frank has a keyboard player already and he's thinking of auditioning another one as well. Why don't you give him a call?' Mars went through a torturous audition, which he sensed was going nowhere, until Frank asked him to sing something. Not one song came to mind. 'So I told him, "Frank, I can't think of anything so I'm going to improvise something". So I just started playing and singing. I have a style of scatting that is very definitely my own and it's coordinated very basically and organically with what I'm playing on the piano. It totally knocked Frank out. He called Gail, his wife, downstairs and said, "Listen to this guy blow". And that saved me. My reading was only adequate for what he wanted but the improv saved me, I'm sure.'[34]

Frank put him on a temporary retainer and gave him some music to learn over the next week. 'A week later, I came back down from Santa Barbara,' he told Robert L. Doerschuk. 'I had learned every piece that he gave me as a solo piano arrangement, even 'The Black Page' and 'Punky's Whips'. He thought I would just learn the chords and some of the melodic licks, but I did everything as if I would do it solo. So he was utterly flabbergasted.'[35]

Perhaps not. 'I'll tell you, the kind of musician I need for the bands that I have doesn't exist,' Frank told Tim Schneckloth early in 1978. 'I need somebody who understands polyrhythms, has good enough execution on the instrument to play all kinds of styles, understands staging, understands rhythm and blues, and understands how a lot of different compositional techniques function.

'The main thing a person has to have is very fast pattern recognition and information storage capability. That's because we play like a two, two-and-a-half-hour show non-stop with everything organised . . . So it requires a lot of memorisation - fast memorisation. You can't spend a year teaching somebody a show.' Frank pointed out that three months constant rehearsal was an expensive investment, 'because it's $13,250 a week for rehearsals - we rehearse with full equipment, full crew and a soundstage. So I prefer people who learn fast.' In order to keep it all on the move, the stage gear required one 22-foot and two 45-foot trucks. 'In Europe we were using two 40s. For every person on stage playing an instrument, there are two other guys in the crew. There's seven people in the band, 21 total travelling. And they all work.'[36]

BABY SNAKES

After a warm-up gig at the University of California in San Diego on September 9, 1977, the band took to the road for the next couple of months, including a four-day stint at the Palladium in New York City that ended with shows on Halloween Night. These shows were recorded on the Record Plant's 24-track mobile facilities, and film crews were also present to shoot footage for Frank's next project, *Baby Snakes*. With sundry backstage japes, including Roy Estrada's interminable liaison with a full-bodied Ms Pinky, interpolated into the performance, the complexity of the music is matched by Bruce Bickford's mind-clenching clay animation, including a sequence in 'Disco Boy' where 'Billy The Mountain' and 'Greggary Peccary' are both briefly glimpsed.

A 'soundtrack' album was eventually released in 1983, containing an introductory conversation between Frank and Warren Cucurullo, and versions of 'Baby Snakes', 'Titties & Beer', 'The Black Page', 'Jones Crusher', 'Disco Boy', 'Dinah-Moe Humm' and 'Punky's Whips'. The film also contained an extended preamble to 'Dirty Love', later released (along with 'Tryin' To Grow A Chin') on *YCDTOSA 6* as 'The Poodle Lecture', in which Frank enumerated God's three mistakes, those being Man, Wo-Man and the Poodle. Having no truck with snakes and apples, Frank recounts how Eve took a fancy to certain parts of the poodle and sent Adam out to work for the money needed to buy some clippers, scissors and the inevitable zircon-encrusted tweezers, with which to give the dog of her dreams 'the disco look that's so popular these days'. Frank squatted on a suitably-primped life-sized replica to show how Eve brought bestiality to the Garden.

This being the site of his previous live New York recordings, he couldn't resist a dig at his previous record company during the preamble to his parody of an English pop-star's recent American hit. Released on *YCDTOSA 6* as 'Is That Guy Kidding Or What?', Frank asked his audience, 'How many of you people feel that rock has gotten entirely too preposterous?' He went on to be moderately scathing about Peter Frampton's 1976 number 2 US hit, 'I'm In You', and put forward an imaginary scenario in which a teenage groupie took her pop star idol back to her appropriately-lit teenage bedroom, removed her own teenage clothes and granted entry to the pop star appendage, only to have the immortal words of Frampton's song whined in her ear. Frank's parody, 'I Have Been In You', typically dispensed with 'in-you-endo' in its tale of bedroom athletics.

He saved his most scathing record company attack for the ad-lib section of 'Titties & Beer'. 'I have been through hell,' he spat. 'Remember, I was signed with Warner Brothers for eight fuckin' years. Now how bad is that?'

He was about to get his answer.

CHAPTER FOURTEEN
LATHER

'I'm here to play an album for you and I'm rapping a little - rapping is one of those words you say when you go on rock 'n' roll radio stations - I'm rapping a little bit at this point to prepare each and every one of you for the grand and glorious experience of getting your little cassette machines out. Because I would like to have you tape record this album off the air. Because this album is not going to be available in stores. Because Warner Brothers is trying to ruin my darn career.'

Frank was sitting in a studio at KROQ in Pasadena. He was about to play *Lather*, a remixed and re-programmed four-album version of the tapes he'd presented to Warner Brothers in March. When the DiscReet contract ran out in June, he'd set about finding a new record company to distribute his product. First he approached and was declined by Capitol (part of the EMI organisation); they used the same law firm as Warner Brothers and pressed Warners' records at the time. Mercury/Phonogram then agreed to release the set on his own Zappa label on October 31.

And then . . . Warner Brothers announced they'd scheduled *Zappa In New York*, as per the DiscReet contract; since *Lather* also contained some of the same performances, Mercury/Phonogram could not issue it. Three hundred box-sets (catalogue number: SRZ 4-1500) had already been produced and were now useless. But Frank had a set of test pressings and he was going to use them. He briefly explained the circumstances to the KROQ audience as they readied their cassette machines.

'Warner Brothers does not have the rights to this material, although it was delivered to them. They refused to pay me for the material and so I claimed a breach of contract and set out to negotiate with some other record companies. And in several instances, Warner Brothers interfered with those negotiations and spoiled the possibility of releasing this material elsewhere. First place they did it was with EMI and the second was with Mercury/Phonogram; they were ready to press the album, the cover was printed. What you're listening to now is actual test pressings that Mercury/Phonogram had prepared. At the last minute, Warner Brothers threatened them with legal proceedings and so they backed out of the deal.

'The way it stands now is my future as a recording artist is dangling in mid-air, pending court procedures which in California can take anywhere from three to five years for civil cases just to get a day in court and get your case heard. So, since I don't think anybody wants to wait three to five years to hear my wonderful music, I've taken it upon myself to come down here and advise anybody interested in the stuff I do to get a cassette machine and tape the album. You can have it for free, just take it right off the radio. Don't buy it, tape it.'

Some time later, wouldn't you know it, a bootleg box-set was issued, including his opening preamble. Some time after that, a double-album bootleg, *Leatherette*, devoted three sides to tracks from *Lather*, while the fourth side featured a 1972 radio interview with Martin Perlich and the complete conversation with KROQ's Jerry Kay.

It was a frustrating time; access to his film and audio archive had been denied him and Warner Brothers' proprietorial attitude towards Frank meant that he'd become a pariah in the record business. 'They had made it impossible for me to get a record contract with anybody,' he told Den Simms. 'There was a period of time where I was kind of locked out of the music business, and since I didn't have a recording studio at that time, and since I didn't have a contract, and I couldn't go into a recording studio, in an act of desperation, I took my four-track and hooked up a bunch of little dipshit equipment here in (my) basement, just like every other garage band guy would do, and I was making some one-man tapes here.'[1]

The only thing to do was to get out on the road. As in previous years, 1978 opened with another European tour, which this time began and ended with shows at London's Hammersmith Odeon. The first of these was a five-night stand, from Tuesday, January 24 to Saturday, January 28. Paul Rambali interviewed Frank for *NME* while final rehearsals were taking place. He opened his piece dramatically: 'There exists a very real possibility that we won't hear any new recordings from Francis Vincent Zappa until at least the turn of this decade.'[2]

The next paragraphs detailed the machinations of managements and record companies, and revealed that 'the fate of *Live In New York* is undecided due to some defamatory material included therein about a certain Punky Meadows'. The Angel story was related, as was a further deterioration in Terry Bozzio's conduct: 'He has lately been seen on stage sporting S&M gear replete with fido studs and butt strap.' It turned out that the hunk in question had heard 'Punky's Whips', had felt flattered and given Frank his permission to release it, but that wasn't enough for Warners.

Later in the conversation, Frank deflected a question about feminist attitudes to his more lubricious material: 'I'm saying simply this: it's as much of a hype as punk rock as far as I'm concerned. Some of the things they wish to achieve are quite noble, but I resent the manner in which they are being advertised. It's not the ideals, it's the packaging. I find it repulsive and think it's an insult to men and demeaning to women.'

Finding his stride - and this being England - he roped in an all-too-familiar hobby horse. 'Punk rock is a phenomenon manufactured by managers. It's almost a matter of survival the way I sense it here - the pressure to be a part of whatever is the going trend. In the States the pressures are different. You still have peer group acceptance pressures, but they're not based on rock as a culture . . . I get the impression that in order to survive in this country you have to be absolutely dedicated to what has been announced as the trend of the day, otherwise you're a nerd - and nobody wants to be a nerd. As an amateur sociologist then, I would say they are in a better mental health condition rock-wise in the States than they are here.'

America wasn't completely healthy, though. As far as learning from the cultural upheavals of the 60s, he was less sanguine. 'They haven't learned some of the most important lessons of the 60s. The single most important one I think is that LSD was a scam promoted by the CIA and that the people in Haight-Ashbury who were idols of people across the world as examples of revolution and outrage and progress were mere dupes of the CIA.' Had the government been experimenting on its own people? 'I think it's a process they wanted to go through to find out what the applications are in terms of controlling segments of the population. It's one thing to use these drugs on enemy soldiers, but what happens in situations in cities?'[2]

It was a theme that Frank had developed in a radio interview with Jim Ladd: 'Look, in the 1950's a teenager was an unwanted commodity. Nobody knew yet that that was the new big consumer market. They were just troublemakers, you know, so teenagers were just sort of swept under the rug. They were the wild teenage thrill seekers and juvenile delinquents, and nobody had any use for them until they found out that those little spare-time jobs that they were getting and the money they were getting for allowances when added up turned out to be billions of dollars a year for certain products. At the point that that was discovered, one of the great truths of business lit up over the heads of all those people in the places where they work on those kind of things.'

According to Frank, the next step was, 'We can't just get their bucks, we have to keep them under control because money means power. If these kids have money then they have power, and if they ever find out that they have power, then we're in trouble, you know, they'll be uncooperative. So they have to be dealt with, and there are ways of dealing with them.'[3]

Rambali found all that hard to believe. 'That's because you're not in America. But the way I see it is that those crooks who wind up being president of the United States and the other smart little persons they have working for them will do anything. They believe that they are the law.' As he'd said in the earlier conversation: 'The best thing that the government has working for them is that the people that they are trying to control are willing to be controlled.'[4]

The idea may have seemed bizarre but the logic was devastating. It prompted Rambali to ask whether Frank considered himself the arch-cynic he was portrayed to be. 'I think being a cynic is the only rational stance to take in a contemporary society. I would call it quite a compliment to be called an arch-cynic; that almost sounds important.'[5]

What was important about his prolonged stay among his favourite people was that the Hammersmith gigs were being recorded for the next album, for which there was as yet no outlet. But not for a live album; improved technology, via The Basing Street Truck, was finally enabling Frank to achieve the (albeit intermediate) goal of recording live backing tracks on multi-track equipment, of sufficient quality to then be overdubbed in the studio with all the embellishments that he could envisage. The ultimate goal for this approach, which would also be achieved, was the combination of musicianship and technical expertise that would mean his compositions could be performed and recorded live with no additional studio work.

Just to keep Frank's prejudice fresh and corrosive, the British press reported a new outrage to add to their catalogue of Zappa indiscretions. The group were leaving Heathrow on their way to a gig in Frankfurt as the Sunday papers reported the arrest of certain members overnight. The *Sunday Express* piece bore the headline, 'Zappa Group In Hotel Uproar'. While Frank had stayed in a hotel 'off Hyde Park', the band were at the Holiday Inn. Frank was quoted: 'Four members of the road crew and one member of my group were taken to Paddington police station after police burst into their hotel rooms this morning. They did not have a warrant. They simply broke open the doors and cut the burglar chains with wire cutters. I understand that a member of the hotel management made a complaint. We didn't smash anything, attack anyone or scream blue murder all night.'[6] A police spokesman said that 'various substances' were found in their rooms. One man was released immediately and the other four were freed on bail 'to report back on February 27 to see if analysis of the substances constitutes an offense'. Nothing more was heard.

During a four day stint in Paris, Frank went down the Metro to find a musician he'd read about in the *New York Herald Tribune*. Harmonica player Sugar Blue and his French girlfriend Cecile were playing blues on the platforms of Odeon station. Frank brought him to the Nouvel Hippodrome, where he jammed in front of 10,000 people. 'Zappa,' he told Phillipe Manoeuvre, 'that mother has a lotta soul. I felt so close to him on stage. I could feel his heart beating while we were playing. He gave me a lot of room to play, and when we went out, he just asked me, "How much do you want?" I sure didn't know what to tell him.'7 Shortly after, Blue played harmonica on the Rolling Stones' 'Miss You'.

COCAINE DECISIONS

Warners finally released *Zappa In New York* on March 3, 1978, five months after its intended release date, only to withdraw it immediately after the first pressing. The company's legal department were still concerned about 'Punky's Whips' and now took exception to some more ad lib remarks about Punky Meadows and Jeff Beck in the badinage between Frank and Terry Bozzio during 'Titties & Beer'. The latter was re-edited and, despite Meadows' consent, 'Punky's Whips' was removed altogether. The excision of almost 11 minutes playing time meant the running order of the first two sides had to be changed and the album was drastically shortened overall.

'They took it out,' an indignant Frank told Hugh Fielder. 'First of all they had no right to tamper with the tapes. Secondly, they didn't pay me for any of the stuff that I delivered to them. I mean, they're just so far in breach of the contract and they're just so grossly unfair.' Reacting to criticism of the short playing time, he said, 'It wasn't my fault. I didn't have any control over it.'8

'Warner Brothers were never interested in giving people value for money,' Frank said to me in 1991. 'From my knowledge, I think that that company was probably more infested with white powder than just about any other in the business at that time. It was an industrialised procedure. They had people that would show up at concerts with suitcases full of drugs.'

The bowdlerised version of *Zappa In New York* was released in Britain the following month but the British company quietly let stocks of the original album and cassette reach the shelves of some Virgin stores. The only light note in the proceedings was an advertisement that featured a picture of a facially-decorated Margaret Thatcher emerging from her Jaguar at the Houses of Parliament with a copy of the album under her arm, alongside the headline, 'I heard *Zappa In New York*, but it didn't do a thing for me.'9

It wasn't until 1991 that the unexpurgated album, with 30 minutes of additional material, was released on a double-CD. For the immediate future, Frank concentrated on the new album, to be called *Sheik Yerbouti*, a pun on K.C. And The Sunshine Band's 1976 chart-topping hit, *(Shake, Shake, Shake) Shake Your Booty*. 'We worked for months on that,' Tommy Mars remembered. 'For instance, on the song 'Baby Snakes', I was watching a *Twilight Zone* on TV late one night and I got this phone call from Frank. He said, "Hi, Tommy, how are you? Feel like doing a little singing tonight?" And I said, "Sure". I came down to (Village Recorders) and did 'Baby Snakes' that night about six times, my own voice on one line, no harmonies, just a straight linear thing.'10

Other songs, like 'Yo' Mama', involved even more work. 'On an orchestrated section of (that) song, the actual things that were reinforced happened at different times. On that guitar solo, there are three different sections from three different concerts, and Frank just juxtaposed them. It was an augmentation of what happened at a live performance, but an actual arrangement that evolved in the studio. He'd say, "Go free, interpret it", and all these countermelodies evolved out of the arrangement that was there.

'Frank wrote that song at the very beginning of the '77 European tour, and it has a personal relevance to me. We were doing this rehearsal in London and Frank was getting very tense. I got fined because I hadn't memorised this little piece called 'Little House I Used To Live In'. I hadn't realised he wanted it totally memorised. So this rehearsal ended in a total fiasco. The next day, he came in with these lyrics: "Maybe you should stay with yo' mama . . ." It was really autobiographic; that's how things evolve with Frank.'11

The majority of the album's 16 tunes would be built up from backing tracks recorded at Hammersmith. Two others, 'Jones Crusher' and 'Jewish Princess', were recorded in similar fashion at the Palladium in New York City, and two instrumentals, 'Rat Tomago' and 'The Sheik Yerbouti Tango' were four-track recordings from the February 15 gig at Berlin's Deutschlandhalle. There were also two typically obtuse spoken interludes, 'What Ever Happened To All The Fun In The World' and 'We've Got To Get Into Something Real', the latter commenting on how the songs were 'two tours old' and incorporating the mention of LEATHER. Finally, there was 'Rubber Shirt', the most perfectly realised example of xenochrony thus far. Frank explained its creation in the sleevenotes and ended with a typically sardonic flourish: 'All of the sensitive, interesting interplay between the bass and drums never actually happened . . .'

Frank took most of the lead vocals, but Terry Bozzio and Adrian Belew each had their features. Some of the material, like 'Broken Hearts Are For Assholes' and 'Tryin' To Grow A Chin', was indeed much older than just two tours. The latter song chimed well with the recent upsurge of punk rock, and 'I'm So Cute' was also specifically written for Terry 'Ted' Bozzio to lampoon the trend. Having already guyed the disco craze with 'Disco Boy', Frank came up with an even better synthesis of pastiche and satire, 'Dancin' Fool'. Two other songs, 'Bobby Brown' and 'Jewish Princess', would each contribute in different ways to the eventual success of the album, making it Frank's biggest seller.

With the sessions completed, auditions and rehearsals began in July for an autumn tour of Europe and America. Both Patrick O'Hearn and Adrian Belew had left, the latter to work with David Bowie. They had met backstage at a German gig, and Bowie had asked Belew to join his band. 'It worked out later that Frank was sort of finished with his thing and it was time for me to go and do something else,' he said in discussion with Steve Vai. 'I remember one night we were playing 'Yo' Mama'. Frank changed the words to, "I think maybe you should stay with your David". Apart from that he never gave me any grief about it. He wished me well and it was very generous of him. I often felt like it was an opportunist move on my part and I wish I hadn't done it, but those things happen. I was young and stupid.'[12]

On the very first day of rehearsals, another major change took place. Terry Bozzio had auditioned with Group 87 before coming to the rehearsal. 'I went in; I'd cut my hair, I was wearing different clothes, I'd just played this audition and been offered a deal with a record company (Columbia). We started to rehearse, me and Pat, and Frank could tell I wasn't really into it. He called me into his office, as he would say – actually we stepped behind the stage and he said, "I think it's time you go off and do your own thing", just like a good father would.'[13]

O'Hearn and Bozzio were replaced by Arthur Barrow and Vinnie Colaiuta, while Belew's place was filled by the return of Denny Walley and the introduction of Ike Willis. Peter Wolf said of Barrow, 'When he got into the band, he could play everything. He just walked in and knew all the old parts, all the old bass lines. He was actually correcting Frank in some places.'[14] Willis was a native of St. Louis, he'd first seen the Mothers at the city's Ambassador Theater in 1974. Three years later, on October 2, 1977, the Zappa band played a concert at Washington University, where Willis was studying. He met Frank after the sound check and auditioned for him in the dressing room, playing Frank's guitar and singing a new song called 'Bamboozled By Love'. They then harmonised on 'Carolina Hardcore Ecstasy' and Frank had made a note of his phone number. 'He just sings his ass off, it's fantastic,' Frank told Christopher Kathman. 'I told him at that time that when we were having auditions, I'd bring him out.'[15]

'Nobody's universal,' Frank told Wayne Manor in an *NME* piece, 'The Monk On Zappa's Back', that never explained its title. 'People have different abilities, and if you're working in a special idiom, you want people who are comfortable in that idiom. There's plenty of stuff for anyone to learn when they come in the band. It's like, I think my band's probably the finest music school in America. It gives you on-the-job training, and if you're lucky enough to get into the school, you get paid while you learn.'

What conversation there was picked over the corpse of *Lather* and detailed the three albums that were to come from Warner Brothers. In a rare instance of candour, Frank talked of his family. 'I've got a brother who sells college textbooks for McGraw-Hill. He spent three years in the Marines. I got another one who's working in an old folks home. ['In the kitchen,' says Gail.] My sister started out by marrying an Okie, and later divorced him and married a former basketball player. She spends her time working in a Photo-Mat.'

There was one prophetic observation, however. 'I see that people are drifting toward the Right today, in a very hypocritical way. They're not really right-wing people. But they figure that the more they look right-wing, the more they'll be able to get away with in the closet. The whole right-wing trend is people who want to look upstanding while they go home and do as much weird stuff as they can get away with.'[16] Was there a scent of Ronald Reagan and Jimmy Swaggart in the wind?

ARE YOU HUNG UP?

Before spending the autumn touring America, the Zappa band came to Europe for seven dates, five in Germany, one in Sweden and one in England. No less than four were open-air festivals, including that in the grounds of Knebworth House which also featured the Boomtown Rats, Peter Gabriel and the Tubes. After the first gig in Ulm on August 26, Frank had intended to stay in Munich, but his request for a piano in his suite could not be met. So, reluctantly, he came to London and took a four-room suite on the fifth floor of the Hyde Park Hotel. Hugh Fielder went to meet the Anglophobe.

'I hate playing in England,' Frank declared. 'I don't mind playing in Europe too much. The audiences on the Continent are pretty good. I can't stand this place, though. It's the people . . . the thing that's always depressed me about the English audience is that they're oriented towards dressing up and queuing up and anything in between that is irrelevant.' Fielder pointed out that he'd sold out six shows on his last visit. 'God knows why,' Frank replied. 'I mean, even when they're clapping it doesn't feel right to me. It's like they like you for the wrong reason.'[17]

In our conversation, Frank's reaction to London audiences proved to be only part of a wider-ranging antagonism. 'On each successive visit,' he said in 1991, 'I saw Britain turning into a Third World country, much like our own here. People being depressed, getting meaner, getting more desperate and things getting more peculiar. Behaviour becoming more peculiar. And that's saying something, because it was plenty peculiar in 1967. Things got meaner and cheaper and dirtier and it started to remind me of the kind of growth decay that happens in large US cities, where things just fall apart. And the main thing that you feel when you arrive in the city is just a big ball of hatred that's not especially directed at anybody or anything, it's just, *Hate lives there.*'

On a lighter note in his interview with Fielder, he was happy to announce that Warner Brothers would not be getting his new album. 'That will be coming out in January and it's probably going to be on Virgin in the UK and it will be on my own label in the United States and Canada.' The British deal wasn't definite, though. 'I don't demand very much. Just give me the money to make a record and make sure that it gets into the stores. With them, there's no sweat; they've got the stores. They're a little bit tight on the money, though.' Nor was Richard Branson very enthusiastic about the ten-album set, taking the same view as Warner Brothers that it represented one unit rather than ten. 'I can't afford that. I've already invested my money in making the thing, so I have to get reimbursed for doing it.'[18]

The prolificness of Frank's musical output had always been a bone of contention with whichever label he was signed to. He explained to Tim Schneckloth, 'record companies, in order to protect their investment, try to avoid putting out more than two albums per year on an artist because they want to milk the sales on each release as thoroughly as possible. I think that's a fantasy in my case because we sell so much in catalogue. Whether the albums becomes a hit when it's first released is irrelevant, because the stuff just keeps selling. People hear about it by word of mouth.'[19]

Another orchestral project, this time with the Vienna Symphony Orchestra, had fallen through. Frank showed Fielder a full orchestral score on which he was still working, having so far completed two movements. 'It was supposed to be for next May. What I'll probably do is to finish the piece off and hire an orchestra and record it.' That would be an expensive proposition, Fielder thought. Frank's reply became one of his most famous aphorisms: 'Well, some rock and roll musicians make a bunch of money and stick it up their noses. I stick mine in my ear.'[20]

The set played by the Zappa band in the early evening of Saturday, September 9 at Knebworth was identical with that at Saarbrucken six days earlier. A bootleg double album, *Saarbrucken 1978*, later became part of *Beat The Boots 1*. Most of the songs came from *Sheik Yerbouti*, although 'Easy Meat', 'Keep It Greasy', 'The Meek Shall Inherit Nothing', 'Bamboozled By Love' and 'Conehead' would appear over the course of several albums, often in radically altered form. 'Conehead' had already changed significantly from the instrumental version played by the previous band on New Years Eve at LA's Pauley Pavilion. It now had lyrics and a repetitive riff similar to that used on 'Muffin Man', but would not appear on record for another three years.

The following week, Warner Brothers released *Studio Tan* in a garish cartoon cover, by *Raw Comix* artist Gary Panter, completely devoid of recording information or personnel details. 'They were doing whatever they could to hurt my career,' Frank said to me. 'You've heard the expression, "You'll never work in this town again"?' At that time, sales had dropped off since *Apostrophe (')* and were averaging between 50,000 and 70,000. The shoddy manner in which *Studio Tan* and the last two albums were dumped on the public seemed to justify Frank's onstage comments, which centred around the basic mantra, 'Warner Brothers sucks'.

Critical reaction was mixed, or in Ian Penman's case, confused. 'Here the texture and dimension - parodies of repression, parodies of techniques to achieve same - are intertwined and cross-referenced until one imitates the other and background is foreground, until attack is lull - and joke is judgement.' Er, yes. 'These are repossessions and deftly engineered dry echoes of older and other work. It still bounces. It could be an anonymous soundtrack (there are no credits) for a Stigwood production of *Uncle Meat*. It's a package, a fun and games machine.'[21]

Part of the album's problem was that most of the material was at least four years old. 'Greggery Peccary' had been written in 1972; its 20-minute duration encompassed a dazzlingly edited combination of orchestral and small group themes, tied to a rambling story that jostled together several of Frank's abiding antipathies. Unlike 'Billy The Mountain', who also puts in a brief appearance, it lacked spontaneity. Dense orchestral arrangements overlaid with long passages of verbose exposition lacked the humour of the earlier piece, not to mention the manic dimension of Flo & Eddie's personalities. In fact, most of one speech, by 'the greatest living philosopher' Quentin Robert de Nameland, had been replaced by Bruce Fowler's trombone solo.

Two of the album's other three tracks featured the 1974 band; 'Revised Music For Guitar And Low-Budget Orchestra' is a self-explanatory reworking of the piece first featured on Jean-Luc Ponty's *King Kong* album; 'REDUNZL' (the vowels were later to be omitted) made full use of George Duke's lush piano harmonies before Frank's guitar solo developed into a group improvisation, which after some more staged 'events' became a fleet piano solo. 'Let Me Take You To The Beach' was an incongruous trifle in this company, satirising the vacuous triviality of the Hit Parade. Engineer Davey Moire's falsetto lead vocal conjures up such masterpieces as the Newbeats' 'Bread And Butter'.

The American section of the tour concentrated on the East Coast for the balance of September and all of October, with the now traditional residency at New York City's Palladium for the four nights up to Halloween. Joining the band on that night for the second time on the tour (the first was in Berlin on September 7) was violinist Lakshmirnarayna Shankar. Originally from Madras, Shankar had been playing violin since the age of five. He came to America in 1969 and studied ethnomusicology at the Wesleyan University. He met John McLaughlin in 1973, during the latter's Sri Chinmoy phase, and two years later the pair formed Shakti, an acoustic quartet which attempted the difficult fusion of classical Indian music and jazz. After three albums, the group had broken up earlier in 1978. Two examples from the Halloween performance, 'Thirteen', in which Frank coaxes the audience to clap in 13/8, and 'Take Your Clothes Off When You Dance', appear on *YCDTOSA 6*.

Another participant that night was Warren Cucurullo, a young guitarist who'd spent the last three years attending every one of Frank's East Coast concerts. He befriended soundman Davey Moire and was eventually introduced to Frank, who was impressed that Cucurullo had learned not only his tunes but many of his guitar solos. Celebrating his birthday one night in a

New York restaurant, Frank introduced him to William Burroughs and Allen Ginsberg, seated at the next table, 'This is Warren, he's a guitar player'. 'After that,' Cucurullo said, 'I spent a lot of time just practicing in my basement.'[22]

His contribution to the Halloween show was reciting 'Ms X', a story he'd first told to Frank in Florida six weeks previously. Towards the end of the year, he received a phone call from Frank telling him about the next European tour and asking him if he'd like to audition for the band. 'I left for California the next day, and then the next thing I knew I was playing the Hammersmith Odeon - plucked right from the basement to the big stage.'[23]

Denied the means to spend weeks at a time in recording studios, Frank concentrated on touring. Tim Schneckloth asked him if he still found it worthwhile. 'It's the greatest thing there is,' Frank replied. 'As a matter of fact, it is the only thing that makes it worthwhile. Some of the drudgery you have to go through on the road is so boring. And once you get a chance to do that . . . I wouldn't even care if there wasn't an audience there. It's just that you've got all the equipment set up, the musicians are there and paid for, it's just the right temperature, the stage is the right colour, it's the right mood. And then you play, and you can create things right there. And fortunately, there are cassettes of it so you have a chance to hear it back later and see if your experiments were successful or what. That's one of the prime reasons for me going out on the road and touring.

'I like playing in hockey rinks,' he added. 'The problem about playing hockey rinks is that it's hard to hear the words. If you're word oriented, okay, that's tough. But that air space you have in there is such a great thing to work with - it's this huge tonnage of air. And when you go 'wham' and hit a big chord, you've taken all that and spewed it over 15,000 people. It's not just a feeling of power. If you want to play really soft, think how soft one note is diluted in the air space of a 15,000 seat hockey rink. That's really soft. And one note played really loud is really loud. So the dynamic range in a place like that - softest note versus the loudest note, the top to bottom of your sculpture - with the right equipment, gives you a chance to do a more interesting and complicated sound event. Forget about whether it's a song or a drum beat or a scream on the microphone or whatever it is - those are sounds that are moving air around. Taken in the purest abstract sense, the opportunities in a large, enclosed, resonant place like that are very interesting.'[24]

An opportunity of a different kind came at the beginning of December. William Burroughs was the subject of the three-day NOVA Convention at New York's Entermedia Theater, during which Laurie Anderson performed, Patti Smith played the clarinet and the Fugs' Ed Sanders read an account of a fictional rock group called J'Accuse. Allen Ginsberg recited 'Punk Rock You're My Big Cry-baby' and Frank read the 'talking asshole' section from Burrough's *Naked Lunch*. Frank and Burroughs were pictured together at the event in *Rolling Stone;* later, over dinner, they discussed the possibility of making a Broadway musical out of Burrough's book, but the project got no further.

TOUCH ME THERE

Frank arrived in London yet again in mid-January 1979 with a full work schedule. The first priority was to record an album with L. Shankar for Zappa Records, his new label to be distributed in America by Polygram. In Britain and the rest of the world, Virgin had disappeared from the frame to be replaced by CBS, with *Sheik Yerbouti* scheduled for release at the beginning of March. There were also rehearsals for the European tour that would begin on February 10 with nine British dates.

As Frank finalised arrangements for his first new album in two years, Warner Brothers divested itself of *Sleep Dirt*. It had originally been titled *Hot Rats III* and took its new title from an acoustic guitar duet between Frank and James 'Bird Legs' Youmans which ends suddenly with Youmans' muttered 'damn!' Frank asks, 'Getting tired?' 'No,' replies Youmans, 'my fingers got stuck.' Three of the tunes come from Frank's science-fiction musical, *Hunchentoot;* 'Flambay', 'Spider Of Destiny' and 'Time Is Money' were recorded in early 1974 at Blood, Sweat And Tears' producer Jim Guercio's Caribou studio in Colorado. The fact that here they sound like backing tracks was confirmed when *Sleep Dirt* was reissued on CD in 1991, with vocals by Thana Harris and Chester Thompson's original drum tracks digitally replaced by Chad Wackerman.

'Regyptian Strut' retains the original band personnel on a slow tune that is all exposition apart from Bruce Fowler's eccentric trombone flourishes. Later in the piece his multiple overdubs confirm Frank's high assessment of his talent. 'Filthy Habits' is a seven-minute exercise in controlled feedback; multiple guitar overdubs, some recorded backwards, howl and whine behind Frank's solo, which itself operates on the verge of constant distortion. Towards the end, Frank adds bursts of keyboard overlays that are reminiscent of the work of pioneer minimalist, Terry Riley.

The last track on the album is also the longest; at 13 minutes, 'The Ocean Is The Only Solution' is a trio improvisation that scurries through a series of complex rhythmic patterns before settling into a fuzz guitar solo over a fast, tumbling riff that probably provided more entertainment for the musicians than for the listener. 'What actually happened,' Terry Bozzio told Andy Greenaway, 'was that Frank, Dave Parlato and I jammed at the Record Plant for about 35 minutes and filled up two reels of tape. Zappa, out of all that material, edited down to about 13 minutes. He played it on a real interesting Fender 12-string that had a pick-up in the neck. He had this glass-shattering 12-string sound – it was really unique.'[25] Parlato's bass track was then replaced by Patrick O'Hearn.

Graced with another cartoon cover by Gary Panter but, like *Studio Tan,* devoid of any recording information, *Sleep Dirt* sounds (as was later proved) unfinished. If the tapes were delivered as put together here, then Frank must have been fulfilling his contract quota. It makes more sense to believe that they were intended as part of an album set like *Lather*, where individual tunes would be contrasted with vocal performances and perhaps gain from the comparison. Lumped together in this arbitrary fashion, the merit of a particular performance, such as 'Filthy Habits', is challenged by the similarity of tempos elsewhere and an absence of the inner logic that the listener expects from a Zappa compilation.

The recording of L. Shankar's debut solo album had been switched to London from California since none of the facilities that Frank normally used was available. Backing tracks were recorded at Advision Studios, which Frank found 'primitive', with a British band consisting of keyboard player James Lascelles, guitarist Phil Palmer, Dave Marquee on bass and drummer Simon Phillips. Overdubs were done at the 'New York standard' AIR Studios and the album was mixed at The Townhouse.

'Touch Me There' explored the microtonal variations of L. Shankar's acoustic and amplified violin work, although the latter more often resembled a bumble bee on valium. The overall tone of the album, exemplified by 'Windy Morning' and 'Love Gone Away', was reflective and curiously unengaging, only igniting on 'Little Stinker' and 'No More Mr Nice Girl'. The latter was one of four collaborations with Frank, including the title track, 'Knee Deep In Heaters', its lyrics rendered almost incomprehensible by Shankar's schoolboy falsetto, and 'Dead Girls Of London'. This last was originally intended to feature Van Morrison's lead vocal, but Warner Brothers vetoed his appearance. His performance was replaced by Frank and Ike Willis harmonising as 'Stucco Homes'. Other, more ethereal vocal embellishment was provided by Vicky Blumenthal and Jenny Lautrec.

These days, rehearsals were supervised by the Clonemeister, the new alias for bassist Arthur Barrow. 'Frank would always show up for the last four hours of rehearsal, and I would tape that part. He'd say to various band members, "Okay, now you do this here, and you make the fart noise there, and you do that there." So, after the rehearsal I'd sit down with a notebook and make notes about who was supposed to make what fart noises and stuff. It was like being a drill sergeant, kind of.

'When Frank was there at the rehearsal and inspired, he would write with the band the way someone else might write at the piano, or with a piece of score paper, or at a computer. It was really amazing how quickly he could get stuff together, and get really good players to interpret it and make it sound like Frank Zappa music. Frank's just about the only guy who did not compromise his music at all, and still make a living at it.'[26]

'He rehearsed us to death,' Peter Wolf averred. 'I've never rehearsed that way in my life, before or since. First, he would lay all this music on you, which was a conglomerate of styles: '50s rock and roll, punk rock, new wave, jazz, Bela Bartók, Greek folk music, and weird 12-tone stuff. You had to put on all these different hats, and be quick and spontaneous about it.'[27]

'Frank loved to test the band members,' Tommy Mars remembered. 'I'll never forget one tour. We were getting ready to go to England. Then, three days before we went out, Frank came to rehearsal and said, "I want every piece in this show to be done reggae. I don't care if we stay here until the tour starts, that's what we're gonna do." So we burned out that night, we burned out the next day. Then, the day before the tour, he comes back all happy and says, "We're not gonna do that reggae anymore". I mean, he put us right in front of the muzzle of the gun, man!

'He was extremely difficult sometimes. He knew exactly what button to push. I saw people who revered him so much, who were very chopsy but who didn't have exactly what he needed, absolutely cremated on the spot by him, in rehearsals, in auditions, onstage. He pushed every boundary personally, sociologically, politically, comedically, and tragically. He couldn't be happy until it was ready to break.'[28]

'Well, I'm a hard taskmaster all the time,' Frank told Nigel Leigh. 'For whatever I do. I don't have any control over the way they perceive me but this is a situation where they get a pay cheque and they either do the job or they don't do the job. I don't hire them to be my buddies.'[29] In another interview, he admitted, 'I'm the worst person you could work for and the best. Yes, there is tyranny and personal abuse. It produces the desired effect.'[30]

CHAPTER FIFTEEN
SHEIK YERBOUTI

A year to the day since the release of *Zappa In New York*, the Zappa visage, swathed in an Arab burnous, peered from the cover of the first album of new material since *Zoot Allures*, released back in October 1976. The contrast between *Sheik Yerbouti* and the albums Warner Brothers were foisting on the public was great. Although the new album contained a number of songs that had been 'toured' for a while, their sometimes scabrous, always scathing lyric content ranged over a number of controversial subjects guaranteed to offend anyone unaccustomed to Frank's withering wit. With the exception of the instrumental features, there was an absence of the complex tempo changes that characterised so much of Frank's music. This time, his messages were delivered hard and straight.

A stately version of 'I Have Been In You' opened Side One, devoid of its explicit onstage prologue. Thereafter, the incompetence of US service industries, anal sex, rapacious women, punk rockers, gender-bending record pluggers, drug addicts, dancing fools and Jewish princesses came under review. Was Frank going for the easy options? Nick Kent thought so. Flourishing his credentials, he stigmatised *Sheik Yerbouti* as 'the same old slop, whether it be the "serious" orchestral flotsam he can flaunt to justify his noxious condescending broadside wildly directed at the poor saps who still think he's some bona-fide genius, or the gross-out whacko "yucks for the bucks" flimflam.'

Barely pausing for a stimulant he went on, 'this is wall-to-wall four-sided dreck that may even actually represent a new look for Zappa's swindling artistic returns so far . . . here is a man obsessed with peddling cheap laughs that, beyond the odd witty couplet or two, aren't worth even a gratuitous smirk most of the time.' Only bad typesetting blunted his scorn: 'Buy this album and you can check you (sic) arsehole-rating.'[1]

After such a review, what better consequence than that people with secure fundaments bought *Sheik Yerbouti* in sufficient quantities for it to reach number 21 in the US album charts and make it Frank's best-selling album, selling more than 1.6 million units world-wide. 'The reason for that was 'Bobby Brown',' he said in 1991. 'If it weren't for some twist of fate where somebody in

Norway decided that they liked that song very much and kept playing it in discos, that's where the whole thing started from.'

'Picture a disco in Norway with people dancing to 'Bobby Brown'. College students got cassettes of it and hooked up speakers in their cars and drove through town blaring this song. It was unreal. And then it went from Scandinavia, a year later, to be a hit in Germany. Not quite with the same rabidity. And you could never even play the record on the air in the United States.'[2]

The explicit story of a record plugger who realigns his sexual preferences after an encounter with a lesbian could never have been a hit in any English-speaking country. The gay community, still in the first flush of its liberation and largely unaware of the harsh fate in store for many of its number, was not amused. Replying to the inevitable accusations of being sexist, misogynistic and homophobic, Frank said, 'Some people miss the joke. In general, I was a convenient enemy and they could get exposure for their causes by coming after me. But I'm not anti-gay . . . I'm a journalist of a sort. I have a right to say what I want to say about any topic. If you don't have a sense of humour, then tough titties.'[3]

'If you looked at the number of songs that I've written and how many characters in the songs are men,' he pointed out to Charles Shaar Murray, 'most of the songs are about men. No men's group ever said, "Hey, how come you're sayin' we're stoopid?" Women are sensitive if you say they're stupid. I like women: women are fine. But - men do bad stuff, women do bad stuff. Who's the worst? You guys arm-wrestle over it. I'm not gonna tell ya.'[4]

Nor was he anti-Semitic, but that didn't deter the Anti-Defamation League of the B'nai B'rith from filing a complaint when 'Jewish Princess', a lubricious catalogue of sexual attributes expected from one of her persuasion, received heavy airplay on California's radio stations. 'They wanted to convince the world that there's no such thing as a Jewish princess, but, I'm sorry, the facts speak for themselves. They asked me to apologise and I refused . . . Well, I didn't make up the idea of a Jewish princess. They exist, so I wrote a song about them. If they don't like it, so what? Italians have princesses, too.'[5] To that end, he announced that his next album would contain the song, 'Catholic Girls'.

He expanded on the subject in conversation with Nigel Leigh: 'I'm making comments about society, and the society that I was commenting on was engaged in what they loved to describe as the sexual revolution - a world of sexual incompetents encountering each other under disco circumstances. Now can't you do songs about that?' But those songs always associated sex with human stupidity. 'Well, have you ever looked at people fucking? Oooo. I mean that's a silly looking thing to begin with. It's silly looking. Let's face it, it looks silly. Why not say so? And from that you could develop a number of theories about it, whether or not it should be celebrated. I mean, so what if it feels good? It's still silly.'[6]

Did he think that he was the cultural enemy of the many pressure groups? 'No. I'm sure they might have had a different viewpoint because anybody who would write the kind of material that I write was a pretty convenient target. I mean, it's pretty easy to hate me for whatever you choose to hate me for. Because I'm virtually unrepentant, and I just don't care.' Did he accept the criticism that he'd dealt insensitively with the subject of female sexuality and female rights? 'I hope that in those instances where I have dealt with that topic that I have been as insensitive to them as I've been to everybody else. I think that my insensitivity is pretty evenly spread around.'[7] Perhaps it was also the case that his records didn't sell in sufficient quantities to warrant a law suit by those he offended.

It was a fact, though, that Frank's sense of humour was becoming increasingly sour, perhaps as a result of the real and perceived slights and injuries that seemed to dog his career during the 70s. George Duke had noticed a change during his tenure with the Mothers. 'The only change I saw in Frank over those years was that he went from being funny/sarcastic to being almost serious/sarcastic. The latter part of the time I was in the band, his sense of humour became kind of vindictive.'[8]

David Sheff asked Frank if there was rhyme or reason behind the subjects he chose to attack. 'Whatever I'm mad at the time,' he replied. 'I like things that work. If something doesn't, the first question you have to ask is, Why? If it's not working and you know why, then you have to ask, "Why isn't somebody doing something about it?" . . . I like carrying things to their most ridiculous extreme, because out there on the fringe is where my type of entertainment lies.'[9]

Mark Ellen, reviewing the first of three Hammersmith gigs on February 17- 19, thought that Frank 'walks the line between the ageing tackiness of his sagas and the sheer complexity of his music . . . it's clear that his lyrics have never veered much from the gross and narrow.' Ellen offered a potted version of Frank's career and the observation that, 'The shock/horror mystique has long since been replaced by "total control".'

The control slipped towards the end of the three-hour show when a member of the audience passed Frank a book. 'He looks delighted. It's passed around the whole band, who all crack up in hysterics. We're treated to an extract – a clinical aid to the canine birth process, advising the use of sterilised scissors.'[10] What Ellen didn't tell *NME* readers was the title of the book and thus its particular significance – *Breeding From Your Poodle* by Margaret Rothery Sheldon and Barbara Lockwood. For once, conceptual continuity had been contrived, but there it was, nonetheless.

The Rolling Stones Mobile was parked outside the theatre and all three nights were recorded. Two new songs, 'For The Young Sophisticate' and 'Bamboozled By Love', and fresh arrangements of 'Brown Shoes Don't Make It' and 'Peaches III', were issued in 1981 on *Tinsel Town Rebellion*. Several songs from February 18 were later included on separate volumes of *You Can't Do That On Stage Anymore*, including a version of 'Don't Eat The Yellow Snow' with bizarre poetic contributions from a distraught young bard in the audience. His second piece, 'Broadmoor', delineated his desire for a 'garden' as bleak and colourless as his diction. As he declaimed 'I want to water that garden with my tears', Denny Walley retorted, 'Oh, you want kindergarten'. The event was recalled three years later at the same venue, with Frank referring to the unfortunate poetaster as 'that asshole'. When he inserted the sequence in a mutant-edit version of 'King Kong' on *YCDTOSA 3*, Frank also included Walley's original comment.

It was events like this that prompted Frank's observation to Nigel Leigh: 'After a certain amount of touring, especially in Europe, the people who would come to the shows understood what the game was. You knew that things could change on the spot, right there on stage. It's not like you would rehearse in the afternoon and say, "Tonight's surprise will be . . ." You try and work with musicians who have the flexibility and the kind of spontaneity that if a musical situation arises, or a social situation arises with somebody in the audience, that they can play off of it and develop it into something else. So those were the kinds of surprises that were being delivered. Things that were unique just to that audience. Just for that concert. At one time only.'[11]

The principal use that Frank made of the Hammersmith tapes was in the compilation of *Shut Up 'N Play Yer Guitar*, three albums of guitar solos first made available in 1981 by mail order only. Half of the 20 tracks came from the Hammersmith recordings; no less than four were solos taken from performances of 'Inca Roads'. One track, 'Pink Napkins', came from a February 1977 performance by the Eddie Jobson/Ray White band, another, 'Ship Ahoy', from the 1976 Japanese tour. The balance would come from the 1980 American tour.

The Spring 1979 European tour was the most extensive Frank had ever undertaken, stretching from February 10 through to April 1, with only ten days off. 'The tours keep getting longer and longer,' he said. 'And I need them more and more and more.' He refused to do a television broadcast on February 20, in between gigs in Brussels and Paris. 'If you don't start having your days off when you come over on these things, your health just starts falling apart.'[12] After finishing in Zurich, the band flew on to Japan for more gigs, before returning to California in mid-April.

Talking about his popularity in Europe, Frank said, 'I think the reason why we're better known there is because of all the US groups that could tour in Europe, we probably did it more frequently, on a regular basis throughout the years, than most of the other US groups. We played regional dates. We took the music right there and stuck it in their face, French provincial dates and lots of small dates in Germany. We played towns outside of London. The big groups would come over and just do the one big show in one town. We went out and played for everybody. One of our best British dates was in Newcastle. If I had to choose one place in England to play, I'd say Newcastle would be my favourite British audience.'

JOE'S GARAGE

The last of the three disputed Warner Brothers albums, *Orchestral Favorites*, was released on May 4, 1979, with the most inappropriate cover art of them all. Gary Panter's cartoon depicted a head with piano keys for teeth, a guitar fretboard for a nose and a stubbled cleft chin in the Desperate Dan mould. Nothing could have better revealed the record company's purpose. It was plain that they had no interest in, nor respect for, the serious side of their former artist's music.

The poster for the original September 1975 concert at UCLA's Royce Hall had promised premiere performances of 'Pedro's Dowry' and 'Bogus Pomp' and both were included here, along with 'Strictly Genteel' (the finale of *200 Motels*), 'Naval Aviation In Art?' and an orchestral arrangement of 'Duke Of Prunes'. The Abnuceals Emuukha Electric Orchestra consisted of 37 musicians, along with Frank on guitar, bassist Dave Parlato, Terry Bozzio on drums and Emil Richards on percussion. The majority of the hired help consisted of brass and woodwind players, with only four string players. The murky sound of the original vinyl issue was cleaned up for its CD reissue, thus enhancing the enthusiasm with which the ensemble approached their unconventional task.

The most adventurous piece was 'Pedro's Dowry', which avoided the regular pulses that drove most of the other compositions. 'Naval Aviation In Art?' was little more than a fragment, an eerie minute or so that contrasted staccato violin events with sustained chords from the woodwinds. This was perhaps the most imaginative piece, the more so for ending just when its ominous and threatening atmosphere had been established. 'Duke Of Prunes' was basically a grandiose framework for a guitar solo that made creative use of feedback. 'Bogus Pomp' shed a humorous light on the sort of episodic writing that goes into film soundtrack music. Some of its themes were first performed by members of the BBC Symphony during the Mothers' Royal Festival Hall appearance way back in October 1968. Three of these pieces would be recorded in 1983 by the London Symphony Orchestra with less that satisfactory results.

Frank was already in the throes of his next multi-album project, *Joe's Garage*, conceived as a three-record set and released as a single album followed by a double-album. The original intention was to record a single of the title song and 'Catholic Girls', his equal opportunity response to 'Jewish Princess'. 'It started out to be just a bunch of songs,' he said. 'Then I figured out a story that would hold 'em together. It's all exercise. It's like doing crossword puzzles. In looking at it I saw that not only did it make a continuous story, but it made a good continuous story.'[13]

Good for a fully-fledged conspiracy theorist, that is. *Act 1*'s gatefold sleeve set forth the various hypotheses that drove the narrative. In simple terms, devoid of the individual targets for Frank's invective, a US President just might seek to abolish music by identifying it as a principal cause of the energy crisis and inflation in general, and further, that people just might think it was a good idea. As Frank admitted in his next paragraph, it was a stupid story, done in the manner of a cheap high school play. The sting in the tail was to point out that, in Iran, music was illegal. The sleeve of the concluding double album developed the idea of 'Total Criminalisation', a Kafka-esque concept whereby a system of surreptitiously promulgated laws ensured that everyone was guilty of something, especially if it had to do with music.

In fact, the story was operating on two levels: overtly, it was working out the above hypotheses; on a more mundane level, some of Frank's perennial bugbears, such as the dumbness of pop music, the bands that played it, the people that watched them, the groupies that serviced them and especially the journalists that wrote about it, lined up to be pilloried one more time.

In order to get through the reams of exposition that were needed to explain both the supposition and the plot line, Frank became The Central Scrutinizer. His voiced EQ'd to sound as if it was issuing from a cheap plastic loud-hailer, he announced it as his responsibility to enforce all the laws that hadn't been passed yet. With a licence to commit mayhem thus granted, the hapless Joe's story unfolded, interrupted by the Scrute's explanations.

Joe is a guitarist in a garage band that regularly annoys the neighbourhood. His Catholic girlfriend, Mary becomes a 'Crew Slut' before taking part in 'The Wet T-shirt Contest'. Meanwhile, Joe is seduced by Lucille, who works at a Jack-In-The-Box concession and generously passes on a social disease which makes his balls feel like a pair of maracas, provoking the perennial question, 'Why Does It Hurt When I Pee?'. Act 1 ends with a rambling reggae version of 'Lucille Has Messed My Mind Up', the title song of Jeff Simmons' *Straight* album. So far, so literal. Thereafter, things get a trifle bizarre.

In *Acts 11 & 111*, the stricken guitarist pays an exorbitant fee for a consultation with L. Ron Hoover, head of the First Church of Appliantology, who deduces that Joe is a Latent Appliance Fetishist. Visiting The Closet, a club where the sexually damaged can interact with kitchen appliances, Joe dresses up as a housewife and learns to speak German. By these circuitous means, 'Stick It Out', a song from Flo & Eddie days, becomes the explicit serenade through which Joe importunes Sy Borg, an XQJ-37 nuclear powered Pan-Sexual Roto-Plooker and a mutant relative of Chunga, the industrial vacuum-cleaner who had her revenge several albums ago. Ike Willis' mother was responsible for the word 'plook', which here receives a meaning quite at variance with what Mrs Willis intended.

Unaware of the (or his) ramifications, Joe plooks Sy to death and is committed to a special prison full of musicians and redundant record executives (from Warner Brothers?) and 'promo personages' (Bobby Brown?) who gang-bang him to the tune of 'Keep It Greasey'. Sorely troubled, Joe lapses into semi-catatonia and dreams of guitar notes. Eventually, he's released into a world without musicians that, in 'Packard Goose', provokes a sort of madness in which his imaginary music is criticised by equally fanciful journalists.

A vision of his long-lost girlfriend, Mary, comes to him and delivers THE AUTHOR'S MESSAGE: 'Information is not knowledge. Knowledge is not wisdom. Wisdom is not truth.' (Okay, so far.) 'Truth is not beauty. Beauty is not love. Love is not music. Music is THE BEST.' Lit from within by this simplistic mantra, Joe consigns all journalists to squat on the Cosmic Utensil and dreams one last imaginary guitar solo, 'Watermelon In Easter Hay', before going to work in the Utility Muffin Research Kitchen, arrogantly applying his fully-charged icing anointment utensil. Festivities are brought to a close with 'A Little Green Rosetta', in which the entire cast gather round their author/director and sing his 'stupid song' in a party atmosphere that deliberately echoes, though less imaginatively, 'America Drinks And Goes Home'.

Because it operates on a number of levels, *Joe's Garage* is a hard record to enjoy, even when its achievements are acknowledged. The story is indeed stupid, its targets are easy and ones that had borne the brunt of Frank's wit many times before. As George Duke had noted, his humour, laced with a large shot of cynicism, was taking on an increasingly bitter and sardonic edge. Sex in his songs had become brutal and demeaning, as if he equated it with what he thought record companies and pop journalists had done to him. 'Packard Goose' is particularly paranoid, referring to all journalists as 'the worst kind of sleaze', dubbing them 'the government's whore' and inviting them to buss his buttocks.

'Catholic Girls' is small beer compared to the explicit 'Jewish Princess', its lyric content subordinated to the plot. To make sure the listener gets the connection, Warren Cucurullo's electric sitar plays part of the latter tune's melody during the fade-out. 'Crew Slut' mentions a group whose name sounds suspiciously like Toto. When remastered for CD, 'Toad-O Line', supposed to emulate one of the group's hits, was blandly retitled 'On The Bus'.

'The Wet T-shirt Contest' ruffled a few feminist feathers. One of Frank's roles in the unfolding melodrama metamorphoses from Father Riley at the local CYO into Buddy Jones, compere of the contest at 'The Brasserie . . . Home of THE TITS'. Nigel Leigh was questioning Frank's motives when he interrupted, 'Think carefully before you laugh or even answer this, that the guy who invented the wet T-shirt contest came up with a bad idea. "We need some more people coming to this bar. How do we get them in? Oh, I'll give $50 to the girl with the biggest tits who will go on stage and let some dumb fuck dump a bucket of water on her with a white T-shirt on, and then we'll sell more beer. What do you think, Billy?" I mean, surely he would have been a failure if it weren't for the fact that there is a virtual species of women in the United States that would kill each other to enter these contests and prevail for $50 or less. Shouldn't we recognise this fact? As Americans, we have to come to grips with this.

'It's a wonderful institution. Look at the people in the audience who experience what they really are interested in. Maybe not to the n'th degree, which would be total removal of the T-shirt. Some places, they do that. But you know, the girls get to fight it out for that $50. The bartender sells more beer. The band gets to watch whatever is going on up close, so long as the water doesn't damage some of their equipment. I mean, that's the only real down side to this.'[14]

Several of the compositions in *Acts 11 & 111* had been around for a while and only required minimal adaptation to be shoe-horned into the story. There was little new writing and what there was provided continuity or formed the framework for Frank's on-going experimentation. It wasn't until five years later that a chance question revealed that, with the exception of 'Watermelon In Easter Hay', all of the guitar solos heard in *Joe's Garage* were xenochronous.

'In the studio, they called it the "Ampex guitar",' Frank told David Mead. 'I had all these quarter-inch tapes of guitar solos that I liked from the '79 tour, and I'd go through my files, see what key a certain solo was in, and just experimentally hit the start button on the playback machine and lay it onto the multi-track.' Any tuning variations were adjusted with a Variable Speed Oscillator. 'We'd wiggle the pitch around to make sure it sounded like it was in the right key.'[15]

If there is a musical reason for *Joe's Garage* to exist, it has to be for the random creativity of its instrumental passages. The one exception, 'Watermelon In Easter Hay', is atypical Zappa, a simple soaring melody that belies its creator. When we talked about the album, I told Frank I thought it was the highlight of the entire album. 'Well, it is,' he replied. 'It's the best song on the album. But *Downbeat* didn't think so. The review in *Downbeat* was so unfavourable towards *Joe's Garage* and especially 'Watermelon In Easter Hay'. The jazzbo reviewer of that album just hated that song. It was supposed to be that character's last imaginary guitar solo before he quits the music business. So it's a sad song.' Ironic, too, that the so-called 'imaginary guitar solo' is the only real one.

The recording of *Joe's Garage* was not without its problems. 'When we first went into the studio, Peter (Wolf) was back in Vienna and Tommy (Mars) started the album off,' Frank told Michael Davis. 'With Tommy, we worked for several days and wound up with two tracks, whereas with Peter, we could do two or three tracks a day. They're equipped differently. Tommy is definitely a creative keyboard player with a good musical mind, but in the discipline department we had some problems. He just can't control himself to sit down and play something simple that's required for a simple song. So Tommy plays on only two songs on all six sides of *Joe's Garage;* the rest of the keyboard work is Peter.

'The first few sessions were very chaotic. I hate to have to act like an umpire or referee and go scream at everybody because they're jamming. I don't pay $200 an hour studio time to have guys go in there and jazz out. If you want to practice, do it at home; don't do it in the studio. The studio is the time to make a record.'[16]

BABY SNAKES

That was probably foremost in Frank's mind throughout the *Joe's Garage* sessions, for with any luck this would be the last time he would be reliant on commercial recording facilities. The Zappa basement was being converted into a recording studio, suitably named the Utility Muffin Research Kitchen. Because of the on-going construction work and the fact that Gail was due to give birth in August, he cancelled the late summer tour that had been scheduled.

The press quoted Frank as saying about their fourth child, 'If it's a boy we'll call him Burt Reynolds and if she's a girl she'll be called Clint Eastwood'. On a Dallas radio interview, he announced, 'If it's a girl, her name will be Peru.' In the event, their second daughter arrived at the beginning of the month and got to be called Diva for possessing the loudest scream in the hospital. 'And it turns out,' Gail told Victoria Balfour, 'that Diva has this incredible voice and she can knock you over from a distance of 30 feet.'[17]

Finishing touches had to be put to the latest concert film, *Baby Snakes*, due to be premiered in New York in December. Once again, Bruce Bickford's clay animation was an integral part of the production. Early in the film, Frank asks the artist how he got into animation; the ensuing conversation shows that, like so many of the people that fascinated Zappa, Bickford has an original but warped mind. 'My first animation,' he says, 'was cars running over the tops of hills. And then I branched out into, well, anything I could do with cars; and the clay people I had in the cars, I started animating.'

Frank then gets caught out in an assumption that trapped many of his own interviewers over the years, the supposition that certain elements when repeated must have meaning. 'There's an image that you use quite frequently in these films,' he says, putting forward a small clay structure that resembles a viaduct leading to a tunnel. 'This image here, would you mind explaining what this image is?'

Bickford replies, 'That was a face originally, but it turned into this bridge, the guy's nose and lips elongated out into this bridge.' A piece of animation illustrates the action.

'Yeah,' Frank presses, 'but you've done this transformation several times. What's that symbol really mean?'

'I don't know,' Bickford replies, mystified by his own invention. 'Noses are easily animatable into something else.'

Another amusing exchange follows. Bickford haltingly describes how one day he accepted 'a few tokes' from a passer-by's joint and went to sit on some rocks on a nearby beach. 'I felt like I was trapped there . . . I was so weak that I couldn't get up and I couldn't walk back to the sand. These rocks had – ', he wavers.

'An unearthly power over you?' Frank prompts.

'Yeah, the magnetism in them or something – They were thrown in there with no regard for their original – well, the original magnetism they'd picked up over the ages as they formed and everything. They were put in contrary to that pattern.'

'How long were you trapped?'

''Bout a half hour.'

'How'd you get away?'

'I finally – well, the effect of the dope wore off.'

Bickford plainly lived his life with the hand brake on. The final sequences of his stop-time animation flash past with such manic energy that the viewer forgets the enormous patience and attention to detail that have gone into their creation. The screen is crowded with mobile clay, each part fastidiously moved a fraction of an inch for each frame. Much of his work deals with the rapid metamorphosis of faces, within themselves or devouring each other, as when one mutates into a hamburger and sucks his neighbour into his bun. At other times, undulating sexual images fill the screen, changing too rapidly to do more than suggest the actions that vault from the viewer's imagination.

There are also several sequences of Frank playing his guitar; in one, he transforms into a demon, in another, his chording hand suddenly sprouts 20 fingers, in yet another, a fingertip becomes a head which then bites a chunk out of another, only to be punched into submission by a third. There are also narrative sequences of figures stumbling through forests and a red car being pursued by others over increasingly rugged terrain. To paraphrase Frank's onstage opinion of some pop superstars, 'This guy is seriously fucked-up.'

Frank was sufficiently impressed to commission *The Amazing Mr Bickford*, a 50-minute video compilation released in 1989 and featuring some of the artist's earliest work and sequences from *The Dub Room Special* and *Baby Snakes*. The soundtrack consisted of music recorded by Kent Nagano and the London Symphony Orchestra and Pierre Boulez and the Ensemble InterContemporain. Six months after Frank's death, Richard Hanson, a teacher at Mifflinburg High School in Pennsylvania, was suspended without pay for screening the video for students in his 11th-grade English class as part of a study of absurdity in art. Following an anonymous complaint about 'pornographic' content, the school board watched the video and by their action proved yet again that art merely reflected life.

Joe's Garage Act 1 was issued on September 17, with a front cover three-quarter profile portrait by Norman Seeff of Frank in black-face makeup, nestling a mop to his cheek. The inside of the gatefold sleeve, designed by John Williams, included a collage of a naked Maya, a sequence from Eadweard Muybridge's photographic explorations of movement, sundry unspecified technical drawings, the Pyramids, fingers on a lute fretboard and a 'Perspective Drawing Of A Garage'. The lyric insert had similar illustrations, but these did have a passing relevance to the songs' content. The photograph of cloth-capped workers wearing gas-masks that adorned the centre-spread didn't need explanation.

The cover portrait of *Acts 11 & 111*, issued two months later on November 19, wittily subverts the supposed symbolism of *Act 1*. Frank, this time face-on to the camera, is having the black-face makeup delicately applied around his eyelids by the makeup girl whose blond head occupies the lower right quadrant of the sleeve. What is the significance of the fact that she has red nail-polish on the fingers of her left hand but none on those of her right? Or was she caught half-way through the application? Who gives a fuck?

The inside gatefold similarly deconstructs the previous artwork. Torn elements of the collage surround the head of a man taken from a medical journal; his transparent skin reveals the skull with the sinus cavities highlighted in a clear reference to Frank's childhood asthma and the radium-tipped swab that was used to treat it. Muffins with generous toppings of icing also surround the face and reoccur in the illustrations that skirt the lyric sheet, ending with an Edwardian picture of a muffin-man, his tray on his head, plying his trade on a suitably-aproned housewife's doorstep.

Throughout the autumn, Frank concentrated on the installation of his studio's equipment and the final print of *Baby Snakes*. He also prepared another triple album, *Warts And All*, compiled from the 1978 Halloween show at the Palladium, New York and the February 1979 shows at London's Hammersmith Odeon. But it seems the market couldn't stand another three-record set just then. Most of the 23 tracks, though not always in the same versions, would appear spread over *Tinseltown Rebellion, You Are What You Is* and the *Shut Up 'N Play Yer Guitar* series, while 'Ancient Armaments' ended up on a single with 'I Don't Want To Get Drafted' during the following year. 'Dead Girls Of London' was set aside yet again, along with 'Magic Fingers', 'Ms X' (Warren Cucurullo's monologue), 'Persona Non Grata' and the return of 'Little House I Used To Live In'. 'Thirteen', featuring L. Shankar on violin, and 'Little Rubber Girl' eventually appeared in the *YCDTOSA* series.

Baby Snakes was premiered at the Victoria Theater, New York on Friday, December 21. Critical opinion was generally dismissive. Tom Carson's review in *The Village Voice* was typical: 'In *Baby Snakes*, Frank Zappa manages to come off as avuncularly benign as David Crosby,' he began. Noting that, at two hours, forty-three minutes, it wasn't the longest rockstar self-indulgence (that accolade went to Bob Dylan's *Renaldo and Clara)*, Carson pilloried *Baby Snakes* as an ego trip, 'but on a picayune (that's 'insignificant', if you're not American), low-rent scale. It may be the first rockstar movie ever designed from the outset as a cult item.'

Flourishing his scalpel, Carson thought that Frank was 'still trying to act as if he symbolises a whole culture, but the culture isn't there anymore; in this movie, it's more like the Lost Patrol. At the same time, by turning himself into warm, lovable Uncle Frank, telling the same jokes over and over for an audience that already knows all the punchlines, he obviates whatever edge his satire might have left. He's become the ageing avatar of the same hippie pieties he once worked to subvert.' Presumably Carson had blocked out the whole of Frank's lecture at the beginning of 'I Have Been In You'. He concluded: 'Once, Zappa built a satirist's career on the idea that all of life was just like high school; now it turns out that all he ever wanted, apparently, was a high school clique of his very own - and on the evidence of *Baby Snakes*, he's found one.'[18]

The high school metaphor is easy to apply to any rock concert, but by the same token, that 'apparently' is a 'prefect' word, designed to imply superiority when incomprehension stalls the critical faculties. Earlier in the review, Carson noted that without Bruce Bickford's 'decorative touches', this was just 'another rock-concert film'. It was easier for him to appreciate the animation work, since the visual is more easily described than the musical. For example, he thought the concert sequences 'some of the best I've seen - cleanly photographed, smoothly edited'; but the music had 'little life to it'. Forgot to listen, eh?

Critics like Carson got caught out by confusing the arbitrary with the meaningful. They should have taken their cue from the opening, speeded-up sequences of Frank using an editing machine, and his questioning of Bruce Bickford, where the point is made that the artist has no responsibility for the way in which others view his work. Frank experimented with film in the same way he did with music. He wanted to see what would happen when separate elements were put together in a certain way. They could just as well be placed in other ways to obtain the same result.

Long-time road manager and 'snorker' Dick Barber made the point when talking about the making of *200 Motels*. 'With Frank, nobody knew what was gonna happen from one night to the next, which was one of the reasons it was exciting and challenging, because nobody knew what was happening. Now, I think Frank, in some way, in a lot of ways, approached the making of *200 Motels* the same way, and so, we kinda ended up in England, and we got this script, but the script was being rewritten by the minute, and I think that was a little frustrating for Tony Palmer. You really can't, and shouldn't, for the most part, make movies on that basis.'[19]

Frank's literal, nuts-and-bolts approach to assembling film denied those expecting meaning the means of their satisfaction. Even the onstage sequences sometimes cut back from tight head shots to reveal Frank stalking the stage apron with cameras on either side of him. At other times, he involves the camera in his cueing of the band, gestures at it with a toy poodle, and during Patrick O'Hearn's bass solo, one cameraman shows Frank instructing another on how to frame his shot. It seemed that at all times, Frank was intent on puncturing the idea that any of this had any meaning beyond what was taking place at the time. Similarly, the animation sequences were prefaced in a way that undermined pretentious interpretation.

Baby Snakes had its faults. Some of the backstage sequences were tedious, unfunny and inconsequential; Roy Estrada, with his demented busby of a haircut, takes far too long doing far too little with his inflatable friend; band members mug and talk to the camera, and carry on 'faggot' badinage with a kaftaned John Smothers. The layered sound sometimes makes the words of the person on camera hard to distinguish; and the fans' contributions add nothing of value or interest. Since its premiere, it has been shown rarely. Two years later, it was awarded the Premier Grand Prix for a musical film at the First International Music Film Festival. Though available on video in America, it has yet to be issued in Europe.

As 1980 began, Frank had been off the road for nine months and hadn't played a gig in America since November 1978. He spent February and early March rehearsing a band that dispensed with Peter Wolf but saw the return of Ray White. Tommy Mars, Ike Willis and Arthur Barrow, who occasionally doubled on keyboards, were retained, while Vinnie Colaiuta was replaced by the nebulous David Logeman. *Keyboard* magazine sent Michael Davis to interview Frank to the cacophony of workmen putting the finishing touches to the Utility Muffin Research Kitchen.

Despite the considerable talents of his current band, Frank was not satisfied.

'I think I'm probably gonna start auditioning again,' he said, 'because I haven't yet found a keyboard player who is "roadable" and who can really read music . . . I'm talking about someone who can look at the most difficult stuff on a page and the notes come flying off; that means less time and trouble teaching the stuff to the rest of the band. Then he would have to be roadable. By that, I mean have the flexibility to go from playing simple backgrounds to really difficult written-out stuff, plus have the attitude so that he would enjoy touring. I haven't had too much luck finding someone who can do all those things because he probably doesn't exist. But maybe there's someone out there and I just haven't found him yet.'

Another problem that he encountered was his keyboard players' lack of understanding when it came to their efforts being used for texture rather than emphasis. 'Well, see, the music is based on contrasts, contrasts between things that are very simple and things that are very complicated . . . This is a problem I face as a composer and an orchestrator; musicians always look at it like anyone who tells them what to play is inhibiting their lifestyle. Once the musicians learn the songs in rehearsal, once they learn the arrangements and we get out on the road, the songs sound good. But as soon as the lights go on and the audience claps a few times, everybody starts adding their own little things. By the end of the tour, a lot of things sound like chaos. This is one of the reasons why some people lose their jobs.'[20]

Perhaps that was what had happened to Peter Wolf. Frank had more to say on the subject of keyboard players' onstage attitudes. 'The rigs I provide for (them) to monitor themselves with are really elaborate. Each guy can sound like a million bucks to himself, but they always crank the bass up so they can rattle their groin while they're doing it . . . The mixer is always telling them to take some bass off, and this makes them unhappy that they can't give themselves a scrotal massage while they're playing. At the end of the show, you have these keyboard players walking around like you'd stabbed them in the heart because the mixer told them to lower the low end out of their setup or told them to play softer.'[21]

Starting with a gig at the Seattle Center Arena on March 25, the Zappa band spent much of 1980 on road, with a European tour sandwiched between two American tours. In the break from mid-July until the end of September, a new album would be recorded, the first to be made in Frank's own custom-built facilities.

CHAPTER SIXTEEN
UTILITY MUFFIN RESEARCH KITCHEN

As his fortunes waxed and waned through the 70s, Frank had always ensured that, within the constraints of available finance and any on-going litigation, the instruments he and the band played and the equipment they used were at the leading edge of whatever technology was available at the time. Nigel Leigh asked to what extent his work had developed in tandem with technology. 'Right along with it,' he replied, 'because in many instances we were the bait, a test site for some of these things, or at least some of the first customers for the objects themselves. There have been a number of items where I bought the prototypes and I used them right away in recordings, like Syn-Drums, for example.

'The guy who invented these things brought them over and showed them to me and I bought 'em right away and started incorporating them into the arrangements. When you're doing electric music, every new device that comes along that allows for the creation of a sound that might not have existed before should be of interest to you. This is to a certain degree contingent on your budget, because none of these things are cheap; and so you take a risk purchasing the new piece of equipment. It might make a really wonderful sound but then explode in your face three weeks later, and the company will be out of business and then you will have laid down a bunch of money. And I've been that route before. But generally speaking, if there's something new and if I think that for the kind of music that I do there's a use for it in my writing, I'll get it.'[1]

He'd been an early experimenter with a wah-wah pedal. 'I think I was one of the first people to use (one). I'd never even heard of Jimi Hendrix at the time I bought mine; I didn't even know who he was.'[2] Later, Jimi's guitar roadie, Howard Parker, gave him the sunburst Strat that Hendrix burned at the Miami Pop Festival, which Frank would pass on to Dweezil. He also used something made for him by Bob Easton called the Electro Wagnerian Emancipator. 'It's a very attractive little device that combines a frequency follower with a device that puts out harmony notes to what you're playing . . . Its main drawback is that the tone that comes out of it is somewhat like a Farfisa organ.'[3]

Frank would also search for different guitar sounds in the studio. Since the

Over-Nite Sensation sessions, he'd used a tiny Pignose practice amp, giving him stadium-quality distortion at low volume which he could then record in stereo for either an ambient sound or so that each track could be separately EQ'd. Alternatively, he could place it in an echo chamber to get that 'hockey rink' resonance.

These and other considerations went into the design of the Utility Muffin Research Kitchen (UMRK). As well as providing him with a range of possibilities when it came to recording his guitar, Frank also ensured that his facility would have a wide variety of keyboards, acoustic and electronic, at his disposal. 'I've got a warehouse full of keyboards,' he informed Michael Davis. 'A lot of my synthesisers are going to be mounted on a semi-permanent basis in my studio. In the control room, there's going to be one master keyboard that's patchable out to the other synthesisers, so that instead of one big toot coming out, you play the keyboard and the individual voices can be played in the live echo chamber through eight speakers going through an air space with stereo microphones in the chamber.'4 Pride of place went to a Bosendorfer Imperial grand piano with its extra octave in the bass, and a Hammond B-3 organ, intended primarily for road use, with a modified keyboard that also drove a Minimoog and a set of Syn-Drums.

Frank enthusiastically embraced the development of synthesiser technology. 'All the heavy duty hardware that a rock and roll touring band would use, I've purchased and supplied to whoever the keyboard guy is who does the tour. So I know basically what the consumer end of the synthesiser stuff is like, even though I'm not a keyboard player and never expect to be.'5 He told *Downbeat* that the string synthesiser was 'the best thing that could happen to pop music because when you consider the attitude of normal string players, even jazz string players, it's so disgusting doing business with them that it's great that somebody has finally invented a box that will help you do away with them and their aura.'6

Tim Schneckloth asked him if it had got any harder to find sounds that wouldn't quickly become bland. 'Absolutely not,' he replied. 'That surface hasn't even been scratched yet. Without even touching a synthesiser, there are so many things you can make with normal instruments, and in a diatonic context. There are so many people who are dashing away from diatonic music in order to give the appearance of being modern - which I think is a waste of time. I've developed different types of notation that accommodate the different things that synthesisers can do . . . If you're a composer or arranger and you want to use the synthesiser, you have to know all the basic language of what the instrument is dealing with . . . so you can communicate with the people who play the instruments.'

What about the people who claimed that all electric instruments, including synthesisers, detracted from the 'humanity' of music? 'People who worry about that are worried about their own image as a person performing on the instrument. In other words, the instrument is merely a subterfuge in order for the musician to communicate his own personal, succulent grandeur to the audience which to me is a disservice to music as an art form. It's the ego of the performer transcending the instrument . . . I don't want to go and see somebody's deep inner hurt in a live performance. I don't want to hear their personal turmoil on a record, either. I like the music.'[7]

Frank had once maintained that Americans hated music but loved entertainment. 'The reason they hate music,' he explained, 'is that they've never stopped to listen to what the musical content is because they're so befuddled by the packaging and merchandising that surround the musical material they've been induced to buy. There's so much peripheral stuff that helped them make their analysis of what the music is . . . The way in which the material is presented is equally important as what's on the record. It's the *garni du jour* way of life . . . Americans have become accustomed to having a *garni du jour* on everything . . . It's equally true of the jazz world. The whole jazz syndrome is smothered in *garni du jour*.'[8]

YOU ARE WHAT YOU IS

UMRK came into commission on a piecemeal basis. One of the first fruits was 'I Don't Want To Get Drafted', a single recorded with Vinnie Colauita on drums and released in May 1980. The idea for the song grew out of a discussion during a rehearsal break. 'We were having a dinner break,' Tommy Mars said, 'and it was just around the time when there might have been the draft in America. Frank was talking about World War Two . . . Then all of a sudden, he was working on [the melody line]; that was like a guitar-solo at the time. So he said, "Put down the burritos, I think we got a new tune, boys". And he started writing the lyrics right out.'[9] On the b-side was a guitar solo, 'Ancient Armaments', taken from the 1978 Halloween show at New York's Palladium and previously slated to appear on the three-album set, *Warts And All*. CBS were happy to release the single in Britain but Mercury-Phonogram declined to distribute it in America.

The Kitchen's first major task was the next album, due for release towards the end of 1980. The Zappa band had been on the road for over three months before the sessions began in July. By that time, much of material had been thoroughly road-tested. From March 25 to May 11, they played 26 dates across the United States; after a ten day break, they then set off to Europe for another 34 dates, ending on July 3 in Munich, the last of 15 gigs in Germany. That gig was later broadcast in America on the *King Biscuit Flour Hour* on June 28, 1981.

As usual, Frank continued to write on the road. On Saturday, May 3 at Boston's Music Hall, he addressed the audience before the last song of the evening: 'Here's the deal. We have a new song here - we have this song that was written about three days ago and we rehearsed it this afternoon. We're getting it together, you know what I mean? We've never played it for anybody before. You guys'll be the first people on the face of the Earth to hear it.' Then he counted the band in on a very tentative version of 'You Are What You Is'. Interestingly, the first verse began, 'A dandy young man from a nice Jewish family'; by the time it had been recorded, the young man had become 'foolish' and his 'fam'ly' middle class.

A significant part of the set consisted of two suites of inter-related songs. 'Society Pages', 'I'm A Beautiful Guy', 'Beauty Knows No Pain', 'Charlie's Enormous Mouth', 'Any Downers' and 'Conehead' were all performed in one unbroken sequence, and in another, 'Mudd Club', 'The Meek Shall Inherit Nothing', 'Heavenly Bank Account', 'Suicide Chump', 'Jumbo Go Away', 'If Only She Woulda' and 'I Don't Wanna Get Drafted'.

Frank's initial intention was to compile a single album, to be called *Crush All Boxes*. Its first side would contain 'Doreen', 'Fine Girl', 'Easy Meat' and 'Goblin Girl', and the second side the 'Society Pages' suite of songs. At some stage that all changed as Frank envisaged a way to re-jig elements of the aborted *Warts And All* in an ambitious set of releases that would emphasise different aspects of his several talents. In the meantime, he set about recording the current band repertoire, adding 'You Are What You Is' and a handful of other songs.

One of these was 'Teen-age Wind', which came about through Arthur Barrow's childhood friendship with Chris Geppert, who grew up to become Christopher Cross and sign a deal with Warner Brothers. His debut album, released in 1980, featured 'Ride Like The Wind', a song that became a Top Five single and earned Cross Grammy awards for Best Record, Best Album and Best Song. Barrow heard it while he was driving to a rehearsal: 'I recognised the voice immediately. I went up to Frank when I got to rehearsal and I said, "I can't believe it! This guy I went to high school with has got a song on the radio." And I started playing it on the piano and singing as much of it as I could remember. Frank says, "Aw, gimme a pencil and paper and I could write a song like that in five minutes" and he whipped out the lyrics to 'Teen-age Wind'. When Cross heard that Frank was writing a take-off of his song, he remarked, "Oh God, I hope he doesn't release (it) while I'm peaking".'[10] Soon after, Frank took to commenting 'I'm peaking, I'm peaking' onstage.

Then there was 'Dumb All Over', a devastating critique on the blind prejudice of institutionalised religion. 'I was on a flight back from Germany when I came up with the idea for the song,' Frank said. 'I scrawled out three pages' worth of ideas on the plane. I couldn't wait to get into the studio to record it.'[11] The song was inspired by the hostage crisis in Iran and the jingoistic fervour motivating various televangelists, modern-day hucksters who'd traded their tents for television stations, to call down God's nuclear wrath on anyone who didn't agree with their particular brand of spiritual guidance.

Frank savaged the notion that religious fanatics of any persuasion could use their book of rules to commit murder for righteousness' sake. The mode of dress might differ, but the call to butchery was the same. Which brought him to his *coup de grâce*. Referring to the Bible's assertion that God made us in his image, logic must dictate that if we were dumb, then God must be dumb and 'maybe even a little ugly on the side'. Little wonder that Frank told Alex Kershaw he was a devout pagan: 'I detest religion for what it has done for the human species . . . The difference between religions and cults is determined by how much real estate is owned . . . Look, how many people died as a result of the Bible compared to the Kama Sutra? There's no competition.'[12]

'Dumb All Over' was placed between 'The Meek Shall Inherit Nothing' and 'Heavenly Bank Account', songs that shone a harsh spotlight on the likes of Jim and Tammy Bakker, Pat Robertson, Oral Roberts, Jerry Falwell and Jimmy Swaggart, televangelists who blurred the distinction between 'pray' and 'prey'. The Bakkers headed a conglomerate called the PTL Club, which stood for Praise The Lord or Pass The Loot, depending on the quality of your faith. Bakker had prayed with President Carter on Air Force One and knew the new president, Ronald Reagan. Unfortunately, in 1980 he also 'knew' Jessica Hahn, a 21-year-old church secretary. At the same time, Tammy Faye was allegedly having knowledge of Gary Paxton, producer of her solo album and of 'Monster Mash'. The scandal didn't break until 1987, after Bakker had paid $265,000 hush money to Hahn, her surname pronounced as in 'enhanced', which is what happened to her breasts before she posed nude for *Playboy*.

'The Meek Shall Inherit Nothing' pointed out that the religious right, hand-in-glove with an administration that relied upon its financial support, was devoted to the pursuit of self-interest. 'Heavenly Bank Account' pilloried Jerry Falwell, creator of the Moral Majority (later renamed Liberty Federation for tax reasons). To make sure the message got through, Frank intoned after the first verse, 'Remember, there's a big difference between kneeling down and bending over'. When performing the song live, he would state unequivocally, 'TAX THE CHURCHES' and 'TAX THE BUSINESSES OWNED BY THE CHURCHES'. 'I think the Moral Majority is weird,' he said. 'I think television religious fanaticism and "send me your money" is weird. I think the people who send the money are *weird*. I think the people who broadcast the shows are *sick*. And I think the people who do the shows are *the worst*.'[13]

This segued into 'Suicide Chump', suicide being 'the sport of chumps' in Frank's mind, sung over a generic boogie shuffle with slide guitar by Denny

Walley. 'Jumbo, Go Away' dealt harshly with the unwanted attentions of an unattractive groupie. 'If Only She Woulda' used a wicked imitation of a Doors vamp, complete with lurching Farfisa organ solo, as an introduction to 'Drafted Again', a reworking of the recent single with Ahmet and Moon singing separate verses.

'Society Pages' and its satire of the complacent matrons who ran small town American society, began a sequence that relentlessly savaged their empty lifestyle, their dumb but attractive offspring and their masochistic willingness to endure anything in the name of 'beauty', leading to 'Charlie's Enormous Mouth', another stark denunciation of drug addiction. 'Any Downers?' evinced another addiction with which the weak-willed avoided the pain of real life, while 'Conehead', drawing some inspiration from the regular *Saturday Night Live* sketches, underlined the banality of the average American couch-potato's humdrum existence.

The album's opening sequence of four songs, starting with 'Teen-age Wind', were not segued. 'Harder Than Your Husband', a song that subverted C&W conventions, was a solo feature for Jimmy Carl Black in his guise as 'Lonesome Cowboy Burt'. Ray White sang lead vocals on 'Doreen', a doo-wop song for the 80s with staccato backing from Frank's guitar. The mix that would have appeared on *Crush All Boxes* faded at the beginning of Frank's blistering guitar solo, which here continued to the backing track's end. 'Goblin Girl' ensured that oral sex would not be forgotten but as it progressed the song became the pretext for a dazzling array of harmonised vocal overdubs which reprised 'Doreen' and ended with a soliloquy for lighting man Coy Featherstone.

While there were guitar solos spread throughout the album's 19 songs, there was just one instrumental, 'Theme From The 3rd Movement Of Sinister Footwear'. Strictly speaking, this wasn't a product of xenochrony; the basis of the piece was the opening instrumental interlude from the late show at New York's Palladium on October 27, 1978, which was to have been released on *Warts And All* as 'Persona Non Grata'. Frank's solo was then transcribed and played again by percussionist Ed Mann and on bass clarinet by David Ocker, who'd also worked on *Sheik Yerbouti*. Careful listening to the stereo reveals another guitar doubling the original improvised melody. This was played by Steve Vai, credited on the album for 'Strat Abuse'.

Vai was a native of Long Island who took guitar lessons from Joe Satriani at high school before studying jazz and classical music at the Berklee College in Boston. Having listened to Frank's music since the age of 13, he set himself the task of transcribing 'The Black Page' and sent the result to Frank, along with a demo tape of his guitar playing. Frank was impressed enough to invite him for an audition. 'I told him that I was 18. He said, "You're what?" - clearly too young to be involved with a high-energy operation like a Frank

Zappa tour. Shortly after that Zappa changed his phone number and I thought I'd been unlucky.'[14] But contact was re-established and Frank asked him to transcribe the guitar solos from *Joe's Garage*. The following year, Vai moved to Los Angeles and Frank got him to add rhythm guitar parts to songs that would end up on *You Are What You Is* and ultimately made him a band member.

'Steve Vai got the job,' he told Tom Mulhern, 'because . . . I could tell that he had a superior musical intelligence and very great guitar chops. And this showed me that there was a possibility to write things that were even harder for that instrument than what had already been used in the band.'[15]

The care and meticulous preparation that went into the creation of 'Sinister Footwear' was typical of the attention paid to every aspect of the project. The power of the messages Frank wanted to convey was matched by a technical excellence not previously available to him. Songs were not only textually inter-related, but linking material ensured that attention was not lost in the transition between tracks. For the first time, the complexity of the music was matched by the layering of vocal overdubs on the extended codas of songs like 'Doreen', 'Goblin Girl' and 'You Are What You Is'. The work of engineers Mark Pinske and Alan Sides was an achievement in itself, but the vision was Frank's.

He was justly proud of UMRK's first project. 'That's a really good album,' he said in 1991. 'The production values on that album are unbelievable. I had just opened the studio and so I had more control over the production elements that I had ever had in the past. Because, before that, if you're going to make an album with a lot of overdubs and if you're renting commercial space from another studio, you either have to block book it and spend a fortune or go in and out on every other day or something like that. And every day that you're not there, somebody is using it and you have to reset the board and relocate the microphones and it's very difficult to keep a continuity of audio texture. So this album was not only recorded there, it was mixed there.'

I remarked that, despite *Sheik Yerbouti's* success, I thought *You Are What You Is* was the better album. Frank nodded, 'I think so, too.'

BARKING PUMPKIN (2)

With Mercury-Phonogram becoming difficult, Frank elected to wait out the end of his distribution contract, even though he'd wanted to release *Crush All Boxes* before the end of the year. Once again there was a significant backlog of material waiting to be issued. It was time to create another label identity. Since Columbia were already handling his product outside America, it made sense to propose that the deal became worldwide. The new label would be called Barking Pumpkin. 'Gail used to smoke,' Frank explained to Don Menn. 'She quit. But she used to smoke Marlboros, and she coughed all the time. And so I had always referred to her as my pumpkin, and so at that point she was a barking pumpkin.'[16] The logo depicted a Halloween pumpkin barking 'arf!' at a suitably startled cat under the company's banner headline.

In the meantime, the Zappa band played almost 40 dates during October and November 1981, crossing America from west to east and taking in three Canadian gigs, before finishing with dates in Berkeley and Santa Monica at the beginning of December. Both the California gigs provided material for *Tinsel Town Rebellion*, slated to be the first Barking Pumpkin release. Vinnie Colaiuta had returned on drums, Bob Harris came in on keyboards, trumpet and 'high vocals', and Steve Vai took along his 'stunt guitar'.

'We toured the US for three months,' Vai said, 'and it was one of the most tiring experiences of my life. I grew up pretty fast. Zappa doesn't tour like the average rock band. He works long, he works hard. I like that. I wasn't used to it, of course, but I really learnt the tour life.'[17] At a price. 'I was a nervous wreck,' he said on another occasion. 'I wasn't eating right, I was sick, I was fooling around all the time. I was 19 years old and I was out there and I got no respect from anybody on the crew. I was under a lot of pressure because the music was so hard to play and I didn't want to make any mistakes. I did - it was inevitable - but the music was extremely hard and I had to keep practicing all the time. But it was all really just nerves. I thought Frank was going to send me home. Why he didn't, I don't know.'[18]

Frank posed a rhetorical question to Matt Resnicoff: 'What is Steve Vai going to do ? As a young musician, how do you get to be unique, when a record company doesn't want to sign unique people? The easiest gig for a unique person is a format where uniqueness is acceptable . . . I always saw him as a thoroughly professional, on-the-case, totally talented, fabulous musician, and you couldn't ask for a better guy to be in your band.'[19] Few other ex-band members received such a glowing endorsement from their employer.

But then, few other band members could transcribe guitar solos the way that Steve Vai could. 'It was a lot of fun,' Vai said, 'because it was like an art project . . . I had an opportunity to explore these twisted notational rhythms. I really got my ears together because I transcribed for four years and it came to the point where I didn't use a guitar anymore or any instrument. My relative pitch got really good. Frank started sending me all sorts of things from lead sheets to orchestra scores where he had orchestrated certain sections, like 'Greggary Peccary'. Other sections weren't orchestrated, they were just put together by Frank and he wanted to have the score for it.'[20]

There was a practical reason for his work as a transcriber. As well as producing albums to be distributed by Columbia, Frank also compiled three albums of guitar solos, which were to be made available through mail order. As Gail explained to Don Menn, 'We were involved in litigation with a major record company. We were virtually prevented from having an income by them. They froze us out. We were an insignificant entity facing this huge corporation. They had Frank's earnings tied up in order to prevent us from fighting them, and on top of that we were fighting old managers. I realised we were going to be in a position where we weren't going to have a lot of money because the legal fees at that point were just phenomenal. Plus we had a lot of money tied up with the current management. So I started a mail-order company.'[21]

Shut Up 'N Play Yer Guitar, Shut Up 'N Play Yer Guitar Some More and *Return of The Son of Shut Up 'N Play Yer Guitar* consisted mainly of solos drawn from live recordings from the 1979 and 1980 tours. Nine of the 20 tracks involved came from the three-day residency at London's Hammersmith Odeon. Six 1980 solos were from gigs in New York City, Dallas, Tulsa, Berkeley and Santa Monica. 'Pink Napkins', a variation on the usual coloured napery, also came from the Hammersmith Odeon, but this was the 1977 five-piece band with Eddie Jobson on keyboards. Even older was 'Ship Ahoy', from a February 1976 gig in Osaka, originally scheduled to appear on *Lather* under the title, 'Duck Duck Goose'. The remaining oddments were 'While You Were Out' and 'Stucco Homes', recorded at UMRK, and 'Canard du Jour', a duet between Jean-Luc Ponty on baritone violin and Frank playing a bouzouki.

The first months of 1981 were spent in mixing these tapes and those for *Tinsel Town Rebellion;* all four were to be released during May. The latter double album used tracks from 1979 first scheduled for *Warts And All*, one studio track, 'Fine Girl', that would have been on *Crush All Boxes*, and several taken from the last tour, predominantly from the December 5 gig at Berkeley's Community Theater. As had become usual, sections of songs and solos were seamlessly intercut from other performances.

'Easy Meat' was taken from the April 29 gig at Philadelphia's Tower Theater. It had been mixed, with 'massive over-dubbage of keyboards on the classical section (all done by Tommy Mars)', as Frank's sleevenote revealed, and sequenced into *Crush All Boxes*. But where that version (later included in the bootleg, *Demo's*) used Frank's original feedback-enhanced guitar solo, the final released track edited from the 'classical' extravaganza into his solo from the December 11 gig at Santa Monica, which, dispensing with feedback, was a more pointillistic and rhythmically diverse performance inspired by Vinnie Colaiuta's hyperactive drumming. Typically, both solos were excellent in their own right.

Tinsel Town's 15 tracks were a confusing combination of the known and the new. There were rehashes of 'Love Of My Life', 'Tell Me You Love Me' and 'I Ain't Got No Heart' recorded at Berkeley, and 'Brown Shoes Don't Make It' and 'Peaches En Regalia' (renamed 'Peaches III' for its radical reorganisation) from the Hammersmith Odeon. Perhaps his new young audience weren't familiar with them, but did they need to be enshrined in vinyl? A more puzzling inclusion was 'Dance Contest', which did little for the listener except to note that the participants unzipped their brains before climbing onstage. 'I'm makin' it up as I go along,' Frank told Den Simms, 'so I think that the people from the audience who come up there, they want that. I don't think that they wanna come onstage and know that I've planned something for them, 'cause then they would feel like a victim. If they come up there, and I'll just cook something up on the spot, I'm gonna invent it based on what I think they can handle, and if I guess wrong, then it's my fault.'[22]

Critics chose to condemn 'Panty Rap' for its perceived chauvinism and bad taste; it was apparently not funny to refer to female body secretions as 'voodoo butter', and as for drawing olfactory gratification from warm undergarments . . . Frank explained the history of panty-gathering: 'A few years ago, in Philadelphia, a girl approached the stage and pitched up this little pair of blue panties. I knew the drummer and one of the other guys in the band liked to sniff girls' underpants, so as soon as she pitched them up, I made the drummer get off the stand and come down and sniff them. He did and immediately pretended to gag and faint and rolled all over the stage. The audience loved it. The girl, however, was somewhat chagrined, but I have it on good authority that the panties were semi-lethal.'[23]

Bad taste, undeniably, but Lyons, Colorado resident Emily James was making a quilt out of the burgeoning stock of donations. She'd specifically asked for them not to be washed, 'thereby maintaining some exquisite sort of organic miasma in the vicinity of the finished work of art', as Frank put it. The fate of the mulch-laden artefact is lost to history. 'At the point where I handed her these garbage cans full of underpants, and she went to work to commit her artistic deed, I didn't speak to her after that,' Frank said in 1991.[24] Lyons had been flattened by a tornado the year before, but there were no reported sightings of migrating underwear. If indeed the quilt was ever finished, its fabric was so uniquely biodegradable that little can now remain.

The two most significant compositions appeared in sequence. First was 'The Blue Light', the most original song on the album and an indication of Frank's will to experiment. The tune was complex, incorporating many changes of tempo; parts of the lyric followed Vinnie Colaiuta's intricate drum fills, others followed speech patterns over more regular accompaniment. Frank's deadpan delivery was punctuated at dramatic intervals by band harmonies emphasising certain phrases.

He used a vocal technique variously identified as *sprechstimme* (speaking voice) or *sprechgesang* (speechsong). Its first notable use was in Humperdinck's 1897 work, *Konigskinder*; Schoenberg used the technique in *Gurrelieder* (1900-11) and *Pierrot Lunaire* (1912), as did Alban Berg in *Wozzeck* (1917-1922).

Frank's adoption of the technique may have been inspired by one of Tommy Mars' quirky habits: 'This is a guy that you could hold a conversation (with) and Tommy could harmonise it while you were talking. You would just follow dialogue with chords.'[25]

'The Blue Light' was a devastating put-down on the hopelessness and timourousness of a generation that spent its time huddling in groups at fast food joints and in squalid clubs. Nor did the psychedelic generation escape. Mention of Donovan and Atlantis moved on to 'the giant underwater pyramid'; at which point Frank extrapolated, 'Excuse me, Todd.' After recording the *RA* album, on which they were pictured in Egyptian dress, Todd Rundgren's band, Utopia, had toured extensively with a stage set that made prominent use of a pyramid.

Frank reiterated his theme towards the end of the song and, as if as an afterthought, spoke-sang, 'You can't even speak your own fucking language.' It was a clear reference back to 'Panty Rap', also recorded at Berkeley, during which a piece of paper had been handed to him, asking him to wear the person's hat. Frank was incredulous: 'How about this, this is a college community, right? "How about wearing", w-e-r-e-i-n-g, never mind.' Unfortunately, the force of his message was dispelled by the musical hoops through which he made it jump. Nor did the audience catch his ominous prediction, 'Death Valley Days straight ahead'.

More attention was paid to the album's title track and its attack on the exploitation of punk music. In another sprechstimme sequence, he noted, 'Did you know that in Tinsel Town the people there think substance is a bore?' But, he went on to explain, this was a system where spectacle was more important than content and it was sustained by 'all those record company pricks' who put musical quality low on their scale of priorities. He was also critical of musicians who forsook 'real' music in order to cash in on the latest trend; 'who gives a fuck if what they play is somewhat insincere'. He may have been out of step with the times, but if Frank was to be a 'boring old fart', he'd make sure that someone noticed the stink.

On April 17 in New York, Frank was able to do his bit for 'real' music by introducing *A Tribute To Edgard Varèse*, an evening of music that celebrated the 90th birthday of his widow, Louise. He'd been invited by Joel Thome, conductor of the Orchestra for Our Time, who visited him in Los Angeles to discuss arrangements and talk about his own music. The concert was to have been held at the Whitney Museum, but at Frank's suggestion it was moved to the Palladium, which had once been an opera house. 'What they were trying to do was get a younger audience to come and hear the music of Varèse . . . The concert was at the Palladium. They were behaving like a rock and roll audience. They sat completely still when the music was being played, but as soon as the music stopped there was pandemonium.'[26]

Frank had thought that he ought to find out some information to pass along to the audience about Varèse, but it turned out that his efforts were unnecessary. It did, however, give him the opportunity to contact Nicholas Slonimsky, the St. Petersburg-born pianist and conductor, who'd overseen the world premiere of Varèse's *Ionisation*, as well as the symphonic works of Charles Ives and Bela Bartók's *First Piano Concerto*. Slonimsky had written several books on music, including the *Lexicon Of Musical Invective* and the *Thesaurus Of Scales And Melodic Patterns*, which had inspired Frank to make contact. A friendship developed that enabled him to grasp the theories behind Slonimsky's ways of creating chords and harmonies.

Around this time, Frank had expected to begin rehearsals with the Residentie Orchestra for a concert of his music as part of the Holland Festival in Amsterdam. After arranging with various organisations including the Dutch government and Columbia Records that sufficient finance would be available, a short European tour was arranged in order to cover salaries and expenses for travel and rehearsal time. Each member of the nine-piece group was to be paid $15,000 for 17 weeks' work. But before the American rehearsals began, two musicians surreptitiously tried to increase their salaries. When this came to light, Frank made it a strictly orchestral event, but not for long. The orchestra committee announced it had hired a lawyer to negotiate a royalty which they expected to be paid over and above the usual session rate. Enough was enough. Having invested $250,000 in preparatory work, Frank withdrew his music, his involvement and his permission from the enterprise.

WHY JOHNNY CAN'T READ

Indeed, as Hunter S. Thompson would say. That was the title of one of the solos on *Return Of The Son Of Shut Up 'N Play Yer Guitar*, which along with its companions, became available for mail order on May 11. *Tinsel Town Rebellion* was released six days later. To general surprise, the mail order albums sold very well right away, while the distributed release struggled. Speaking two years later, Frank said, 'Actually, they have surprised everybody because the quantity that we sold mail-order went into a profit within two weeks of being out there. That is, they paid for the cost of manufacturing within two weeks.' Asked if any follow-up albums were likely, Frank pointed out, 'I'm not funded by any foundation or grants or any money from the sky, so what comes in gets transferred again into the next product that goes out. And I can only spend the money to make the next product versus the profit that comes in on the previous one.'[27]

There was also the matter of rehearsing a new band for an autumn 1981 tour of America. Chad Wackerman was engaged to replace the venal Vinnie Colaiuta, Bobby Martin came in on keyboards, saxophone and vocals and Ed Mann returned on percussion. Steve Vai, Tommy Mars and Ray White kept their places, but Arthur Barrow was replaced by Scott Thunes. Thunes' guitarist brother Derek had rung Frank in the hope of securing an audition. Frank informed him that he didn't need a guitarist but he was looking for a bass player; Derek unselfishly suggested his older brother. It took three auditions and the memorising of 'Mo 'n Herb's Vacation' for Scott to secure the post.

You Are What You Is was released in September 1981, just prior to the three California gigs that began an intensive tour taking in more than 50 dates in just over three months. Frank had made a video for the title track but it had been banned by MTV for including a Ronald Reagan lookalike who was eventually strapped into an electric chair. The album's gatefold sleeve included a bizarre article, written for *Newsweek* but rejected for being too 'idiosyncratic'.

Headed 'Say Cheese', it suggested that modern America was wilfully deluding itself into accepting a number of fictions about its status and that its self-regard prevented it from acknowledging a woeful lack of true values or accomplishments. 'No society has managed to invest more time and energy in the perpetuation of the fiction that it is moral, sane and wholesome than our current crop of Modern Americans.' In addition, these Modern Americans behaved as if intelligence was some sort of hideous deformity. In order not to be ostracised as intelligent, the population was prepared to be guided by COMMITTEE CHEESE, UNION CHEESE and, worst of all, ACCOUNTANT CHEESE.

In this proscribed society, art was judged by its financial cost and, along with 'taste' and 'the public interest', was 'all tied like a tin can to the wagging tail of the sacred Prime Rate Poodle'. Frank concluded, Yes, Virginia . . . there is a FREE LUNCH. We are eating it now. Can I get you a napkin? The implication was that it was already too late to reverse the insidious progress of state-controlled aesthetic judgement. The deeply ironic tone of the piece and its allusive terminology rendered it incomprehensible to many, thus making it 'subversive' and probably 'unpatriotic' in the minds of the Moral Majority. The article was dated April 1, 1981, but Frank wasn't fooling. However, he was being idiosyncratic, and that was enough for *Newsweek* to protect its readership from the pain of original thought.

CHAPTER SEVENTEEN
DROWNING WITCH

How many of those that came to a Zappa concert thought about what Frank tried to bring to their attention? For many, it was the opportunity to see a highly talented and regimented band being put through its paces for a couple of hours. And during the evening, they'd get to sing along with 'Bobby Brown' or 'Broken Hearts Are For Assholes', with the prospect of 'Dinah-Moe Humm' or 'Muffin Man' as an encore. For all of his sarcasm, Frank adopted a paternal attitude towards his young audiences. Old enough to be their father, he delighted them by ridiculing political figures their parents believed in and the antics of pop stars whose shows they nevertheless attended with equal enthusiasm. During the show, many rock conventions were so accurately satirised that at least part of the audience may not have noticed the difference.

Frank's hectoring tone was reminiscent of their teachers, but in his case, you got the music as well. Sometimes, though, people went too far. Arthur Barrow recalled an incident at an East Coast gig: 'I was standing near Frank on the stage and he was playing one of his long guitar solos. He was just there enjoying himself he had his eyes closed, playing away. And I look at him, and all of a sudden he's like knocked back. I think, Oh my God, he's been shot or something. He almost fell over. And it turns out somebody from the upper level seats had thrown a pint vodka bottle and it struck him on the shoulder. It didn't really hurt him, but it scared him.

'He was so great at this, I guess it was all those years of handling an audience. He really knew how to do it. He says, "Hey, wait a minute, stop the music. Everybody stop playing." So we just stopped. And he said, "Turn on the lights. I wanna find out who threw that bottle at me." And the light guy starts flicking the spotlight around the audience. "No, no, I don't mean the spotlights, I mean the fucking house lights, turn on the big light" . . . And people sort of pointed their fingers in a certain direction, the security guys walked up there and they found the guy, and they took him off. Because Frank says, "We're not playing another note until the guy who threw that bottle at me goes to jail". They went and got him and took him off and then we resumed playing.'[1]

Another unfortunate went too far at the Santa Monica Civic Center on

December 11, 1981. The band were playing 'Broken Hearts Are For Assholes' and had just begun the last verse when someone threw popcorn onto the stage. 'Stop! Stop!' Frank shouted to the band. 'That was very wrong to do. Bring that man back and make him lick this shit up.' Smothers was detailed to lift the culprit by his ankles and run his face through the mess. When he was brought to the stage, Frank exclaimed, 'All right! Now at last, the attention that you so justly deserve! Step right up, introduce yourself and prepare to dine as you've never dined before.' The plaintiff babbled some nonsense and tried to protest, but Frank just said, 'Get your face in it, buddy.' As a struggle ensued, he made sure that there was no violence. After an 'enormous napkin' had cleared up the residue, he led the band into the last verse.

The Santa Monica gig was notable for the appearance of Nicholas Slonimsky during 'A Pound For A Brown On The Bus'. Frank brought the band down behind him and addressed the audience: 'Ladies and gentlemen, I'd like to introduce you to a real national treasure, Nicholas Slonimsky. He's 83 years old. If there's any musicians in the audience, then you know who Mr Slonimsky is. If you're not a musician, well, let's see, how can I put it to you? This man has not only conducted the world premieres of many of the greatest works of modern classical music, but he's the author of many books, including the bible of improvisation, the *Thesaurus Of Scales And Patterns* [published when Frank was six years old] . . . Besides writing these books, Mr Slonimsky plays the piano and that's what he's gonna do right now.'

With that, the octogenarian launched into the 51st and final piece from his *Minitudes*, his left hand stabbing descending triads while his right scrabbled across the treble keys with surprising energy. His solo was brief but dramatic and was greeted with cheers from the audience. 'To my surprise,' he noted in his autobiography, *Perfect Pitch*, 'I sensed a growing consanguinity with my youthful audience as I played. My fortissimo ending brought out screams and whistles the like of which I had never imagined possible.'[2] As he left the stage, Tommy Mars sketched the melody line of 'Young At Heart'. 'The concert was a great success,' Slonimsky told Don Menn. 'Usually I have just a hundred or two hundred people, but this was a huge audience, and they shouted and everything!'[3] The bemused musical lexicographer later wrote, 'Dancing Zappa, wild audience, and befuddled me – I felt like an intruder in a mad scene from *Alice In Wonderland*. I had entered my Age of Absurdity.'[4]

There were guest vocalists at each of the day's two shows. At the first, young Ahmet made his debut, singing his own composition, 'Frogs With Dirty Little Lips'. Lisa Popeil illuminated several songs at the second show, her voice equal parts operatic and athletic. 'We were having an open call for drummers,' Frank told Den Simms. While her drummer boyfriend was auditioning for him, Tommy Mars discovered that Lisa could sing, sight read and play the piano. Frank was duly impressed when she sight-sang 'Be-Bop

Tango'. 'And so she attended a few of the rehearsals, I guess for about a week, and there were some things that she could do, and do very well, and other things that she couldn't, and it just turned out that there were more of the things that she couldn't do, that we needed, for a second keyboard position in the band.'⁵ Lisa showed her vocal expertise on her semi-improvised 'Life Story' (included on *YCDTOSA 6*), 'Teen-age Prostitute' and 'The Dangerous Kitchen'.

'Teen-age Prostitute' became part of the next album, *Ship Arriving Too Late To Save A Drowning Witch*. The title came from *Droodles*, a book of minimalist cartoons by Roger Price, first published in 1953. The one that Frank chose consisted of just five lines, one of which denoted the horizon. The prow of a ship juts in from the left, while a steeply-pitched triangle represented a witch's conical hat. The congruence of the slanting lines suggests a large 'Z'. To assist the motif, the letters of 'Zappa' are represented where appropriate as circles, straight lines and triangles. 'I always liked the picture,' Frank said, 'and recently I tried to find the guy who did it, and found out that he lived about ten miles away from me, and I bought permission to use the picture on the cover of the album.'⁶

Once again, the marriage of live and studio recordings was for the most part unnoticeable, except at the end of 'Teenage Prostitute', where audience applause denoted the end of the album. *Drowning Witch* itself betrayed none of the time-consuming editing that had gone into its production. 'Do you know how many edits there are in *Drowning Witch*?' Frank asked Tom Mulhern. 'Fifteen! That song is a basic track from 15 different cities. And some of the edits are like two bars long. And they're written parts - all that fast stuff. It was very difficult for all the guys to play that correctly . . . So there was no one perfect performance from any city. What I did was go through a whole tour's worth of tape and listen to every version of it and grab every section that was reasonably correct, put together a basic track, and then added the rest of the orchestration to it in the studio.'⁷

Such microscopic attention to detail was only possible now that Frank took adequate recording facilities with him on the road. In 1980, he'd upgraded from four-track to an eight-track machine. For the 1981 tour, he travelled with a 24-track recorder. During 1982, he bought the Beach Boys' mobile truck and stocked it with three Ampex 24-tracks, with one as a standby in case either of the others broke down. The only drawback to this system was the time it took to locate and construct a backing track.

VALLEY GIRL

An indication of the average gestation period of a Zappa tune could be gleaned from the creation of 'Valley Girl'. 'It was a riff that started off at a soundcheck about a year before,' Frank said, 'and I had been piddling with it for a long time.'⁸ Then, at the end of a drum tracking session with Chad Wackerman, Frank got an idea for a background riff and decided to get it on tape before he forgot it. 'So I went out to the studio with him, and in about a half an hour, we had put down this backing track, which didn't have any words or any idea of where it was gonna go, and it was maybe a couple of months later that I got the idea for what the words might be for this thing, and at the end of one of the vocal sessions for *Thing-Fish*, I had Ike, Ray and Bob Harris sing the chorus. A few weeks later I got the idea to have my daughter go out and do this monologue on top of it. The last thing that was added was the bass part, and then it was mixed. We went off on a tour in 1982. We're in Europe, touring around, and I find out that I've got a hit record . . . by accident!'⁹

Ship Arriving Too Late To Save A Drowning Witch was released as the band set off to Europe at the beginning of May. As well as revisiting the northern strongholds of Zappa fervour, this time there were to be 11 Italian gigs. Throughout its two and a half months, the tour was dogged by natural disasters, technical problems and belligerent audiences. The May 23 Kiel concert lasted just ten minutes because the band were being pelted with various objects. Heavy rain stopped the gig at Mannheim on June 6, and the June 17 show in Lille was cancelled after the soundcheck.

The tour concluded at Palermo in Sicily on July 14; here a full-scale riot, with police firing tear gas into a volatile crowd, erupted after 30 minutes. Frank commemorated the event with two tracks on *YCDTOSA 3;* the band were playing 'Cocaine Decisions' when the first tear gas grenade was fired. Frank wrote, 'The Army and the local Police (who didn't like each other, and who were completely unco-ordinated) began a random process of blasting these little presents into the crowd. We could see fires in the distant bleachers. Tear gas seeped onto the stage.' The band segued into 'Nigger Business' and John Smothers had to wipe the tears from Ray White's eyes while he was playing. It was the last show that the 1982 band would perform.

'That was our last European tour,' Frank said the following month. 'It's too expensive to play, too expensive to travel around, and with the anti-American sentiment around, it is hard to go onstage and do what you do with the emotional freight that is attendant to European attitudes toward American foreign policy.'¹⁰

That foreign policy, dictated by the CIA and Defense Department vultures perched on Ronald Reagan's shoulders, included trying to keep leftist guerrillas from seizing control of El Salvador, while bankrolling the Contras in their bid to overthrow the Sandanista government in Nicaragua. In his attempts not to be the 'wimp' he'd accused his predecessor Jimmy Carter of being, Reagan was convinced the following year to send troops into the Lebanon, where Israel and the PLO were religiously killing each other. His action resulted in a car bomb that destroyed the American Embassy in Beirut and 241 Marines inside.

Material from the tour made up the second disc of *YCTOSA 5;* the ill-fated Geneva show provided a number of its 13 tracks, with the balance from Munich, Balzano and Frankfurt. Frank was generous in his notes: 'The '82 band could play beautifully when it wanted to. It is unfortunate that the audiences of the time didn't understand that we had no intention of posing as targets for their assorted "love offerings" cast onto the stage [in Milan they threw used hypodermic syringes].' Frank himself was in good form, as his solos on 'Easy Meat', 'RDNZL', 'A Pound For A Brown On The Bus', and a reggae version of 'The Black Page #2' with the guitar riff of 'Ya Hozna' running behind it, showed. Even though the CD exceeded 70 minutes, an air of disappointment was evoked by 'Geneva Farewell', as Frank first warns the audience to stop throwing objects onstage, and when they continue, announces, 'House lights. The concert's over.'

By way of consolation, he was well on his way to having a hit by the time he returned to California. 'With 'Valley Girl',' he told Charles Shaar Murray, 'my daughter did a radio interview and brought along an acetate of the song. They played it on the air, and the phones went crazy. The station held on to the acetate and kept playing it, and the thing was such an instant grassroots hit that other stations were taping it off the air and playing it. It didn't sell a lot - maybe 350,000 copies - and the album *Ship Arriving Too Late To Save A Drowning Witch* maybe did 125,000 units; but sociologically it was the most important record of 1982 in the United States.'[11]

What began as a satirical gibe at a generation of teenage girls whose chosen habitat was the shopping mall, and who spoke a form of English that foresaw the advent of Loyd Grossman, had been taken at face value as a celebration of a dystopian way of life. 'I'm not too thrilled about the (San Fernando) Valley as an aesthetic concept,' Frank admitted, 'to me, [it] represents a number of very evil things.'[12] Moon revealed the origin of her bizarre dialogue: 'I would go to bar mitzvahs and come back speaking Valley lingo that everyone at the bar mitzvah was speaking and the song came out of that.'[13]

Her father was slightly bemused by the song's success: 'Who would have thought in their *wildest dreams* that a record like that would drive people *crazy*?'[14] But he was reluctantly good-humoured about it: 'First, it's not my fault,' he told Tom Mulhern, 'they didn't buy that record because it had my name on it. They bought it because they liked Moon's voice. It's got nothing to do with the song or the performance. It has everything to do with the American public wanting to have some new syndrome to identify with. And they got it . . . you wouldn't believe what kinds of things will be coming out with the words 'Valley Girl' on them. You name it, everything from lunch boxes to cosmetics, including a talking Valley Girl doll in February.'[15]

No doubt it said 'Bag your face' and 'Gag me with a spoon' or some of the other like totally bitchen expressions that drawled from the lips of Encino cheerleaders. Nicholas Slonimsky used another, 'Grody to the max', as the name of his mischievous cat. The 14-year-old Moon suffered the slings and arrows of outrageous fame. 'The people at my school are pretty supportive,' she said. 'But the ones I never was very friendly with and the ones I didn't like are really negative. They finally have a chance to categorise me. They call me a soc or a snob - God knows what.'[16]

'We've had calls from Universal, United Artists, even Norman Lear asking to do a film on 'Valley Girl,' her father added. 'If we do [it] as a movie, she'll be in it, so she'll have to miss some school. But she'll have a tutor. I refuse to let her just walk away from school.'[17] In the event, *Valley Girl* the film starred Nicholas Cage and Deborah Foreman in a tale of forbidden romance between a Val and the typecast Cage as a Hollywood punk.

Meanwhile, the guitar albums continued to sell well. Because of the way the deal with Columbia was structured, the company had the right to release them commercially as a three-record set outside America. 'That did really well in Europe,' Frank said, 'and suddenly they started importing them into the United States.' All those who'd bought the albums mail-order got upset, to the extent that Frank had to release them as a box-set himself.

'They pressed 5,000 sets to begin with, and they went immediately. So, they ordered another 7,000. It's kind of an unusual item since it is fairly expensive, it's in a box, it's hard to rack, and you wouldn't think there'd be much demand for it because it is instrumental music by some guy who is not normally recognised as being a musician. People think of me as some kind of deranged comedian. So CBS was kind of surprised that there were that many orders coming in.'[18] They were happier about 'Valley Girl', which eventually reached number 32 in the singles chart; and although it contained some demanding music, *Ship Arriving Too Late To Save A Drowning Witch* climbed to number 23 in the *Billboard* album charts.

Despite putting out albums that demonstrated his guitar playing, when he came off the road Frank hardly touched one at all. 'The only time I play my guitar is when I know I'm going to tour,' he said. 'I practice a little bit before we go into rehearsal, to get the calluses built up again. Then I play during rehearsals, and when we get out on the road, I usually practice an hour a day before each show. Once the tour is over, I don't touch it.'[19]

'I really like the instrument and I really like to play,' he added, 'but when the responsibility for running the business rests on my shoulders, there isn't any time to practice.' Nor did he feel the need to wear it on stage all the time. 'I'm not a very good singer and I don't have very good breath control. And the weight of the guitar on your shoulder pushes down on your lungs. I find it easier to sing in tune with the other guys onstage if I don't have that weight on my body . . . Why dirty up the arrangement, which is planned to be concise and accurate, by randomly whacking a couple of chords or a couple of extra tweezy notes just because that's what everybody else would do? The music isn't designed that way. That's not the reason why I have the thing out there. It's something to make music on. And I really don't care what I look like out there as long as I can get my work done.'[20]

BOGUS POMP

In the second half of 1982, Frank concerned himself with a number of orchestral projects. *Sinister Footwear* was to receive its world premiere in the spring of 1984 with the Berkeley Symphony Orchestra and the Oakland Ballet Company. *The Perfect Stranger* was a commission from Pierre Boulez, to be premiered in Paris on January 9, 1984, with his Ensemble InterContemporain, with some other Zappa compositions. 'Right now, we don't have any guarantee that even if he conducts the premiere that it will get recorded,' Frank said in 1982. 'And I'm interested in getting it recorded so that I can hear it. It's never enough just to hear it played once live in a hall. You may be able to listen to the stuff carefully so that you can go further and advance your craftsmanship, but it's just a little bit hard to do that by hearing it only once, so I do want to get it recorded.'[21]

First, there was the preparation of scores for his collaboration with the London Symphony Orchestra. It would entail a performance in London's Barbican Hall on January 11, 1983, followed by three days of recording of 'Envelopes', 'Mo 'n Herb's Vacation', 'Bob In Dacron', 'Sad Jane', 'Pedro's Dowry', 'Bogus Pomp' and 'Strictly Genteel'. The orchestra and the location were both reluctant compromises. The concert was originally scheduled to take place at New York's Lincoln Center with the Syracuse Symphony Orchestra, 'but they decided to hose me by doubling the price in a couple of days', Frank told Robin Denselow, when the reporter visited his home. His next choice had been the BBC Symphony Orchestra, but they were unavailable. 'It will be exciting to hear them for the first time, if they are played right,' Frank added. He admitted to Denselow that the scores were very difficult and that the LSO had a chance to make musical history, because what was required from them in the score was 'quite unusual'.[22]

Frank took Ed Mann, Chad Wackerman and clarinettist David Ocker, the featured soloist in 'Mo 'n Herb's Vacation', with him. The entourage was completed by engineer Mark Pinske, who had recorded the 1982 tour. 'The entire orchestral thing is on my own budget,' Frank said. 'I've had requests from orchestras all over the world asking to play music, but basically it comes down to one thing: They want me to pay for it . . . What I'm hoping to do is have [the LSO] rehearse it for about a week, and it may turn into something that they will keep in their repertoire, and it will continue to be played especially after the record comes out because then it will be something that will sell tickets for them.'23

But then, no British institution was going to grant Frank's dreams, least of all the tabloid press. 'Zappa takes the dance out of ballet' announced the *Daily Express* on January 7, 1983. 'The 42-year-old musician said of his ballets without dancers: "The scenarios and plot-line will be described in the programme. When the music has been heard, a choreographer can come forward."' That wouldn't happen on the Barbican stage, as Frank discovered when he first entered the hall. A row with the organisers ensued; 'It is tiny and pitifully inappropriate,' Frank told them.24 At a later press conference, he added, 'Well, having seen the stage I'd rather get it over with as quickly as possible and do the recording. The sort of audience that will go to see classical music concerts and even rock groups in England are just trying to be cool anyway.'25

Frank enlisted Kent Nagano, conductor of the Berkeley Symphony Orchestra, to realise his scores. Nagano had been aware of him since 1967 but hadn't realised there was more to Frank than the Mothers until he visited some friends at Pierre Boulez's Institut de Recherche et Coordination Acoustique/Musique (IRCAM) in Paris. There he noticed some of Frank's compositions in a list of future works and learned of the *Perfect Stranger* project. Back in the States, the two met backstage at a Zappa concert and Frank showed him some scores. 'I looked at them and realised they were far too complicated for me to comprehend just sitting there,' Nagano said.

'These kinds of musical syntaxes usually take a master's degree to even grapple with, and even then, most composers with degrees don't necessarily have the inspiration to go along with their knowledge,' he added. Nagano asked if he could perform Frank's music with the Berkeley Symphony, but Frank had another purpose in mind. Four months after their initial meeting, Nagano got a phone call asking if he'd be interested in conducting some of Frank's music with the LSO. 'It was much more than "would I be interested?"' he told Andy Greenaway. 'I considered it a real privilege, a real honour to be able to work with someone like Frank. We did some initial rehearsals together at his home in Los Angeles, and there I realised it was indeed going to be an extremely exciting project. For my knowledge of his music and his incredible musicianship, I knew that for him it was just as important to have music performed as close to perfection as possible as it was for me.'26

Nagano compared what Frank was doing to the work of Pierre Boulez, but Frank didn't agree. 'Boulez writes complex rhythms,' he told Denselow, 'but they are mathematically derived, while the rhythms I have are derived from speech patterns . . . they should have the same sort of flow that a conversation would have, but when you notate that in terms of rhythmic values, sometimes it looks extremely terrifying on paper.' His orchestral works contained a 'purely original system for balancing the tension zones and relaxing zones'.[27]

'The evening of the performance, I had butterflies in my stomach,' Nagano admitted, 'but it was more a combination of anxiety and enthusiasm than actual fear. There was definitely a feeling that something enormous was about to happen. The reception was pretty predictably unpredictable in that the hall was half-filled with normal LSO concertgoers and half-filled with Frank Zappa enthusiasts, some of whom had never seen a symphony orchestra before. Because of that mix of listeners, there was an electric tension in the air, since people had no idea what to expect. But the London Symphony was 100% behind the concert and behind Frank, and they played extremely well.'[28]

The *Daily Mail* reviewer evidently didn't notice. Under the headline, 'Zappa keeps the hippies hushed', he fluted, 'Many feared a riot as the American premiered his two new ballets - without dancers - with a concert by the London Symphony Orchestra at the Barbican Centre. Instead, there was a cathedral-like reverence from the 2,000 capacity crowd as long-haired denim-clad hippies from the sixties mingled with dinner-jacketed classics lovers . . . his loyal fans seemed happy - even though it was hard to tell the difference between the orchestra tuning up and the cacophany [sic] that followed.'[29]

In *The Times*, Richard Williams showed considerably more awareness. He began his review, 'Frank Zappa was the first rock musician to saturate his work with irony, setting a fashion so widely copied that the music has practically drowned in self-awareness. It also makes his music interesting to deal with in critical terms, since it is often difficult to guess his intention and thereby assess his achievement.' He thought that Frank's music was never wholly serious nor totally given up to satire, parody and ridicule. 'To maintain such ambiguity is an achievement of its own, although some may feel that it closes off the opportunity for emotional expression. Perhaps that was never his aim.

'The first half ('Envelopes' and 'Mo 'n Herb's Vacation'),' he thought, 'was hugely depressing.' There were echoes of Charles Ives, Bartók and Varèse, Williams gauged, but none of the 'new harmonic technique' promised in the programme. 'The remainder of the programme was less ambitious, less diffuse, and not surprisingly, more enjoyable.' 'Bogus Pomp' 'began with broad parodies of Hollywood movie music and ended, to the merriment of the orchestra, with visual and musical slapstick. The safest music had fared best, always an unsatisfying conclusion.'[30]

Afterwards, Frank said, 'I'm glad people liked it but it wasn't a very accurate performance of the music. There were a lot of wrong notes in the show and the acoustics of the place were really shitty. If they liked it then the record will kill them because only on the record will you hear what the things are really supposed to be.' He was grudgingly appreciative of the orchestra:

'The LSO has an air of professionalism above and beyond most other orchestras, which is not a lot, but I've been associated with a few. I like the attitude of the LSO and whatever the liabilities might be from some of the individual performers, or the attitude of some guys in the orchestra, the net result of working with them was really positive.'[31]

The following day, the massed forces of the LSO made their way to Twickenham Film Studio. 'Frank was right there next to me,' Kent Nagano remembered. 'He demonstrated that he had impeccable ears and absolute command of the scores . . . I include Frank in the category of composers who are keenly in tune with their own work, how it's being rehearsed, how it's developing, and who can participate and help correct the wrong notes, make suggestions, and change phrasing on the spot in ways that might be easier or more musical to play.'[32]

There was some 90 minutes of music to be recorded over the course of three days. Under normal circumstances, for musicians of the LSO's supposed standard, that would have been within the bounds of accomplishment. But not for Frank's music. In his note for Volume One of the recordings, he noted that 'as with every performance of new music, errors will occur. Every effort has been made to remove these, but without a much larger budget for rehearsal and recording time, the possibility of perfection in a premiere situation such as this is somewhat remote.'

Four years later, when the second volume was issued, he was brutally honest about the circumstances of the last piece to be recorded, 'Strictly Genteel'. 'The performance included here was recorded in the last hour of the last session of the last night . . . with no possibility of overtime (at any price) to correct mistakes. During the final "rest period" just before the big push to get a good take, the entire trumpet section decided to visit a pub across the street. They returned 15 minutes late. No recording could be done without them. The orchestra refused to spend another 15 minutes at the end of the session to make up for their glowing brass section neighbours. I have done as much as possible to enhance this fine British "craftsmanship" (at least 50 edits in 6.53), but to no avail . . . the "human element" remains intact.'

Nagano was diplomatic: 'Costs make Frank's works very difficult for a traditional institution to mount. They call for huge orchestras – much larger than normal, and the scores are expensive to produce. They're difficult from a technical standpoint, and that requires much more rehearsal time than a standard repertoire piece.'[33] Fewer visits to the pub and a professional observation of working hours, especially when the composer is footing the bill, would also have been appreciated.

INFIDELS

Before Christmas, Frank had given Robin Denselow a list of his projects:

'There's a new album, *The Man From Utopia*, due out in two weeks, then I've just finished three film treatments and a treatment for a Broadway show. I've made a deal for an animated TV show on 'Valley Girl'. I've finished an 88-minute film, *Baby Snakes*, involving live concert footage and animation, there are two other 90-minute videos . . . I've waded through 300 of the 400 reels of tape from our last tour and there's enough for five albums there. . .'[34]

He also told of a late-night visitor one recent December night: 'I get a lot of weird calls [at home], and someone suddenly called up saying, "This is Bob Dylan, I want to play you my new songs." Now, I've never met him and I don't know his voice, but I looked at the video screen to see who was at the gate, and there, in the freezing cold, was a figure with no coat and an open shirt. I sent someone down to check to make sure it was not a Charles Manson, but it was him.'

Dylan was led down to the studio, where he sat at the piano and played 11 songs and then asked Frank to produce his next album. 'It could be funny,' Frank grinned. 'It's so ridiculous and off the wall that I feel I should do it. He doesn't have much of a sense of humour, but his new sounds are nice, so I'd like to produce them, though it would be a bit of an adjustment. I said he should sub-contract out the songs to Giorgio Moroder. I said he should do a complete synthesiser track and Dylan should play guitar and harmonica over the top.'[35]

For Dylan, that would have been over the top. He later maintained that the project foundered because Frank asked for too much money and wanted to use his own musicians. In any event, Frank didn't hear from him again and the new album, *Infidels*, was recorded with co-producer Mark Knopfler and Mick Taylor on guitars, and Robbie Shakespeare and Sly Dunbar provided the propulsion.

By then, there were two new Zappa albums on the market. *The Man From Utopia*, as good a description of the position Frank found himself in as any, was released in March 1983. Its cover painting, by Gaetano Liberatore, depicted a massively-muscled and snarling Frank as a clone of 'RanXerox', the robotic hero of a political comic strip 'Tanino' drew for the Italian magazine, *Frigidaire*. His left hand has crushed the neck of his Stratocaster, while with the right he tries to swat the mosquitoes that beset the band at the Parco Redecesio in Milan. Behind him, a signpost indicates some of the other Italian towns the band played in.

The back cover, showing the scene from behind 'FranXerox', was even more detailed. The location has switched to Palermo at the start of the riot. Tear gas drifts across the crowd as police buckle on their shields. In left foreground, John Smothers is crushing a photographer's head alongside two furtive cocaine sniffers ('Cocaine Decisions' opened the album). To the right, Pope John Paul gestures from a throne carried by Swiss guards. In front of him, a bare-breasted woman holds aloft a rolled copy of *Frigidaire* in a pose that echoes the Statue of Liberty. Italy had just beaten Germany in the World Cup, so a banner announces '3-1 Vaffanculo'; telling the Germans to 'fuck off' must have been a novel experience.

For some Zappa fans, the cover was more attractive than the contents. Songs like 'Cocaine Decisions' (another broadside aimed at Warner Brothers) and 'Stick Together', which attacked the mob-ruled union movement, were in the Zappa mainstream, as was the medley of two doo-wop songs, 'The Man From Utopia' and 'Mary Lou'. Less listener-friendly were three excursions into sprechstimme, 'The Dangerous Kitchen', 'The Radio Is Broken' and 'The Jazz Discharge Party Hats'. The musical achievement, particularly in the first two numbers, was considerable, but their value as entertainment, even at the first listening, was questionable.

'We have this thing called meltdown,' Frank told Rick Davies, 'where, depending on what's in the news that day, or what happened in the audience during the show, I'd start talking in a singsong tone of voice and then Tommy Mars would chop changes behind it. Now that's very freeform, kind of like 'The Dangerous Kitchen' or 'The Jazz Discharge Party Hats'; those are both meltdown events. In the case of 'Dangerous Kitchen', it's a fixed set of lyrics that has variable pitches and variable rhythms. In the case of 'The Jazz Discharge Party Hats', it was completely spontaneous, 100% improvised by me and the band. It ended up right on the spot in this concert in Illinois. So that type of rampant behaviour is good as a contrast, but I think that for today's audience you can't go out and do a whole evening of random behaviour. They're not going to tolerate it; they want to see a structured show.'[36]

The tortuous vocal line in 'The Dangerous Kitchen' was transcribed by Steve Vai, who then overdubbed an acoustic guitar part on the live recording, which featured Vinnie Colaiuta on drums. 'It's not 100% accurate, as a matter of fact,' Frank pointed out to David Mead, 'because if you play the pitches of his transcription without the vocal, there are certain things that just sound a little bit weird. I'd give it 99%, though.

'When you're transcribing something to publish in a magazine, that's one thing. But when you're transcribing it and you know that within a day or so you're going to be overdubbing on the track, and you're going to be sight-reading your own transcription, and it's got to synch up exactly with what's on the track - that's when you'll really know whether you're a good transcriber or not. But that's how he did it; he wrote it out, he came in, we turned on the tape, he read it and he did it in two or three takes. He even put in a string-scratch for when I laughed! I went Huh, huh, huh and he's got that little 'scrape, scrape, scrape' in there. He nailed everything.'[37]

'The Radio Is Broken' was a studio creation which interspersed a dialogue between Frank and Bobby Martin on the subject of shoddy sci-fi B movies over a complicated rhythm passage that had Scott Thunes' bass utilising the riff from The Knack's 'My Sharona'. It was the sort of 'audio junk sculpture' with which Frank liked to tease his fans; The Knack had recorded 'My Sharona' at Village Recorders while he was there cutting *Joe's Garage*. The song's composer, Doug Fieger, claimed Frank as 'a big, big influence in my life. I met him one time, and he insulted me. It was at an airport. It was good-natured, but he was ever the iconoclast and the kind of "grumpy old man" . . . I gave him a Knack button, and I said, "We're gonna be a big band." And he said, "So what!"'[38]

'The Jazz Discharge Party Hats', again with Colaiuta on drums, is probably the most tasteless song in Frank's whole catalogue. The song concerned the band's visit to Albuquerque, New Mexico and two unnamed band members' attempts to pooch some local college girls. The story of a panty-sniffing session while one of the girls skinny-dipped in the hotel pool gets just a little too graphic ('He told me later the stuff in the bottom was like punching an eclair'). There is no way of telling what Frank's attitude is to the events he recounts, except when he refers to the panty-sniffing fetish as 'part of a great American Tradition'.

There were three short instrumentals on *The Man From Utopia*, none over-arranged. 'We Are Not Alone' was an updated echo of 50s R&B bands, featuring the massed saxophones of Marty Krystall. Frank referred to 'Moggio' as 'a very complicated instrumental for the full ensemble, featuring Steve Vai playing some very hard guitar stuff'. The title came courtesy of his daughter: 'One day, when Diva was real young,' he told Den Simms, 'she crawled into bed with us, and I was going to bed, like, seven o'clock in the morning, and she had been sleeping in bed with Gail during the night. As I got into bed, she was just waking up, and she was telling me about this dream that she had, that she had a tiny, little father named "Moggio" who lived under the pillow . . . and gave me this complete scenario about this character that she was familiar with.'[39]

Most interesting of all was 'Tink Walks Amok', a showcase for Arthur Barrow's bass-playing. It was originally a band piece, 'Thirteen', that was renamed when Frank learned Barrow's nickname from Christopher Cross, at a time when neither were peaking. 'The band versions of it were much cooler than the album track,' was Barrow's modest opinion. 'We did it by starting to a click track, then I put down a basic bass track. Then I overdubbed bunches of other tracks, micro bass and some other stuff. We were sitting in the studio with the tape rolling. Frank would say, "OK, move the whole pattern up to the D-string, get ready, NOW!" All while the tape was rolling. That's the way it is on the record.'[40]

When the album was digitally remixed for CD, the air of cold calculation in much of the material was accentuated, rendering an already difficult record appreciably harder to enjoy. The original running order was changed and an extra track, 'Luigi & The Wise Guys', an inconsequential a cappella doo-wop parody that accused a crew member of being a dork, was added. Released to mail order at the same time was a picture disc of the *Baby Snakes* soundtrack, beginning with the original track from *Sheik Yerbouti* and versions of 'Titties 'n' Beer', 'The Black Page #2', 'Jones Crusher', 'Disco Boy', 'Dinah-Moh Humm' and 'Punky's Whips' from the 1978 Halloween concert. The set was remixed and formally released three years later.

CHAPTER EIGHTEEN
SYSTEMS OF EDGES

Frank may have felt he was at some sort of impasse as the early months of 1983 transpired. There was progress with his 'serious' music but also a disheartening failure of nerve and execution by the orchestral forces at his disposal. After recording with the LSO, Frank got an opportunity to conduct an orchestra in public when he was asked by the San Francisco Contemporary Chamber Musicians to take part in an Edgar Varèse Memorial Concert on February 9. The first half of the evening was conducted by Jean Louis Le Roux; in the second half, Frank conducted *Ionisation* and *Integrales* and pieces by Anton Webern.

'The orchestra is the ultimate instrument,' he wrote in *The Real Frank Zappa Book*, 'and conducting one is an unbelievable sensation . . . From the podium (if the orchestra is playing well), the music sounds so good that if you listen to it, you'll fuck up. When I'm conducting, I have to force myself not to listen, and think about what I'm doing with my hand and where the cues go.'[1]

On the band front, tour schedules had become more extensive and demanding, their costs secured by a never-ending series of bank loans. The 1982 tour had suffered from circumstances beyond his control, making the treadmill that he'd fashioned for himself, of touring to earn revenue to finance UMRK to produce albums that needed to be promoted by another tour, even more burdensome. He was also frustrated by the persistence of bootleggers that made capital from his gigs. He was unwilling to persist in basing each tour on new material, filled out with songs from previous albums. 'I stopped doing that because people usually bootlegged it, and they'd have it out in the market before I'd even have an album out,' he told Rick Davies.[2]

Nor would there be a 1983 band tour. 'Well, whenever we go off the road, there isn't any band,' Frank told *Guitar Player*. 'Everybody is hired for the tour; nobody is on a yearly salary. I used to do it differently years ago: everybody was employed, and they got the same amount of money every week whether they worked or not. And some of the guys said, "I'd rather get paid more money just for the time I'm on the road". And I said, "Fine", and that's the way it is now. So when they're not on the road with me, they go out and do other work. It's going to be a while before I'm back on the road, so it's good they have other work.' As for Frank: 'I have a lot of things to do that can't be done while you're on the road. We've got video and movie stuff happening right now, and you can't be a touring musician and still have control over that stuff.'³

He was about to embark on a project, ambitious even by his own standards. After years of legal wrangling with MGM–Verve and Warner Brothers, he'd finally got back all the tapes and masters of the early Mothers albums. He was asked if he still listened to his old albums. 'Well,' he replied, 'I'll be listening to those things a whole lot because we plan to re-release the entire catalogue of my albums next May. 'We're remixing everything . . . I don't know whether we'll be able to pull it off in time because there's an awful lot of work to be done to meet the deadline, but I'm hoping by Mother's Day to have five boxes with seven albums in each of them, covering the entire catalogue. And we'll divide them up so that the first box is like all the early Mothers stuff plus one extra disc of material from that era that's never been released before. And the same goes for the rest of the boxes: each will have one disc of things that were done during that time that never got released.

'All the stuff is either going to be remastered, as is the case with the things that already have a good mix, or completely remixed. This includes 4-track, early 8-track or early 16-track or anything done when science wasn't there to make it sound right.'⁴ The task was even bigger than he envisaged, and *The Old Masters Box One* would not be released until April 1985. A contributory factor in the delay was a decision that would prove to be controversial with Zappa enthusiasts. This was the removal of the original bass and drum tracks from both *We're Only In It For The Money* and *Cruising With Ruben And The Jets*. One reason put forward was that the oxide on the original multi-tracks was crumbling away and affecting the sound quality.

Arthur Barrow, who played the new bass parts, was the first to express misgivings: 'I had mixed feelings about it. On the one hand, as a musician, I'm always happy to be employed and doing sessions is always fun. But on the other hand, I did try to talk Frank out of it the best I could. I said, "Are you sure you want to do this?" He said, "I don't like the old bass and drum tracks."' Apart from the aural contrast between the original sound and the pristine digital precision of the new recordings, there was the anomaly of Barrow's use of the 'My Sharona' riff during 'Flower Punk', since The Knack's song had not been released until 12 years after *We're Only In It For The Money*.

'Actually,' Barrow added, 'how could the oxide be falling off the tape on one track and not on other tracks? But it's Frank's album. It's his music. He can certainly do what he likes with it. But I think it would be nice for those of us that like the original version, to put that out also . . . As for *Ruben And The Jets*, I kinda think that's bad too. Because one of the coolest things about that album originally was the tape loops for the drums. It sounded like a machine, it was a great sound.'[5]

The answer to several of Frank's current frustrations was another machine. For years he'd been accustomed to keeping pace with the developments in synthesiser technology. Though not professing to be a keyboard player, he made himself conversant with the potential of each innovation as it became available. But the Synclavier had applications beyond the scope of his other equipment. 'You see,' Frank told Paul Gilby, 'the thing that got me hooked on the Synclavier was the music-printing aspect of it. Before getting that, I would carry manuscript paper around with me in my briefcase and write music on the road, in a hotel or on an aeroplane. It was a very manual procedure where, having come off the road, I would collate my ideas and then write out the new arrangement and that would go to a copyist, and so on. It was really expensive, very time-consuming, and at the end you really didn't know what you were going to get till you heard it played.'[6]

In conversation with Rick Davies, he elaborated on the process: 'Then the musician takes his part and under the baton of the conductor attempts to interpret what you dreamed up in the first place. And this interpretation is subject to such questions as how much time they have for rehearsal, which is based on how much money they have to lose, and the acoustics of the hall in which the thing is going to be played. So basically your chances, as a composer writing for human beings, of getting your idea accurately performed are really not too good. Not good at all, unless you write very simple music, which I do not.'[7]

Manufactured by New England Digital, the Synclavier had been developed as a composer's tool, enabling its operator to test melodic structures and the voicing of arrangements. With his inquiring mind, Frank's interest rapidly became an addiction: 'When I first got it I probably did the same thing that a lot of people do when they buy a complex piece of equipment - I said, "Oh my God, do I have to read all those big books?" So I didn't! . . . But on the other hand I did happen to hire people who had read them, and they did all the stuff that I didn't want to do. What I wanted to do right away was write music on it, not learn how to write computer programmes. I still don't know how to do that and I will probably never bother to find out, because it took me about two or three months before I could turn round and say, "I can type music into that!"

'I remember I had a guy (Steve DiFuria) operating the machine and the way it happened was - and, boy, how this man suffered! I was working on a piece and I had to get the musical information into the computer. Since I didn't know how to type it in, I had to sit next to him and say, "Make that one a C, make the next one a G, etc." Then one day he said, "Look, Frank . . . if you would just do this, then I wouldn't have to sit here!" So I said, "Okay, let me try", and it only took about a day to learn the process. From that point on he couldn't even get into the room to use the machine because I was there day and night!

'You see, once you learn how to do this stuff, it's dangerously addictive. If you love music, and you desire the ability to write down your music and then push a button and hear it played back to you right away - the Synclavier is the instrument for you.'[8]

For someone obsessively involved in creating music, capable of sustaining 16 to 18-hour days of intensive work, the Synclavier was a godsend. 'You see,' he explained, 'when I'm composing, my main idea often starts with various musical theories and I ask myself what happens if I do this or that, and what are the physical limits of what a listener can comprehend in terms of rhythm? How big is the "data universe" that people can take in and still perceive it as a musical composition? That's the direction I'm going in.'[9]

The trouble was, once the programming aspects of the machine were mastered, the number of musical problems he could set himself proliferated alarmingly. Ideas flowed onto disc and sometimes waited years to be completed or adapted into other compositions. 'For example,' he told Don Menn, 'when I first bought the Synclavier, it wasn't even a sampling machine, and I started writing things for it that just used the FM synthesis. The main charm with [it] at that time was the power of its sequencer and the fact that you could have multi-tracks and things colliding with each other. So some of the pieces that were started even in the pre-sampling days . . . have gone through permutations over the years and still haven't been released yet.'[10]

He explained the Synclavier in layman's terms to Nigel Leigh: 'It expedites everything. All the different mechanical aspects of putting a piece together - it's like a musical word processor that would read to you. Like if you were writing a novel, for example, on a computer and the word processor helps you to move your paragraphs around and do all that stuff, and when it was all done, you'd push a button that would read your book to you. That's kind of what the Synclavier does.'[11]

THE PERFECT STRANGER

On the conventional front, *The London Symphony Orchestra/Zappa Vol. 1* was released in America on June 9. Despite Frank's caveat about errors in the performances of 'Sad Jane', 'Pedro's Dowry', 'Envelopes' and 'Mo 'n Herb's Vacation', it would be hard for anyone but the composer to notice. What does strike the untutored ear is that there are frequent instances of whole sections of the 100-strong band being unoccupied, and that in general the opportunity to engage the full sonority of such a large aggregation has been missed. The LSO's performance of 'Pedro's Dowry' is more cumbersome than that by a 40-piece band on *Orchestral Favorites*. Similarly, 'Envelopes' is taken at a more deliberate tempo than the version on *Ship Arriving Too Late To Save A Drowning Witch*, making what was potentially bizarre almost contemplative.

'Sad Jane', the least bombastic of all Frank's orchestral pieces, based in part on a 1968 guitar solo transcribed by Ian Underwood, is very much in the same vein, even when Chad Wackerman's overloud drumkit provides a more regular pulse. For much of its duration, the piece alternates between passages for strings, woodwind and brass, and rarely uses the LSO's full resources. 'Mo 'n Herb's Vacation' is in three movements, the first a feature for David Ocker's clarinet, closely followed by Chad Wackerman's drumkit and supported by woodwinds. Violins lead off the second movement, playing long sliding notes reminiscent of Gyorgy Ligeti. For the first time, the listener becomes aware of the orchestra's fullness. But once again, the sequential nature of the writing doesn't allow the impression to last. The final movement opens with a convulsive flourish before the angular melody line passes around the sections of the orchestra. For much of its 13 minutes, it combines a long series of ominously eventful episodes that finally resolve in a tumbling climax incorporating blasts from a klaxon horn.

It's as if with this record, and *Volume 2* released in September 1987, Frank is laying to rest the urge to emulate the techniques of the composers who sparked his youthful interest, and thus their influence. From now on, he would be able to work in a medium that was not available to his musical antecedents; he could create his own compositional language, exploring tonal and rhythmic theories that were inconceivable at the time of Varèse's death. The older man had been excited by the possibilities of electronic sound, an alien universe which he strived to embrace. But the embryonic resources at his disposal could provide no more than the crudest of wave forms with few inherent musical qualities. The Synclavier, even in its basic form, let Frank's imagination take flight in an infinity of directions.

'Every composer has some image in his mind of what he wants his stuff to sound like,' he said, 'not just the composition, but the overall tonal quality of what he's writing. In my head I have an audio image, not just of the notes, but of the way the notes will sound played in an idealised air space, which is something you can't get in the real world. The closest you can get to it is a digital recording with digital control over imaginary audio ambience.'

'The moment you get your hands on a piece of equipment like this,' he added, 'where you can modify known instruments in ways that human beings just never do, such as add notes to the top and bottom of the range, or allow a piano to perform pitch-bends or vibrato, even basic things like that will cause you to rethink the existing musical universe. The other thing you get to do is invent sounds from scratch. Of course, that opens up a wide range.'[12]

It was this potential to explore the unknown that also motivated the eminent composer/conductor Pierre Boulez to create L'Institut de Recherche et Coordination Acoustique/Musique (IRCAM) at the Centre Georges Pompidou in Paris. The building of the £9 million music resource centre stemmed from a meeting between Boulez and the French President in 1970, at which Boulez explained his vision of the music of the future. Pompidou was so taken with the idea that he agreed to a continuous subsidy of £2 million a year to maintain the two-and-a-half tier underground complex of offices, laboratories, studios and computer room.

The Institut opened in 1977; the Italian composer Luciano Berio was made head of the electro-acoustic department, the Yugoslav composer Vinko Globokar researched the potentialities of voices and instruments, and Jean-Claude Risset oversaw the computer section. In 1980, Boulez sacked these and many other employees and took on a younger team better able to make the technology user-friendly for visiting composers. A year later, the resident Italian computer expert, Giuseppe di Giugno, invented the 4X, a digital signal processor capable of 200 million operations per second.

Frank was said to be 'enthralled' by the 4X, which he used to develop ideas for *The Perfect Stranger*, before its premiere at the Theatre de la Ville in Paris on January 9, 1984, played by Boulez's Ensemble InterContemporain. The 29-strong chamber group also gave performances of 'Dupree's Paradise' and 'Naval Aviation In Art?', as well as works by Carl Ruggles, Elliott Carter and Charles Ives. The three Zappa compositions were then recorded over the next two days at IRCAM. Rumours persisted that there was a falling-out between the conductor and the composer, which served to explain why the resulting album became an amalgam of human and electronic resources. But since only three works were rehearsed and performed, that doesn't seem likely.

Once again, Frank was not satisfied with their live performance. He thought the Ensemble under-rehearsed and he was most unwilling to take the bow that Boulez forced upon him. 'I was sitting on a chair off to the side of the stage during the concert,' he wrote in his autobiography, 'and I could see the sweat squirting out of the musicians' foreheads.' He went on to describe how everyone present at such occasions has to take a chance, with the composer most at risk, subject to inaccurate performance, leadership and the audience's lack of awareness. Not only that, 'even though the programme says World Premiere, that usually means Last Performance'.[13]

Boulez was said to be 'attracted by the energy and spontaneity of some pop artists'. 'They have not the mass of education and repertoire that paralyses many musicians,' he said. 'They are not afraid to experiment. With scores like Zappa's I have the opportunity of breaking down musical ghettos in a dignified way. That is a good thing.'[14] Whether Frank was a willing participant in the great man's crusade went unrecorded. But he was able to have a closer relationship with the Ensemble. 'First of all,' he told Don Menn, 'there were fewer of them, so you could actually have memorable conversations with them. And a number of them had asked me to write solos for them. One of the brass players was also the head of a brass quintet that worked within Boulez's Ensemble InterContemporain. And he wanted me to write some brass music. And usually percussionists will come up to me and ask me for music. I never did manage to do any of those things, because they all take time.'[15]

On the album sleeve, Frank wrote a scenario for each of the compositions. *The Perfect Stranger* depicted a licentious dalliance witnessed by Patricia, a dog sitting in a high chair, between a 'slovenly' housewife, a door to door salesman and his 'faithful gypsy-mutant industrial vacuum cleaner'. Their *ménage à trois* is delineated in woodwinds and violins, while percussion and muted trombones depict 'the spiritual qualities of chrome, rubber, electricity and household tidiness '. The Ensemble attack the piece with apparent gusto, as they do *Dupree's Paradise*. Only 'Naval Aviation In Art?' suffers from a certain staidness in a performance that fails to emulate the ominous qualities of that, a whole minute shorter, on *Orchestral Favorites*.

Frank returned to America with the tapes and spent the next three months compiling the Synclavier pieces that would make up the completed album. These were 'The Girl In The Magnesium Dress', 'Outside Now', 'Again', 'Love Story' and 'Jonestown'. The first piece was another example of Frank's perverse and enquiring mind, in that it was composed by using what he referred to as 'digital dust'. This was his name for the normally unseen instruction codes that told the machine how to operate. One set were called 'G numbers', which came into use if a guitar was interfaced with the Synclavier. Frank and his engineers found a way to transform these 'points in time' into note blanks. 'So we converted this dust into something that I could then edit for pitch, and the dust indicated a rhythm. So what I did was take the rhythm of the dust and impose pitch data on the dust and thereby move the inaudible G number into the world of audibility with a pitch name on it.'[16]

'The Girl In The Magnesium Dress' employed tones akin to the sound of marimbas and glockenspiels which chatter across the stereo. The aural effect was the equivalent of drops of mercury merging and separating over an undulating surface. Similar effects could be heard in both 'Love Story' and 'Jonestown'. The former, just one minute long, Frank described as 'an elderly Republican couple attempting sex while break-dancing', the brittle crumbling sounds resembling detuned zithers. Frank called 'Jonestown' 'a boring, ugly dance evoking the essential nature of all religions'. It referred to the 1978 'Jonestown massacre' perpetrated by a charismatic preacher who styled himself the 'Rev. Jim Jones'. A native of Indiana, he moved to California in 1967 and joined the People's Temple in San Francisco in 1971. Hounded for alleged abuses against his followers, in 1977 Jones took them to Guyana and set up

Jonestown in the North West district, close to the Venezuelan border.

On November 14, 1978, US Representative Leo Ryan of California brought newsmen and relatives to the commune to conduct an unofficial investigation. Four days later, Ryan and 14 defectors were ambushed on Jones' orders at the nearby airstrip. Ryan and four others (three of them newsmen) were killed. Aware that more investigations would now follow, Jones put into effect a plan for mass suicide which he'd rehearsed with his brainwashed followers several times before. Large tubs of Gatorade, laced with cyanide, were prepared; all present drank the lethal preparation, parents dosing their children. In all, 913 misguided people died, 276 of them children. Jones was found shot through the head, in a manner indicating that it wasn't a self-inflicted wound. Unfortunately, it hadn't been done until after last orders.

'Jonestown' establishes a bleak aural landscape of tremulous sustained chords that imply paranoia. Percussion effects cut through the stereo but the principal elements are raw, gouging metallic sounds that increase during the middle section of the seven-minute piece, accompanied by siren-like ascending notes. The effect is other-worldly and threatening, maintaining an absence of hope that underscores the tragedy of the real event and Frank's own opinion of the perniciousness of all forms of religion.

FRANCESCO ZAPPA

Cyanide was still on his mind when he delivered the keynote speech at the 19th Annual Festival Conference of the American Society of University Composers held at Ohio State University in Columbus on April 4-8. After referring to himself as a 'buffoon', he proceeded to puncture any complacency in the room, calling their (and his) work 'baffling, insipid packages of inconsequential poot'. He told them that popular American musical taste was determined by Debbie, the 13-year-old daughter of 'Average, God-Fearing American White Folk', unwitting dupes of 'the people in the Secret Office Where They Run Everything From'. Frank reiterated his belief that serious contemporary composers were superfluous to American society and should remove themselves from the world before it removed them. He suggested that ASUC change its name to 'We-Suck' and 'get some cyanide and swizzle it into the punch bowl with some of that white wine "artistic" people really go for, and Bite The Big One.'[17]

'I was at this little podium,' Frank told Den Simms, 'and then, on the stage with me, seated in chairs was the music faculty, sitting like a bunch of puppets onstage, and they didn't know what I was going to say and they did not enjoy it. Actually, there was quite a bit of backlash at the subsequent banquet, where I was forced to sit at a table with some of the composers that had attended. The drunker they got, they started attacking me at the table. It was really quite laughable.'[18] There were no reports of unrest when 'Naval Aviation In Art?',

'Black Page #2' and 'The Perfect Stranger', were performed later by Relache, the Columbus Symphony and the Pro Musica Chamber Orchestra.

On May 20, he spoke about 'Mo 'n Herb's Vacation' when he was the subject of the 'Speaking Of Music' series held in the sensory museum, the Exploratorium, in San Francisco's Palace of Fine Arts. He played a number of Synclavier pieces, including those to be featured on *The Perfect Stranger*, as well as tracks from other planned albums. There were also excerpts from another ongoing Synclavier project which focused on the works of the 18th Century Milanese cellist and composer, Francesco Zappa. Frank wrote a brief play, *Francesco, The Almost Fictional Life Of An Obscure Italian Composer*, which was read by Calvin Ahlgren and later featured in the video, *Does Humor Belong In Music?*

Frank's namesake was discovered by Gail while browsing through the *Grove Dictionary of Music and Musicians*. Music scores were provided by Michael Keller from the Music Library at UCLA in Berkeley, which were then typed into the Synclavier by David Ocker. 'Then, on the first day, after he typed in Op. 1 and we listened to it, I thought, "Hey, that's a nice tune. I wonder what the rest of it sounds like?",' Frank said. '[David Ocker] spent about a month typing in a huge amount of these string trios - they were all string trios, by the way. They sounded nice, so I thought, "Why not make an album out of it?"

'It was written for two violins and an upright bass - not exactly the world's most appealing audio combination. Even if I had suitable synthesiser replicas for those instruments, I'm not sure that would have made the most interesting album. So I just added a little technicolor to it and let the music speak for itself.'[19]

Frank's own music did more than that when the Berkeley Symphony Orchestra, conducted by Kent Nagano, held 'A Zappa Affair' on June 15/6 in the Zellerbach Auditorium on the Berkeley campus of the University of California. Frank's symphonic works were performed as ballets using members of the Oakland Ballet, who wielded large marionettes made by John Gilkerson for the San Francisco Miniature Theater. The programme consisted of 'Bob In Dacron', 'Sad Jane', 'Mo 'n Herb's Vacation', 'Sinister Footwear' and 'Pedro's Dowry'. The same programme was repeated four days later at the San Jose Center for Performing Arts.

During the month, rehearsals began for the 'Twentieth Anniversary World Tour', beginning in Los Angeles with a five-day stint at the Palace Theater on July 18 and continuing with dates in the Midwest and on the Eastern Seaboard. Video cameras recorded the August 25/6 gigs at The Pier in New York City and *Does Humor Belong In Music?* was released the following year. Thereafter, in the first week of September, a series of European dates took the band through Belgium, Germany, Scandinavia, Holland, France, Spain,

Austria and Italy, before returning to the USA towards the end of October. More dates in America and Canada would culminate on December 23, back in Los Angeles at the Universal Amphitheater.

Ray White, Bobby Martin, Scott Thunes and Chad Wackerman were retained; Napoleon Murphy Brock and Ike Willis returned but Tommy Mars was replaced by Alan Zavod, late of Jean Luc Ponty's band. There would be no more 'stunt guitar', since Steve Vai had already begun a successful solo career. Brock lasted only two weeks, his indulgence in chemical enhancement disqualifying him from further employment.

A typical set contained material from all eras of the various Zappa bands, from 'Trouble Every Day' to 'The Dangerous Kitchen'. Newer compositions like 'What's New In Baltimore?', 'Ride My Face To Chicago', 'Truck Driver Divorce' and 'Hot Plate Heaven At The Green Hotel', and selections from the forthcoming *Thing-Fish*, were interspersed throughout the average evening. Two of the recent additions that also became concert favourites, one a tune that had gone through numerous identities before becoming known as 'Let's Move To Cleveland', the other the almost invariable set-closer, 'Whipping Post', illustrated in different ways Frank's ability to draw from the totality of his experience.

The first grew out of a commission he'd received in 1968 from a concert violinist whose name has gone undocumented. 'I never completed the piece for violin and piano,' Frank told Den Simms, 'but there was enough of a group of sketches for the thing, that I could, at the point where I had a band who could actually play it, I could build a stage arrangement . . . The first band that tried to play it was the [1976] band with Roy Estrada, Terry Bozzio, Napoleon and Andre Lewis . . . and at that time, it was called *Canard Du Jour*.'[20]

It was also played in the 1980 band with Vinnie Colaiuta on drums. At his insistence, the title changed to 'Young And Mond' and was given its 'world premiere' at the Berkeley Community Theatre on April 1, 1980. 'A guy who wears a leisure suit with an enormous medallion, that's 'mond', according to Colaiuta,' Frank said.[21] A rather deliberate performance in Cologne by the 1982 band was included on the bootleg *As An Am*, which was issued in *Beat The Boots Box One*.

When it became part of the 1984 repertoire, the title had changed once again, variously spelt as 'Creega Bondolo' or 'Kreegah Bandolo'. This, claimed Ike Willis, was the sort of cod native language to be found in Edgar Rice Burroughs' Tarzan books. 'And then, "Bon-do-lay-boffo-bonto" was contributed by Ray White, who asserted that it was a Swahili expression meaning "white people taste good" or "white people are good eating" or something,' Frank added. One of the best live performances in this guise, performed at the Saratoga Springs Arts Center on September 1, was included on the bootleg *Big Mother Is Watching You.*

Tiring of that nonsense, the band then sang, 'Let's move to . . .' wherever the gig was taking place, or anything else that sprang to mind. 'It could be anything. You get a bunch of syllables that'll fit that part of the song, and you just sing it. That audience in Cleveland was so good, that's the reason we sang it at the end of that performance . . . 'Let's Move To Cleveland'.' Zappa played Cleveland twice during the 1984 tour, on August 12 and November 14. Since the tune is identified on several European bootlegs from the tour as *Kreegah Bandolo*, it's safe to assume that the title change took place on the latter date.

'Whipping Post' also enjoyed a long gestation period. It began at the Mothers gig in Helsinki on September 22, 1974. The moment is captured on *YCDTOSA 2*, when a member of the audience shouts out "Whipping Post!". After some jocular confusion, Frank admits that the band doesn't know it. 'Sing me 'Whipping Post',' he suggests, 'and then maybe we'll play it with you.' After a perfunctory yodel from the hall, he says, 'Judging from the way you sang it, it must be a John Cage composition, right?' Then the band play a suitably altered version of 'Montana'.

'We didn't know it,' he said later, 'and I felt kind of bad that we couldn't just play it and blow the guy's socks off. So when Bobby Martin joined the band, and I found out that he knew how to sing that song, I said, "We are definitely going to be prepared for the next time somebody wants 'Whipping Post' - in fact we're going to play it before somebody even asks for it." I've got probably 30 different versions of it on tape from concerts all around the world, and one of them is going to be the 'Whipping Post' - the apex 'Whipping Post' of the century.'[22]

THEM OR US

Before the end of the 1984 tour, no less than four albums were released. Having spent almost 18 months off the road, Frank had built up a backlog of product, brought about in part by the fact that he'd fallen out with CBS. Once again, a major company had apparently indulged in some 'creative accounting'. The search for a new distributor was further hampered by management troubles. 'You see,' Gail said, 'in about 1984, we'd gotten into a situation where we were really subsidising Frank's manager. He owed us a lot of money, and so in order to keep the business going we were taking care of all his outstanding debts, and I was getting very agitated with that. Things weren't working in an efficient way, Frank was on the road, and the shit hit the fan.

'He fired the manager, and I took over the business, and the first thing I did was fire everybody that worked for us. The lawyers, accountants - I just said, "That's it, I don't want any help from any of those people", and went out and found replacement parts. I took over in 1985, and it was trial by fire. It took several years to get through the outstanding nasties.' With a $12,000 bank loan, she bought two computers, fed in a mailing list and sent out a questionnaire which also offered a Barking Pumpkin T-shirt for sale. 'I made the $12,000 back right away. I set up this company, which we called Barfko-Swill, which Frank named. I had my sister and this guy who worked for Frank in production and myself, and we sat on our living room floor stuffing envelopes full of T-shirts.'[23]

Distribution deals were agreed with MCA in America and EMI for the rest of the world. Angel Records, an EMI subsidiary, released *The Perfect Stranger* in America on August 23, 1984. *Francesco Zappa* was released in November, with a typically pedantic artist credit to the 'Barking Pumpkin Digital Gratification Consort'. These and the double album *Them Or Us*, released on December 21, used the paintings of 'American Artist: Donald Roller Wilson'. Each one portrayed the dog Patricia, wearing dark glasses and a red dress with a white lace collar.

Wilson exhibited a visual wit and originality that easily equated with Frank's own. He worked in a style that combined bizarre photo-realism with the sort of reflected light that imbued the paintings of Georges De La Tour. Each painting was dated, numbered and timed, presumably on its completion, and given an enigmatic title (in capital letters) that varied in length and oddity. The title of that used for *The Perfect Stranger*, painted on February 1, 1983, ran to 18 lines; by contrast, *Francesco Zappa* sported a harshly-light portrait fashioned on August 22, titled: 'PATRICIA SAW RICHARD ACROSS THE ROOM AND WAS CERTAIN MRS JENKINS HAD TURNED HIM GREEN'.

Them Or Us showed Patricia standing against a wall between two small wall brackets on which a Heinz Ketchup bottle and a baby's milk bottle, with teat attached, stood. These latter had stood on the cluttered table beside Patricia's high-chair on the cover of *The Perfect Stranger*. The rear cover of the double album had a sepia portrait of Frank, his chest-hair sprouting coyly from the cleavage of his double-breasted linen jacket. His left hand, encased in a green oven glove, was raised in a clenched-fist power salute. We know who 'us' are, but 'them' could be any one of the Reagan administration, the fundamentalist right, the major record companies, or all three and more besides.

Any hypothetical identifications are not reflected in the song texts, however. Sandwiched between the cheesy doo-wop of the Channels' 'The Closer You Are' and the Allman Brothers' 'Whipping Post' is a collection of songs that simultaneously celebrate and denigrate their subjects. 'In France' is sung by Johnny 'Guitar' Watson in a wired, impatient parody of soul techniques, as he tackles pissoirs, standing toilets and 'mystery blow-jobs'. Ahmet's 'Frogs With Dirty Little Lips' carries a distant echo of francophobia in its conclusion, 'Dirty little frogs is what you eat'.

The relentless, chain-saw guitar riff that drives 'Ya Hozna' was used as a background element during Frank's solo in 'The Black Page #2' on the 1982 tour. Here it supports three separate backward vocal tracks taken from 'Sofa #2', 'Lonely Little Girl' and Moon's 'Valley Girl' aerobics work-out from a version of 'I Don't Wanna Get Drafted' used on the demo tape of 'Thing-Fish'. Steve Vai plays a solo that shows he never needed xenochrony to hear outlandish harmonies. The resurrection of 'Sharleena' from *Chunga's Revenge* contains the first of two solos by the 14-year-old Dweezil, showing commendable dexterity for someone with two years' experience of playing the guitar, albeit with teachers of the calibre of Steve Vai and Eddie Van Halen.

The latter's fibrillating, hyperactive style can be heard in Dweezil's solo in 'Stevie's Spanking', providing a contrast to Vai's fluid but lurching, hammered-on fretboard athletics. The song tells of Vai's November 1981 encounter with the generously-proportioned Laurel Fishman and his efforts to gratify her taste for sex with inanimate objects, in this case a hairbrush and a banana. Such was her belief in the efficacy of this behaviour that Laurel willingly gave Frank written permission to use her real name in the lyrics and was interviewed on video. 'I've had many enjoyable afternoons in the grocery store that have resulted in enjoyable evenings,' she told him.

Frank's own guitar has its say in 'Sinister Footwear 11', 'Marque Son's Chicken' and 'Them Or Us', all recorded live with the 1982 band, the latter taken from a performance of 'The Black Page' in Bolzano, Italy on July 3. With the exception of 'Baby, Take Your Teeth Out' (also issued as a single), 'The Planet Of My Dreams' and 'Be In My Video', all the tracks were recorded, in whole or in part, during the 1981/2 tours. Some, like 'Frogs With Dirty Little Lips', performed at the Santa Monica Civic Centre on December 11, 1981, and Frank's guitar solo in 'Truck Driver Divorce', taken from *Zoot Allures* at The Ritz, New York exactly a month earlier and mixed xenochronously with other backing tracks, can be accurately dated.

In the case of 'The Planet Of My Dreams', it consisted of a 1974 backing track of George Duke and Patrick O'Hearn on which Chad Wackerman's drums were later overdubbed. This was yet another song from *Hunchentoot*, its offhand brevity masking a serious message. Despite disillusionment with a world of ineffective education and military proliferation, Bob Harris's vocal states that he won't despair and 'CHEAT like ALL THE REST'. Then the composer declares himself with the words, 'I'll just keep on with what I do the best!'

For many of Frank's fans, that was playing the guitar - even though his opinion of his own work was typically scathing. 'During the 1984 tour,' Frank noted in his autobiography, 'I would usually play eight solos per night (five nights a week, times six months), and out of that there might have been 20 solos that were musically worthwhile enough to put on a record. The rest of it was garbage. It's not that I wasn't trying to play something; most of it just didn't come off.'[24]

That's borne out by the fact that of the 65 tracks taken from the 1984 tour that found their way onto various volumes of *You Can't Do That On Stage Anymore*, *Does Humor Belong In Music?* and *Guitar*, roughly 20 are instrumentals. The latter was the 1988 double-CD follow-up to *Shut Up 'N Play Yer Guitar*, which contained 32 solos taken from the 1979, 1981/2 and 1984 tours. Even though Frank plainly set himself the highest standards, it's interesting to note that no less than 14 solos on *Guitar* come from the 1984 tour.

Unlike the video of 14 songs shot at the Pier in New York City, the CD version of *Does Humor Belong In Music?*, released in England in 1986, is made up of ten tracks from nine locations. Some are whole performances, but most are composites of up to four separate recordings. As usual, it's not easy to notice the edits, although Frank appeared to have a cavalier attitude to the sanctity of a performance. 'Let's Move To Cleveland' consists of a piano solo from St. Petersburg, Florida, a drum solo from Vancouver and Frank's solo from Amherst College in Lowell, Massachusetts, with the introduction and coda from Los Angeles. However, *YCDTOSA 4* contains another portion of the Amherst performance, featuring solos by Archie Shepp and Alan Zavod.

The CD also contains a version of 'Whippin' Post', with a guitar solo by Dweezil, taken from the Los Angeles gig on December 23, 'the last song of the last show of the last tour'. Whatever his intentions may have been, Frank could not have realised that when he laid down his guitar at the end of the show, he wouldn't pick it up again for almost four years.

CHAPTER NINETEEN
THING-FISH

'The simple thought behind *Thing-Fish*,' Frank told me in 1991, 'is that somebody manufactured a disease called AIDS and they tested it. They were developing it as a weapon and they tested it on convicts, the same way as they used to do experiments on black inmates, using syphilis. That's documented. They used to do these experiments with syphilis on black inmates in US prisons. That's fact. So we take it one step further and they're concocting the special disease which is genetically specific to get rid of "all highly rhythmic individuals and sissy boys". So I postulate that they do this test in a prison and part of the test backfires and these mutants are created.'

Just another conspiracy theory? In his autobiography, Frank cites passages from *A Higher Form Of Killing*, a book by Jeremy Paxman and Robert Harris in which an Army manual is quoted on the feasibility of manufacturing 'ethnic chemical weapons', and a 1969 Senate appropriations hearing that was addressed by an unidentified speaker looking for funds to develop a virus that would be 'refractory' (i.e., resist treatment) to the human immunological system. None of the names of those involved is mentioned or whether money was allocated. Could such ghoulish research be possible in the jewel of Western civilisation?

Consider the Tuskegee experiment, briefly mentioned in an episode of the television series on the paranormal, *The X Files*; this was a projected six-month study of syphilitics in the communities around the small agricultural town in Macon County, Georgia in 1932. Its aim was to monitor the course of the disease, without the benefit of medicine, in 400 black males. Two Public Health Service doctors, Raymond Vonderlehr and Taliaferro Clark, were supposedly seeking a cure and offered 'special free treatment' to the men, who in reality got everything but their syphilis treated. Clark retired a year later, leaving Vonderlehr clear to extend the study for the duration of the subjects' lives.

Because of the isolation and backwardness of these communities, no one bothered to inform the victims of their involvement in an experiment nor was their consent sought. 'Informed consent was not the vogue in those days,' Dr. Sidney Olansky, who worked on the project in the 50s, said by way of belated justification. 'We have no compunction about sending our youth to war in the national interest,' Dr. John Cutler claimed. 'And it was in the national interest to know as much about syphilis as quickly as possible'[1]

The study was not officially terminated until 1972, by which time more than 100 had died as a direct result of the disease. The survivors were paid compensation of up to $32,500 each, but none of the doctors involved was prosecuted or even reprimanded. Nor did any of them consider the programme racist or immoral or even criminal, even though the Nuremberg trials had exposed the Nazis' genetic experiments. In the 50s, the PHS launched a nationwide anti-syphilis campaign - except in Tuskegee. 'Well,' said Olansky with logic worthy of Josef Mengele, 'if we'd given them penicillin, there'd have been no Tuskegee study.'[2]

'We have a batch of religious fanatics now in the United States,' Frank told *Today*, 'who believe that Armageddon is a Biblical necessity.' One such was the Jubilee Tabernacle in Amarillo, Texas, where all America's nuclear weapons were made. Its leader, Reverend Royce Elms preached that nuclear war would destroy the world. But, in an event called the Rapture, God would scoop his chosen people into the clouds just before the first bomb went off.

Back on earth, Frank continued, 'A few years ago, genetic engineering became a huge stock market issue. It was suddenly possible to mutate bacteria and produce super-specific germs which would affect only certain ethnic groups. You then have a really cheap cost-effective way of putting your enemies' lights out without damaging real estate. Now, put this power in the hands of a very wealthy religious fundamentalist and it presents him with some mind-blowing possibilities, like producing a disease to stop people having sex. After all, fundamentalists believe that sex is a sin, especially the way that gay guys do it. Weird? Well, I don't think so. Especially after the rhetoric flying around when AIDS was first "discovered". Religious leaders like Pat Buchanan and Jerry Falwell were gleefully claiming that it was divine retribution from God - it gets rid of gays, prostitutes and intravenous drug users.'[3]

Little wonder that when *Thing-Fish* was conceived as a satire on Broadway musicals, the wind that came 'rushin' down the plains' bore something weightier than Rodgers & Hammerstein's chocolate-box platitudes. The 'Original Cast Recording' three-LP box-set, with libretto, was released on December 21, 1984. It had been at least two years in the making, even though a third of its tracks were reworked versions of material from *Zoot Allures*, *Tinsel Town Rebellion*, *Drowning Witch* and *You Are What You Is*. Three songs from the latter album made the final cut, but a demo tape exists with a further six selections suitably altered.

The central role of *Thing-Fish* was taken by Ike Willis. The name was adapted from Kingfish, a character from the 50s US television series, *Amos & Andy*, played by ex-prize fighter Tim Moore. Frank referred to Thing-Fish's grotesque language as a 'pseudo-negrocious dialect'. Willis himself helped shape the dialogue: 'In my family, we sort of joke around with dialects, and what it sounded like to me was Paul Laurence Dunbar. He was a black poet from the late 19th century who used to write poems in dialect like that . . . I asked Frank if he had ever heard of this guy, and he said, "No", so I started giving him examples of Dunbar's work, and eventually, that ended up being a big influence on the Thing-Fish dialect.'

Willis confirms the malleable nature of the original script. 'We put everything together in song form first, and things were structured like that, but the thing was, it changed every day, because the script grew every day. Frank would come in with a revised script. A lot of the things we'd leave, but there might be certain things he wasn't quite satisfied with, or I wasn't quite satisfied with. Mostly him, of course, since he is the boss. Through that kind of tweezage, it got much better. It got tighter.'⁴

In fact, the AIDS premise is swiftly dispatched in the 'Prologue', in which Thing-Fish lectures the tiny 'Sister Ob'Dewlla 'X' on the 'potium' that the 'Evil Prince' has fed to the 'San Quentim' inmates in their mashed potato. When nothing happens, the rest of the 'potium' is added to a shipment of 'Galoot Co-Log-Nuh' and within a month 'fagnits be droppin'' off like flies'. But the hardier prison inmates have mutated into 'Mammy Nuns', with 'head like a potato . . . lips like a duck', wearing voluminous gingham skirts and an apron referred to as a 'nakkin'.

The majority of the ensuing action concerns Harry and Rhonda, two members of the audience convinced that any show with coloured folk in it guarantees 'GOOD, SOLID, MUSICAL ENTERTAINMENT'. They are co-opted into the action, which quickly degenerates into fetishism and bizarre sexual athletics. Each is confronted by an alter ego, Harry-As-A-Boy and Artificial Rhonda, the latter marking the return of 'Ms. Pinky'. 'Briefcase Boogie' finds Harry in S&M gear, a chain hanging from his pierced nipples, craving 'homo-sectional' knowledge of Sister Ob'Dewlla 'X'. Meanwhile, an outraged Rhonda in a rubber body suit screws her briefcase and uses her fountain pen as an anal dildo. By the penultimate song, 'Drop Dead', she has become a caricature feminist, berating her husband as an 'all-American cocksucker' and indulging in the self-referential triumphalism that all zealots chant as a mantra.

It's hard to know what to make of *Thing-Fish*. The idea that inspires it, that government-funded genetic research is killing specific sections of the community – or that such research might be happening at all – has far more potential for controversy than the tawdry little drama that follows. By its familiarity, the reworking of so much recent material undermines whatever strengths the plot possesses. The potentially promising clash of ideas could have engendered satire of a higher order, but the action narrows down to some rather desperately perverse behaviour by cardboard characters mouthing platitudes.

Because of its mix-and-match construction, *Thing-Fish* ultimately disappoints. It's impossible not to feel short-changed by the percentage of recycled songs. Nor is much to be gained from the new material. Most consists of dirge-like vamps over which Thing-Fish narrates the convoluted plot while Harry and Rhonda and their miniature clones act out the consequences. Some songs, like 'The Evil Prince', 'Brown Moses' and 'He's So Gay' were already in the touring repertoire.

It did have the distinction of containing Frank's first use of the Synclavier. 'Listen to 'The Crab-Grass Baby', which opens Act Two,' he pointed out. 'The background vocals are a repeated vocal chant with this computer singing over it. The computer voice is done with a little card that fits into an IBM computer, and the stereo background vocals were our first attempt at stereo sampling using the mono system.'[5] More Synclavier introduces the following track, 'The White Boy Troubles'.

Frank had trouble of his own with Barking Pumpkin's distributor, MCA Records. A woman in the Quality Control department had heard the test pressings of *Thing-Fish* and complained. Consequently, MCA had withdrawn from the deal and a hasty agreement made with EMI for *Them Or Us* and *Thing-Fish* to be distributed in America by Capitol. All this prompted Frank to include a warning sticker on the inner sleeve:

'WARNING/GUARANTEE: This album contains material which a truly free society would neither fear nor suppress.

In some socially retarded areas, religious fanatics and ultra-conservative political organisations violate your First Amendment Rights by attempting to censor rock & roll albums. We feel that this is un-Constitutional and un-American.

As an alternative to these government-supported programs (designed to keep you docile and ignorant) Barking Pumpkin is pleased to provide stimulating digital audio entertainment for those of you who have outgrown the ordinary.

The language and concepts contained herein are GUARANTEED NOT TO CAUSE ETERNAL TORMENT IN THE PLACE WHERE THE GUY WITH THE HORNS AND POINTED STICK CONDUCTS HIS BUSINESS. This guarantee is as real as the threats of the video fundamentalists who use attacks on rock music in their attempt to transform America into a nation of check-mailing nincompoops (in the name of Jesus Christ). If there is a hell, its fires wait for them, not us.'

It was his first salvo in a war of words that would occupy a lot of his time during 1985.

PORN WARS

In 1984, the diminutive symbol then known as Prince starred in *Purple Rain*, a film that gaudily recorded one small person's escape from impoverished origins onto the broad uplands of world recognition through music. The soundtrack album yielded three hit singles, the title track, 'Let's Go Crazy' and 'When Doves Cry'. But it was 'Darling Nikki' which inspired the right-wing backlash that perennially lies in wait for errant rock 'n' rollers.

Mary Elizabeth Gore, wife of the Democratic senator for Tennessee, Al Gore, and known by her childhood nickname, Tipper, bought the album for her eight-year-old daughter and was 'shocked' to learn that one verse of the song referred to the said Nikki masturbating with a magazine in a hotel lobby. Recognising a threat to the entire fabric of American society, she convened a meeting of like-minded friends who, like her, just happened to have influential husbands, including Susan Baker, wife of Treasury Secretary James Baker, Pam Howar and Sally Nevius, wed to prominent Washington captains of industry. Together they formed the Parents' Music Resource Center (PMRC), with Howar as its president.

Their first action was to write to Stanley Gortikov, president of the Recording Industry Association of America (RIAA) to demand that the industry instigate a rating system for records similar to that used by the film industry. The suggested categories were: 'X' for 'profane or sexually explicit', 'O' for 'occult', 'D/A' for 'drugs or alcohol' and 'V' for 'violent'. Although this coven of self-appointed moral guardians had no power or mandate, their hands were close to the organs of power, and that made them hard to ignore. One of their male members, Allan Bloom, said that the PMRC only wanted to promote art that was 'noble, delicate and sublime'. Frank had a reply for that: 'This is not a noble, delicate and sublime country. This is a mess run by criminals. Performers who are doing the crude, vulgar and repulsive things Bloom doesn't enjoy are only commenting on that fact.'[6]

'We're not censors,' Gore claimed. 'We want a tool from the industry that is peddling this stuff to children, a consumer tool with which parents can make an informed decision on what to buy. What we're talking about is a sick new strain of rock music glorifying everything from forced sex to bondage to rape.'[7] She cited Prince's 'Darling Nikki' and Judas Priest's 'Eat Me Alive', which she reckoned was about 'oral sex at gunpoint'.

On August 5, Gortikov wrote a reply which essentially rejected their demands, since they involved 'complications that would make compliance impossible'. However, he indicated that his members would consider developing a sticker which would advise concerned parents of a record's explicit content. With this concession, the industry implicitly accepted that censorship was necessary. By the merest of coincidences, H.R. 2911, a bill to impose a blank tape tax, was at the committee stage in Congress. This tax would effectively penalise the home taper and benefit no-one but the industry itself. 'If they could've got the Congress to pass that,' Frank said later, 'they would've picked up a quarter of a billion dollars a year in found money, and it would've been collected for them by the US government.'[8] It seemed that a trade-off was in the wind.

That wasn't enough for the PMRC. The 'Washington wives' met with Edward Fritts, President of the National Association of Broadcasters (NAB), after his wife attended one of their lectures. Panicking, he requested that record labels send lyric sheets with new releases to all radio stations to help programme directors choose what should be broadcast. Not everyone was willing to join the lemmings in their rush over the cliff. Charlie Kendall, of New York's WNEW-FM, reckoned, 'We know what the lyrics are to the songs we play, and I know what my community can take. There is always gonna be an element that doesn't like rock 'n' roll. But as long as I keep it clean and within FCC guidelines, I say "Fuck 'em".'[9]

Frank wrote an open letter to *Cashbox*, entitled 'Extortion Pure And Simple', spelling out the possible connivance whereby the Constitution's First Amendment guarantee of free speech might be compromised by the record industry's lust for revenue. He also wrote to President Reagan, that pious paragon of American virtues who in the early 50s had loyally fingered his fellow actors as Communist sympathisers to McCarthy's HUAC committee while others kept their council. 'The PMRC is an unlicensed lobbying group,' Frank wrote, 'comporting itself outrageously. While threatening an entire industry with the wrath of their husbands' powerful committees, they blithely spew frogwash and innuendo with the assistance of an utterly captivated media.'[10]

In August, Frank debated the issue with PMRC representative Kandy Stroud in Washington, DC on CBS television's *Nightwatch*, in front of a live audience. During a question-and-answer session, a local DJ noted that the proposals smacked of the secret radio blacklist of the 60s. His comment never made the transmission. A week later, Frank was being interviewed on WNEW in New York when the DJ admitted to having seen a blacklist; it was hardly surprising that he refused to admit it under oath.

The PMRC's proposal was heard by the Senate committee for Science, Commerce and Transportation on September 19. Among those giving depositions were Frank, John Denver and Dee Snider, lead singer of Twisted Sister, whose 'We're Not Gonna Take It' was on the PMRC's 'Filthy Fifteen' list, along with W.A.S.P.'s '(Animal) Fuck Like A Beast', Sheena Easton's 'Sugar Walls' and AC/DC's 'Let Me Put My Love Into You'. 'The atmosphere there was really very strange,' Frank said, 'because the hearing itself was such a mongrelisation . . . There were 50 still photographers and something like 30 video teams. It was a big media event.'[11]

Frank's statement revealed the instinct of a raptor; the PMRC's proposal was 'an ill-conceived piece of nonsense', their demands the equivalent of 'treating dandruff by decapitation'. 'Taken as a whole,' he went on, 'the complete list of PMRC demands reads like an instruction manual for some sinister kind of "toilet training programme" to housebreak ALL composers and performers because of the lyrics of a few. Ladies, how dare you?'

He pointed out that the PMRC had no members, but it raised money by mail, had tax-exempt status and was advocating what amounted to restraint of trade. How could it be proper that three senators on the committee he was addressing had wives who were 'non-members' of the PMRC? Whatever happened to 'conflict of interest'? How long before another fanatic demanded the letter 'J' be affixed to anything written or performed by a Jew? 'What hazards await the unfortunate retailer who accidentally sells an 'O' rated record to somebody's little Johnny? Nobody in Washington seemed to care when Christian Terrorists bombed abortion clinics in the name of Jesus. Will you care when the 'friends of the wives of big brother' blow up the shopping mall? Bad facts make bad law,' he asserted, 'and people who write bad laws are in my opinion more dangerous than songwriters who celebrate sexuality.'

He was then questioned by individual senators, with the exception of the splenetic Senator Slade Gorton, who denounced his statement as 'boorish, incredibly and insensitively insulting' and doubted his ability to understand the Constitution. By contrast, Senator Gore was almost friendly, expressing his esteem for Frank's music before repeating that no legislation or regulation was being suggested. Senator James Exon of Nebraska made a perceptive aside; 'I wonder, Mr Chairman, if we're not talking about federal regulation, and we're not talking about federal legislation, what is the reason for these hearings?'.[12] No legislation followed. Nor did H.R. 2911 become law. But 'Parental Advisory' stickers began to appear and, as Frank predicted, record distributors and retailers began to arbitrarily ban product they thought should be stickered and some states tried to make it illegal to even sell stickered albums.

Flushed with victory, Tipper Gore turned her attention to rock videos. 'I'm disturbed by the portrayal of women and the graphic violence on MTV,' she said. The PMRC also wanted offensive album covers kept from public view and warnings to be issued about rock concerts they found tantamount to 'burlesque shows'. 'We're going to have to put a national organisation in place, on a state-by-state basis,' Gore envisaged. 'We're seeking a coalition with the PTA, the American Academy of Pediatrics, labour, anyone who is willing to help.'[13] For a while it seemed that Frank's prediction in *Thing-Fish* would come true: 'Only the boring and bland shall survive!'

THE MOTHERS OF PREVENTION

His reaction to the hearing was to hastily compile *Frank Zappa Meets The Mothers Of Prevention*, an album of band and Synclavier material released during October. Its focus was a 12-minute sound collage entitled 'Porn Wars'. Employing the same techniques with which he'd assembled 'The Chrome-Plate Megaphone Of Destiny', Frank used the voices of Senators Danforth, Hollings, Trible, Hawkins, Exon, Gorton, Gore and the crusading Tipper herself, editing their words with jump cuts and speeded-up repeats to emphasise the dread weight of their self-righteous pomposity.

Key phrases were used as loops to interrupt and underpin various statements. Most prominent was Senator Paula Hawkins' 'fire and chains and other objectionable tools of gratification in some twisted minds', spoken in a robotic monotone that eerily resembled Pamela Zarubica's Suzie Creamcheese. Frank termed her 'the Nancy Reagan lookalike from Florida - she had the reputation of being the least effective senator, she was really a disaster'.[14] Other phrases included Senator Hollings' 'outrageous filth' and 'maybe I could make a good rock star', and an unattributed (Bobby Martin?) 'bend up and smell my anal vapour'. Synclavier excerpts propelled sections of the verbal tirade, while two short passages from the *Lumpy Gravy* piano conversations and one from *Thing-Fish* formed a surreal and ironically prophetic counterpoint.

As well as Barking Pumpkin's usual 'Warning/Guarantee', Frank printed the First Amendment of the Constitution on the inner sleeve. Underneath it was Senator Hollings' assertion, almost inaudible on the record, that '. . . if I could find some way constitutionally to do away with it I would'. Such a statement by any one of the artists being pilloried, or by Frank himself, would have been regarded as tantamount to treason. Apparently, the PMRC and its toadies had a moral imperative to ignore any law or statute in order to achieve their ends.

'Porn Wars' was a scathing response to the PMRC hearing, but the same inspired haste that created it couldn't compile an album of comparable and consistent quality. The first side of *Mothers Of Prevention* comprised four band tracks of some vintage, since both Steve Vai and Tommy Mars were present. The two songs, ' We're Turning Again' and 'Yo Cats', were both mean-spirited affairs. The first was an almost petulant attack on 60s revivalism; Frank set the scene with some withering comments on the hippie ethos ('1967: drug-crazed youth discovered vagrancy as a way of life'), before Ike Willis in Thing-Fish mode laid into Jim Morrison, Keith Moon, the Mamas and the Papas and particularly Jimi Hendrix.

'Yo Cats' continued the assault, taking on the session musician mentality. 'Well, a "Yo Cat" is beyond being a sight-reading cretin,' Frank averred. 'A "Yo guy" is part of this special species that popped up in Hollywood studios -

the A-team mentality . . . A handful of guys get all the work. That's the A-team. And they do it day in, day out, three sessions a day; they grind it out. And one must ask at the end of the day: Was it music? Did they care?'15 Co-written by Frank and Tommy Mars, it was sung by Ike Willis with smug glibness: 'I play shit but I love that loot.'

Both instrumentals, 'Alien Orifice' and 'What's New In Baltimore?', proved Frank's musicians were anything but 'Yo Cats'. Ed Mann's chattering xylophone led the pointillistic melody of 'Orifice' before Frank contributed a typically fluent, and probably xenochronous, guitar solo. Percussion also led off 'Baltimore', a rather mechanical studio-bound version that failed to breathe life into the shifting metres of its opening theme. Frank's guitar played the almost stately title theme which resembled 'Watermelon In Easter Hay' in its uncharacteristic romanticism. Live versions, like that on 1986's *Does Humor Belong In Music?*, were taken at a faster pace and featured a vocal chorus on the title phrase.

Two Synclavier pieces sandwiched 'Porn Wars': 'Little Beige Sambo' proceeded at a relentless clip, employing organ- and harp-like tones on a theme that could have graced *Uncle Meat*, even if the lightning-fast percussive flourishes would have needed the use of a vari-speed control. 'Aerobics In Bondage' was slower and in some ways ironic after the effusion of senatorial pronouncements. Sampled tom-toms and cymbals added a realistic context.

The European version of the album was issued in February 1986 minus 'Porn Wars', which Frank deemed 'uninteresting to listeners outside the US'. His note continued, 'This special European edition contains three new songs not available in the US album. We hope you appreciate the difference.' 'Not that much' might have been a typical response. 'One Man - One Vote' and 'H.R. 2911' were both realised on Synclavier. The first acted as a preview for 1986's *Jazz From Hell*, bearing a broad similarity to one of its most notable tracks, 'G-Spot Tornado'. 'H.R. 2911' was cut from the same musical cloth as the piece which added its dread deliberate rhythm to the central section of 'Porn Wars'.

Least impressive of all was 'I Don't Even Care', co-written with Johnny 'Guitar' Watson and consisting of a stolid and repetitive backing track over which Watson and a vocal chorus chanted the title. Stretched beyond four minutes, Watson struggled with his ad-libs, at one point asserting that 'the cow jumped over the moon'. Ray White joined in towards the end and easily outshone Watson's flagging spontaneity. The arbitrary nature of the track served to underline that 'Porn Wars' was fundamental to the original compilation; without it, *Mothers Of Prevention* became a divided, almost schizophrenic entity divested of its heart. The 1990 CD reissue, which combined the material from both vinyl releases, wisely placed 'Porn Wars' at the beginning, setting the tone for what followed.

During the succeeding months, by his own estimation, Frank did as many as 300 talk shows and interviews on the subject of censorship, spending up to $70,000 on phone-calls, travel and print costs for what he termed 'The Z-Pack', an on-going dossier of cuttings and comment, available free from Barfko-Swill. His most powerful weapon was his withering scorn. 'They can't stand for people not to take them seriously,' he said. 'They hate to be laughed at. If they weren't so fucking dangerous, it would be fun to laugh at them all the time, but sometimes you have to take into account how much damage they can do.'[16]

'The people who want to censor do not care about saving your children,' he told David Sheff. 'They care about one thing - getting re-elected. Let's face it, folks: Politicians in the United States are the scum of the earth. We have to go after them individually because they're varmints. The legislation they are passing, piece by piece, converts America into a police state.'[17]

NONE OF THE ABOVE

Although he turned into a tireless campaigner against the forces of repression, other more fruitful work was not neglected. April had seen the premiere of another major Zappa work, *None Of The Above*, commissioned by the Kronos String Quartet. The group played the first movement on KPFA's 'Morning Concert' on April 8. It was followed by a Synclavier version of the same movement and a rehearsal/discussion of the work. Four days later, they gave the world premiere of the complete 20-minute work at the Herbst Theater in San Francisco. The performance was repeated at UCLA's Schoenberg Hall in Los Angeles on April 19, and in Arhus, Denmark on April 28.

Within days, there was a second Zappa premiere. This time, the Aspen Wind Quintet performed *Time's Beach* at the Alice Tully Hall in New York's Lincoln Center. The original work was in three movements but when it was to be repeated, at Washington's Coolidge Auditorium, the composer suggested that the first movement be omitted. 'As winners of the (Walter W.) Naumberg Award, we were awarded a commission, to commission an American composer,' said the group's oboist, Claudia Kuntz. 'We felt that Frank Zappa was the quintessential American composer encompassing a wide range of musical experiences, and we felt that he was a really great musician of our time.'[18]

April had also seen the release of *The Old Masters Box One*, containing all the Verve albums, except *Mothermania*, and a *Mystery Disc*, which anthologised selected moments from Frank's musical past and the earliest incarnations of the Mothers. Once the *Mothers Of Prevention* was out of the way, he set about compiling the CD version of *Does Humor Belong In Music?* from recordings of the 1984 tour. For undisclosed reasons, this CD-only release appeared early in

1986 in England and Germany and was not made generally available until 1995.

Whatever the explanation, it was another example of Frank's willingness to embrace new technology. Another was the deal he negotiated at this time with Rykodisc for the pioneering CD label to reissue the majority of his back catalogue. The company had been mooted at the 1983 MIDEM in Cannes, and president Don Rose had Zappa in mind even then. 'He was high among the list of appropriate artists for early CD release,' he said, 'and one of my first ideas. He was a pioneer in digital recording. He had purchased one of the first Sony multi-track digital recording machine, and was one of the first popular artists to commit to digital. And he was well-known as an innovator - both musically and technologically . . . So it made perfect sense for us to go after such a forward-thinking artist who controlled his own material and was already digital-friendly.'[19]

In 1986, the CD market was still in its development stages, and it was hard for fringe artists like Frank to get releases in the new format. Capitol distributed Barking Pumpkin but they weren't interested in manufacturing CDs of Zappa material. Rose saw an opportunity for his fledgling company, based in Salem, Mass. 'I hadn't even heard of them before,' said Frank. 'Then here's this guy named Don Rose who knew something about my catalogue and was interested, and it was like one cottage industry talking to another.'[20]

Billboard reported the deal early in February but the initial eight-title release didn't take place until the following autumn. 'It was probably the biggest back-catalogue issue by a single artist on CD at the time,' said Rose. 'Frank insisted that they come out simultaneously for greater impact. We went along with him only to find out he was right.'[21]

It was the sort of conviction that drew Frank to fight off yet another censorship attack, this time by the moralising vote-catchers of his home state. The Maryland House of Delegates had passed a bill which, if ratified, would alter the state's existing pornography statutes to include records, tapes and CDs. To become law, it had to be heard by the Maryland State Senate Judiciary Committee. Frank, accompanied by Bruce Bereano representing the RIAA, attended the hearing on February 14, having met delegates at a cocktail party the previous evening and secured recantations of their votes from five of them.

The bill was proposed by Delegate Judith Toth, who along with Delegate Joseph Owens demonstrated a rabid variant of the PMRC's sanctimonious moral guardianship of the nation's young. Toth called her bill 'constitutional'; 'And stop worrying about [children's] "civil rights". Start worrying about their mental health and the health of our society.' Owens declared that rock music was 'mass child abuse', while Toth maintained that 'these records' advocated 'incest', 'rape' and 'sexual violence'. 'You've got to read this stuff to know just how dirty it is,' she chided.

In his testimony, Frank pointed out that to refer to rock music as 'mass child abuse' was 'sky-high rhetoric'. Once again, he prompted general laughter as he pilloried the bill's proposed banning of anything that depicted 'illicit sex'. In Maryland, that apparently included human (but not animal) masturbation, 'sexual intercourse or sodomy', the 'fondling or other erotic touching of human genitals' and the female nipple. 'Now, I like nipples,' he averred, 'I think they look nice.' So did babies, who got to have that 'nozzle' right in front of their faces. 'You grow up with it, so to speak - and then you grow up to live in the state of Maryland and they won't let you see that little brown nozzle anymore.'

With this and other testimony, the bill was rejected. The April 9 edition of the *Evening Standard* called it 'A Win For Zappa'. On the phone from Los Angeles, Frank was quoted, 'I get asked all the time to run for President. If I ever decided to go into politics, I would jump right in.' The zealous Toth was undeterred; she'd reintroduce the bill and 'bring the record industry to its knees'. But she'd have to reckon with Frank. 'I've got a personal stake in all this,' he told Josef Woodard. 'I'm a record company owner, I'm a composer, I'm a publisher, I'm an artist, and these people are fucking with my business . . . I went there speaking as a private individual on my own behalf, not on behalf of the industry, not on behalf of any other artists, just me as a businessman. In a true conservative attitude, I want the federal government off my back.'[22]

ELECTRIC HOEDOWN

Back at UMRK, he and engineer Bob Stone were producing Dweezil's first album, *Havin' A Bad Day*, which was released by Barking Pumpkin in August. Apart from adorning several of his father's gigs, Dweezil had made his recording debut four years earlier in 1982. With assistance from Steve Vai and his sister, Moon, he'd recorded a single, 'My Mother Is A Space Cadet' and 'Crunchy Water'. Now he was backed by Scott Thunes and Chad Wackerman on an album of bludgeoning guitar rock defined by the influences whom he acknowledged on the sleeve, Eddie Van Halen, Randy Rhoads, David Lee Roth and Steven Tyler. Moon sang 'You Can't Ruin Me' and 'Let's Talk About It', but like Dweezil's own vocals, these were rather drowned in the mix.

Most intriguing were two instrumentals, 'The Pirate Song' and 'Electric Hoedown', the latter inspired by Eddie Van Halen's solo from 'Cathedral', that hinted at the sort of original thought expected of a Zappa. 'I wanted the first record to sound like a digital garage band,' Dweezil told *Guitar World*. 'I wanted it to be straight-ahead honest, with no slick production.'[23] That could be heard on *Miami Vice* actor Don Johnson's solo album, *Heartbeat*; Dweezil contributed some feedback frenzy to 'The Last Sound Love Makes'.

Frank divided the rest of his time between preparing *The Old Masters Box Two* for release in October and an album of new Synclavier material. The second anthology of remastered albums covered the period from *Uncle Meat* to *Just Another Band From L.A.*, and included another *Mystery Disc*. The first side was made up of some 20 minutes from the Mothers' Royal Festival Hall appearance on October 28, 1968, while the second featured studio out-takes like 'Agency Man' from 1967 and 'Wedding Dress Song'/'Handsome Cabin Boy' from the *Uncle Meat* sessions, sundry live excerpts and oddities like 'The Story Of Willie The Pimp'.

Synclavier technology had improved significantly since Frank had acquired the basic system in 1983. For him, the most important development was the sampling unit that allowed him to stockpile recordings of musical instruments, which he could then recombine and modulate in whichever ways his inquiring mind fancied. Grasping that the Synclavier divided sound up into segments or 'frames', affecting pitch variations in the same way that film recorded movement, Frank realised that he could create sounds that were beyond human contrivance.

The process was laborious. First the samples were recorded in digital stereo on a Sony 1610 machine, then Frank's assistant, Bob Rice, entered them in the Synclavier, one side at a time. Then the stereo sides had to be matched up, the sample trimmed and catalogued. Interviewed for *Keyboard* in December, Frank admitted that Rice was probably eight months behind on sample trimming. 'As the samples get trimmed and organised, I build them into various types of patches, according to what composition I'm working on. We have things called pintos, which are mix-and-match patches. Instead of having a patch that is just a saxophone, for example, you can have a patch that is a few notes of the sax, a few of a clarinet, a few of an oboe, a few of a trombone, all different instruments, appearing on different notes, all of them on the keyboard.'[24]

In addition, up to four harmony parts which moved in different directions but eventually resolved could be assembled in each patch. These were called 'evolvers' or 'resolvers'. '"Evolvers" are timbres that start with one kind of sound in re-synthesis,' Frank explained, 'and you take a certain number of frames from that, and they cross-fade into another timbre. For example, a horn could fade into a clarinet and then into a string section over a pre-determined time. "Resolvers" are a classification of sound which has some sort of melody line built into it, but all under control of one key on the keyboard.'[25]

What he hadn't done was to sample his own guitar playing, although Dweezil had done an exhaustive session. 'A guitar player I may be, but when I first went to one of those music equipment conventions in New York City and saw the Synclavier system, I tried out the guitar interface and it wasn't really for me . . . I haven't been satisfied with it, generally because of the way I play, known as I am for being incredibly slovenly with my technique of rubbing fingers all over everything!'[26]

Given the amount of work required just to formulate the sounds from which its tunes could be assembled, it's hardly surprising that it took eight months to complete *Jazz From Hell*. Frank had an analogy for the process: 'Sculpture is a subtractive medium, and you start off with more than you wind up with. So the analogy here is that the raw material that I'm working with is whatever is in my imagination versus what samples are at my disposal. And building the mountain is building your collection of samples.'[27]

It was expensive keeping pace with the flow of software. 'Before you can make (a Synclavier) do what you hear on *Jazz From Hell*,' he told *Keyboard*, 'you've got to spend a quarter of a million dollars.'[28] He took pride in the fact that he'd not applied for any foundation grant money to finance his operation. It was solely financed from record sales. 'But as the record sales go down, so does the amount of money that I can turn around and re-invest into the hardware - which has a price that's steadily rising - and it squeezes me into a weird kind of position, because it keeps me constantly in debt to the bank to pay off loans in advance to buy the equipment.'[29]

Jazz From Hell consisted of seven Synclavier pieces and one guitar solo, 'St. Etienne', recorded in that city on May 28, 1982. The solo, played while Frank sat cross-legged on a stool, was captured on video by Thomas Nordegg and included in *Video From Hell*. The rest of the album showed the phenomenal progress Frank had made in his enhancement of the Synclavier's resources. 'Night School' represented the ideal transition from the old music to the new. Beginning with a complete but sonically fragmented drumkit and sustained by a three-note bass pulse, lush piano chords echoed by synthesised strings provided a floating backdrop for a 'solo' that in previous years would have been played on a guitar but here was a combination of grand piano and trumpet, complete with pitch-bends.

Similar innovatory skill was evident throughout, leavened by the humour to be expected on a Zappa record. The frenetic attack of 'G-Spot Tornado' simultaneously mocked the expected consequence of caressing that erogenous area of the vagina and the 'scratch' techniques of disco DJ's, with a melody that resembled a tap-dancer on acid. 'The Beltway Bandits' had a scurrying mechanical melody line that for Frank symbolised the Washington pressure groups and 'think tanks' that preyed on the Reagan administration. 'While You Were Art II' rearranged 'While You Were Out', a guitar solo from *Shut Up 'N Play Yer Guitar*. The complex arrangement used a technique Frank called 'hocketing' (also known as *klangfarbenmelodie*), whereby the melody is broken down into segments each played by a different instrument or sound.

He'd first used it in 'Zolar Czakl' on *Uncle Meat*, and also used it here on 'Damp Ankles', where it was complimented by ambient sound and 'industrial' samples.

The title track parodies what Frank referred to as 'noodling', his term for the formless wandering which some jazz musicians characterised as improvisation. Asked if *Jazz From Hell* was an ironic reference to the PMRC's assertion that rock music contained satanic messages, Frank replied, 'No. You know the expression: if there's somebody in show-business and he's an asshole, he can be referred to as an Entertainer from Hell. It arrived from that type of concept. This is it. If this is Jazz, then it's *Jazz From Hell*.'[30]

The album excited a lot of media interest and Frank made the front cover of the February 1987 editions of *Keyboard*, *Music Technology* and *Sound On Sound*. The latter magazine talked to Frank in November at the 1986 AES Convention in Los Angeles, at which he played tracks from the album. 'The sequences that I will be demonstrating on the Synclavier at today's show are very tame by my standards,' he told Paul Gilby. 'They've been chosen because they are the most accessible of the pieces I'm working on. The rest of my stuff is mathematical and very strange and it's definitely not foot-tapping stuff!'[31]

In *Music Technology*, he gave some idea of his prodigious work-load. 'There's tons of stuff planned for future recordings. *You Can't Do That On Stage Anymore* is a ten-record box, a live collection that I've been working on for the last 22 years. I have a huge collection of tapes and stuff, and I've been going through the final examples of strange stuff that happened on stage with all the different bands. And there is the sequel to *Lumpy Gravy*, which is done. That's an amazing piece. It's all the missing dialogue that will help you understand it. If there is anything to understand about *Lumpy Gravy*, this is all the missing components . . . Then there's another guitar box coming out, there's a three-record box called the *Helsinki Concert*, which was done in 1974 with George Duke. *The London Symphony Volume Two* will be out shortly . . . I've got three albums of Synclavier chamber music. It's done, it's just sitting there.'[32]

As usual with Frank's scheduling, things didn't quite work out the way he envisaged them that day. But what it did prove was that he wasn't 'just sitting there'. He was too shrewd not to realise the value of his massive archives. The best way to generate the income he needed to finance his Synclavier habit was to make some small part of that available to the legion of fans who made up the Barking Pumpkin and Barfko-Swill mailing lists and others around the world whose reaction to a new Frank Zappa album could out-pant Pavlov's dog.

CHAPTER TWENTY
ONCE AGAIN, WITHOUT THE NET

What held good for records also went for video. During the first six months of 1987, Frank prepared the first releases from his own company, Honker Home Video. The idea came from Waleed Ali, head of MPI Home Video; his company had stepped into the breach in 1984, when Sony Video had refused to release *Does Humor Belong In Music?* without a warning sticker. 'For obvious political reasons, the whole idea of stickering original home video product was something that rubbed me the wrong way,' said Ali. 'What was interesting about Frank's idea for a label – and we shared it with him – was the idea of really exploiting home video for everything that it stood for, which was the last bastion of the ability to deliver truth and points of view.'[1]

The last bastion? Let's hear it again for sky-high rhetoric. Frank didn't want his profile added to Mount Rushmore, he meant to make money. His first releases would be the three-hour version of *Baby Snakes* and *Video From Hell*, a sampler of intended Honker product, including *Uncle Meat*, *An American Dissident* and *You Can't Do That On Stage Anymore*. Only *Uncle Meat* would appear before his death. 'I think that it's a mistake to assume that everybody in the US who watches television, likes what they watch,' he said. 'There's a substantial portion of the American public that watches broadcast TV and wishes they were getting a little bit more bang for their buck – or a little bit more content.'[2]

More content was a by-product of the April 1987 interview in *Guitar World*. Editor Noe Goldwasser had visited UMRK to plan a 34-minute cassette called *The Guitar World According To Frank Zappa*, to be offered with their July edition. In the course of the interview, Frank induced journalistic trauma by admitting that he hadn't touched a guitar for two years. 'The problem is, most of the best stuff that I will physically be able to do on the guitar is already on tape. You just haven't heard it yet. I mean, I don't have much incentive to play it.'[3]

He went into more detail while talking with Paul Zollo: 'I didn't think there was any great demand in the marketplace for what I do on the guitar. I mean, why should I bust my chops, so to speak? There's plenty of people who play faster than I do, there's plenty of people who dance around more than I do, and there was nobody doing what I was doing on Synclavier. Rather than stand in line and be just another redundant guitar player plying his trade in the music business, I thought I'd better come up with something new.'4

Another new endeavour was a projected television show. In mid-March, he met with ABC network representatives to discuss *Night School*, his concept for a weekday late-night programme. The aim was to show raw, uncut news footage, point out what had been deleted or ignored and speculate on the reasons for each omission. A live band would be in the studio, the musicians doubling as actors in 'pre-enactments' of the 'possible social consequences' of specific news items. There would also be an opportunity to purchase a $25 degree for a Psychology Course dealing in sexually related topics for $100, students could graduate cum laude. The show would carry the warning: 'This programme deals with reality, using easy to understand colloquial American Language. If you fear (or have difficulty accepting) either of the above, feel free to change the channel.'5

Frank had enlisted the participation of Daniel Schorr, a senior newscaster/journalist with CBS and National Public Radio. Schorr, as 'Professor Of Recent History', would be in a Washington studio, while Frank and the band would be in Los Angeles. He'd first contacted Schorr's Washington office in August 1986. 'Why me,' Schorr wrote later, 'a senior citizen totally alien to the rock culture? Ah, because the "kids" didn't trust their contemporaries and saw in me an incorruptible maverick like him.'6

Given the nature of what Frank intended, it's little wonder that neither ABC nor any other television network would touch his idea. The wonder was that they saw him at all, and he probably had the PMRC and the Maryland Senate to thank for that. His appearances before the various Committees had made good (if dangerous) television and those who knew of him as a 'wild man of rock' were surprised by his eloquence. He soon found himself on the celebrity quote list. 'Every time somebody wants an opposing point of view, they call me up,' he told Rick Davies. 'Unfortunately, they do call to get an opposing point of view, because before I started doing it, there was no opposition . . . I do at least one interview a week on the PMRC, and some weeks five.'7

He'd found a different way to deal with another *bête noire*, the religious Right. Papers were filed in Montgomery, Alabama for the incorporation of a new religion, the Church of American Secular Humanism, or CASH for short. It was Frank's response to a judgement handed down in the state by Judge Brevard Hand, that Alabama schools were riddled with Secular Humanism, thereby violating the civil rights of decent Christian folks who wanted their children to grow up book-burning, beer-swilling, gun-toting, God-fearing Commie-haters in their image. Frank countered that since it hadn't been officially recognised as a religion, it was about time it was. He parodied the judge's ruling in his 'Tenets of Faith', and paraphrased the odious

Oliver North (the bungling patriotic mastermind of Irangate, the 'arms for hostages' scandal during which the Gipper showed he couldn't remember the lies he'd been programmed to tell) by stating that his 'religion' would be 'an off-the-shelf, stand-alone, self-financing organisation, capable of worldwide covert action'.[8]

Barking Pumpkin re-released *Joe's Garage* as a box-set in June, and *London Symphony Orchestra Volume 2* in September. *The Old Masters Box Three* was prepared for release in December. *Baby Snakes* and *Video From Hell* also appeared that month and were advertised in *Billboard*. Frank was pictured in garish jacket and bow-tie, his hair tweezed vertically in Eraserhead mode, wearing a pair of 'No-D' glasses. These were explained: 'HONKER NO-D GLASSES provide opaque cardboard protection for viewers who fear exposure to unexpectedly mind-boggling theoretical concepts. They are reversible for protection against heavy-metal video radiation, and, by poking out the convenient perforations, little peek-a-boo flaps can be created, accommodating the young sophisticate.

'HONKER believes that WHAT YOU WATCH and WHEN YOU WATCH IT should be a matter of personal choice, and such decisions are not appropriately made by third parties or organised pressure groups. Nonetheless, for the deranged few who feel that censorship is a good idea, HONKER provides NO-D GLASSES so they can do it to themselves.'[9]

While all these projects were being worked on through the summer, he told *SongTalk*, 'I keep [a guitar] sitting next to my chair in the studio and I occasionally pluck around on it, but I'm only barely getting some calluses back.'[10] A tour was in the offing. Exploratory rehearsals began in October, with Bobby Martin, Ray White, Ike Willis, Ed Mann, Scott Thunes and Chad Wackerman. Tommy Mars was present for a week, but pulled out. Ominously, one of his reasons was that he was 'having a problem with Scott Thunes'. Ray White also disappeared early on, summoned away by a phone call. Nothing more was heard from him.

Howard Kaylan and Mark Volman attended several early rehearsals, but they had an aversion to revisiting the material they'd sung with him more than a decade before. 'We had spent 15 years cleaning up ourselves for the public,' Volman said. 'It took doing a lot of children's projects,' Kaylan added. 'We wrote for television and we were radio personalities in Los Angeles, and we got very, very mainstream, and by the time Frank came back to us and asked us to rejoin the group, we had finally, finally broken all those negative barriers [of having been Flo & Eddie].'[11] Nor did they like Frank's overt political stance and the fact that this would be a 'Zappa' tour and not the Mothers Of Invention. And they'd be giving up a healthy income as the Turtles. Some fans sighed with relief.

Mike Keneally, a Long Island-born guitarist living in San Diego, heard about the rehearsals and phoned up for an audition. He'd played piano since the age of seven and picked up the guitar four years later. Although he was no sight-reader, his knowledge of Frank's music carried him through the initial audition. At its end, Frank told him, 'Come back on Monday so that the rest of the band can witness your particular splendour.' After rehearsing for most of the following week, Frank decided not to wait for Ray White and told Keneally the good news.

TOURING CAN MAKE YOU CRAZY

In the final weeks of rehearsals, ten hours a day for five days a week, a horn section was added, which consisted of Walt Fowler, trumpet, Bruce Fowler, trombone, Paul Carman on alto, soprano and baritone saxes, Albert Wing, tenor sax, and Kurt McGettrick on baritone and contrabass clarinet. The first leg of the tour was scheduled to begin in Albany, New York on February 2, 1988, taking in 27 locations on the Eastern Seaboard and as far west as Detroit and Chicago, and ending in Uniondale, NY on March 25. Several of the gigs, like those in New York City, Washington, Philadelphia and Detroit, were three-day stints. After a two-week break, the tour continued on to Europe, where 43 dates in France, Germany, England, Scandinavia, Spain and Italy occupied all of April, May and the first ten days of June. There should have been a further ten-week US tour, taking in the South and the West Coast, but the band self-destructed before the final leg could begin.

Later, with bitter hindsight, Frank would say this was the best band he'd ever taken on the road. 'I'd been very happy with that band,' he told David Mead, 'the audiences really liked it too, and the reviewers thought it was great. It was unique because it combined a very strong five-piece horn section with all kinds of electronic stuff, with effects on the percussion section, on the drums, multiple keyboards – a very interesting blend of this horn harmony and very strange sound effects.'[12]

The harmony didn't extend to the band's personalities, though. The problem emanated from Scott Thunes' role as 'clonemeister', a role previously performed by Ed Mann and Arthur Barrow. 'He's very abrasive,' said Mike Keneally. 'He's very honest. He's brutal. He's blunt. And when he was in charge of running the rehearsals in Frank's absence, these qualities came to the fore, but it was in service of getting the job done.'[13] 'If it's not the right energy, it doesn't work, somehow,' Ed Mann reckoned. 'It's a difficult position for the guy who has to run the band, and Scott, to his defence, was in that position, and he took it very seriously, and everybody else didn't wanna hear it.'[14]

Mann played down the exact nature of his role in what happened. 'The others all decided that they hated Scott's guts,' Frank explained, 'it was very weird. Basically the ringleader was Ed Mann, and he and Chad Wackerman decided that Scott had to go, and they brought about most of the discontent in the band.'15 Perhaps two dictators was one too many. 'Scott has a unique personality,' Frank told Matt Resnicoff. 'He also has unique musical skills. I like the way he plays and I like him as a person, but other people don't. He has a very difficult personality: he refuses to be cordial. He won't do small talk. And he's odd. So what?'16

Everyone got odd, that's what. On the last German date, promoter John Jackson presented the band with a big cake with all their names on it. One of the ringleaders sneaked off stage and scraped the bass player's name off the cake. Things were obviously going badly awry. Frank polled the band and discovered that no one, apart from Mike Keneally, wanted to work with Thunes. 'If you replace anybody in a band that has rehearsed for four months, you've gotta go back into rehearsal. I couldn't replace Scott to assuage everybody in the band who hated him. There's no bass player who could have done that job. The repertoire was so large, the workings of the show so complex, you had to know so much - there was no way. So I had to lose the income of all those dates . . . Everybody on that tour got paid but me; I lost $400,000.'17

It was an expensive show to mount, involving five trucks, two buses, and some 43 people. 'And we weren't doing fireworks or anything spectacular out there, it was like a basic touring package: enough lights to see the show, enough PA to hear the music and enough crew to set up the gear. It's not like taking a glamourous entourage out there; just was not a money-making proposition. In a way, I'm glad I did it, though, just because of some of the musical things that did get recorded.'18 But it hadn't been easy. 'I just spent the last six weeks of the tour trying to wend my way through this garbage that was going on onstage. On a good night, the ideas I had for guitar solos came out. On a bad night, it was me versus the band. The audience didn't really know, but it was another example of the kind of thing that made me want to put the guitar down in the first place.'19

Several months later, all those that supposedly couldn't bear being on stage with Thunes admitted they'd made a mistake and fell over themselves to apologise to him. No wonder Frank was disgusted. 'If that band had stayed together all this time,' he said in 1991, 'not only would it be the most outrageous touring band on the planet, but I'd still be playing guitar . . . And one of the most egregious things: One of the sax players who'd been complaining that Scott didn't give him enough support on his solos after he heard *The Best Band You Never Heard In Your Life*, he came over here and said, "Oh, he sounds good, man". Stuff like that makes me sick.'20

The pity was that this band's repertoire was the most eclectic and comprehensive he'd ever attempted. There were songs from every era of the Mothers and subsequent bands, and a raft of cover versions, from Lennon &

McCartney's 'I Am The Walrus' and Page & Plant's 'Stairway To Heaven' to Stravinsky's *L'Histoire du Soldat* and Ravel's *Bolero*. 'I always liked *Bolero*,' Frank said. 'I think that it's really one of the best melodies ever written.'[21] The new songs addressed America's current religious/political stew, satirising Nixon, Reagan and Bush, along with the Rev. Jesse Jackson, Pat Robertson, Jim and Tammy Bakker. Michael Jackson, who now owned Northern Songs, the Beatles' publishing company, was the object of ridicule in 'Why Don't You Like Me?', a withering re-write of 'Tell Me You Love Me' from *Chunga's Revenge*.

The most fruitful source of derision was Jimmy Swaggart. When Jim Bakker's knowledge of Jessica Hahn was finally revealed in 1987, Swaggart was his loudest and most righteous accuser. His vehemence increased when Bakker was convicted of defrauding his followers of some $158 million and sentenced to 45 years imprisonment by Maximum Bob Potter, the Judge Roy Bean of his generation. Bakker wasn't Swaggart's first prey. In July 1986, he'd denounced fellow Assemblies of God minister Marvin Gorman as an adulterer. The following year, Gorman learned of his denouncer's visits to the Texas Motel in Metairie, across the parish line from New Orleans, for unspecified 'relief'. Gorman hired a private detective, and on October 17 caught Swaggart outside the Travel Inn, where he'd just been professionally entertained.

Another prostitute, Debra Murphree, told WVUE-TV, 'He told me to get naked and maybe lay on the bed and pose for him . . . To me, I think he's kind of perverted . . . talking about some of the things that we talked about in the rooms, you know, I wouldn't want him around my children.'[22] She wasn't alone in that thought. Another minister in Ferriday, Louisiana, hometown of Swaggart and his cousin, Jerry Lee Lewis, was forced to leave his parish. Jerry Lee's sister, Frankie Jean, was quoted, 'We call it the crime of the century. This poor little Assemblies of God man was arrested over here. They say he raped his two daughters, and they're lookin' at the parakeet.'[23]

Swaggart spent months avoiding his promised public confession. Eventually Gorman took his evidence, including photographs, to the Assemblies of God headquarters in Springfield, Missouri, Swaggart was banned from preaching, first for three months and then a year. On the first Sunday of Lent, February 21, 1988, he made a tearful, histrionic public confession in front of his wife and a stunned television audience. Vengeance might have been the Lord's, but Frank's was as swift and gleefully condign. In Poughkeepsie, New York, two days later, he debuted 'Swaggart' versions of 'More Trouble Every Day' and 'Penguin In Bondage'. By March 8 in Pittsburgh, there was a 'Swaggart' version of 'Lonesome Cowboy Burt'. Most damaging of all, and regrettably unreleaseable, were adaptations of three classic Beatles songs, which showed up a week later at the Royal Oak Music Hall in Troy, on the outskirts of Detroit; 'Norwegian Wood' became 'Norwegian Jim', 'Lucy In The Sky

With Diamonds' was recast as 'Louisiana Hooker With Herpes', while 'Strawberry Fields Forever' masqueraded as the 'Texas Motel'.

Other songs were written in response to specific news items and performed only once. 'Promiscuous', from the February 26 Detroit gig was about Surgeon General C. Everett Koop, a rather ludicrous figure affecting quasi-military dress who assured the American public that AIDS had started in Africa, when some poor unfortunate had been infected by the blood of 'a little green monkey'. Frank had a nickname for him: 'Dr. God! . . . What the fuck is this shit, okay? And besides, he's a Reagan appointee. That's strike number one. Strike number two is the Dr. God suit - no explanation given. Why does he look like an admiral? Is he the Admiral of Health? And I question any medical advice given by a man who joins the PMRC onstage during their symposium and talks about anal sex while they talk about backwards masking.'[24]

YOU CAN'T DO THAT ON STAGE ANYMORE

While the tour pursued its inexorable course, records continued to appear. In April, Barking Pumpkin released *Guitar*, the double-album follow-up to *Shut Up 'N Play Yer Guitar*, consisting of solos from the 1981/2 and 1984 tours, with two from 1979, one of them the original version of 'Outside Now', which began life as a solo in 'City Of Tiny Lites'. The following month, Rykodisc issued a 2-CD version with an additional 13 tracks. At the same time, Barking Pumpkin released a double-album sampler for the *You Can't Do That On Stage Anymore* series which Frank had announced the previous February. Then, it had been on ten albums, now it was to be a 13-hour series of six 2-CD sets.

'The aesthetic goals of the series,' he told William Ruhlmann, 'have more to do with the growth of the music and a celebration of the good parts of live performance. There are a lot of good things to be said about playing on the stage in terms of unique events that will happen only for that particular audience and if you've got a tape running and you've captured it, you've got a little miracle on your hands . . . Sometimes the recording quality is not as good as some other version of it, but I want to put as much of the unique stuff in there as possible.'[25]

YCDTOSA 1 traversed the years from 1969 to 1984 in the course of 28 tracks. Since he'd always been an incisive and creative editor, Frank juxtaposed bands of different eras, in this case sequentially but on later volumes, within the context of a single song. 'So that you have the feeling that you're at a concert, but it's an impossible concert. There's no way you could ever see all these people onstage at the same time, but if you've got a fairly decent imagination, you could especially put the earphones on and be at a show that spans, what, 25 years, with some of the most amazing musicians that were ever put onto a record and there they are, just performing their little hearts out for you.'26

Having lost so much money, Frank had no intention of losing any time; he set about selecting and mixing tracks for *Broadway The Hard Way*, bringing together the new songs from the tour and some others that hadn't yet appeared in America. In his notes for the *YCDTOSA* sampler, Frank expressed the hope that it provided 'some incentive for the acquisition of a CD player'. With *Broadway*, he reinforced that message by creating two very different packages. The Barking Pumpkin vinyl album released in October contained nine tracks; the Rykodisc CD added a further eight, among them versions of 'Hot Plate Heaven At The Green Hotel' and 'Outside Now', Oliver Nelson's 'Stolen Moments', and Sting singing a hastily-contrived arrangement of 'Murder By Numbers' recorded in Chicago on March 3.

The overtly political nature of much of the material reflected the fact that this was an election year. The 'virtually brain dead'27 Reagan had come to the end of his second term and now the Republicans intended to elevate Vice-President George Bush to the Oval Office. The Democrats conspired to ensure his victory by nominating the ineffectual Michael Dukakis, brother of actress Olympia, one of Cher's co-stars in *Moonstruck*. The Libertarian Party had offered to make Frank its presidential candidate, but he'd refused. 'I read the Libertarian platform and I said, "Basically, you guys are closet anarchists. If you could have your way, there wouldn't be any government at all."'28

Instead, he tried to contact Dukakis's advertising people with some 32 ideas for television commercials. 'I thought the best way to start reducing the effect of the Republican disinformation campaign was to run a series of spots that called into question who these fucking people think they are. So one of the spots had a guy - obviously a Republican - standing on a lawn in front of a mansion, saying, "I'm a Republican, and I care about the environment". He points to his house: "My environment".29

'Bush-Quayle is a scandal waiting to happen,' he told Kurt Loder. In October 1980, Bush had met with Iranian representatives in Paris, allegedly to offer a $5 billion arms deal in return for delaying the release of American hostages until after Reagan had defeated Jimmy Carter in the 1980 presidential election. If that came to light, Frank thought, it might lead to another impeachment. 'And then you'll see the real reason for Dan Quayle being pasted onto the ticket: he's the lowest form of impeachment insurance.'30 When as President he was asked about tax rises, Bush said, 'Watch my lips', while keeping his mouth shut. By the same token, Quayle only opened his mouth to change feet; sometime later, and on television, he would attempt to correct a child's spelling of 'potato' by adding an 'e' at the end.

Then there was the 'religious right'. 'Come on, let's call a spade a spade here,' Frank spat. 'These fuckers are fascists. Fascists with a cross.'31 'What has

happened to the presidency as an institution in the United States is a disaster,'
he told the *Los Angeles Times*. 'It's not a matter of conservative versus liberal,
it's a matter of fascist versus freedom. Because what you've seen for the last
eight years is bunting-encrusted fascism waving a flag in one hand and a cross
in the other.'[32]

Broadway The Hard Way attacked what he regarded as an insidious threat to
all sorts of freedoms. 'Rhymin' Man' characterised the posturing Rev. Jesse
Jackson and his Presidential pretensions. 'When The Lie's So Big' was about
another Presidential hopeful, Rev. Pat Robertson, who told his audiences he
was on a mission from God to lead the Republican Party. 'Jesus Thinks You're
A Jerk' was a nine-minute assault on both Robertson and Jim Bakker. Ike
Willis' monologue rattled skeletons in Robertson's cupboard, including a
'love-child' and his claim of 'honourable' service in the Korean War, when a
phone call to his father, a US Senator, had got him off the troopship.

Even 'What Kind Of Girl' contained rewritten verses with veiled and overt
references to Robertson, Swaggart and Ed Meese, the one-time Attorney
General who swung both ways on the Irangate. Nelson Riddle's 'The
Untouchables' contained another Ike Willis monologue vilifying various
Reagan henchmen, including Admiral Poindexter, Oliver North, Michael
Deaver and William Casey, all forced to leave high office or White House
employ for their nefarious exploits.

Their leader was further lampooned in the sleeve artwork. Using another
shot from the Honker advertising campaign, a quote from Reagan's address to
the 1988 Republican Convention was sprayed on Frank's 'office' wall: 'Facts
are stupid things.' His former chief of staff Donald Regan coined the
memorable phrase, 'The Presidential mind is not cluttered with facts.' In *Death
Of A Salesman*, Frances FitzGerald noted that Reagan's mind 'contained a
number of precepts, each one backed up by a quotient of anecdotes and
personal reminiscences – some of which had a basis in fact.'[33] He was indeed
the personification of his dictum.

Broadway The Hard Way was released in October, along with *YCDTOSA 2*,
subtitled *The Helsinki Concert*. This latter proved Frank's enduring regard for
the 1974 band. In the booklet note he wrote, 'This band had a lot of skill (and
miserable touring equipment – it was always breaking down, and full of hums
and buzzes). In spite of this, it has remained one of the audience's favorite
ensembles, and so, for those of you who crave what they used to do, we
present a full concert with a little bit of everything – including stuff that you
can't do on stage anymore.' The fact that it contained much the same
repertoire as *Roxy & Elsewhere* didn't matter; 'the ultra-fast tempos on the
more difficult tunes demonstrate what happens when a band has played the
material for a year, and is so comfortable with it they could probably perform
it blindfolded'.[34]

022

2

Releasing *The Helsinki Concert* created something of a rod for his back, at least in interviews, since everyone wanted to know if there would be more such releases. Matt Groening seemed to be siding with the bootleggers when he expressed his pleasure at hearing a complete show. 'That to me is excruciating,' Frank replied, 'because when I've listened to those, it's hard for me to imagine one show that had so many good things in it that you'd want to release the whole show.'[35] The bootleggers and their customers thought otherwise.

ONCE UPON A TIME

As well as documenting a 25-year career on record, Frank was also preparing *The Real Frank Zappa Book* for publication in May 1989, an idiosyncratic combination of selective autobiography and polemical discourse. In this he was helped by Peter Occhiogrosso, who taped their conversations and then transcribed and edited them onto floppy disc. These were then re-edited by Frank and the resulting manuscript was sent to Ann Patty of Poseidon Press in New York. 'If you're gonna do a biography of a rock star, you probably can't get one more interesting than this one,' she said. 'It's a good mission in life.'[36]

The book's autobiographical sections were somewhat reticent and quickly over; thereafter, Frank's thoughts ranged far and wide on subjects that exercised his interest, exemplified by chapter headings such as 'All About Schmucks', 'Marriage (As A Dada Concept)', 'Porn Wars' and 'Church & State'. With typically mordant humour, the penultimate chapter was titled 'Failure' and listed some Zappa projects, including the *Night School* television show, that had come to nothing. In it, Frank was pragmatic about the inevitability of failure. 'I would say that my entire life has been one massive failure,' he'd said two years earlier. 'I live with failure everyday because I can't do the things that I really want to do . . . I enjoy sitting down here [in the studio] all by myself typing on the Synclavier. I can do twelve hours and love it. And I know that ultimately it doesn't mean a thing that I did it. It's useless. That's okay; it makes me feel good.'[37]

In dedicating the book to 'Gail, the kids, Stephen Hawking and Ko-Ko', he recorded that the manuscript was finished in the early morning of August 23. In Chapter 19, 'The Last Word', he noted that he finished reading the first galley proofs on the even earlier morning of Christmas Day, generating 'an eye-popping headache' in the process. In winding up, he couldn't resist a few last barbs against Ted Turner's CNN network, Surgeon General Koop and Ronald Reagan. 'Would a Kind And Loving God let an asshole like that (and all his fabulous appointees) escape unpunished after eight years of Constitutional desecration?'[38] You betcha.

The December 24 edition of *Billboard* had a video supplement in which

Honker advertised their forthcoming videos, *Uncle Meat* and *The True Story of Frank Zappa's 200 Motels*, to be released on January 31, 1989. The advert, parodying *E.T.*, bore the headline, 'The Story That Touched The Weird'. Frank was shown in a chunky pink sweater, scratching his ear with the prehensile thumb of a silver lurex glove. Along with *Does Humor Belong In Music?*, there were now five Zappa videos on the market.

In February Gail's brainchild, Joe's Garage, opened. The three-room rehearsal facility was created in the warehouse that for 15 years Frank had used to store band equipment. It was run by Marque Coy, Frank's monitor engineer since 1981. The name was his idea, too. 'The Zappas didn't know what they were going to call it,' he told Don Menn. 'I said, "Well, you own the name." They said, "What do you mean?" I said, "The line in the song goes: 'You can jam at Joe's Garage. . .' Let's call it 'Joe's Garage'."'[39] Acts 1 and 2 were the large and small rehearsal rooms, while Act 3 housed a 24-track studio linked for audio and video with the other rooms.

The new year saw Frank working as hard as ever. 'Even though I've got a busy schedule editing albums and doing all the mechanical stuff to stay in that part of the record business, I still manage 30 hours a week on the Synclavier,' he told William Ruhlmann.[40] But by his own admission, Frank spent 'virtually 100 per cent' of his time until November 1989 mixing and editing the 1988 tour tapes. This amounted to approximately 1,970 takes of 120 titles. 'Out of that, somebody has to decide which parts of which song are the best version available from any given city, remember it, tell the engineer to mix this city to match that city and then glue it together to make the album. You don't farm that out to anyone else, so that's what I've been doing here.'[41]

'The only time I took time off was for four trips to Russia and one trip to Czechoslovakia,' he told Gary Steel. 'After the Czech trip, I was side-tracked into some foreign trade stuff that I'm doing with my Why Not? company. It's a Delaware corporation chartered to licensing, consulting and social engineering . . . When I went over there, I met all these very interesting people who wanted to do a wide range of business things with people from the West, and there was no way for them to get in touch . . . kind of like a dating service. Find out what somebody wants over there and try to find 'em a partner over here.'[42]

His initial February visit came about after Dennis Berardi, owner of Kramer Guitars, told him he was thinking of opening a factory in what was then the Soviet Union. 'I told him he was crazy,' Frank told Neil Cohen. 'I knew exactly what everybody else in the United States of America knew at the time about the Soviet Union – nothing. You can't know anything unless you go over there and look at it. IT'S ANOTHER PLANET.' There were further visits in March, April and May. 'I was not prepared for the amount of data I was receiving. I was given an education in [the] politics, sociology, and anthropology of the Soviet Union that you couldn't buy anyplace else.'[43]

Part of that education, and something that may have dampened his relish for the new-found role of entrepreneur, was that Russian businessmen had an altogether different approach to negotiation, honed in the thriving black market that formed such a vital but debilitating part of the Soviet economy. Frank met the director of the Luzhniky Sports Complex in Moscow, who told him he wanted to add a hotel, casino and shops to the site. Frank put him in touch with Wesray Capital, a New Jersey-based investment firm. But when Wesray indicated its interest, the Luzhniky director doubled his price.

'Until there is an increase in knowledge as far as how the deals work and the idea that WESTERN CAPITAL IS NOT A PRESENT THAT COMES FROM HEAVEN AND LANDS ON YOUR DOORSTEP AND SUDDENLY WONDERFUL THINGS HAPPEN, nobody is going to invest a nickel in there unless they're going to get a profit out of it,' Frank said. 'And profit is another word they don't understand.'[44] Other schemes faltered in similar ways, initial enthusiasm worn down by mistrust, misunderstanding and the dread weight of Russian bureaucracy. One small success was a San Fernando Valley jewellery maker who was put in touch with several suppliers of amber. 'It would be frustrating if this was the only thing I did for a living,' Frank admitted. 'I probably would be crazy if by every Friday I had to post a deal someplace. But since I do have another source of income, I don't have to worry.'[45]

The most surprising aspect of Frank's visits was the realisation of how much he was appreciated in a country where none of his records had been officially released. While being shown around the Stosnomic (or Stass Namin) Centre in Gorky Park, he was introduced to a Siberian R&B band. 'I walked in and I thought the guy was going to have a heart attack; he couldn't speak for spluttering. Through an interpreter, he says, "Look at this", and opens his wallet, shows me a photo of his house in Siberia. He's got all of my records on the rack, posters of me on the wall . . . You never know who's listening or why they're listening.'[46]

On November 12, at the end of his mammoth mixing session, a crowd estimated by the press at 20,000 but Frank thought was five times larger listened to him at a pro-choice rally at Rancho Park in Los Angeles. The choice was for abortion, but Frank reckoned that more than womens' rights were at issue. 'It should be clear from recent events that the enemy that America must face is not the Communists over there. It is those deranged right-wing lunatics right here in America. Make no mistake about this. Those people you see on the freeway with the fish on the back of the car - that's the enemy . . . You can't let these lunatics change the way things work around here.'

He then led the crowd in a typically acerbic prayer: 'Dear sweet Jesus, don't listen to those other guys. They are not Christians, they are practising voodoo. Not long ago they prayed to you and demanded the death of a Supreme Court Justice. What's that got to do with Christianity, huh?' 'Well, I think they needed to have that [humour],' he said later, 'because the proceeding was pretty fucking serious up to that point . . . the kind of character I am, I can get up there and get away with that. I think that somebody else doing it woulda been perceived as out of place, but I thought it was the right thing to do, and so, I did it.'[47]

Those that didn't attend the rally could listen to *You Can't Do That On Stage Volume 3*, which was largely devoted to the 1984 band. It included Dweezil and his father onstage at the tour's final L.A. gig for a version of 'Sharleena', 'Chana In De Bushwop', co-written by Diva and her father, and a medley of 'Bobby Brown' and 'Keep It Greasey' during which Ike Willis' repeated chant of 'Hi-ho Silver!' reduced Frank to a giggling jelly. As he wrote in the booklet notes, 'Just a little more proof that touring can make you crazy.'

With the mixing of the 1988 tapes complete, the UMRK mixing desk was set up to do Synclavier mixes. Frank had been commissioned to write the music to accompany Jacques Cousteau's television film about the Exxon Valdez Alaskan oil disaster, *Outrage At Valdez*. The writing incorporated a small disaster of its own. It was a last minute request which meant that Frank had to write without any reference to pictorial content. 'I knew kind of what the scenes were gonna be, so I started sketching the stuff out before I even got the videotape.'[48] He cued his music to the coded videotape he then received, only to discover that this wasn't the final 'drop frame code', necessitating two days frantic remixing.

Cousteau would be in Russia when Frank travelled to Moscow once more on January 15, 1990. He would be accompanied by a camera crew from the Financial News Network, who'd hired him to host three *Focus* programmes on Soviet business opportunities when he returned. 'I'm going to get video coverage of all the weird stuff that I've seen in Moscow,' he told Eric Buxton, 'and even if I never get any of it on television, it'll certainly make an interesting Honker product, because I'll show people a view of the Soviet Union they never dreamed of before.'[49]

The most significant part of this trip was his first visit to Czechoslovakia. In January 1989, he'd been visited at home by Michael Kocab, a Czech composer and musician who offered to have one of Frank's orchestral scores played by the country's Philharmonic Orchestra. 'He was part of the student protest movement, one of the people who was speaking out against the government, and he invited me to Prague.'[50] The country's Velvet Revolution took place in November 1989 and the Civic Forum took over. When Frank landed at Prague's Ruzyne Airport on January 21, Vaclav Havel was president and Michael Kocab was a member of the Czech parliament, in charge of overseeing the departure of the Soviet military.

Over the course of his visit, Frank was fêted by musicians, fans and the president, who expressed his admiration for *Bongo Fury*. He met 'underground' artists at the Krivan Hotel, visited Havel at Hradcany Castle, attended a party at which he sang with the Plastic People Of The Universe, one of the bands present. He appeared on a television programme, *Kontakt*, during which Minister of Culture Milan Lukes announced that Frank had been appointed to represent the government for trade, tourism and culture.

Unfortunately, over lunch Havel mentioned that Vice-President Dan Quayle was to visit the country. 'I expressed the opinion that I thought it was unfortunate that a person such as President Havel should have to bear the company of somebody as stupid as Dan Quayle for even a few moments of his life. The next thing I know, Quayle doesn't come. Instead, (Secretary of State) James Baker III (husband of Susan, co-founder of the PMRC) re-routes his trip to Moscow so that he can come blasting into Prague and literally lay down the law to the Czech government. He says, 'You can either do business with the United States or you can do business with Zappa. What'll it be?'[51] Within six weeks, Frank had been reduced to an unofficial emissary for culture.

'I'll tell you what the circumstances were,' Frank said to me, 'because there have been two people that have told me that they saw the meeting and they heard what he said. One of them almost did a television interview. I went out and got a camera crew. From the day that the guy told me what had happened to the next day when I got the crew, somebody had gotten hold of him and he refused to talk when the camera crew was in there. He absolutely verified that pressure was applied to the Czech government for them not to do business with me.'

On February 26, Frank hosted his first programme on FNN, *Frank Zappa's Wild Wild East*, analysing real estate opportunities in Moscow with a senior Russian economist and conducting a phone-in discussion about Soviet agriculture with a Carolina tractor-maker. Others featured included the heads of the Luzhniky Sports Complex and the Soviet Director's Guild, a senior administrator at the TASS news agency, and Mikhail Afanasiev, a director of Moscow's Imemo Institute. One New York banker who'd had meetings with Frank reckoned, 'He's a perfect Adam-Smithian capitalist. He knows that in the end self-interest [Frank would receive five per cent of any completed deals] is a lot better in pursuing things than altruism. But his biggest motivation behind all this is really to help these people; it isn't to make a buck.'[52]

CHAPTER TWENTY ONE
THE TORTURE NEVER STOPS

Something far more unpleasant than a petulant government official with an insulted wife came to light in the spring of 1990. 'I'd been feeling sick for a number of years,' Frank told David Sheff, 'but nobody diagnosed it. Then I got really ill and had to go to the hospital in an emergency. While I was in there, they did some tests and found out it had been there for anywhere from eight to ten years, growing undetected by any of my previous doctors. By the time they found it, it was inoperable.'[1]

'It' was a tumour in Frank's prostate, the gland surrounding the neck of the bladder whose function is to release the fluid that carries the semen. At the time, deaths in America from cancer of the prostate were over 30,000 a year; in Britain, where the figure was 9,000, doctors identified it as the second biggest cancer killer among British men. Prostate cancer is hormone dependent and if the level of male hormones is reduced by either physical or medical castration, the malignant tissue will shrink. Although Frank's tumour initially responded to treatment, it soon developed beyond hormonal control.

'When I went into the hospital, the cancer had grown to where I could no longer take a piss. In order for me just to survive, they had to poke a hole in my bladder. I spent more than a year with a hose coming out of my bladder and a bag tied to my leg. That'll keep you from travelling. I went through radiation and that fucked me up pretty good. They were supposed to give me twelve shots of that, but I got to number eleven and I was so sick that I said I couldn't go back. The result of the radiation was that the tumour was shrunken to the point where I could get rid of the bag and could piss again, but there were bad side effects.'[2]

The immediate cancellation of all Frank's public activities set off rumours about his health. It would have been a busy summer. In June he'd been scheduled to attend a contemporary music festival, *Meeting Of The World* in Finland, while in September he was to be in France, where a concert of his works was being staged in Lyon. He'd also been invited to Prague in June for Czechoslovakia's first presidential election. Frank sent his regrets for not attending. 'I really support Havel's idea of establishing a government that has an aesthetic, as well as an economic, ethic. But right now the best thing I can do is to stay away.'³ Few knew it was the only thing he could do.

Events were lending macabre significance to *You Can't Do That On Stage Anymore*. What came about through financial strictures and a sea-change in Frank's musical career had become a physical reality. A further irony was that this was his twenty-fifth year in the music business. In their May 19 issue, *Billboard* celebrated the fact with a 16-page supplement. Largely written by Drew Wheeler and designed by Cal Schenkel, it contained an interview and articles on his career, his family and his business.

Rykodisc took the centre spread to advertise the last batch of releases from Frank's back catalogue, including *Fillmore East, You Are What You Is* and *Sheik Yerbouti*. An entire pressing run of *Sheik Yerbouti* had to be destroyed when it was discovered that 'Yo' Mama' had lost some ten minutes of its original 12 minutes 38 seconds running time. *YCDTOSA 4*, slated for November 4 release, was postponed. It had been announced in the September ICE (International CD Exchange) as well as a 4-CD set from the 1988 tour, entitled *The Best Band You Never Heard In Your Life*. Other projects included *The Lost Episodes*, comprising studio outtakes from the early years; *Lumpy Gravy, Phase 3*, later known as *Civilization, Phaze 3;* and *Ahead Of Their Time*, the Mothers' Royal Festival Hall gig from October 28, 1968: 'I think there's a market for this, since it's probably the most interesting of all the archival tapes.'⁴

Asked whether the Zappa vault was a bottomless pit, Frank replied: 'I'm trying to bring that phase of my release schedule to an end as soon as possible, to get the best of the archival stuff into some kind of release form and move on to concentrating on the new stuff I'm working on today. Also, because I don't have any plans to tour again, I'd like to bring an end to this whole phase of live band tapes . . . At the same time that I'm putting these together, I'm still composing new pieces; there's all kinds of different work in progress.'⁵

The fourth Biennale de la Danse was held in Lyon between September 13 and October 6; Dancing Zappa was presented by the Orchestre de l'Opera de Lyon and the Lyon Opera Ballet at the Maurice Ravel Auditorium for five nights, beginning September 20. Robert Hughes conducted 'The Perfect Stranger' and 'Bogus Pomp'. There were four pre-recorded songs, 'Trouble Comin' Every Day', 'Plastic People', 'I'm The Slime' and 'Why Don'tcha Do Me Right', and Kent Nagano took up the baton to conduct 'Strictly Genteel'.

Back in Los Angeles, Frank worked as hard as his health permitted. 'The minute somebody tells you you have cancer, your life changes dramatically, whether you beat it or you don't,' he said. 'It's like you have a fucking brand put on you. As far as the American medical profession goes, you're just meat. It complicates your life because you have to fight for your life every single day, besides doing your shit. To do the music is complicated enough, but to think of doing things that involve travel and other kinds of physical stress is too much. Whatever medication you take fucks you up, too.'⁶

On October 26/7, he was interviewed by Co de Kloet for a four-hour radio programme, *Supplement*, to be transmitted by Dutch NOS radio on December 21, Frank's fiftieth birthday. When asked what music he listened to, Frank replied, 'I'm making music, not listening to it. The only time I have to listen to it is when I'm not watching the news. So, given the choice between listening to music and watching the news, I usually watch the news these days.'[7]

The main reason for watching the news was the developing situation in the Middle East. Throughout the 80s, Iran and Iraq had been at war, and America had pumped billions of dollars into Iraqi leader Saddam Hussein's war effort. By 1988 the conflict abated, with both sides exhausted. To generate finance, Hussein demanded that OPEC countries cut their oil production, increasing the price and thus Iraq's income. Led by Saudi Arabia and Kuwait, his Arab brothers refused. He then demanded from Kuwait the return of certain oilfields and strategic islands lost to Iraq when the existing boundaries between the countries were established in 1922.

Hussein's warlike intentions were no secret; the US Ambassador to Iraq told him that America 'had no opinion' on what it saw as a boundary dispute. Hussein's forces seized Kuwait on August 2, taking control of one fifth of the world's oil reserves. Given America's proprietary attitude towards Middle East oil, the Bush administration could no longer just send lawyers, guns and money. Troops arrived in Saudi Arabia and ultimatums were issued. Frank saw through his country's motives. 'They're not going there to protect democracy, because Kuwait is not a democracy and neither is Saudi Arabia. Both of these countries have very, very strict regimes, and to listen to speeches giving any other reason for this force in the Gulf other than protecting US oil interests is totally fake.'[8]

Interviewed by Trevor Lofts and Steven Homan four days before his birthday, he warmed to his theme: '. . . when they start talking about, "Well, it's just about aggression. You know, the very idea that somebody would just go charging into somebody else's country." Wait a minute! Yesterday was the first anniversary of 'Operation Just Cause', when we went blasting into Panama to arrest their president [Mañuel Noriega]! For what? So we can stick him in jail and tape his conversations?'[9] The resulting conflict, named Desert Storm, was brief, environmentally catastrophic and ultimately inconclusive.

WHEN NO ONE WAS NO ONE

Frank was also feeling contained. Dweezil had been on tour in Australia, accompanied by Ahmet; at the same time, Gail, with Diva in tow, was having meetings with Festival Records. 'We were seriously discussing the possibility of moving my business down there, and I told Gail to look for some property.' He visited the Australian consulate in Los Angeles to see what incentives their government might offer to move his business to Australia. He also wanted to discuss a project he'd had in mind for some time, of setting up a modern-day Bauhaus where artists of all types could meet and co-operate. 'After I'd explained to [this man] all the things I was interested in, he began with his lecture about Australian unions. He basically made it very clear that nothing that I ever wanted to do in life could ever be done in Australia because of [the] union situation.'[10]

Birthdays were going to be important events from now on, and for his fiftieth Frank bought himself a brand new Synclavier 9600. 'It's twice as big, in terms of storage,' he told Den Simms, 'and it also has a direct to disc system, so it can do a lot more than the old one.'[11] However, it was going to necessitate getting a new mixing console, in order to accommodate the increase in sound quality. That, in turn, was going to put back the mixing of any Synclavier material until it was installed.

On the record front, Frank announced *The Best Band You Never Heard In Your Life* had been reduced to a 2-CD set, but the remaining material would become another 2-CD set, *Make A Jazz Noise Here*. The one piece of bad news was that *Ahead Of Their Time* was on indefinite hold, largely due to the settlement of the lawsuit with the original Mothers, which had been on-going since February 1985. In it, the Mothers had staked their claim to 'unpaid royalties' earned from the reissue of the albums which featured them. 'All I want,' Jimmy Carl Black told the *Austin Chronicle*, 'is what's coming to me, and that could be a lot of money. I don't want any of Frank's, I just want what's coming to me. I think that's only fair.'[12] That was only a part of the $16.4 million mentioned in the lawsuit.

Details of the settlement were not made public, but Frank picked up the tab for the legal fees and *Ahead Of Their Time* went into turnaround. 'I'm not sure I want to spend my life trying to make those guys any more famous than they already are,' he said. 'I just think that it was such a stupid thing to begin with, and even though it's all over, as far as I'm concerned, there's plenty of hard feelings on my side.'[13] Eventually, he relented and *Ahead Of Their Time* was issued in April 1993.

The Best Band You Never Heard In Your Life was also issued in April. Its 28 tracks combined 'concert favourites and obscure album cuts, along with deranged versions of cover tunes and a few premiere recordings'. Frank's note continued, 'In a world where most of the "big groups" go on stage and pretend to sing and play, we proudly present this quaint little audio artefact. Yes, once upon a time, live musicians actually sang and played this.'

The musicianship was indeed dazzling, as those who'd witnessed the shows already knew. The versatility and skill of his musicians was matched by the breadth of their repertoire. The 'cover tunes' included Johnny Cash's 'Ring Of Fire', 'I Left My Heart In San Francisco', Ravel's *Bolero*, 'When Irish Eyes

Are Smiling' and the themes from *The Godfather* and *Bonanza*. There was also Ike Willis' *Thing-Fish* medley of 'Purple Haze' and 'Sunshine Of Your Love' (the latter with Mike Keneally's bizarre 'Johnny Cash' for good measure), from a soundcheck in Linz, and Led Zeppelin's 'Stairway To Heaven', with the brass section playing Jimmy Page's original guitar solo note for note.

Toward the end of the second CD, there were 'Swaggart' versions of 'Lonesome Cowboy Burt', 'More Trouble Every Day' and 'Penguin In Bondage', during which Frank provoked as much laughter onstage as there was in the audience by incorporating various details of Swaggart's disgrace into the lyrics. 'A Few Moments With Brother A. West' was a cod 'sermon' from the man who'd illustrated *The Real Frank Zappa Book*. Frank announced later in the show that the 'sermon' was in fact a satire on the spurious moral hysteria of the religious Right.

On Monday April 15, Frank appeared on Berkeley's Radio KPFA for a combined interview and phone-in with Charles Amirkhanian, the inventor of a musical form he called 'text-sound', during which he revealed that he might enter the following year's Presidential race. 'I don't want to be connected with any party. In fact, I think that the condition of politics in the United States right now is so drastic that any thinking individual who still says he belongs to a party is just kidding himself, because neither party is doing anything for anybody except their buddies.'[14] Thereafter, for several months there was talk of a feasibility study, which fell victim to the weight of work and Frank's uncertain health.

During a second appearance on Amirkhanian's programme on Monday May 20, there was mention of what was to be the last major event in Frank's musical life. 'On Thursday, there's a group of people who are coming to visit me from Germany, and they've invited me to write a major piece for the Frankfurt Festival for 1992.'[15] At the meeting with Dr. Dieter Rexroth, in charge of the Festival, film-maker Henning Lohner and Andreas Molich-Zebhauser, manager of the Ensemble Modern, it was agreed that instead of one large orchestral work, Frank would prepare a set of compositions, some of which would receive their premiere. The 18-strong Ensemble would come to Los Angeles for two weeks in July, so that both parties could assess the potential of their collaboration.

Another project nearing fruition was a stage presentation of *Broadway The Hard Way*, already postponed twice from October 1990 and March 1991. It was the brainchild of conductor Joel Thome, with whom Frank had collaborated ten years previously on a tribute to Varèse. By May, the project had broadened. 'Almost two years have gone by [since the original idea],' Mike Keneally explained, 'and so it makes more sense to do a lot more music from a lot more phases of Frank's career'[16] 'This is a wonderful opportunity to pay tribute to Frank,' said Thome. 'He's such an important force in music with such a passionate vision, so it's our way of saying, "Thank you".'[17] By September, the show had been retitled *Zappa's Universe* and Zappanauts would be attending The Ritz in New York City for four days beginning on Thursday, November 7.

Make A Jazz Noise Here, released in June, concentrated on instrumentals, including 'Big Swifty', 'King Kong', 'Dupree's Paradise' and 'Strictly Genteel', which gave individual members of the band generous solo space. 'When Yuppies Go To Hell' was an outstanding representation of the group improvisation that took place every night. The almost 15-minute collage began with a theme written during the tour which Frank entitled 'Dessicated', while later parts were taken from performances of 'A Pound For A Brown On The Bus'. Scott Thunes contributed arrangements of the Royal March from Stravinsky's *L'Histoire Du Soldat* and the theme from Bartók's *Piano Concerto No. 3*. Unfortunately, copyright problems with these and Ravel's *Bolero* on *Best Band* subsequently led to public apologies and a temporary withdrawal of stock.

As *Make A Jazz Noise Here* was released, Jimmy Swaggart was caught with another prostitute. 'It comes out on the market,' Frank said to me, 'and they catch him again. Some things never change.' *You Can't Do That On Stage Anymore 4* was issued at the same time. Its time-frame ran from 1969 to 1988, with almost half the tracks taken from 1984 performances. Of particular interest were the original 1976 version of 'The Torture Never Stops' with Captain Beefheart's vocal, a guest appearance by saxophonist Archie Shepp on 'Let's Move To Cleveland', and the marathon guitar duel with Steve Vai on a Rome recording of 'Stevie's Spanking'.

On June 20, Frank flew to Russia once more, and four days later arrived in Prague to join the celebrations marking the departure of Soviet armed forces from Czechoslovakia. Later, at a concert headed by Michael Kocab's group, The Prague Selection, he strapped on a Fender Strat for the first time in three years, soloing on a reggae instrumental. Before playing, he told the audience, 'I'm sure you already know it, but this is just the beginning of your new future in this country, and as you confront the new changes that will take place, please try to keep your country unique. Don't change into something else. Keep it unique.'[18] At the next election, the country split into the Czech Republic and Slovakia.

A few days later, he journeyed on to Hungary, where the mayor of Budapest, Gabor Demszky, repaid the courtesy he'd received when he'd been a guest at Frank's house earlier in the year. Once again, he took up his guitar to perform with a local band at the Tabanban, near Budapest. Photographs taken during the visit hint at the toll the cancer treatment was taking on Frank, overweight and with a haunted look in his eyes when not in the public gaze. While his hair was as luxuriant and unruly as ever, his sideburns were white, his moustache grey-flecked. It was as if the ageing process was accelerating.

Frank returned via France and London, where on July 3 he appeared on BBC Radio 4's *Midweek* with guests including the Chieftains. Presenter Libby Purves asked about his Presidential aspirations and Frank replied he was still doing 'a feasibility study'. Nine days later, in a recorded interview for Radio 1's *News 91*, he commented, 'We had kind of a chimpmaster turned President for eight years, and now we have a spymaster turned President . . . We've seen the results in the US of a world invented for us by a former used car salesman, and you can see the result of that. So, how can a person from the world of culture make it any worse than it already is?'[19]

By then, he and the Ensemble Modern were ensconced in Joe's Garage, rehearsing and improvising. During a two-week stay, the musicians were also 'sampled' at UMRK, so that Frank's eventual compositions, developed in the Synclavier, would reflect their individual capabilities. At the same time, the Ensemble's copyist, Ali Askin, was recruited to prepare arrangements of previous Zappa work for inclusion in the 90-minute programme. Frank responded to the musicians' enthusiasm with some bizarre experimentation. 'There are two people in this group who play didgeridoos,' he told Don Menn. 'One of them is the woman from Australia who is also the oboe player [Catherine Milliken] . . . I imagined this awful sound that could be created if one were to take a didgeridoo and play it into a partially-filled coffee pot. And I asked her whether she would do it. She said yes, and let me say, it is truly nauseating. I was laughing so much I had to leave the room.'[20]

Zappa fans didn't laugh when a set of Zappa bootlegs was released in October. Rhino had announced in March that they'd teamed up with Frank on a separate deal for a 10-LP box-set entitled *Beat The Boots!*. Release on the Foo-eee label had first been scheduled for June. Frank had his reasons: 'The only real answer to bootlegging is the use of tactical nuclear weapons but short of that, the Foo-eee project is the most humane solution. In a 25-year career, I've experienced the phenomenon of vast quantities of boots being recorded, really bad recordings that pissed me off . . . That's a pretty strong motivation to get back at these guys, and that's where I got the idea to bootleg the boots.'[21]

The final selection, made by the Zappa office from albums supplied by Rhino employee Tom Brown, comprised, *As An Am* (New York, 1981), *Live At The Ark* (Boston, 1968), *Freaks & Motherfuckers* (New York, 1971), *Unmitigated Audacity* (Indiana, 1974), *Any Way The Wind Blows* (Paris, 1979), *'Tis The Season To Be Jelly* (Stockholm, 1967), *Saarbrucken 1978* and *Piquantique* (Stockholm/Sydney, 1973). The vinyl and cassette versions came in a cardboard box with a T-shirt and button, the eight CDs in just their jewel-cases. 'I haven't heard them myself, nor do I intend to,' said Frank. 'I make no claim that any of the material contained on these records is of any musical value whatsoever. Besides, if you want crap, now you can get fully authorised affordable crap, and maybe put some sleazebag out of business.'[22]

In November, *Zappa's Universe* brought together the Orchestra Of Our Time, conducted by Joel Thome, vocal groups The Persuasions and Rockapella, and a band consisting of Mike Keneally, Scott Thunes, keyboardists Mats Oberg and Marc Ziegenhagen, drummer Morgan Agren and percussionist Jonathan Haas. Guests included Steve Vai, Denny Walley, Dale Bozzio, Lorin Hollander, and Moon, Diva and Dweezil. Each show, featuring some 30 of Frank's compositions, began with a performance of Erik Satie's *Socrate*, a work Thome thought appropriate. 'In Satie, all the works add up to a single, powerful, evolving idea. A similar thing happens with Zappa. Taken together, Frank's works add up to one extraordinary opera.'[23]

The first concert was filmed for video release, and both this and the second night were recorded for CD release by Verve. Both packages were issued in 1993, and as usual with Zappa releases, their contents were sufficiently dissimilar to make it necessary for fans to buy both. Drew Wheeler thought 'Thome's orchestrations had the right Zappaesque flair,'[24] taking particular notice of 'Nite School', 'Waka-Jawaka' and 'Brown Shoes Don't Make It'. Richard Gehr picked out the same three numbers in his review, reckoning that the first sounded 'like a skittering skateboarder hanging ten on an ice floe'.[25]

Frank had been expected to attend, but mechanical problems with his plane and the onset of flu kept him in California. Even so, Moon and Dweezil had a more serious task when they called a press conference at The Ritz on the afternoon of the first performance. 'We're here to make a statement on behalf of our family,' Moon began. 'Although Frank was looking forward to being here and really intended to be here, unfortunately he's not here. As many of you know he's been diagnosed by journalists as having cancer. We'd like you to know his doctors have diagnosed prostate cancer which he's been fighting successfully and he has been feeling well and working too hard and planned to attend. Up until the last minute we were still hoping he would feel well enough to get on a plane and come here. There are occasional periods where he's not feeling as well and it's really unfortunate it happened to coincide with this event.'[26]

So the news was finally out. Newspaper reports had Frank at death's door with weeks to live. The truth, though serious, was less alarming. 'Although a bad day rolls around every couple of weeks, it hasn't interrupted his work schedule, which is feverish to say the least,' said Frank's publicist, Sean Mahoney. 'The stories of him being in the hospital in critical condition are totally exaggerated. He's in the studio most of the day, and when he's not, he's glued to C-SPAN or CNN.'[28]

Apart from preparing the final volumes of *You Can't Do That On Stage Anymore*, Frank was hard at work on the scores for the Frankfurt Festival. I talked with him during the afternoon of November 30. For the first three hours, we talked about his career, and then our conversation moved on to wider topics, including what he saw as the 'plague' of 'affirmative action' and the breakdown of an education system which produced school-leavers who were 'ignorant with style'. 'It's 52% illiteracy here in the United States by the latest estimate. When you figure that that number is arrived at by averaging things out, that means that in some places the literacy is 99%, in other places it's 9% or 2%. Hollywood is probably at the lower end of the scale.'

Why did no one pursue excellence anymore? 'They don't dare. Excellence costs money and not everybody can do it. There is no governmental mandate that every manufacturer should have a certain number of people that are excellent. You must have a certain number of people of a certain colour and a certain sex but none of them must be excellent. In fact, if they are, you're in big trouble.

'How can you compete with countries that make products which are in fact excellent, when you have a non-excellent workforce, with non-excellent designers and non-excellent managers making non-excellent decisions to steer the path into a non-excellent future? You got it, we got it. It's because Thatcher and Reagan took all those rides in that fucking golf-cart together. I just want to know which one had their hand on the little steering stick.' A bit later, he added, 'The damage has been done to this country since Reagan took office – actually, the shit hit the fan with Richard Nixon, the first major imperial presidency. And then Reagan and now Bush, this pitiful, ignorant . . . ,' he let out an anguished sigh, 'it just makes my flesh crawl to think of what he's doing in there.'

As 1992 began, there was talk of a second *Beat The Boots!* set to be released in May, comprising *Disconnected Synapses* (Paris, 1970), *Tengo Na Minchia Tanta* (New York, 1970), *Electric Aunt Jemima* (Denver, 1968), *At The Circus* (Munich, 1978), *Swiss Cheese/Fire!* (Montreux, 1971), *Our Man In Nirvana* (Fullerton, 1968) and *Conceptual Continuity* (Detroit, 1976). Since its release, the first vinyl set had gone through three pressing runs totalling 20,000 units. Geoff Gans, art director of the project, had been nominated for a Grammy in the 'best album art' category. Despite the sales, Frank's opinion had not improved: 'Let's say you had a turd. If you took the turd and buffed it, you'd still have a turd. And that's what you have with these releases – a digital replication of a buffed turd.'[28]

During the same interview, he anticipated the September concerts: 'This is a special thing for me. The Frankfurt Festival is investing an enormous amount of money to do an entire week of my music . . . I think the project in

Frankfurt is going to open the door for a lot more work in the classical music field. You know, if you're my age, that's not a bad age to be a classical composer. But it's a terrible age to be a rock 'n' roll musician.'[29]

The Ensemble Modern concerts were now set for September 17-19 at Frankfurt's Alte Oper, September 22/3 in Berlin's Philharmonie, and September 26-28 in Vienna's Konzerthaus. In addition, the Junge Deutsche Philharmonie would perform 'Bogus Pomp' at the Alte Oper on September 20. With some reluctance, Frank had acquiesced in naming the concerts *The Yellow Shark*. On seeing the yellow fibreglass fish in Frank's listening room, Andreas Molich-Zebhauser had taken it as an appropriate symbol for the event, even if its sailfin identified it as a marlin. He took its humorous representation of a predator to be a metaphor for some of Frank's own character traits. Made from a surfboard, it had been created in 1986 by Mark Beam and left in the Zappas' driveway as an anonymous Christmas present.

On July 13, Frank, accompanied by Gail and Moon, flew to Frankfurt for two weeks of preliminary rehearsals with the Ensemble. Eight days later, he held a press conference at the Hotel Frankfurter Hof, telling reporters that each concert would be 'an evening of entertainment, with a lot of different aspects to it'. All of the shows in the concert series would be recorded live, and with improvisation taking place every night. 'We think that by the time that all of the material is collected, it will be enough for two CDs.' Asked if this was the end of his career as a rock 'n' roll musician, he laughed and replied, 'God, I hope so. At 51, I better be looking for another job.'[30]

The final volumes of *You Can't Do That On Stage Anymore* were released in August. 5,000 copies of *YCDTOSA 5 & 6* came in a pink storage box that could house all six double-CDs. Fans with less money could buy *YCDTOSA 5* straight away but had to wait until November to get *YCDTOSA 6* as a separate item. *YCDTOSA 5* devoted one disc to the 1982 band with Steve Vai. For the other disc, he showcased the 1969 band, adding a 1965 Fillmore West recording by the original band with Elliot Ingber. Noting the sound was not exactly 'hi-fi', he'd compiled the tracks 'for the amusement of those collectors who still believe that the only "good' material was performed by those early line-ups'.[32] Disc One of *YCDTOSA 6* featured songs 'dealing generally with the topic of sex (safe and otherwise)', including 'The M.O.I. Anti-Smut Loyalty Oath', 'The Madison Panty-Sniffing Festival', 'Make A Sex Noise' and 'I Have Been In You'. There was an aroma of Halloween to Disc Two, with six of its 15 tracks recorded over several such nights at New York's Palladium. The monumental series bowed out with a 1981 Halloween version of 'Strictly Genteel'.

Frank returned to Frankfurt early in September for final rehearsals with the Ensemble Modern. Matters were complicated by the use of a six-channel playback system which surrounded the audience for which each musician was miked up and channelled to a particular speaker. A further refinement was 'the hoop', a ring of six microphones which could be lowered over a musician's head, so that the house mixer could cross-fade from the entire Ensemble down to one instrument. There was also the Canadian dance troupe, La La La Human Steps, three male and three female dancers who Frank had seen on video and requested their involvement.

The final programme fully repaid the effort put in by everyone involved. Many compositions received their world premieres: 'Amnerika', 'Beat The Reaper' (for Synclavier and dancers), 'Food Gathering In Post-Industrial America', 'Get Whitey', 'N-Lite' (for Synclavier), 'Pentagon Afternoon', 'Ruth Is Sleeping' (for two pianos), and 'Welcome To The United States'. There were also new arrangements of 'Dog/Meat', 'Be-Bop Tango', 'G-Spot Tornado', 'The Girl In The Magnesium Dress', 'None Of The Above' (for string quartet), 'Outrage At Valdez', 'A Pound For A Brown On The Bus' and 'Times Beach' (for wind quintet).

On the opening night, Frank conducted the improvised *Overture* and later, 'Food Gathering' and 'Welcome To The United States'. Otherwise, Peter Rundel, the Ensemble's usual conductor, led the proceedings. The evening's climax was a manic performance of 'G-Spot Tornado' with dancers and an even faster encore of the same piece minus the dance troupe. An ailing Frank received a standing ovation from the audience. The news that he wouldn't attend the second night came as no surprise, although the rest of the Zappa family were present, as they were for each concert. 'If I hadn't been sick,' he said later, 'the experience would have been exhilarating. Unfortunately, I felt so excruciatingly shitty that it was hard to walk, to just get up onto the stage, to sit, to stand up. You can't enjoy yourself when you're sick, no matter how enthusiastic the audience.'[31] He was able to attend the final Frankfurt performance, but then had to return home on September 22, missing the performances in Berlin and Vienna.

The first night was videotaped and broadcast live on Premiere, Germany's pay television channel. *Peefeeyatko*, Henning Lohner's film about Frank, was shown in the foyer of the Alter Oper each evening. In the run-up to the shows, German television showed a pair of documentaries, *Anything, Any Place, Any Time, For No Reason At All* and *Kulturplus*, covering the preparations for *The Yellow Shark*. The final section of *Anything* contained an unreleased 1988 guitar solo accompanying footage of the L.A. riots incited by the police beating of Rodney King. 'We had television sets in the bar during intermission showing the finest of American cultural entertainment. On one set, nonstop riot. On another, nonstop televangelists. On another, C-SPAN. On another, Desert Storm. You got to have your light beer and watch the American media at its finest.'[32]

Health had become the determining factor in his work rate. 'Some days you can do more than others. Part of the problem is that it hurts to sit some days, and this work is done sitting at a computer terminal. I used to be able to work 16, 18 hours a day and just get up from my chair and go to sleep and go back to work, and it was fine. But some days I can't work at all. Some days I can work two hours. Some days I can work ten.'[33]

Before leaving for Frankfurt, he'd prepared *Playground Psychotics* for release in October, a double-CD combining 1971 gigs by the Flo & Eddie band at the Fillmore East, UCLA's Pauley Pavilion and the ill-fated Rainbow Theatre, with on-the-road dialogue recorded by Frank and Mark Volman and sections of soundtrack from *The True Story Of 200 Motels* video. Taking its title from a chance remark by Jeff Simmons, the collection's highlights were a 30-minute version of 'Billy The Mountain' and Frank's mix of the jam session with John Lennon and Yoko Ono. As Frank noted, the latter was 'substantially different' from what had appeared on *Some Time In New York City*.

ZAPPA!

Throughout the previous spring, as preparations for the Frankfurt Festival went ahead, Frank had also been interviewed for a special magazine to be jointly published by *Guitar Player* and *Keyboard*. Beginning in April, editor Don Menn conducted a series of talks with Frank, culminating in a week of interviews during June. From being a tribute to Frank's career, the project grew to encompass the whole of his enterprises. As well as interviews with every member of the Zappa family, all his technical staff at UMRK and Joe's Garage explained their functions. Nicholas Slonimsky, Kent Nagano and Andreas Molich-Zebhauser lent their weight to Frank's status as a leading American composer, while Warren De Martini and Aynsley Dunbar reinforced his rock credentials. In all, Menn recorded between 40 and 60 hours of material, some with assistance from *The Simpsons* cartoonist Matt Groening, from which the 100-page *Zappa!* was culled.

As public awareness of his condition increased, he had to contend with the attentions of the world's press. He told David Sheff he'd become 'very time-budget conscious. Certain things are very time-consuming and the time spent doing them is productive. Other things are time-consuming and it's like being hijacked. I have a low tolerance for wasting time. I try not to be irritable about it, but it's my main concern. I'm trying to live my life the same way that I lived it before.'[34]

At the time of the interview, he was 40 pounds overweight, 'a walking balloon', from medication that filled him up with water. 'The week before last I found myself in the hospital for three days riddled with morphine. That was definitely an experience I don't want to repeat. When I got out, it took almost ten days to get the residue of all the drugs they'd given me out of my body.' Worst of all was the effect that drugs had on his ability to make decisions of any kind. 'If you can't trust your own judgement, that's really hard. When you're writing music, every note you put down is a judgement call.'35

In February 1993, an impromptu recording *soirée* was arranged, bringing together the disparate forces of The Chieftains, L. Shankar, Terry Bozzio, Johnny 'Guitar' Watson and a trio of Tuvan throat singers, brought along by Matt Groening. The session was videotaped by a BBC crew for inclusion in a BBC2 *Late Show* tribute that was broadcast on Thursday, March 11. The 40-minute programme combined archive film and video footage and interviews with Groening, Jim 'Motorhead' Sherwood, Ruth Underwood, Steve Vai, Dweezil and Ahmet. For his own interview, Frank appeared wan and bloated but his tongue was as sharp as ever, even if his humour was now more waspish than cynical.

It was increasingly apparent that only so many projects would be completed before his health deteriorated completely. 'I used to be a night owl, but now I'm usually in bed by six or seven in the evening. It's hard for me to work a real long day anymore. I'm up at 6.30 in the morning. If I can do a 12-hour shift, then I feel I'm really doing something.'36 Critical judgement was hard to sustain. 'During one period, I was working on some pieces that I let go before their time. Since they hadn't been released yet, as I gradually felt better, I went back and worked on them to make sure that the level of competence was maintained.'37 Projects included the on-going *Civilization: Phaze III, The Lost Episodes* and *Dance Me This*, an album of Synclavier music designed for modern dance groups. The first had become an 'Opera Pantomime' which Frank hoped would be performed in May 1994 as part of the Vienna Festival.

Other plans included further collaboration with the Ensemble Modern. Andreas Molich-Zebhauser discussed the possibility of Frank preparing a 22-minute video for a concert the group would play in Cologne in May, and there was talk of the Ensemble playing an evening of Zappa 'theatrical works' such as 'Billy The Mountain' and 'Brown Shoes Don't Make It' in May 1995. In July, he and the Ensemble recorded *The Rage And The Fury: The Music Of Edgard Varèse*. 'Frank didn't want to call it a tribute,' said engineer Spencer Chrislu. 'He felt Varèse is completely misunderstood, and he didn't think the music had ever been performed properly. At one point,' Chrislu added, 'Frank told the Ensemble, "You're all wonderful, technical musicians. But now it's time to put some eyebrows on it." He wanted them to feel the music and get in touch with the emotions waiting to come out of it.'38

As Spring became Summer, his face adorned the covers of a number of magazines, among them *Rock CD*, *Guitarist*, *Cutting Edge* and the weekend supplement of *The Guardian*. For the cover of *Pulse*, photographer Aldo Mauro managed to get a fully-bearded Frank to smile, but the sombre portrait inside caught a more haunted and pained expression. He also submitted to a *Playboy* interview but didn't make the cover. Inevitably, interviewers brought up the subject of his health, with varying degrees of tact. Asked by Joe Jackson if his condition was terminal, Frank replied, 'Everything is terminal. But as to the question of whether it is in the short term, the only thing I can say it that I hope not. It all depends. That's why, right now, I've got to leave you and go into my bedroom and have a blood transfusion.'[39]

Alex Kershaw eschewed a direct question but portrayed the reality of Frank's condition: 'The real Frank Zappa finally stands up, simply a man racked with pain, awash with drugs, and slowly climbs up stone steps leading to the kitchen, his fingers gripping the brick wall as if he were clinging to life itself.'[40] Earlier in their conversation, Frank had disparaged the recent election that had put a Democrat, Bill Clinton, into the White House. One outcome had been the resignation of Tipper Gore from the PMRC, now that husband Al was Vice-President. 'The media likes to give the illusion that [she] and I are mortal enemies. That's not a fact. She sent me a sweet letter when she heard I was sick, and I appreciate that.'[41]

As 1993 drew towards its close, so did Frank's life. 'Even when he couldn't get out of bed much, I would go up and see him,' said Chrislu, 'and he would want a full report of what was being done in the studio. He definitely wanted to be part of it.'[42] *The Yellow Shark* was issued to critical acclaim on November 2: Frank Zappa the American composer had finally found a group of musicians who were capable of accurately interpreting some of his most difficult music. When he became bedridden, friends from the old days would gather at his bedside and listen with him to the doo-wop records that had been his early inspiration and an enduring pleasure.

On Monday, December 6, the Zappa family issued a statement: 'Composer Frank Zappa left for his final tour just before 6.00 pm on Saturday, December 4, 1993, and was buried Sunday, December 5, 1993, during a private ceremony attended by the family. He was with his wife Gail and four children, Moon, Dweezil, Ahmet and Diva at home in Los Angeles at the time of his death.'

CHAPTER TWENTY TWO
OUTRO

Here lies a cavalier of fame,
Whose dauntless courage soar'd so high,
That death, which can the boldest tame,
He scorn'd to flatter, or to fly.
A constant bugbear to the bad,
His might the world in arms defy'd,
And in his life though counted mad,
He in his perfect senses dy'd.

Don Quixote, Book Four, Chapter 21
Miguel de Cervantes
(Translated by Tobias Smollett, 1755)

Both the *Los Angeles Times* and the *Daily News* put Frank's death on the front pages of their December 6 editions. To one, he was the 'Iconoclast of Rock', to the other, an 'Offbeat musician–composer'. Both quoted friend and journalist Rip Rense, 'As a musician, as a composer he was absolutely driven. The man lived to create art. If he loved anything better than art, it was his life, it was his family.' The announcement came too late for the British daily press, but Monday's *Evening Standard* ran a piece that paraphrased quotes from the *Daily News*.

The following day, the *Calendar* section of the *Los Angeles Times* carried an appreciation by Daniel Schorr, senior news analyst for National Public Radio. In a piece that had been commissioned some months in advance, he described how he and Frank had become friends. 'It took me a long time to realise that behind the angry dirty words about conspiratorial government and the mediocrity of the world around him was hidden a true musical genius who cared a lot about young people. Like a Pied Piper, he wanted to use music to lead young people to an interest in politics.'

Schorr went on: 'Frank also liked being contrary. If you talked about his success, he said he was a failure. If you noted his popularity, he said he was lonely. Maybe he was. The world around him contained too much crassness, too much mediocrity, too much homogenization. It could not offer enough scope for his enormous creativity and individuality. So he denounced it with dirty words. But, I imagine that the quickest thing about Frank Zappa to fade from memory will be all the windmills at which he tilted. What will be remembered is his restless search for new forms, his open mind for new musical meanings. And his dedication to "kids", his own and the world's.'₁

A penchant for 'dirty words' and mythologised dirty deeds were an inescapable ingredient in British press obituaries, which varied from sound-bite trivia in *The Sun* to comprehensive coverage in *The Times*, with an obituary (which called him 'an obstreperous and delightfully barking mad spirit'), a perceptive appreciation by music journalist David Toop and an article on prostate cancer. Every journal struggled to make a coherent whole of Frank's many disparate achievements. Typically, the *Daily Mail* called him 'America's sonic satirist', 'brilliantly avant garde, he never outgrew a fondness for smut'.

In the *Daily Mirror*, *The Guardian*, *The Independent* and the following weekend's *Sunday Times*, Frank was the 'father of invention'; for *Today*, he was the 'rock perfectionist who didn't care how he was remembered'. All referred to his fight against censorship and his defiant political stance. The *Daily Express* repeated a 1988 quote from LA's *Daily News:* 'I was asked, "Don't you think you should be more subtle in your approach?" With reading and listening comprehension where they are in the United States, it is time to get out the baseball bat.'

While several papers mentioned it, the *Daily Telegraph* reproduced the 'Phi Zappa Krappa' poster alongside Charles Shaar Murray's appreciation. Robin Denselow quoted Frank on the subject in *The Guardian:* 'I'm very famous, but the number of people who know my music as opposed to seeing a poster of me sitting on the toilet is very disproportionate.' In the same edition, Adam Sweeting thought 'Zappa was too inquisitive and provocative to be easily pigeonholed, and it will take years for his achievements to be fully appreciated'.

Back in Los Angeles, Jack Skelley began his *LA Reader* obituary: 'Frank Zappa was the strange uncle in the family of late-20th-century music. Misunderstood by most of the relatives but held in awe by those too young or tolerant to be put off, he was never given his proper seat at the table.' *People* managed to extract a suitable coffee-table cliché from Alice Cooper: 'Everybody that was considered a genius, from the Beatles to Brian Wilson, looked to Zappa as the genius.'

Further afield, the December 20 *New Yorker* had two tributes: Matt Groening reckoned, 'What kept me and so many other people percolating to Zappa's music for the past 27 years was the thrill of hitching a ride with a critical mind that was always pushing into uncharted territory.' Vaclav Havel evinced Frank's stature in the Czech underground and his sincere interest in the country's future as a democratic state. 'I thought of Frank Zappa as a friend. Meeting him was like entering a different world from the one I live in as President. Whenever I feel like escaping from that world – in my mind, at least – I think of him.'

The February *Musician* carried tributes from ex-bandmembers Mark Volman, Ruth Underwood, Bruce Fowler, Adrian Belew, Chad Wackerman and Mike Keneally, as well as (Miss) Pamela Des Barres, Cal Schenkel, Matt Groening and Daniel Schorr. Pierre Boulez called Frank 'an exceptional figure' in both the pop and classical worlds. 'His musicianship was very extensive. He did not say much but he knew much more than one could have thought.' Mike Keneally was infuriated that Frank had been misunderstood: 'He was always fond of saying that his life was a series of failures. Every artist has a lot of projects that never quite get off the ground. But when you see what he did accomplish and how many people it reached, I'd say that his career was a massive success.' Joel Thome was succinct: 'The silence of Frank's voice is deafening; the sound of his music will live forever.'

Considering the abrasive nature of his relationship with *Rolling Stone*, the magazine's five-page tribute in RS 674, written by David Fricke, was generous. Or perhaps it was compensation for the fact that, though a nominee for the 1994 awards, they'd neglected to induct him into the Rock & Roll Hall of Fame while he was still alive. After all, his opinion of such events was scathing: 'Taste is reinforced by what gets broadcast, and it's reinforced by who receives those stupid awards on those horrible award shows that keep coming up over and over and over again.'[2] When the likelihood of him boycotting or disparaging the event was gone, he was inducted into the hallowed portals on January 12, 1995, with Moon accepting on her father's behalf. By an exquisite irony, the inductor was Lou Reed, who called Frank 'a force for reason and honesty in a business deficient in these areas'. *Downbeat* critics had elected him with less ceremony into their own Hall of Fame in September 1994.

A more celestial honour had been bestowed in July, when Minor Planet 3834 was designated Zappafrank. Dr John Scialli, a psychiatrist from Phoenix, Arizona, had intended to attach Frank's name to one of the three known planets to orbit another star, a pulsar in the Virgo constellation. However, a radio contest opted for naming them after the Three Stooges. In the end, an asteroid discovered in May 1980 by L. Brozek at Klet Observatory in Czechoslovakia was donated, in recognition of the fact that Frank had been regarded as 'a symbol of democracy and freedom' during the Soviet occupation of the country.

Another albeit transient memorial arrived on American television screens on March 5, 1994, when a new cartoon series debuted on the USA Network. *Duckman*, his tubular head topped off with an extended quiff of orange hair, his eyes set in spectacles half-way down his beak, was a 'Private Dick/Family Man'. That family consisted of Aunt Bernice, twin sister of his dead (by his own hand) wife Beatrice, children Ajax, Charles and Mambo, 'three sons in two bodies', and the comatose Grandmama, whose only utterances were skirt-fluttering farts.

Created by the animators of *The Simpsons*, the first episode, *I, Duckman*, had Frank Zappa all over it. The opening sequence featured Senator Paula Hawkins' 'fire and chains' soliloquy from 'Porn Wars' as well as 'Let's Make The Water Turn Black', and the soundtrack ended with Louis Cuneo's maniacal laughter. It was 'Dedicated with fond memories to Frank Zappa'. Frank's music was used 'by appointment to Her Majesty The Scarlet Pimpernel', while original music was provided by Scott Wilk and Todd Yvega. Dweezil supplied the voice of Ajax, a polite but mentally challenged teenager who couldn't always remember not to knock on his own bedroom door.

IT JUST MIGHT BE A ONE SHOT DEAL

In the brief time since his death it's not possible to quantify Frank Zappa's achievements or what impact his compositions, of all kinds, will have on the history of music. Throughout his career, he maintained that he wrote music in order to hear what it sounded like. We bought his records to see whether we liked them. That was the contract. The pragmatism of his methods of composition indicated that the results shouldn't bear the weight of anything other than musical analysis.

Those who dip their hand in the bran-tub of philosophical reasoning to bring forth a gaudy package of deeper meaning in Frank's music should bear in mind the words of Robert De Niro's character Michael in *The Deer Hunter*, as he gesticulates with a bullet: 'This is this. It ain't somethin' else. This is this.' Frank told his last interviewer the colour purple was just the combination of red and blue. It had no other significance, and liking its hue revealed nothing about an individual's character. Similarly, Frank's significance is how he lived and the music he wrote. Any attempt to force that through a distorting prism of supposition and speculation is unlikely to bear consumable fruit.

Frank's 'serious' orchestral music was written under the influence of Varèse, Stravinsky, Webern and others. Nicholas Slonimsky found 'the configuration of notes and contrapuntal combinations' of his scores 'remarkably Varesian'.3 As such they weren't innovative, but whether Frank was an original or a *pasticheur* ultimately doesn't matter. Where he was innovative was in the way he applied his compositional skills to explore the Synclavier's potential, its capacity to create new sound textures and bizarre melodies, above all its capacity to create complex rhythms beyond human execution. One interviewer noted, 'He exults in the heady freedom that his instrument confers'. 'I've done things like 88 tuplets: 88 notes in the space of three quarter notes as a regular feature, played versus 35 notes. Thirty-five over 88!' What does that do to you? he was asked. 'What does it do ? It makes me want to dance!'4

'Machines like this have made it possible for me to hear things I never dreamed I would hear in terms of air molecules in life,' he added. As the available software became more sophisticated, so his ideas and explorations proliferated. *Civilization Phaze III*, his last major original work and one it had taken him more than a decade to complete, was released a year after his death. In it, he tied up the loose ends that *Lumpy Gravy* had left dangling 26 years previously and provided a chilling soundscape to underline his contention that society's evils had worsened in the interim. 'I think it's very much about finishing his life,' Gail told the *Los Angeles Times*. 'He said that after he finished this, he had nothing more to do. I asked him, "Is there anything else you want to tell me about?" He said, "No. I've done everything that I can."'5

Each disc of the 2-CD set contains a major composition, 'Beat The Reaper' and 'N-Lite', the latter a continuous 18-minute work in six parts. To scotch speculation about its title, he explained, 'It was put together out of two unrelated sequences. There's a group of notes in front of this one sequence that just happens to sound like 'In The Navy' from that Village People song. You don't realise it until it's gone by, and then – that's 'In The Navy'! So that's the 'N' and the 'Lite' part is this sequence that was basically a bunch of very fast and short synthesiser pockets that had the computer title, 'Thousand Points of Light'.'6

Phaze III is the proof that, before he died, Frank had stepped across the threshold of a new musical vocabulary, which hopefully won't have died with him. 'There is nothing else in contemporary music like it,' Matt Groening asserted. 'It's very thick and dense and overpowering. Even if you think you know Frank Zappa's music, I don't think anybody could be sufficiently prepared for the powerhouse that this thing represents.'7 'I think [it] has a lot to do with Frank knowing that he wasn't going to be able to realise a lot of the things that he wanted to,' Gail said. 'I don't think he was in a hurry, as much as he was pragmatic and said, "I can do this". I see it as a big-time "Thanks for the Memories" in some ways.'8

There was no such sentiment on Frank's behalf for the world that he was leaving. It had long since lost any power to impress or surprise him. During his BBC2 interview, he'd held up a glossy magazine, *Future Sex*, and said, 'Look, here it is the 90s, here's where we are. Shouldn't somebody say something about people who will buy $1,000 dildo things that they plug into their computer to do stuff to them with 3-D goggles attached to it?' Then, he used the situation to deliver a warning: 'I think that if you need a $1,000 dildo with a helmet, you'd better get it. Get it now. Wear it to work. Stay happy.

Because the 90s are not going to be a happy time. This may be your last chance.'9

He'd made a more serious observation three years before: 'I think that what is being lost during this tail end of the 20th century is the will on the part of the average American to be an individual. The people seem to be too willing to just conform and be moulded into some bland, obedient nothingness.' 10 Despite his pessimism about the future, he'd made sure that his family would be provided for. On October 7, 1994, Rykodisc announced it had purchased the entire Zappa catalogue of more than 60 albums from the Zappa Family Trust. The price was undisclosed but in order to gain sole ownership, Rykodisc had to undergo a $44 million corporate restructuring. *Billboard* reported the purchase in its October 29 edition, during which it mentioned that Frank had remastered the albums for a second time, including an original two-track master of *We're Only In It For The Money* to replace the overdubbed version. The deal also covered a number of then unissued projects, including *The Lost Episodes* and *Have I Offended Anyone?*.

By her own admission, Gail had evinced little interest in selling the catalogue, but Frank had been adamant. 'He said, "I want you out of this business. I want you to relax and have a good time",' she told Drew Wheeler. 'I very much appreciate that he was so forceful about establishing how he wanted it sold.'11

How has America fared since he left on his last tour? In one of his last interviews, Frank anathematised its politics: 'Hypocrisy is not the special province of any one party or movement. It seems to be rampant everywhere. The Republicans represent pure unbridled evil and the Democrats wish they were Republicans. Up until this [1992] election, they hadn't proved they had the mechanical skills to execute the kind of trickery that makes the Republicans what they are.'12

On April 22, 1994, 14 days after Kurt Cobain achieved nirvana with the aid of a 20-gauge shotgun, Richard Nixon made a slightly more dignified exit. His funeral was an over-emotional orgy of tributes to a dignified statesman of unimpeachable character, rather than that of the only president forced to resign office to avoid impeachment. Hunter S. Thompson redressed the balance in *Rolling Stone*: 'He was a swine of a man and a jabbering dupe of a president. Nixon was so crooked that he needed servants to help him screw his pants on every morning. Even his funeral was illegal. He was queer in the deepest way. His body should have been burned in a trash bin.'13 'Dickie's Such An Asshole' wasn't part of the funerary music.

'There's been an incredible rise in racist and fascist attitudes here,' Frank told Dan Ouellette, 'most them being helped along by the Republican Party. That Republican National Party Convention last summer [1992] was just unbelievable. Even the set decor looked like a Nuremberg rally. Hatemongers like Pat Buchanan and Pat Robertson and the rest of the featured speakers were convinced they were going to win again.'14

When Bill Clinton proved to be as unfortunate a President as Jimmy Carter, the previous Democratic incumbent, the Republicans took their revenge in the 1994 mid-term elections, gaining possession of the Senate and the House of Representatives. In a landslide victory on November 8, Newt Gingrich deposed Democrat Tom Foley to became the first Republican Speaker of the House for several decades. He immediately announced his 'Contract With America', a programme of reforms that prompted his identification by one political commentator as 'a talented reactionary in the vengeful tradition of Gov. George Wallace and Sen. Joseph McCarthy'.15

One of the few Republican aspirants to fail was Oliver North, the man who'd avoided punishment for lying to Congress over the Iran–Contra scandal on a legal technicality. He and Democrat Charles Robb turned the Virginia election into a slanging match. North couldn't even be gracious in defeat, neglecting to wish his opponent well as tradition demanded. Perhaps his disappointment stemmed from the fact that he thought he'd had God on his side, or at least His earthly manifestation in the person of Pat Robertson, failed presidential candidate in 1988 and the dubious hero of 'When The Lie's So Big' and 'Jesus Thinks You're A Jerk'. Robertson regrouped after his failure and formed the Christian Coalition in 1989, dedicated to 'reclaiming America' for the religious right. Its executive director, Ralph Reed, announced after the election that 44 of 52 new Republican House members had been elected with its support. The 'fascists with a cross' are still on the march and they mean to keep their cash from the undeserving poor. But this time around, Frank Zappa won't be there to add his weight to the drive to neuter Gingrich and his self-serving crusaders.

That wasn't the only proof that gullibility and blind allegiance are still mainstays of the American psyche. In the summer of 1994, a film starring Tom Hanks, 'a half-wit's version of the American Dream'16, took an initial $240 million at the American box office. The book by Winston Groom on which it was based satirised the very things that its audience scarfed up as readily and unquestioningly as they did their Diet Coke and popcorn. And when Oscar time came around, Hanks clutched the trophy that confirmed that acting stupid brought rich rewards.

It was 'Valley Girl' gone nationwide. And it begged the question:

Whatever would Frank Zappa have made of *Forrest Gump* ?

NOTES

INTRO
1. *The Wire* 34/5, 1986, "The All American Composer", interview by Steve Lyons and Batya Friedman,
2. *Playboy* 1982, '20 Questions Frank and Moon Unit Zappa', interview by David and Victoria Sheff.

CHAPTER ONE WHAT'S NEW IN BALTIMORE
1. *No Commercial Potential*, David Walley (Dutton, 1972).
2. *Spin*, July 1991, 'Signs Of The Times', interview by Bob Guccione, Jr.
3. BBC-TV interview by Nigel Leigh.
4. *Los Angeles Times Magazine*, October 30, 1988, "Democracy's Pitchman", interview by Joe Morgenstern.
5. ibid. .
6. See Note 1.
7. See Note 2.
8. BBC-TV interview by Nigel Leigh.
9. *Society Pages* 6, 'Ode To Gravity'.
10. BBC-TV interview by Nigel Leigh.
11. *Playboy* April 1993, 'The Playboy Interview', by David Sheff.
12. ibid.
13. *Bat Chain Puller* 'Rock & Roll In The Age Of Celebrity' (St. Martin's Press, 1990), 1988 interview by Kurt Loder
14. BBC-TV interview by Nigel Leigh.
15. *Beat The Boots! Vol. 2* (Foo-eee Records) Scrapbook.
16. *Playboy* April 1993, interview by David Sheff.
17. BBC-TV interview by Nigel Leigh.
18. *Guitarist* June 1993, 'Unholy Mother', interview by David Mead.
19. BBC-TV interview by Nigel Leigh.
20. ibid.
21. *SongTalk* Vol. 4, Issue 1, 'The SongTalk Interview' by Paul Zollo.
22. *Zappa!* (Miller Freeman, 1992), 'The Mother Of All Interviews'.
23. *The Real Frank Zappa Book* by Frank Zappa with Peter Occhiogrosso (Poseidon Press, 1989). This is actually adapted from 'Edgar Varèse, Idol Of My Youth', which Frank wrote for the June 1971 issue of *Stereo Review* .
24. See Note 21.
25. *Frank Zappa In His Own Words*, edited by Miles (Omnibus Press, 1993), unattributed 1970 interview.
26. *Los Angeles Times Magazine* October 30, 1988, 'Democracy's Pitchman', by Joe Morgenstern.
27. BBC-TV interview by Nigel Leigh.
28. See Note 25.
29. BBC-TV interview by Nigel Leigh.
30. See Note 17.
31 See Note 14.
32. *No Commercial Potential*, David Walley (Dutton, 1972).
33. Q December 1989, 'Frank's Wild Years', by Andy Gill.
34. ibid.
35. *Pulse*, August 1993, 'A Rare Interview With Pop's Philosopher-King', interview by Dan Ouellette.
36. See Note 21.
37. ibid.
38. BBC TV interview by Nigel Leigh.
39. See Note 31.
40. *Society Pages* 8, quote from TV interview, 'Class Of The 20th Century', (A&E Network).
41. See Note 22.

42. *Rolling Stone* July 20, 1968, 'The Rolling Stone Interview', by Jerry Hopkins.
43. See Note 14.

CHAPTER TWO CRUISING FOR BURGERS
1. *NME* August 9, 1986, 'Go Van Go!', interview by Kristine McKenna.
2. *Interview*, 'Don Van Vliet Captain Beefheart', interview by John Yau.
3. *Rolling Stone* 38, May 14, 1970, 'The Odyssey Of Captain Beefheart' by Langdon Winner.
4. BBC-TV interview by Nigel Leigh.
5. ibid.
6. *Guitarist* June 1993, 'Unholy Mother', interview by David Mead.
7. BBC-TV interview by Nigel Leigh.
8. *Rolling Stone* July 20, 1968, 'The Rolling Stone Interview', by Jerry Hopkins.
9. See Note 6.
10. BBC-TV interview by Nigel Leigh.
11. *Zappa!* (Miller Freeman, 1992), 'The Mother Of All Interviews'.
12. *T'Mershi Duween*
13. *Society Pages* 10, 'Corrections and Clarifications'.
14. See Note 11.
15. *Beat The Boots! Vol. 2* (Foo-eee Records) Scrapbook
16. BBC-TV interview by Nigel Leigh.
17. ibid.
18. See Note 15.
19. See Note 11.
20. *Goldmine* January 27, 1989, 'Moving On To Phase Three', interview by William Ruhlmann.
21. ibid.
22. ibid.
23. See Note 15.
24. ibid.
25. See Note 20.
26. *T'Mershi Duween*
27. *Pulse!* August 1993, 'A Rare Interview with Pop's Philosopher King', by Dan Ouellette.
28. *Society Pages* 10, 'Corrections and Clarifications', quote from a November 27, 1968 interview by Les Carter on KPPC radio.
29. *No Commercial Potential* by David Walley (Dutton, 1972).
30. ibid.
31. BBC-TV interview by Nigel Leigh.
32. ibid.
33. ibid.
34. ibid.
35. ibid.
36. ibid.
37. See Note 29.
38. *ZigZag* 53, 'The Earliest Days Of The Mothers Just Another Band From L.A.', Unattributed interview in Pete Frame Family Tree.
39. *Rolling Stone* July 20, 1968, 'The Rolling Stone Interview' by Jerry Hopkins.
40. BBC-TV interview by Nigel Leigh.
41. ibid.

CHAPTER THREE PROJECT/OBJECT
1. *Rolling Stone* July 20, 1968, 'The Rolling Stone Interview', by Jerry Hopkins.
2. *ZigZag* 53, 'The Earliest Days Of The Mothers Just Another Band From L.A.' Unattributed interview in Pete Frame Family Tree.
3. *Beat The Boots Vol. 2* Scrapbook.
4. See Note 2.
5. See Note 1.
6. See Note 2
7. *The Age Of Rock: Sounds of the American Cultural Revolution* edited by Jonathan Eisen, 'Zappa And The

Mothers: Ugly Can Be Beautiful', by Sally Kempton. Reprinted from *Village Voice* .
8. Q December 1989, 'Frank's Wild Years', interview by Andy Gill.
9. See Note 1.
10. See Note 2
11. ibid.
12. *No Commercial Potential* by David Walley (Dutton, 1972).
13. *Psychedelic Psounds* written and compiled by Allan Vorda (Borderline Productions, 1994), Bryan Maclean interview February 22-24, 1993 by Neal Skok.
14. *Society Pages* 1, 'Corrections and Clarifications', quoted from booklet notes to *Old Masters, Box One* .
15. *Melody Maker* interview.
16. *The Real Frank Zappa Book* by Frank Zappa with Peter Ochiogrosso (Poseidon Press, 1989).
17. BBC-TV interview by Nigel Leigh.
18. BBC-TV interview by Nigel Leigh.
19. See Note 10.
20. BBC-TV interview by Nigel Leigh.
21. See Note 1.
22. ibid.
23. ibid.
24. ibid.
25. ibid.
26. See Note 2
27. *NME* January 26, 1974, 'Kicks In The Ear Zappa On His Musical Motivation', interview by Jim Smith.
28. Victoria Winston interview, November 1994.
29. ibid.
30. See Note 2.
31. ibid.
32. ibid.
33. See Note 1.
34. See Note 2.
35. See Note 16.
36. Victoria Winston interview, November 1994.
37. *Goldmine* November 26, 1993, 'Living and Dying in L.A.' by Steve Roeser.
38. *The Rock Giants* edited by Pauline Rivelli and Robert Levin (World, 1970), 'Jefferson Airplane' by Frank Kofsky, originally published January 1968.
39. See Note 1.
40. BBC-TV interview by Nigel Leigh.
41. Victoria Winston interview, November 1994.
42. *Rock Giants* edited by Pauline Rivelli and Robert Levin (World Publishing, 1970), 'Frank Zappa: The Mothers Of Invention', interview by Frank Kofsky, September 1967.
43. See Note 2.
44. *When The Music Mattered Rock in the 1960s* by Bruce Pollock (Holt, Rinehart and Winston, 1983).
45. Q July 1993, 'Party On, Dudes!', interview by Mat Snow.
46. *Bill Graham Presents My Life Inside Rock And Out* by Bill Graham and Robert Greenfield (Delta, 1992).
47. ibid.
48. *Los Angeles Free Press* 114 September 16, 1966, original review quoted in Mothers advertisement.

CHAPTER FOUR FREAK OUT!
1. *Beat The Boots Vol. 2* Scrapbook.
2. ibid.
3. *Los Angeles Times Calendar*, August 7, 1966, 'Popular Records: Pass Aspirin, Please', record review by Pete Johnson.
4. *Los Angeles Free Press* 114 September 16, 1966, original review quoted in Mothers advertisement.
5. *The Rock Giants* edited by Pauline Rivelli and Robert Levin, 'Frank Zappa: The Mothers Of Invention', interview by Frank Kofsky, September 1967.
6. *Uncovering The Sixties The Life & Times Of The Underground Press* by Abe Peck (Pantheon, 1985).
7. ibid.
8. See Note 1.

9. ibid.

10. *Los Angeles Free Press* 114 September 16, 1966, *Washington Post* undated, 'Top Tunes', interview by Ronnie Oberman, quoted in Mothers advertisement.

11. *Bat Chain Puller Rock & Roll In The Age Of Celebrity* by Kurt Loder (St. Martin's Press, 1990), interview in Philadelphia, February 1988.

12. *Detroit Free Press* July 15, 1966, 'Look Out Plastic People The Mothers Have Arrived', interview by Reb Foster.

13. ibid.

14. *Rock Wives* by Victoria Balfour (Beach Tree Books, 1986).

15. ibid.

16. ibid.

17. *Billboard 25th Anniversary Supplement* May 19, 1990, 'Just Plain Folks' by Drew Wheeler.

18. *The Real Frank Zappa Book* by Frank Zappa with Peter Ochiogrosso (Poseidon, 1989).

19. *Rock Odyssey A Chronicle Of The Sixties* by Ian Whitcomb (Dolphin, 1983).

20. BBC TV interview by Nigel Leigh.

21. *Record Mirror* December 16, 1967, 'Frank Zappa - the *Hitler* of song, says Eric'

22. BBC-TV interview by Nigel Leigh.

23. *Los Angeles Free Press* 106, July 29, 1966, 'Guambo Is An Act Of Love - Mothers, Happenings, Dancing', by Jerry Hopkins.

24. ibid.

25. *Los Angeles Free Press* 110, August 26, 1966.

26. *Los Angeles Free Press*, review quoted in Mothers advertisement.

27. *ZigZag*, 'Huge Stars Big Hearts And Little Feat The Exploits Of Lowell George', interview by Andy Childs.

28. *Los Angeles Free Press* 113, September 9, 1966.

29. *Los Angeles Free Press* 117, October 14, 1966, 'Tinsel Town' by Sean McGregor..

30. *Los Angeles Free Press* 119, October 28, 1966, 'M.O.I. Literary Review: Mothers Mourn McGregor's Cop Out'.

31. *Los Angeles Free Press* 130, January 13, 1967, 'Why Kids Have Taken Protest Into Streets', interview by Raymond Gruenther.

32. *Los Angeles Free Press* 128, December 30, 1966, 'Zappa Zaps The Big Lie', interview by Lisa Williams.

33. ibid.

34. *ZigZag* 53, 'The Earliest Days Of The Mothers Just Another Band From L.A.', unattributed interview in Pete Frame Family Tree.

35. ibid.

36. BBC-TV interview by Nigel Leigh.

37. See Note 5.

38. *Let It Rock* June 1975, 'What Did You Do In The Revolution, Dada?', by Karl Dallas, quote from 1967 *International Times* article.

39. See Note 5.

40. *Leatherette*, 1972 radio interview with Martin Perlich.

41. *The Lives & Times Of Zappa & The Mothers* (Babylon Books).

42. ibid.

43. ibid.

CHAPTER FIVE LUMPY GRAVY

1. *Playboy* April 1993, 'The Playboy Interview' by David Sheff.

2. *Zappa!* (Miller Freeman, 1992), 'The Mother Of All Interviews'.

3. *Los Angeles Free Press* 134, February 10, 1967, 'Zappa Freakers Return', concert review by Nat Freedland.

4. *Rolling Stone* April 27, 1968, 'Mothers' Lament: They Called Us Entertainment" by Sue C. Clark.

5. ibid.

6. *Broken Record The Inside Story Of The Grammy Awards* by Henry Schipper (Birch Lane Press, 1992). The back of the dust jacket contains an alphabetical list of significant winners, including Alabama, Debby Boone (you remember), The Chipmunks and B.J. Thomas. The list ends with Yes and Pinchas Zukerman. Henry, shame on you.

7. BBC-TV interview by Nigel Leigh.

8. *The Independent On Sunday* July 7, 1991, 'Blinded By The Hype' by Simon Garfield.

9. BBC-TV interview by Nigel Leigh.
10. *Bat Chain Puller Rock & Roll In The Age Of Celebrity* by Kurt Loder (St. Martin's Press, 1990).
11. *Billboard 25th Anniversary Supplement* May 19, 1990, 'Just Plain Folks' by Drew Wheeler.
12. *Guitarist* June 1994, 'The *Guitarist* Interview' by David Mead.
13. *Downbeat* October 30, 1969, 'Frank Zappa: The Mother of Us All', interview by Larry Kart.
14. *The Rock Giants* edited by Pauline Rivelli and Robert Levin (World, 1970), 'Frank Zappa: The Mothers Of Invention', interview by Frank Kofsky, September 1967.
15. *The Wire* 34/5, 'The All American Composer', interview by Steve Lyons and Batya Friedman.
16. *The Age Of Rock Sounds of the American Cultural Revolution* edited by Jonathan Eisen (Vintage, 1969), 'In Person: The Mothers Of Invention' by Doon Arbus. Reprinted from an issue of *Cheetah* .
17. ibid.
18. *Music Maker* October 1967, 'Speaking Of Mothers, Meet Frank', by Valerie Wilmer.
19. BBC-TV interview by Nigel Leigh.
20. ibid.
21. See Note 15.
22. *When The Music Mattered Rock In The 1960s* by Bruce Pollock (Holt, Rinehart Winston, 1983).
23. *Rolling Stone* July 20, 1968, 'The Rolling Stone Interview' by Jerry Hopkins.
24. See Note 13.
25. ibid.
26. See Note 22.
27. See Note 22.
28. *Goldmine* January 27, 1989, 'Moving On To Phase Three', interview by William Ruhlmann.
29. See Note 13.
30. See Note 27.
31. *Music Technology* February 1987, 'Father Of Invention', interview by Rick Davies.
32. See Note 9.
33. See Note 11.

CHAPTER SIX DEAD GIRLS IN LONDON
1. *Melody Maker* June 24, 1967, 'Mothers Here In October'.
2. *Melody Maker* August 26, 1967, 'Meet the Boss Mother sussing out Britain', by Nick Jones.
3. *Melody Maker* September 2, 1967, 'Zappa Must Be Joking!'.
4. ibid., 'The Raver'.
5. *Daily Sketch* August 22, 1967, 'My World of Pop' by Ann Nightingale, 'Why this bearded Mother isn't flower powered'.
6. *The Observer Review* August 20, 1967, 'Advertising is beautiful'.
7. *Intro* September 23, 1967, 'In It For The Money'.
8. *Record Mirror* September 2, 1967, 'Frank Zappa of the Mothers of Invention - the Hard Guy who doesn't radiate love. . .', interview by David Griffiths.
9. *Melody Maker* August 26, 1967, 'Meet A Mother!'
10. *Daily Sketch* September 19, 1967, 'Musically It's A Freak-Out'.
11. *The Sun* September 18, 1967, 'Wild'.
12. *Evening News* September 19, 1967, "Mother' Frank settles it - Yes, his hair is real'.
13. *Sunday Mirror* September 24, 1967, 'Mothers Stun 'Em', concert review by Bernard McElwaine.
14. *Melody Maker* September 30, 1967, 'Mothers - Almost A Freak Out, Not A Love In, Definitely A Send-Up!', concert review by Nick Jones.
15. *NME* September 30, 1967, 'Mothers Woo In-Crowd', concert review by 'J.W.'.
16. BBC-TV interview by Nigel Leigh.
17. ibid.
18. *T'Mershi Duween* 38, 'Miles Of Zappa: Interview 30.5.69, Part One', interview by Miles..
19. *The Age Of Rock: Sounds of the American Cultural Revolution* edited by Jonathan Eisen, 'Ugly Can Be Beautiful' by Sally Kempton. Reprinted from *Village Voice* .
20. ibid.
21. *Saturday Evening Post* January 13, 1968, 'Does This Mother Know Best?' by W.H. Manville.
22. *Musician* February 1994, 'Frank Zappa', Interviews by Scott Isler, Jim Macnie, Kristine McKenna, Mark Rowland, Roy Trakin and Josef Woodard.
23. *Late Show Special*, BBC-2 March 11, 1993.

24. *Los Angeles Times* March 18, 1968, 'More Polemics From Pop Satirist', record review by Pete Johnson.
25. *Melody Maker* June 15, 1968, 'Zappa masterminds a Mothers' masterpiece', record review by Bob Houston.
26. *The Rock Giants* edited by Pauline Rivelli and Robert Levin (World, 1970), 'My Brother Is an Italian Mother' by C.R. Zappa, originally published August 1968.
27. ibid.
28. *Newsweek* June 3, 1968, 'Zapping With Zappa'.
29. *Rolling Stone* June 22, 1968, record review by Jim Miller.
30. *Rolling Stone* July 20, 1968, 'The Rolling Stone Interview' by Jerry Hopkins.
31. *Beat The Boots Vol. 2* Scrapbook.

CHAPTER SEVEN OUR BIZARRE RELATIONSHIP

1. *Melody Maker* October 5, 1968, 'Reviled, revered Mother Superior', interview by Chris Welch.
2. *Rolling Stone* February 15, 1969, 'The Plaster Casters'.
3. ibid.
4. *Evening Standard* September 24, 1968.
5. *The Guardian* October 14, 1968, 'Chief Mother of Invention' by Stacy Waddy.
6. *Der Abend* October 17, 1968, 'The Toys Are All Broken' by Helmut Kopetzky. Translated by Norman Darwen.
7. *ZigZag* 3, 'ZigZag Unzips Frank Zappa Interviewed by Dick Lawson at the Royal Albert Hall.
8. *Daily Sketch* November 5, 1968. The review continued, "Or the Incredible String Band - two musicians incredible indeed, from Scotland. They're knocking everyone out here and in America."
9. *Mojo* March 1994, 'The Grand Wazoo', interview by Miles.
10. *Beat The Boots Vol. 2* Scrapbook.
11. *Downbeat* October 30, 1969, 'Frank Zappa: The Mother Of Us All', by Larry Kart.
12. *I'm With The Band Confessions Of A Groupie* by Pamela Des Barres (William Morrow, 1987).
13. See Note 2.
14. ibid.
15. ibid.
16. See Note 11.
17. *ZigZag*, 'The answer is blowing in the wind: "I think they're going to have to get more kites"', interview by Ben Edmunds.
18. ibid.
19. *Zappa!* (Miller Freeman, 1992), 'The Mother Of All Interviews'.
20. BBC-TV interview by Nigel Leigh.
21. Unattributed interview, November 8, 1969.
22. See Note 7.
23. See Note 17.
24. See Note 9.
25. *Days In The Life Voices From the English Underground 1961-1971* by Jonathon Green (William Heinemann, 1988).
26. *Daily Sketch* May 28 1969, 'Mr. Zappa didn't have the LSE rolling in the aisles, just Julie Felix sitting there'. The opportunistic Miss Felix was a folk singer who claimed to be an old friend of Frank's. "I wanted to keep out of the limelight so I sat on the floor," she said.
27. *Daily Mirror* June 7, 1969.
28. *Daily Mail* June 5, 1969, 'ZAPPA Your mother couldn't be more wrong about him' by Virginia Ironside.
29. *Beat Instrumental* July 1969, 'Frank Zappa Father Of The Mothers', interview by 'M.H.'.
30. ibid.
31. See Note 11.
32. See Note 7.
33. See Note 30.
34. See Note 7.
35. See Note 30.
36. See Note 11.
37. *NME* December 5, 1970, 'Metamorphosis Of Frank Zappa', interview by Richard Green.
38. *Goldmine* January 27, 1989, 'Moving On To Phase Three', interview by William Ruhlmann.

CHAPTER EIGHT SHUT UP 'N PLAY YOUR GUITAR
1. *NME* February 1, 1975, 'This here's LOWELL GEORGE', 'excited gibbering' by Pete Erskine.
2. *ZigZag* 3, 'ZigZag Unzips Zappa', interview by Dick Lawson.
3. *Downbeat* May 1, 1969, 'Caught In The Act', concert review by Alan Heineman.
4. *Rolling Stone* October 18, 1969, 'Mothers' Day Has Finally Come', by Jerry Hopkins.
5. unattributed interview, published November 8, 1969.
6. *Music Technology*, February 1987, 'Father Of Invention', interview by Rick Davies.
7. *Rolling Stone* March 7, 1970, review of *Hot Rats* by Lester Bangs.
8. BBC-TV interview by Nigel Leigh.
9. *No Commercial Potential* (E.P. Dutton & Co. Inc., 1972).
10. ibid.
11. *Goldmine* January 27,1989, 'Moving On To Phase Three', interview by William Ruhlmann.
12. *NME* February 27, 1970, 'You Don't Always Eat If You Only Play For Fun', interview by Richard Green.
13. unattributed interview, published November 8, 1969.
14. *The Hollywood Reporter*, January 21, 1970, 'Sound Track' by Kathy Orloff.
15. *NME* December 5, 1970, 'Metamorphosis Of Frank Zappa', interview by Richard Green.
16. *Friends* July 10, 1970, 'Hot Waxx!.
17. See Note 10.
18. See Note 14.
19. See Note 13.
20. *Rolling Stone* July 9, 1970, 'What Zappa Did To Zubin Mehta', concert review by David Felton.
21. *Zappa!* (Miller Freeman, 1992), 'The Mother Of All Interviews'.
22. ibid.
23. *Rolling Stone* September 16, 1971, 'Kaylan: Mother Was A Turtle', interview by Harold Bronson.
24. *Society Pages* 10, 'Happy Together, Part Two', interview by Co de Kloet.
25. *Friends* July 10, 1970, 'Hot Waxx!'.
26. See Note 13.
27. *Evening News* July 1, 1970, 'Peter Cole's Beat'.
28. *NME* July 4, 1970, 'Shrewd, But With A Lot Of Heart', interview by Richard Green and Allan McDougall.
29. *Musician* November 1991, 'Poetic Justice - Frank Zappa Puts Us In Our Place', interview by Matt Resnicoff.

CHAPTER NINE WEASELS RIPPED MY FLESH
1 *Rolling Stone* November 14, 1991, '100 Classic Album Covers'.
2. *Disc* November 28, 1970.
3. *NME* December 5, 1970, 'Metamorphosis Of Frank Zappa', interview by Richard Green.
4. *NME* December 5, 1970, 'Zappa at his bizarre best', concert review by Roy Carr.
5. See Note 3.
6. *Sunday Mirror* January 10, 1971, 'Let It Zip, Says Zappa'.
7. *NME* January 16, 1971, 'Establishment Versus The Underground', report by Richard Green.
8. *Born Under A Bad Sign* by Tony Palmer (William Kimber, 1970) .
9. *The Observer* March 28, 1971, 'Frank Zappa, The Royal Philharmonic And Me...', Tony Palmer 'reports on 10 apocalyptic days in which (*200 Motels*) was made'.
10. *Rolling Stone* September 16, 1971, 'Kaylan: Mother Was A Turtle', interview by Harold Bronson.
11. *Rolling Stone* December 21, 1972, 'Keith Moon: One-Man Wrecking Crew', interview by Jerry Hopkins.
12. *T'Mershi Duween* 37, 'Miles Of Zappa', interview conducted November 14, 1970 by Miles.
13. *The Times* February 9, 1971, 'Obscenity in banned pop show is denied', by Peter Waymark.
14. *The Daily Telegraph* February 10, 1971, 'Orchestra used by pop group 'as cover for filth', by James Wightman.
15. ibid.
16. See Note 13.
17. *Daily Express* February 9, 1971, ''Too dirty' pop group banned at Albert Hall', by David Wigg and Norman Luck.

18. *NME* February 27, 1971, 'You Don't Always Eat If You Only Play For Fun', interview by Richard Green.

19. *Leatherette*, bootleg album, including radio interview by Martin Perlich.

20. *NME* November 27, 1971, 'Frank Talking', interview by Roy Carr.

21. See Note 10.

22. *Rolling Stone* September 30, 1971, record review by Lester Bangs.

23. *NME* December 4, 1971, 'Frank talking about his next film', interview by Roy Carr.

24. *Society Pages* 4, 'A walk down memory lane with Dick Barber', interview by Bruce Burnett.

25. See Note 10.

26. *Los Angeles Times* October 30, 1971, "'Motels' a Rock 'n' Roll Tour on Film", review by Robert Hilburn.

27. *New York Times* November 11, 1971, 'Frank Zappa's Surrealist '200 Motels'', review by Vincent Canby.

28. *NME* November 6, 1971, 'He directed it but ... Tony Palmer Slams Zappa 'Motels' Film'.

29. See Note 20.

30. ibid.

CHAPTER TEN SMOKE ON THE WATER

1. *Zappa!* (Miller Freeman, 1992), 'The Mother Of All Interviews'.

2. *Society Pages* 11, 'Happy Together, Part Three', interview by Co de Kloet.

3. *Q* December 1989, 'Duh duh durh, duh duh *du durrh!*', article by Mat Snow..

4. ibid.

5. BBC-TV interview by Nigel Leigh.

6. *Society Pages* 4, 'A walk down memory lane with Dick Barber', interview by Bruce Burnett.

7. *Musician* February 1994, 'Frank Zappa 1940-1993', interviews by Scott Isler, Jim Macnie, Kristine McKenna, Mark Rowland, Roy Trakin and Josef Woodard.

8. Interview with Howard Thompson, 1993.

9. *Musician* February 1994, 'Frank Zappa 1940-1993', interviews by Scott Isler, Jim Macnie, Kristine McKenna, Mark Rowland, Roy Trakin and Josef Woodard.

10. *Daily Express* December 11, 1971, 'Pop star k.o.'d in attack', by Express Staff Reporter.

11. *Daily Mirror* December 14, 1971, 'Injured pop star is out for a month'.

12. *Society Pages* 11, 'Happy Together, Part Three', interview by Co de Kloet.

13. *Musician* February 1994, 'Frank Zappa 1940-1993'.

14. *Daily Mail* January 7, 1972, 'Forced rest'.

15. *NME* February 5, 1972, 'Forget the leg a while. It's ZAPPA on rock, porn and blues', interview by Keith Altham.

16. *NME* February 12, 1972, 'Zappa on Death, Rock Writers, Money', interview by Keith Altham.

17. *NME* February 12, 1972, 'Svengali Zappa and a horrible freak called Beefheart', interview by Roy Carr.

18. ibid.

19. *Daily Telegraph* March 20, 1972, 'Zappa sues over theatre attack'.

20. *NME* November 30, 1974, 'How to complete the subbing and layout of a very long Frank Zappa Lookin' Back', 'An atonal extravagonzo by Charles Shaar Murray'.

21. *Leatherette*, bootleg album including radio interview by Martin Perlich.

22. Internet transcript of October 22, 1988 interview by Bob Marshall.

23. See Note 12.

24. *NME* June 3, 1972, 'Turning Turtle Zappa's men branch out', interview by Roy Carr.

25. *NME* September 1, 1973, 'Penguins in bondage and other perversions', interview by Charles Shaar Murray.

26. *Disc* September 2, 1972, 'Zappa – Mother of 20', interview by Caroline Boucher.

27. *NME* September 2, 1972, 'Mothers Day Fearless Frank tells what he'll lay on you at the Oval concert', interview by Danny Holloway.

28. See Note 26.

29. See Note 27.

30. *NME* September 2, 1972, 'Everything you always wanted to know about the Mothers... but were afraid to ask.' article by Ian McDonald.

31. *Evening News* September 14, 1972, 'Susan says sorry to Frank'.

32. *The Road Goes On Forever* (Elm Tree Books/Hamish Hamilton, 1982), 'The Foulk Brothers: Pop Promoting Blues', by Philip Norman.

33. ibid.

34. *Viva! Zappa* (Omnibus Press, 1985), text quoted by Dominique Chevalier.

35. ibid.

CHAPTER ELEVEN OVERNITE SENSATION

1. *NME* September 1, 1973, 'Penguins in bondage and other perversions', interview by Charles Shaar Murray.

2. *NME* April 17, 1976, 'At last the truth can be told FRANK ZAPPA has no underwear', interview by 'Cherry Ripe'.

3. *Washington Star News* November 11, 1972, 'Zappa Genius on Horn', concert review by Richard Harrington.

4. *Keyboard* April 1994, 'The Zappa Legacy', interview by Robert L. Doerschuk.

5. *Rolling Stone* July 4, 1974, 'Zappa: Continuity Is The Mothers' Mother', interview by Barry Hansen.

6. *NME* August 25, 1973, 'Godmother', interview by Charles Shaar Murray.

7. BBC-TV interview by Nigel Leigh.

8. See Note 2.

9. *Rolling Stone* December 20,1973, record review by Arthur Schmidt.

10. *NME* September 1, 1973, record review by Charles Shaar Murray.

11. *The Lives & Times Of Zappa & The Mothers* (Babylon Books), 'Dirty Frank', reviewed by 'CR'.

12. *Crawdaddy* December 1973, record review by Noe Goldwasser.

13. *Zappa!* (Miller Freeman, 1992), The Mother Of All Interviews'.

14. *Musician* February 1994, 'Frank Zappa 1940-1933'.

15. ibid.

16. *NME* August 25, 1973, 'Godmother' and *NME* September 1, 1973, 'Penguins in bondage and other perversions', interview by Charles Shaar Murray.

17. *NME* September 22, 1973, concert review by Charles Shaar Murray.

18. *The Sun* August 20, 1973, 'Zapped!'.

19. *NME* January 26, 1974, 'Kicks in the ear', interview by Jim Smith.

20. See Note 13.

21. *Los Angeles Herald-Examiner* December 11, 1973, 'Zappa's rock for 'True Freaks'', concert review by Robert A Kemnitz.

22. *Variety* December 11, 1973.

23. *Guitar Player* January 1977, 'One Size Fits All', interview by Steve Rosen.

24. *Rolling Stone* June 6, 1974, record review by Gordon Fletcher.

25. *Rolling Stone* August 1, 1974, Random Note.

26. *Goldmine* January 27, 1989, 'Moving On To Phase Three', interview by William Ruhlmann.

27. *NME* April 6, 1974, 'The unsightly debris of Francis Vincent Zappa', record review by Ian McDonald.

28. *NME* May 25, 1974, 'Mothers' Day memories', interview by Barbara Charone.

29. *Rock Wives* (Beech Tree Books, 1986), by Victoria Balfour.

30. See Note 5.

31. ibid.

32. ibid.

33. *NME* September 14, 1974, 'The Great Brassiere Conspiracy'.

34. ibid.

35. *Evening News* October 2, 1974, 'Zappa – is it goodbye for ever?, Pop column by John Blake.

36. *NME* October 5, 1974, 'Relax, Frank. We ain't no liggers. A few of us just came to join in...And to help you finish up any leftover wine an' stuff', article by Charles Shaar Murray.

37. *Melody Maker* October 5, 1974, 'Monsieur Zappa's rock circus', article by Allan Jones.

38. See Note 4.

39. See Note 26.

CHAPTER TWELVE ONE SIZE FITS ALL

1. *NME* November 30, 1974, 'How to complete the subbing and lay out of a very long Frank Zappa Looking Back' by Charles Shaar Murray.

2. *Melody Maker*, November 9, 1974, 'Caught in the Act'.

3. *Society Pages* 7, 'He's A Human Being. He Has Emotions, Just Like Us', Pt. 2, interview by Den Simms and Rob Samler.

4. *NME* April 26, 1975, "What is a groupie?' asked his Lordship', Report by Mick Farren.

5. *Guitar Player* January 1977. 'One Size Fits All', interview by Steve Rosen.

6. *Keyboard* April 1994, 'The Zappa Legacy' by Robert L. Doerschuk.

7. *Musician* February 1994, 'Frank Zappa 1940-1993', interviews conducted by Scott Isler, Jim Macnie, Kristine McKenna, Mark Rowland, Roy Trakin and Josef Woodward.

8. ibid.

9. *T'Mershi Duween* 28, 'One More Time For The World', interview by Andy Greenaway.

10. BBC-TV interview by Nigel Leigh.

11. See Note 4.

12. *Rolling Stone* July 3, 1975, 'Zappa and the Captain Cook'.

13. ibid.

14. See Note 4.

15. ibid.

16. *Evening Standard* April 16, 1975, 'Rock star Zappa defends his lyrics'.

17. *Evening News* April 16, 1975, 'I won't hear Zappa record, says Judge'.

18. *Let It Rock* June 1975, 'The Truth - The Whole Truth - And Nothing But The Cheeseburger', court report by Michael Gray.

19. *Evening Standard* April 17, 1975, 'Zappa case: 'Pop is 80 p.c. sex' by Gordon Corner.

20. *Daily Mirror* April 19, 1975, 'Pop, Sex . .And That Man Zappa'.

21. *Daily Mirror* April 22, 1975, 'The Zany World of Zappa'.

22. *The Guardian* April 30, 1975.

23. *The Times* June 11, 1975, 'No damages for pop star over cancelled show'.

24. *Daily Mirror* June 11, 1975, '£20,000 shocker for a rocker'.

25. *Rolling Stone* July 3, 1975, 'Zappa and the Captain Cook' by Steve Weitzman.

26. ibid.

27. BBC-TV interview by Nigel Leigh.

28. ibid.

29. See Note 3.

30. *Melody Maker* July 12, 1975, 'One Size fits some'.

31. *NME* July 19, 1975, '... but Frank - you made the pants too long'.

32. *Guitar Player* February 1983, 'Not Exactly Duane Allman', interview by Tom Mulhern.

33. *The Wire* 34/5, 'The All American Composer', interview by Steve Lyons and Batya Friedman.

34. *NME* November 22, 1975, 'Frank & The Captain The Legal Pitfalls Of Having Fun', by Miles.

35. *T'Mershi Duween* 28, 'One More Time For The World', interview by Andy Greenaway.

36. ibid.

37. See Note 3.

38. BBC-TV interview by Nigel Leigh.

39. ibid.

40. *T'Mershi Duween* 43, 'Zapparap Number 29 - The Songs 3', compiled by Andy Greenaway.

41. *NME* April 17, 1976, 'At Last The Truth Can Be Told FRANK ZAPPA Has No Underwear', by Cherry Ripe. Congratulations, honey.

42. ibid.

43. *NME* April 26, 1975, "What is a groupie?' asked his Lordship', Report by Mick Farren.

44. See Note 42.

CHAPTER THIRTEEN ZOOT ALLURES

1. *Guitar Player* January 1977, 'One Size Fits All'.

2. ibid.

3. *Downbeat* May 18, 1978, 'Garni du Jour, Lizard King Peotry and Slime,' interview by Tim (call me cravat) Schneckloth.

4. *Daily Mirror* February 14, 1977, 'Sheer Torture but Zappa has it all taped'.

5. *NME* March 5 1977, 'O.K. Frank - Let It Roll . . . The Frank Zzzzzzzappa Snore-In,' interview (of sorts) by Chris Salewicz.

6. ibid.

7. *Guitar Player* January 1977, 'One Size Fits All', interview by Steve Rosen.

8. ibid.

9. BBC-TV interview by Nigel Leigh.

10. *NME* December 4, 1976, 'Any Resemblance Is Purely Conceptual', interview by Miles.
11. *NME* November 20, 1976, 'Beefheart Discovers 'World's Greatest Band' Sensation', interview by Miles.
12. See Note 10.
13. *Keyboard* April 1994, 'The Zappa Legacy', interview by Robert L. Doerschuk.
14. ibid.
15. *NME* August 21, 1976, 'The Boy With The Lobotomy', interview by Chris Salewicz.
16. *T'Mershi Duween* 28, 'One More Time For The World', interview by Andy Greenaway.
17. See Note 10.
18. ibid.
19. *Sounds* September 9, 1978, 'I hate playing in England', interview by Hugh Fielder.
20. ibid.
21. *Downbeat* May 18, 1978, 'Garni Du Jour, Lizard King Poetry And Slime', interview by Tim Schneckloth.
22. See Note 13.
23. BBC-TV interview by Nigel Leigh.
24. *NME* December 4, 1976, 'Any Resemblance Is Purely Conceptual', interview by Miles.
25. See Note 25.
26. *The Times* February 11, 1977, concert review by Clive Bennett.
27. *NME* February 19, 1977, 'Torture Mama & The Open Brain', concert review by Miles.
28. ibid.
29. See Note 5.
30. *NME* May 7, 1977, 'Zappa sues previous licensees of Rainbow'.
31. *Guitar* February 1994, 'Frank's Garage, Close encounters with five guitarists of the Zappa kind', interview by H.P. Newquist.
32. *Keyboard* June 1980, 'Little Band We Used To Play In', interview by Michael Davis.
33. ibid.
34. ibid.
35. See Note 13.
36. See Note 21.

CHAPTER FOURTEEN LATHER

1. *Society Pages* 2, 'They're Doing The Interview Of The Century', by Eric Buxton, Rob Samler and Den Simms.
2. *NME* January 28, 1978, 'Stern Words In Knightsbridge', interview by Paul Rambali.
3. ibid.
4. *Nuggets* April/May 1977, 'Zappa On Air', interview by Jim Ladd.
5. See Note 2.
6. *Sunday Express* January 29, 1978, 'Zappa Group In Hotel Uproar'.
7. *NME* September 23, 1978, 'Stones Harpist Located Down Paris Subway', interview by Phillipe Manoeuvre.
8. *Sounds*, September 9, 1978, 'I hate playing in England', interview by Hugh Fielder.
9. *NME* April 22, 1978, advert for *Zappa In New York* .
10. *Keyboard* June 1980, 'Little Band We Used To Play In', interview by Michael Davis.
11. ibid.
12. *Guitar* January 1994, 'Brothers Of Invention, Steve Vai as interviewed by Adrian Belew'.
13. *T'Mershi Duween* 28, 'One More Time For The World', interview by Andy Greenaway.
14. See Note 10.
15. Frank Zappa interview by Christopher Cathman.
16. *NME* July 22, 1978, 'The Monk On Zappa's Back', interview by Wayne Manor.
17. See Note 8.
18. ibid.
19. *Downbeat* May 18, 1978, "Garni Du Jour, Lizard King Poetry and Slime', interview by Tim Schneckloth.
20. See Note 8.
21. *NME* September 30, 1978, 'Aunt Meat?', record review by Ian Penman.
22. *Guitar* February 1994, 'Frank's Garage, Close encounters with five guitarists of the Zappa kind',

interview by H.P. Newquist.

23. ibid.

24. See Note 19.

25. *T'Mershi Duween* 28, 'One More Time For The World', interview by Andy Greenaway.

26. *A Definitive Tribute To Frank Zappa*, (Miller Freeman, Inc., 1994), 'The Clonemeister Speaks', interview by Ernie Rideout.

27. *Keyboard* April 1994, 'The Zappa Legacy', interview by Robert L. Doerschuk.

28. ibid.

29. BBC-TV interview by Nigel Leigh.

30. *Evening Standard* January 24, 1978, 'Zap, zap, Zappa is back in town!', interview by James Johnson.

CHAPTER FIFTEEN SHEIK YERBOUTI

1. *NME* February 1979, 'Overly sub-standard', record review by Nick Kent.

2. *The Wire* 34/5, 'The All American Composer', interview by Steve Lyons and Batya Friedman.

3. *Playboy* April 1993, 'The Playboy Interview', by David Sheff.

4. *The Observer* September 3, 1979, 'Frankly a freak', interview by Charles Shaar Murray.

5. See Note 3.

6. BBC-TV interview by Nigel Leigh.

7. ibid.

8. *Keyboard* April 1994, 'The Zappa Legacy', interview by Robert L. Doerschuk.

9. See Note 3.

10. *NME* February 24, 1979, 'A tasty change from so-so soup', concert review by Mark Ellen.

11. BBC-TV interview by Nigel Leigh.

12. ibid.

13. *Bam* October 5, 1979, 'Frank Zappa Vs. The World!', interview by Michael Branton..

14. BBC-tv interview by Nigel Leigh.

15. *Guitarist* June 1993, 'Unholy Mother', interview by David Mead.

16. *Keyboard* June 1980, 'Little Band We Used To Play In', interview by Michael Davis.

17. *Rock Wives* (Beech Tree Books, 1986) by Victoria Balfour.

18. *Village Voice* January 7, 1980, 'Zapped Again', film review by Tom Carson. Reprinted in *Society Pages* 4.

19. *Society Pages* 4, 'A walk down memory lane with Dick Barber', interview by Bruce Burnett.

20. See Note 16.

21. ibid.

CHAPTER SIXTEEN UTILITY MUFFIN RESEARCH KITCHEN

1. BBC-TV interview by Nigel Leigh.

2. *Guitar Player* January 1977, 'One Size Fits All', interview by Steve Rosen.

3. ibid.

4. *Keyboard* June 1980, 'Little Band We Used To Play In', interview by Michael Davis.

5. *Keyboard* February 1987, 'Sample This!' by Jim Aikin & Bob Doerschuk.

6. *Downbeat* January 13, 1977, 'Electronic Projections', compiled by Arnold Jay Smith/Bob Henschen.

7. *Downbeat* May 18, 1978, 'Garni du Jour, Lizard King Poetry and Slime', interview by Tim Schneckloth.

8. ibid.

9. *T'Mershi Duween* 20, 'A Mars A Day...', interview by Axel Wunsch and Aad Hoogesteger.

10. *T'Mershi Duween* 28, 'Tink Walks Amok: The Arthur Barrow Interview', by Slev Uunofski, Tom Brown and Tom Troccoli.

11. *Pulse!* August 1993, 'A Rare Interview With Pop's Philosopher-King', by Dan Ouellette.

12. *The Guardian Weekend* May 15, 1993, 'FRANK, Fearless and still fighting', interview by Alex Kershaw.

13. *Creem* November 1982, 'Only In It For The Money? Frank & Moon Zappa Go AM', interview by Michael Goldberg.

14. *Metal Hammer* Vol. 5 No. 24, Nov. 19-Dec. 2, 1990, 'History Of A Hero', interview by Robert 'Arie' Heeg.

15. *Guitar Player* February 1983, 'Not Exactly Duane Allman', interview by Tom Mulhern.

16. *Zappa!* (Miller Freeman, 1992), 'The Mother Of All Interviews'.

17. See Note 14.

18. *Guitar* February 1994, 'Frank's Garage Close encounters with five guitarists of the Zappa king', interview by H.P. Newquist.

19. *Musician* November 1991, 'Poetic Justice Frank Zappa Puts Us In Our Place', interview by Matt Resnicoff.

20. *Guitar* January 1994, 'Brothers Of Invention Steve Vai as interviewed by Adrian Belew'.

21. *Zappa!* (Miller Freeman, 1992), 'How It All Works Gail Zappa', interview by Don Menn.

22. *Society Pages* 7, 'He's A Human Being. He has Emotions, Just Like Us Part 2', interview by Den Simms and Rob Samler.

23. *Playboy* November 1982, '20 Questions: Frank and Moon Unit Zappa', interview by David and Victoria Sheff.

24. *Society Pages* 6, 'Ode To Gravity', radio interview April 15, 1991 by Charles Amirkhanian.

25. BBC-TV interview by Nigel Leigh.

26. See Note 16.

27. See Note 15.

CHAPTER SEVENTEEN DROWNING WITCH

1. *MOJO* 4, March 1994, 'The Addams Family', interview by Dave Dimartino.

2. *Perfect Pitch A Life Story* by Nicholas Slonimsky (Oxford University Press, 1988).

3. *Zappa!* (Miller Freeman, 1992), interview by Don Menn.

4. See Note 2.

5. *Society Pages* 3, 'They're Doing The Interview Of The Century', by Den Simms, Rob Samler and Eric Buxton.

6. *Society Pages* 4, 'Didja Know...?', interview with 'Charlie'', Goteburg, Sweden, May 10, 1982.

7. *Guitar Player* February 1983, 'Not Exactly Duane Allman', interview by Tom Mulhern.

8. ibid.

9. *Society Pages* 9, 'Interview From Iceland (Where They Love The Grand Wazoo)', radio interview March 23, 1992 by Jon Benediktsson and Kolbeinn Arnason.

10. See Note 7.

11. *The Observer* September 3, 1989, 'Frankly a freak', interview by Charles Shaar Murray.

12. *Creem* November 1982, 'Only In It For The Money? Frank & Moon Zappa go AM', interview by Michael Goldberg.

13. ibid.

14. ibid.

15. See Note 7.

16. *Playboy* November 1982, '20 Questions: Frank and Moon Unit Zappa', interview by David and Victoria Sheff.

17. ibid.

18. See Note 7.

19. ibid.

20. ibid.

21. ibid.

22. *The Guardian* January 11, 1983, 'The father of invention', interview by Robin Denselow.

23. See Note 7.

24. *Daily Express* January 7, 1983, 'Zappa takes the dance out of ballet'.

25. *NME* January 15, 1983, 'Frank goes straight', interview by Gavin Martin.

26. *T'Mershi Duween* 16, 'He's conducting the interview of. . . a lunchtime?!', interview by Andy Greenaway.

27. See Note 22.

28. *Zappa!* (Miller Freeman, 1992), Kent Nagano, interviewed by Don Menn.

29. *Daily Mail* January 12, 1983, 'Zappa keeps the hippies hushed'.

30. *The Times* January 12, 1983, 'In search of the composer', concert review by Richard Williams.

31. BBC TV interview by Nigel Leigh.

32. See Note 28.

33. ibid.

34. See Note 22.

35. ibid.

36. *Music Technology* February 1987, 'Father of Invention', interview by Rick Davies.

37. *Guitarist* June 1993, 'Unholy Mother', interview by David Mead.

38. *Discoveries* 82, March 1995, 'The Knack' interview by Paul Gabriel.

39. *Society Pages* 2, "They're Doing The Interview Of The Century Part 2', interview by Den Simms, Rob Samler and Eric Buxton.
40. *T'Mershi Duween* 28, 'Tink Walks Amok: The Arthur Barrow Interview', by Slev Uunofski, Tom Brown and Tom Troccoli.

CHAPTER EIGHTEEN SYSTEMS OF EDGES
1. *The Real Frank Zappa Book* by Frank Zappa with Peter Occhiogrosso (Poseidon Press, 1989).
2. *Music Technology* February 1987, 'Father Of Invention', interview by Rick Davies.
3. *Guitar Player* February 1983, 'Not Exactly Duane Allman', interview by Tom Mulhern.
4. ibid.
5. *T'Mershi Duween* 28, 'Tink Walks Amok - The Arthur Barrow Interview' by Slev Uunofski, Tom Brown and Tom Troccoli.
6. *Sound On Sound* February 1987, 'Frank Zappa Jazz From Hell', interview by Paul Gilby.
7. See Note 2.
8. See Note 6.
9. ibid.
10. *Zappa!* (Miller Freeman, 1992), 'The Mother Of All Interviews'.
11. BBC-TV interview by Nigel Leigh.
12. *Keyboard* February 1987, 'Sample This!', by Jim Aikin & Bob Doerschuk.
13. See Note 1.
14. *Sunday Times Magazine* February 1985, 'Boulez And The Well Tempered 4X', by Norman Lebrecht.
15. See Note 10.
16. ibid.
17. See Note 1.
18. *Society Pages* 2, "They're Doing The Interview Of The Century', by Den Simms, Rob Samler and Eric Buxton.
19. See Note 12.
20. See Note 18.
21. ibid.
22. *Guitar Player* February 1983, 'Not Exactly Duane Allman', interview by Tom Mulhern.
23. *Zappa!* (Miller Freeman, 1992), 'How It All Works Gail Zappa' by Don Menn.
24. See Note 1.

CHAPTER NINETEEN THING-FISH
1. *The Times Saturday Review* August 8, 1992, 'Victims Of A Diseased Society' by Charlie Smith.
2. ibid.
3. *Today* January 9, 1987, 'Listen With Mother How Zappa swapped freaking out for speaking out' by Jonathan Ashby and David Thornton.
4. *Society Pages* 4, 'Speak Up, Ike, An' 'Spress Yourself', interview by Matthew Galaher.
5. *Keyboard* February 1987, 'Sample This!', by Jim Aikin and Bob Doerschuk.
6. *The Guardian* April 20, 1988, 'Don't wait for the cuckoo', interview by Ed Vulliamy.
7. *Rolling Stone* September 12, 1985, 'Furore over rock lyrics intensifies', by Robert Love.
8. *Society Pages* 3, 'Zappa On Censorship', radio interview June 21, 1990 by J.B. Peterson for station KPFK.
9. See Note 6.
10.. *The Real Frank Zappa Book* by Frank Zappa with Peter Ochiogrosso (Poseidon Press, 1989).
11. ibid.
12. See Note 9.
13. See Note 7
14. *Zappa!* (Miller Freeman, 1992), 'The Mother Of All Interviews'.
15. *Musician* November 1991, 'Poetic Justice Frank Zappa Puts Us In Our Place', interview by Matt Resnicoff.
16. See Note 14.
17. *Playboy* April 1993, 'The Playboy Interview', by David Sheff.
18. *Society Pages* 11, 'The Yellow Shark History In The Making'.
19. *Billboard* May 19, 1990, '25th Anniversary Supplement', 'Zappa: Leading the way in digital & CD technologies' by Jim Bessman.
20. ibid.

21. ibid.

22. *Relix* Vol. 21, No. 2, 'Forever Frank' by Roger Len Smith.

23. *Guitar World* July 1987, 'The Importance Of Being Dweezil', by Bud Scoppa.

24. See Note 5.

25. *Sound On Sound* February 1987, 'Frank Zappa Jazz From Hell' by Paul Gilby.

26. ibid.

27. See Note 14.

28. See Note 5.

29. See Note 14.

30. *Music Technology* February 1987, 'Father Of Invention', interview by Rick Davies.

31. See Note 23.

32. See Note 28.

CHAPTER TWENTY ONCE AGAIN, WITHOUT THE NET

1. *Billboard 25th Anniversary Supplement* , May 19, 1990, 'We Are What We Watch' by Drew Wheeler.

2. ibid.

3. *Guitar World* April 1987, 'Zappa's Inferno', by Noe Goldwasser.

4. *Song Talk* Vol.4, Issue 1, 'The Song Talk Interview' by Paul Zollo.

5. *The Real Frank Zappa Book* by Frank Zappa with Peter Ochiogrosso, (Poseidon Press, 1989).

6. *Los Angeles Times* Calendar December 7, 1993, 'Frank Zappa: A Maverick Pied Piper' by Daniel Schorr.

7. *Music Technology* February 1987, 'Father Of Invention', interview by Rick Davies.

8. See Note 5.

9. *Billboard* December 19, 1987, advertisement 'We Are What We Watch'.

10. See Note 4.

11. *Society Pages* 11, 'Happy Together Part Three', interview by Co de Kloet.

12. *Guitarist* June 1993, 'Unholy Mother', interview by David Mead.

13. *Society Pages* 6, 'Would You Like Some Fries With That Interview?', by Martin De Jong, Piet Doelder, Aad Hoogesteger, Uli Mrosek and Axel Wunsh.

14. *Society Pages* 6, 'Ed Mann In Germany', interview by Aad Hoogesteger and Axel Wunsh.

15. See Note 12.

16. *Musician* November 1991, 'Poetic Justice Frank Zappa Puts Us In Our Place', by Matt Resnicoff.

17. ibid.

18. *Musician* September 1988, 'Hey Frank, Where You Goin' With That Guitar In Your Hand', by Alan di Perna.

19. *Musician* September 1988, 'Hey Frank, Where You Goin' With That Guitar In Your Hand', by Alan di Perna.

20. See Note 16.

21. *Society Pages* 6, 'Ode To Gravity', radio interview April 15, 1991 by Charles Amirkhanian.

22. *Rolling Stone* July 14-28, 1988, 'False Messiah' by Lawrence Wright.

23. ibid.

24. *Bat Chain Puller Rock & Roll In The Age of Celebrity* by Kurt Loder (St. Martin's Press, 1990). Original interview, Philadelphia, February 1988.

25. *Goldmine* January 27, 1989, 'Moving On To Phase Three', interview by William Ruhlmann.

26. ibid.

27. *Rolling Stone* February 25, 1988, 'Death Of A Salesman How Reagan Failed', by Frances Fitzgerald.

28. See Note 24.

29. ibid.

30. ibid.

31. ibid.

32. *Los Angeles Times Magazine* October 30, 1988, 'Democracy's Pitchman' by Joe Morgenstern.

33. See Note 27.

34. *You Can't Do That On Stage Anymore Vol. 2*, 'The Helsinki Concert'.

35. *Zappa!* (Miller Freeman, 1992), 'The Mother Of All Interviews'.

36. *Society Pages?* Poseidon Press Ann Patty quote: It's a good mission in life.

37. *The Wire* 34/5, 'The All American Composer', interview by Steve Lyons and Batya Friedman.

38. See Note 5.

39. *Zappa!* (Miller Freeman, 1992), 'Marque Coy Patron Saint At Joe's Garage', by Don Menn.

40. See Note 27.

41. *Los Angeles Times Magazine* October 30, 1988, 'Democracy's Pitchman', by Joe Morgenstern.

42. *T'Mershi Duween* 20, 'Way Down In New Zealand: FZ Talks To Gary Steel 5.12.90'.

43. *Continental Profiles* May 1990, 'Wanna Do A Deal?', interview by Neil Cohen, reproduced in *Society Pages* 3.

44. ibid.

45. ibid.

46. See Note 42.

47. *Society Pages* 3, 'They're Doing The Interview Of The Century, Part 3', interview by Den Simms and Rob Samler.

48. *Society Pages* 7, 'He's A Human Being. He Has Emotions, Just Like Us', interview by Den Simms and Rob Samler.

49. *Society Pages* 2, 'They're Doing The Interview Of The Century, Part 2', by Den Simms, Rob Samler and Eric Buxton.

50. ibid.

51. BBC-TV interview by Nigel Leigh.

52. *Sunday Times Business World* November 4, 1990, 'Zappa Transformed' by Richard Guilliatt.

CHAPTER TWENTY ONE THE TORTURE NEVER STOPS

1. *Playboy* April 1993, 'The Playboy Interview' by David Sheff.

2. ibid.

3. *Society Pages* 3, 'Zappa Zapped As Trade Rep', by Lawrence E. Joseph, reprinted from *New York Times Business World* , July 10, 1990.

4. *ICE (International CD Exchange)* September 1990, quoted in *Society Pages* 3.

5. ibid.

6. See Note 1.

7. *The Supplement Tape* SPZ10, c. 1990, Siesta Productions.

8. *Society Pages* 5, 'More Wit And Wisdom From Frank Zappa', interview by Co de Kloet, October 26, 1990.

9. *Society Pages* 5, 'Movin' To Australia Soon?', interview by Trevor Lofts and Steven Homan.

10. ibid.

11. *Society Pages* 6, 'He's A Human Being. He Has Emotions Just Like Us',
interview by Den Simms and Rob Samler.

12. *Goldmine* January 16, 1987, 'Hi, boys and girls, I'm Jimmy Carl Black and I'm the Indian of the group - Interview with a Mother' by Jack Ortman, reprinted from the *Austin Chronicle* .

13. See Note 11.

14. *Society Pages* 6, 'Ode To Gravity', radio interview April 15, 1991 by Charles Amirkhanian.

15. ibid.

16. *Society Pages* 6, 'Would You Like Some Fries With That Interview?', by Martin De Jong, Piet Doelder, Aad Hoogesteger, Uli Mrosek and Axel Wunsh.

17. *Society Pages* 7, 'Hot Poop! News & Spoos!', interview with Joel Thome by Rob Samler.

18. *Society Pages* 7, 'Hot Poop! News & Spoos!'

19. *T'Mershi Duween* 20, 'Zapparap: For Real!', transcribed by Darren Prosser.

20. *Zappa!* (Miller Freeman, 1992), 'The Mother Of All Interviews'.

21. *Society Pages* 5, 'Frank Sez Foo-eee To Boots!', by Tom Troccoli, Cynthia Littlejohn and Den Simms.

22. ibid.

23. *Keyboard* February 1992, 'Happy Birthday, Frank!' by Robert L. Doerschuk..

24. *Billboard* December 7, 1991, 'Zappa's Universe', concert review by Drew Wheeler.

25. *Village Voice* review.

26. *Society Pages* 8, 'Hot Poop! Newz & Spooz!'.

27. *Rolling Stone* January 9, 1992, 'Frank Zappa Stricken With Cancer', by Kim Neely.

28. *Society Pages* 9, 'Hot Poop! Newz & Spooz!', original quote in *Music Express* .

29. ibid.

30. *Society Pages* 10, 'The Yellow Shark A Preview', Research: Thomas 'Leppo' Oppel.

31. *Pulse!* August 1993, 'A Rare Interview With Pop's Philosopher-King', by Dan Ouellette.

32. See Note 1.

33. ibid.

34. ibid.

35. ibid.

36. See Note 31.

37. See Note 1.

38. *LA Times.*

39. *Rock CD* 12, 'Frank's Wild Years', interview by Joe Jackson.

40. *The Observer Weekend* May 15, 1993, 'Frank Fearless and still fighting', interview by Alex Kershaw.

41. ibid.

42. *LA Times.*

CHAPTER TWENTY TWO OUTRO

1. *Los Angeles Times Calendar* December 7, 1993, 'Frank Zappa: A Maverick Pied Piper' by Daniel Schorr.

2. BBC-tv interview by Nigel Leigh.

3. *Perfect Pitch A Life Story* by Nicholas Slonimsky (Oxford University Press, 1988).

4. *Los Angeles Times Magazine* October 30, 1988, 'Democracy's Pitchman', Joe Morgenstern.

5. *Los Angeles Times* December 6, 1994, "Civilization' a la Zappa' by Rip Rense.

6. ibid.

7. ibid.

8. ibid.

9. BBC-TV interview by Nigel Leigh.

10. *Society Pages* 5, 'More Wit And Wisdom From Frank Zappa', radio interview with National Radio of Sweden, December 20, 1990.

11. *Billboard.*

12. *The Guardian Weekend* May 15, 1993, 'Frank Fearless and still fighting', interview by Alex Kershaw.

13. *Rolling Stone* June 16, 1994, 'He Was A Crook' by Hunter S. Thompson.

14. *Pulse!* August 1993, 'A Rare Interview with Pop's Philosopher King', by Dan Ouellette.

15. (William Grieder quote re: Gingrich talented reactionary).

16. (*Empire* quote re: *Forrest Gump*).

DISCOGRAPHY: ORIGINAL ALBUMS

Freak Out!
LP: Verve V(6) 5005 CD:

Absolutely Free
LP: Verve V(6) 5013 CD:

We're Only In It For The Money
LP: Verve V(6) 5045 CD:

Lumpy Gravy
LP: Verve V(6) 8741 CD:

Cruisin' With Ruben And The Jets
LP: Verve V6 5055 CD:

Uncle Meat
LP: Bizarre MS 2024 CD:

Mothermania
LP: Verve V6 5068

The Worst Of The Mothers
LP: MGM SE 4754

The **** Of The Mothers
LP: Verve V6 5074

The Mothers Of Invention
LP: MGM GAS 112

Pregnant
LP: Verve 235 6049

Hot Rats
LP: Bizarre RS 6356 CD:

Burnt Weeny Sandwich
LP: Bizarre RS 6370 CD:

Weasels Ripped My Flesh
LP: Bizarre RS 2028 CD:

Chunga's Revenge
LP: Bizarre MS 2030 CD:

Fillmore East - June 1971
LP: Bizarre MS 2042 CD:

200 Motels
LP: United Artists UAS 9956

Just Another Band From L.A.
LP: Bizarre MS 2075 CD:

Waka/Jawaka
LP: Bizarre MS 2094 CD:

The Grand Wazoo
LP: Bizarre MS 2093 CD:

Over-Nite Sensation
LP: DiscReet MS 2149 CD:

Apostrophe (').
LP: DiscReet DS 2175 CD:

Roxy & Elsewhere
LP: DiscReet DS 2202 CD:

One Size Fits All
LP: DiscReet DS 2216 CD:
Bongo Fury
LP: DiscReet DS 2234 CD:
Zoot Allures
LP: Warner Bros DS 2970 CD:
Zappa In New York
LP: DiscReet DS 2290 CD:
Studio Tan
LP: DiscReet DS 2291 CD:
Sleep Dirt
LP: DiscReet DS 2292 CD:
Sheik Yerbouti
LP: Zappa SRZ 21501 CD:
Orchestral Favorites
LP: DiscReet DS 2294 CD:
Joe's Garage Act I
LP: Zappa SRZ 11603
Joe's Garage Acts II & III
LP: Zappa SRZ 11502
Tinsel Town Rebellion
LP: Barking Pumpkin PW 237336 CD:
Shut Up'n Play Yer Guitar
LP: Barking Pumpkin BPR 1111
Shut Up'n Play Yer Guitar Some More
LP: Barking Pumpkin BPR 1112
Return Of The Son Of Shut Up'n Play Yer Guitar
LP: Barking Pumpkin BPR 1113
You Are What You Is
LP: Barking Pumpkin PW 237537 CD:
Shut Up'n Play Yer Guitar (3lp Box).
LP: Barking Pumpkin W3X 38289 CD:
Ship Arriving Too Late To Save A Drowning Witch
LP: Barking Pumpkin FW 38066 CD:
The Man From Utopia
LP: Barking Pumpkin FW 38404 CD:
Baby Snakes
LP: Barking Pumpkin BPR 1115 CD:
London Symphony Orchestra Vol. 1
LP: Barking Pumpkin FW 38820
The Perfect Stranger
LP: Angel 38170 CD:
Them Or Us
LP: Barking Pumpkin SVB 074200 CD:
Francesco Zappa
LP: Barking Pumpkin ST 74202 CD:
Thing-Fish
LP: Barking Pumpkin SKC 074201 CD:
The Old Masters Box I
LP: Barking Pumpkin BPR 7777
Frank Zappa Meets The Mothers Of Prevention
LP: Barking Pumpkin ST 74203 CD:
Does Humor Belong In Music?
CD: EMI CDP 7461882
The Old Masters Box II
LP: Barking Pumpkin BPR 8888
Jazz From Hell

LP: Barking Pumpkin ST 74205 CD:
London Symphony Orchestra Vol. 2
LP: Barking Pumpkin SJ 74207
Joe's Garage Acts I, II & III
LP: Barking Pumpkin SWCL 74206 CD:
The Guitar World According To Frank Zappa
Cass: Barking Pumpkin GW 002
The Old Masters Box III
LP: Barking Pumpkin BPR 9999
Guitar
LP: Barking Pumpkin BPR 74212 CD:
You Can't Do That On Stage Anymore Sampler
LP: Barking Pumpkin BPRD 174213
You Can't Do That On Stage Anymore Volume 1
CD: Rykodisc
Broadway The Hard Way
LP: Barking Pumpkin D 174218 CD:
You Can't Do That On Stage Anymore Volume 2
LP: Barking Pumpkin BPR 74217 CD:
You Can't Do That On Stage Anymore Volume 3
CD: Rykodisc
The Best Band You Never Heard In Your Life
CD: Rykodisc
You Can't Do That On Stage Anymore Volume 4
CD: Rykodisc
Make A Jazz Noise Here
CD: Rykodisc

Beat The Boots Box 1
LP: Foo-eee RI 70907
As An Am
The Ark
Freaks & Motherfuckers
Unmitigated Audacity
Anyway The Wind Blows
'Tis The Season To Be Jelly
Saarbrucken '78
Piquantique

You Can't Do That On Stage Anymore Volume 5
CD: Rykodisc
You Can't Do That On Stage Anymore Volume 6
CD: Rykodisc

Beat The Boots Box 2
LP: Foo-eee RI 70372
Disconnected Synapses
Tengo Na Minchia Tanta
Electric Aunt Jemima
At The Circus
Swiss Cheese/Fire!
Our Man In Nirvana
Conceptual Continuity
Playground Psychotics
CD: Rykodisc

The Yellow Shark
CD: Rykodisc
Civilization Phaze III
CD: Barking Pumpkin
Strictly Commercial
LP: Rykodisc
CD: Rykodisc

In 1995 the entire catalogue was expertly redesigned, repackaged and reissued on CD by Rykodisc. No corners were cut and Ryko have to be congratulated for this sympathetic and ambitious reissue programme. The complete catalogue number listing is standard for both USA and the UK.

Freak Out!
RCD/RAC 10501
Absolutely Free
RCD/RAC 10502
We're Only In It For The Money
RCD/RAC/RALP 10503
Lumpy Gravy
RCD 10504
Cruising With Ruben & The Jets
RCD 10505
Uncle Meat
RCD/RAC 10506/7
Hot Rats
RCD/RAC 10508
Burnt Weeny Sandwich
RCD 10509
Weasels Ripped My Flesh
RCD/RAC 10510
Chunga's Revenge
RCD 10511
Fillmore East, June 1971
RCD/RAC 10512
200 Motels
RCD 10513/14
Just Another Band From L.A.
RCD 10515
Waka/Jawaka
RCD 10516
The Grand Wazoo
RCD 10517
Over-Nite Sensation
RCD/RAC 10518
Apostrophe (')
RCD/RAC 10519
Apostrophe(') Audio-Phile series
RCD 80519
Roxy & Elsewhere
RCD/RAC 10520
One Size Fits All
RCD/RAC 10521

One Size Fits All Audio-Phile series
RCD 80521
Bongo Fury
RCD/RAC 10522
Zoot Allures
RCD/RAC 10523
Zappa In New York
RCD 10524/25
Studio Tan
RCD 10526
Sleep Dirt
RCD 10527
Sheik Yerbouti
RCD/RAC 10528
Orchestral Favorites
RCD 10529
Joe's Garage Acts I, II & III
RCD/RAC 10530/31
Tinsel Town Rebellion
RCD 10532
Shut Up 'N Play Yer Guitar
RCD 10533/34/35
You Are What You Is
RCD 10536
Ship Arriving Too Late To Save A Drowning Witch
RCD 10537
The Man From Utopia
RCD 10538
Baby Snakes
RCD/RAC 10539
London Symphony Orchestra Vol. I & II
RCD 10540/41
Boulez Conducts Zappa: The Perfect Stranger
RCD 10542
Them Or Us
RCD 10543
Thing-Fish
RCD 10544/45
Francesco Zappa
RCD 10546
Frank Zappa Meets The Mothers Of Prevention
RCD 10547
Does Humor Belong In Music?
RCD 10548
Jazz From Hell
RCD 10549
Guitar
RCD 10550/51
Broadway The Hard Way
RCD 10552
The Best Band You Never Heard In Your Life
RCD 10653/54
Make A Jazz Noise Here
RCD 10555/56
Playground Psychotics
RCD 10557/58
Ahead Of Their Time
RCD 10559

The Yellow Shark
RCD/RAC 40560
You Can't Do That On Stage Anymore Vol. 1
RCD 10561/62
You Can't Do That On Stage Anymore Vol. 2
RCD 10563/64
You Can't Do That On Stage Anymore Vol. 3
RCD 10565/66
You Can't Do That On Stage Anymore Vol. 4
RCD 10567/68
You Can't Do That On Stage Anymore Vol. 5
RCD 10569/70

You Can't Do That On Stage Anymore Vol. 6
RCD 10571/72
Strictly Commercial (The Best Of Frank Zappa)
RCD/RAC 40600
The Lost Episodes
RCD 40573
Läther
RCD 10574/76
Have I Offended Someone?
RCD 10577
Strictly Genteel: A Classical Introduction To Frank Zappa
RCD 10578

BIBLIOGRAPHY

Frank Zappa Fanzines and reference works:
Society Pages *The Magazine of The International Frank Zappa Society* Rob Samler and Den Simms P.O. Box 395, Deer Park, NY 11729-0395, USA
T'Mershi Duween *Zappa Fanzine* Fred Tomsett P.O.Box 86, Sheffield S11 8XN, England
The Torchum Never Stops Vols. 1 to 4 The Torture Team Germany, 1991/2

Books
The American Age U.S. Foreign Policy At Home And Abroad 1750 To The Present Second Edition Walter LaFeber (Norton, 1994).
American Heartbeat: Travels from Woodstock to San Jose by Song Title Mick Brown (Michael Joseph, 1993).
The Age Of Rock: Sounds of the American Cultural Revolution edited by Jonathan Eisen (Vintage Books, 1969).
Bat Chain Puller: Rock & Roll In The Age Of Celebrity Kurt Loder (St. Martin's Press, 1990).
Born Under A Bad Sign: Illustrations/Ralph Steadman Tony Palmer (William Kimber, 1970).
Broken Record: The Inside Story Of The Grammy Awards Henry Schipper (Birch Lane Press, 1992).
Captain Beefheart The Man And His Music: Second Revised Edition C.D. Webb (Kosher Pig Publications, 1989).
Days In The Life: Voices From The English Underground 1961-1971 Jonathon Green (Heinemann, 1988).
Experimental Pop: Frontiers Of The Rock Era Billy Bergman and Richard Horn (Blandford Press, 1985).
Hollywood Rock: A Guide to Rock'n'Roll in the Movies Marshall Crenshaw (Plexus, 1994).
I'm With The Band: Confessions Of A Groupie Pamela Des Barres (Jove, 1988).
The Lives & Times of Zappa & The Mothers (Babylon Books).
Mother! The Frank Zappa Story Michael Gray (Plexus, 1993).
No Commercial Potential: The Saga of Frank Zappa & The Mothers Of Invention David Walley (Dutton, 1972).
Perfect Pitch: A Life Story Nicholas Slonimsky (Oxford, 1988).
The Real Frank Zappa Book Frank Zappa with Peter Occhiogrosso (Poseidon Press, 1989).
The Road Goes On Forever: The Foulk Brothers: Pop Promoting Blues Philip Norman (Elm Tree/Hamish Hamilton, 1982).
Rock Day By Day Steve Smith & The Diagram Group (Guinness Publishing, 1987).
The Rock Giants Edited by Pauline Rivelli and Robert Levin (The World Publishing Company, 1970).
Rock Odyssey: A Chronicle of the Sixties Ian Whitcomb (Dolphin, 1983).
Rock Wives The Hard Lives and Good Times of the Wives, Girlfriends, and Groupies of Rock And Roll: Victoria Balfour (Beech Tree Books, 1986).
The Rolling Stone Rock'n'Roll Reader Edited by Ben Fong-Torres (Bantam, 1974).
Science Fiction In The Cinema John Baxter (The Tantivy Press, 1970).
Shots From The Hip Charles Shaar Murray (Penguin, 1991).
The Smithsonian Guide To Historic America: Virginia And The Capital Region (Stewart, Tabori & Chang, 1989).
Uncovering The Sixties: The Life & Times Of The Underground Press Abe Peck (Pantheon, 1985).
Via Zappa! Dominic Chevalier (Omnibus Press, 1985).
When The Music Mattered: Rock In The 1960s Bruce Pollock (Holt, Rinehart and Winston, 1983).
Frank Zappa - A Visual Documentary by Miles (Omnibus Press, 1993).
Frank Zappa In His Own Words Compiled by Miles (Omnibus Press, 1993).

SELECTED INDEX